20.00

D1602722

Wills and Administrations

of

SURRY COUNTY, VIRGINIA

1671-1750

Wills and Administrations
of
SURRY COUNTY, VIRGINIA

1671-1750

By *Eliza Timberlake Davis*

Reprinted in an Improved Format

With a New Index by
Thomas L. Hollowak

Baltimore
GENEALOGICAL PUBLISHING CO., INC.
1980

Originally published: Smithfield, Virginia, 1955
Reprinted in an improved format and with a new index by
Genealogical Publishing Co., Inc.
Baltimore, 1980
Copyright © 1980
Genealogical Publishing Co., Inc.
Baltimore, Maryland
All Rights Reserved
Library of Congress Catalogue Card Number 80-67936
International Standard Book Number 0-8063-0899-0
Made in the United States of America

NOTE

SURRY COUNTY, as it now is, was originally the part of James City County that lay on the south side of the James River. Surry County was formed out of James City County in 1652, and some of the settlers at Jamestown owned land on the Surry side and some of the colonists at Surry owned land at Jamestown. Most of these people were from England, adventurers seeking their fortune in a strange land.

ELIZA TIMBERLAKE DAVIS
Smithfield, Virginia
1955

WILLS AND ADMINISTRATIONS
OF
SURRY COUNTY, VIRGINIA
1671 - 1750

ABORDS, Amaro: Leg.- Mary Brotherton, Timothy Isriell, Micaell Jarrett, Timothy Isriell, Sr., and makes him Exer. 14 July, 1677. Wit: Alex. Richardson, Tho. Edwards. Bk. 2, p. 141.

ADAMS, James: Est.- Sarah Adams, Exerx. Signed: James Chappell, Robert Jones, Charles Briggs. 8 July 1720. Book 7, p. 277.

ADAMS, James: Est.- Sarah Kimball and Joseph Kimball, Exers. Signed: Thos. Holt, John Newsum. 14 Dec. 1725. Book 3, p. 86.

ADAMS, Peter: Est.- James Hugato, Admr. Signed: Wm. Newsum, Mathew Swann, William Chambers. 10 May 1687. Bk. 3, p. 86.

ADAMS, Peter: Leg.- Bequeaths to son Thomas Adams a tract of land which did belong to Samuel Clements, 170 acres. To son, William Adams the tract of land I now live on. If either of my sons should depart this life without lawful issue, or both die without lawful issue, all my lands are to be divided between my three daughters, Mary, Eliza, and Susannah. Gives bequest to sons and daughters various household furnishings, feather beds, furniture, pewter dishes, pots, pans, etc. Gives to son Thomas twenty shillings in the hands of Joan Bagly, 26 lb. 6 d. in the charge of a law suit in the hands of Thos. Howell. Bequeaths a negro to son Thomas - an exchange of slaves and to go to Thomas when Thomas is sixteen and William have a negro girl bought for him and all my children be for themselves at sixteen years and enjoy their Estates. My two sons Thomas and William to be put in school till they can read and wright very well. My desire is that my three daughters, Mary, Eliza, and Susannah have the use of my Plantation until my son Thos. is sixteen, if they stay single, but if they marry that they immediately go off and my son, Thomas, then have the Plantation untill my son William is sixteen years old. I give my wife, Ann and five children, Mary, Eliza. Susannah, Thos. and William all the rest of my Estate to be equally divided. Makes wife, Ann, Exerx. Wit: William Edwards, Samuel Judkins. D.: 21 March, 1734. P.: 17 March, 1735. Book 8, p. 574.

ADAMS, Thomas: Leg.- To Son, Peter Adams, 2 negroes, Labor of negro woman to wife for her life, then to son, William Adams, Gives Peter Adams household furniture when he is 21 years old, six lbs. in money and money towards his Education in learning to read and Write. To son, Peter, my gun. My will is that the remaining part of my Estate be equally divided among my wife and two children Wm. & Peter. Each to have all equal parts. Appoints Wife Exerx. 1 Feb., 1734. P.: 21 May, 1735. Wit: William Marriett, Miles Louis. Presented by Ann Adams, Exerx. Book 8, p. 495.

ADAMS, Thos.: Est.- By Ann Adams. 11 Jan., 1735. P.: 18 June, 1735. Wit: Robert Gray, Wm. Warren, Jno. Warren. Book 8, p. 503.

ADKINS, Richard: Est.- Joane Adkins, Admrx. Signed: John

Warren, Thos. Cotton, Wm. Nance, Wm. Edwards. 1 July, 1679.
Book 2, p. 19.

ADKINS, Thomas: Leg.- To son, Thomas Adkins, plantation and
land I live on. To son, Richard Adkins, land adjoining
Thomas, taken up with Peter Bagley, when Son is eighteen.
Son, William, Daus. Jane, Eliza Adkins - Eliza, wife to
Joseph Harris and wife to Thos. Dunn each a sow. Dau.
Joan Adkins comb and looking glass. Daus., Mary and Rachel Ad-
kins, cow each, wife, Eliza Adkins, rest of personal Est.
and Exer. 26 May, 1711. Probated: 20 June, 1711. Wit:
George Nicholson, George Rochell, Thos. Dunn. Bk. 6, p. 61.

ALDERSON, William: Leg.- Est. divided in two parts. To wife,
Jillian and daughter, Elizabeth. If daughter die, her part
to her mother, if she is living, if not to next of kin.
Makes wife Exerx. D.: 24 Jan., 1683. Probated: 4 March,
1683-4. Wit: Robert Ruffin, William Newsum. Bk. 2, p. 348.

ALLEN, Arthur: Lawnes Creek Parish. Constitutes and appts. my
most Dear and Tender wife, Katherine, and Dutyfull Son,
John, Exer. and Exerx. of last will and Test. To wife, who
is daughter of Capt. Lawrence Baker late of this county,
deceased, for her natural life, at her decease. I give and
bequeath the Manor House of ye said, Dividend with all appurtenances thereto belonging with all Land lying on East
side of second Swamp on ye South Side of branch which
issues from place called Hurtleberry Pocoson -- Then through
the pasture near sd, Manor House untill it falls into the
Swamp which comes from the plantation of Mr. Thomas Drew to
my son James and his heirs, etc. and from want of such heirs
to my son, Joseph and his heirs, etc. and from want of such
heirs to my Son, Arthur and his heirs, etc. I give and
Bequeath to my Son, John, that part of 1000 acres-granted to
me by Patt, dates 29 Apr. 1692, which lyeth on the West Side
of Second Swamp in this part of county; and from want of
heirs to my son, Arthur and the remaining part of sd, Patt,
lying on ye East Side of Second Swamp I give and Bequeath to
my son, James and his heirs. To sd. Son, John 200 acres
situated near the mouth of Upper Chipoakes Creek--bounded
North by James River and South into the woods the same
granted to me by patent 28 Sept. 1681, and also to Son, John
100 acres of land, part of 200 acres purchased of Madam
Sarah Bland, by Deed of Lease and Release dated the 20 Oct.
1704, the sd. 100 acres bounded--Southerly upon a Patt. of
200 acres long since granted to my father, Arthur Allen,
Late of the county, deceased, Easterly on a Drane and Bottom
--named Crabtree Bottom--to Billison's Swamp near the Mill
Dam--northerly to Thomas Hart's Line marked tree--to my own
land, purchased of Mr. Dunston to above Patt. of 200 acres,
to him my son, John, etc., also 150 acres in Lawnes Creek
Psh. purchased of Arthur Long, late of the county, deceased,
and now in tenure of John and Anselm Baley, and for want of
heirs to my Son, Joseph. To my son, Arthur Allen, 1300
acres lately purchased by me of Madam Sarah Bland 13 Nov.
1707, also 100 acres purchased of Madam Sarah Bland, 12 Oct.
1704, for 200 acres more or less and whereas the other part
already bequeathed to Son, John, and for want of heirs both
parts to son, Joseph. To Sons Arthur and Joseph 1800 acres
granted to me by patent 25 April 1705 South side main
Blackwater Swamp in ye county of Isle of Wight, the upper
half and commonly called Coppahaunch. To Son Arthur and ye
lower half called Warreeke to my son, Joseph and fr. want of
heirs to Son Arthur, and to Son, Joseph plantation at Round

2

Hill in ye Upper Parrish Isle of Wight County whereon Darby Bohoon now lives 270 acres and survey in Mr. Secretary's Office. I give and bequeath to my dau. Elizabeth, the wife of Wm. Bridger 360 acres of land situate in a place called --Rount Hill in ye Upper Psh. Isle of Wight Co -- immediately after her decease I give and bequeath the said 360 acres to my nephew, Joseph Bridger and his heirs. Give wife four slaves (names them) my watch, her chamber furniture, and twenty pounds sterling. To Son John three slaves (names them) and my scriptore. Dau. Katherine three slaves, (named) Son James three slaves (named) and biggest cane. Son Arthur three slaves (named) "My other cane". Dau. Ann, three slaves, Dau. Mary three slaves, Son Joseph three slaves. Sister, Joan Proctor I slave, sister Elizabeth Jackman and my son-in-law Wm. Bridger a sum of twenty shillings. To Wife one-third of all land I possess for and during her natural life, together with former bequeasts and horse and side saddle of her choice. To grand children Joseph and Martha Bridger two slaves -- at their Mother's decease, and their Mother, my dau., Elizabeth Bridger--. to my two grandsons, William and Samuell Bridger when twenty-one yrs. old, to each a small Silver Tankard. Will Daughter's son Lower Chipoakes Creek to be furnished-- rest of Estate after debts and legacies are paid, to my wife and seven children, John, Katherine, James, Arthur, Ann, Mary and Joseph. Wife Katherine and Son John Exer. D.: 16 Feb., 1709. Probated: 5 Sept., 1710. Wit: Thomas Holt, Thos. Waller, Wm. Drew, Jno. Baley, Arthur Blair, Jno. Wilson. Book 6, p. 33.

ALLEN, Arthur: Est.- By Arthur Smith, Jr. and Elizabeth his wife. Signed by Elizabeth Smith and James Bray. 20 July, 1736. Book 8, p. 713.

ALLEN (ALLIN), Elizabeth: Bequeath to friend, Thomas Alstin my house and land. To Hannah Seward bed and furniture, side saddle, clothes, cotton ready spun, etc. To Ann Collier an Iron pot. To Mary Penington two suites of cloathes of Virginia cloth, one other black suite, the other gown facet with collier and a cop. To Mary Knot one-half dozen pewter plates. To Thomas Hawkes twenty shillings for a years schooling. To Goddaughter, Elizabeth Evans a gold ring. The rest of my Estate to Thos. Alstin who I do make my sole Exer. 2 Feb., 1735-6. Prob.: 18 Feb., 1735. Wit: James Rookings, Tabitha Niblet. Book 8, p. 565.

ALLEN, James: Leg.- To Brother, Arthur Allen, 1400 acres of land granted to me by Pattent 25 Apr. 1701 situate on South Side main Blackwater Swamp part in Surry and part in Isle of Wight, except 700 acres of land which I have sold to Thos. Pittman and Samuell Lancaster and 300 acres which I have sold to Robert Lancaster, Jr. and also 200 acres of land which I have sold to Joseph Wall, all of which said three parcels of land on part are part of above patent, and I give then to my loving brother John Allen, and his heirs, etc. and he confirm the three pieces of land to said parties as soon as possible after my decease. Bequeaths negro slaves to loving mother, Katherine Allen, for her life, at her death to brother, Joseph. To Margaret Coker, wife of John Coker 1000 lbs. tobo. To couzen, Arthur Bridger, when he is 21 to be paid by Exers. and small silver Tankard val. four pounds. Rest of Estate to be divided between all my brothers and sisters viz: Elizabeth Bridger, wife of Wm. Bridger, John Allen, Arthur

3

Allen, Ann Allen, Mary Allen, and Joseph Allen. All to receive legacy at 18 years. Makes brother, John Allen, Exer.
24 Jan., 1711. P.: 20 Feb., 1711. Wit: Thomas Drew,
Richard Taylor. Book 6, p. 97.

ALLEN, James: Leg.- To Thos. Bray, James Bray, Wm. Allen,
Arthur Smith, Frances Bray, Elizabeth Bray, James Bridger
and Joseph Bridger each a gold ring. To John Cornwell, son
of Jacob Cornwell, 12 lbs. 10 shillings when 21 years old,
if he die before that age to his two sisters, Mary and
Mourning. To sister Catherine Cooke rest of my Estate at
her death to my brother-in-law, Benjamin Cooke, at his
death, funds for a Parish School for poor children as
profits of Estate will afford. Brother-in-law, Benjamin
Cooke, exer. 6 Aug., 1744. P.: 20 March, 1744. Wit:
Wm. Shelly, Richard Smith. Book 9, p. 494.

ALLEN, John: Leg.- I give and bequeath to my Eldest Son, John
Allen, when he shall attain age of twenty-one years one
shilling sterling money of England to be paid by Exers.
hereafter names and no more -- I give and bequeath to my
daughter, Sarah, household good and an equal part of the
residue of my Estate to be given her immediately after my
decease and all her Mother's clothes, lately deceased, and
for the rest of my Estate here, and elsewhere to be equally
divided amongst my three youngest children to each one-
third part to be paid by my Exers. when they are eighteen
years old, and to the girl when she shall come to sixteen
years or day of marriage. Appoints Nathaniel Harrison
Exer. Wit: John Wapoole, Mary Wapoole. 19 Dec., 1699.
P.: 7 Sept., 1700. Book 5, p. 211.

ALLEN, John: Leg.- I give to my nephew, James Bridger, 250
lbs. current money to be paid him at 25 years old, 35 lbs.
to be laid out in Communion Plate for the Lower Church of
the Psh. of Southwarke in Surry County and like sum 35 lbs.
sterling to be laid out in Communion Plate for the Parish
of Albermarle in Surry County for the service & the parish
church or of either of the Chappels as the Church Wardons
shall think fit. I give Mrs. Mourning Thomas, house-
keeper, 100 lbs. current money over and above her wages now
due. My Exers. to employ her to look after the Family at
my dwelling plantation in the same manner she has been em-
ployed by me. I desire the piece of ground where my wife
and children be interred, after my death, may be hand-
somely walled in with Brick and the Tombstones which came
lately from England to set up in a handsome manner over my
wife's grave and it is my earnest desire that the said wall
be always kept in good repair by those who shall enjoy my
Estate. To my nephew, James Allen, 50 lbs. current money
and a like sum to my niece, Catherine Cooke. To James
Harrison, who now lives with me, 20 lbs. current money at
the age of twenty-two. I give my friend Mr. Jas. Baker,
one of my Exers., my gold watch, wearing apparel, etc. I
give my late wife's wearing apparel to be equally divided
between her sisters, Mrs. Roscow and Mrs. Daingerfield. I
give to Miss Mary Roscow, the daughter of Coll. Wm. Roscow
the Gold Watch that was my late wife's. All the rest of my
Estate real and personal to my nephew, Wm. Allen, Son of my
brother, Joseph Allen, deceased. My nephew not to have
Estate until he is 21 years old. In the meantime friend,
James Baker, see after my whole Estate. One of my Exers.
hereafter named, and James Baker to reside with his family
upon my dwelling plantation and he and his family main-

4

tained out of my Est. and receive also 10% Appts. James
Baker Exer. and Capt. John Ruffin Exer. the same privileges
as James Baker, during time aforesaid nephew Wm. Allen,
shall be under age. He to be at the College until he is
21. D.: 5 March, 1741. P.: 21 April, 1742. Wit:
Patrick Adams, Auf. Claiborne, Thomas Wharton, James
Harrison, James Boyd, Charles Henry Jones. Book 9, p. 405.

ALLEN, Joseph: Est.- Court appointed the following to appraise
the estate, Daniel Epps, James Sammon and James Portch, and
William Tomlinson. Appraisement offered by Ingumbred
Anderson and Eliza., his wife. 25 Nov., 1717 - 18 Dec.,
1717. Book 7, p. 84.

ALLEN, Stephen: Est.- To Jas. Forbush for his passage back to
England. Pd. Capt. Watkins, Brother, Allen, Wm. Skinner,
Mr. Wm. Williams, Mr. George Proctor, John Phillips, Lewis
Williams, John Hunnicutt, Wm. Hardy and Mr. Sherwood.
9 Jan., 1675. Signed: Robert Caufield. Book 2, p. 104.

ALLEN, Thomas: Leg.- To wife, Elizabeth Allen my whole estate.
Wit: Wm. Rookings, John Collins. D.: 30 March, 1733.
P.: 20 Feb., 1733. Book 8, p. 353.

ALSOBROOK, Samuel: Est.- Mr. John Thompson, Admr. Signed:
Nicholas Witherington, Geo. Foster, Will. Forman. 4 May,
1697. Book 5, p. 127.

AMOS, William: Est.- Of London dead, his widow Mary Amos de-
sires to receive of Elizabeth Whitaker dau. of Elizabeth
Whitaker of Denbigh, in Warwick County, Virginia, all land
due her, as relict of William Amos. Coll. John Allen,
Attorney. 20 May, 1672. Signed: Adam Graves, George
Wray, David Bray, Joseph Bradby. Book 7, p. 444.

AMRY, Thomas: Est.- Inventory by his wife, Ruth Amry. Sworn
before Capt. Charles Barham. 25 Apr., 1676. Signed by
Randall Holt, Jno. Goring. Fra. Hogwood received of
Edward Warren Est. for Mary Creed. Test: Wm. Thomas.
29 Mar., 1676. Book 2, p. 115.

ANDERSON, John: Leg.- To Wife, Mary, my whole estate having no
other relatives. Bequest to Richard and John King, Jr.
according to bargain. Wit: John King, Richard King. D.:
5 Oct., 1722. Prob.: 21 Nov., 1722. Book 7, p. 425.

ANDREWS, Bartholomew: Leg.- To Couzen, Bartholomew Andrews,
Son of Robert Andrews, my plantation where I now live with
all the land thereto belonging after death of my wife Elizabeth. If he die without heirs then the plantation to next
ensuing heir of the aforesaid Robert Andrews, father of
aforesaid Bartholomew Andrews and to remain in his genera-
tion forever. If said Bartholomew desires to settle a
plantation after he is come of age before decease of my
wife then choose my place below the plantation in the Swamp
and there he live freely to make a plantation. My still to
Wife Elizabeth for life and a negro at her death to my
Cousin, Bartholomew Andrews. Cousin, Elizabeth Andrews
1 shilling. To my negro Tom, a gun which he uses and his
fiddle, his bed, etc., and my negro Tom, free, after
my wife's decease. I give to Wm. Proctor a gun when 18
unless my wife live until he is 21 then shall serve his
full time. To my loving wife, Elizabeth, all my personal
estate and make her Exerx. Wit: Wm. Boldin, Nicholas

Proctor, Robert Gully. 28 Nov., 1720. Probated: 18 May,
1726. Book 8, p. 637.

ANDREWS, Benjamin: Leg.- Son, William Andrews, the plantation
where I now live and all the land thereto. Rest of Est.
divided between Son, Wm. and Daughter, Ann. Daughter Ann
Andrews 5 lbs. Friends, Edward Bagley, Jr. and John
Simmons, Jr. Exers. Wit: John Simmons, Robert Snipes, Ed.
Bayley. 14 Sept., 1736. P.: 20 Oct., 1736. Book 8,
p. 637.

ANDREWS, David: Est.- David Andrews swore to the true inventory of his father's estate. 3 Sept., 1692. P.: 6 Sept.,
Signed by Geo. Foster, Robert Warren. Book 4, p. 276.

ANDREWS, David, Jr.: Est.- Signed: Thomas Warren, James
Davis, John Cooke, James Nicholson. 20 March, 1716.
Book 7, p. 53.

ANDREWS, Elizabeth: Leg.- Cousin, Bartholomew Andrews, son of
Robert Andrews land on John Shahankon Swamp. My former
husband, Nathaniel Roberts, will 19 April, 1693 gave me
above estate. To Margaret Further, dau. of Geo. Further
pewter dishes. To Mary Long, widow of George Long wearing
apparel. To Cousin Bartholomew Andrews, Son of Robert rest
of my Estate and make him Exer. Wit: Henry Sowerby,
Robert Jordon. D.: 29 Nov., 1735. P.: 18 Nov., 1741.
Book 9, p. 392.

ANDREWS, Richard: Leg.- Sons, William, David and Richard
Andrews. Daughter, Elizabeth Wrenn. Daughter, Mary Morroll. The three sons made Exers. of estate. D.: 17 Sept.,
1750. P.: 20 Nov., 1750. Wit: William Clinch. Book 9,
p. 665.

ANDREWS, Robert: Leg.- Son Joseph Andrews land on Cypress
Swamp bounded by Great Branch -- Dividing line between my
land and my brother, Thomas Andrews, land, on a branch
called Little Branch. Son Wm. Andrews his part of my estate which he has already received. To Bartholomew
Andrews two shillings. To Son Benjamin Andrews my plantation where I now live and 170 acres joining the said
plantation, cattle, etc. To my daughter, Susannah Ray, her
part of my estate which she is already possessed of.
Daughter, Sarah Barker the same. Daughter, Catherine Barker the same also. Daughter, Elizabeth Battle also.
Daughter, Ann a cow and calf. Wife and at her death to
daughter, Amie. Wife Exerx. Wit: Wm. Bolden, Deborah
King, Elizabeth Bolden. 18 Feb., 1725-6. Prob.: 16 Oct.,
1728. Book 7, p. 868.

ANDREWS, Thomas: Leg.- Son, John Andrews, plantation where I
now live and all Land belonging. Daughter, Jean, a small
part of plantation while she is single. To Wife a decent
living out of my estate. To daughter Lucy Snipes furniture.
Son Thomas all that he is already possessed of. To Daughter Mary Thornton all that she is already possessed of. To
Daughters Ollaf and Martha ten shillings each. John Andrews as Exer. of estate. Wit: John Simmons, Thos. Bayley,
Ed. Bayley. D.: 21 Jan., 1736. Probated: 15 March,
1737. Book 8, p. 807.

ANDREWS, Thomas, Sr.: Leg.- Son, Thomas Andrews, a parcell of
land beginning at a branch called Great Branch thence down

Swamp to the end of my land. Son, Robert Andrews, my plantation which I now live upon with all the rest of my land which in my will is not disposed of. To Wife, Dorothy, all my personal estate and privilege of one-half the plantation during her life and makes her Exerx. Wit: Ed. Bayley, Barth. Andrews. D.: 5 March, 1688. P.: 21 Oct., 1693. Book 4, p. 341.

ATKINSON, John: Leg.- Bequest to Son, Absolom Atkinson, the plantation where I now dwell and land belonging, 100 acres, only that my wife, Elizabeth shall have use and profitts of the plantation for her life. Gives Son, Absolom, Troopers Arms and great Bible, cattle, etc. To Son, John Atkinson, one "Neck of Land lying in Isle of Wight County, 100 acres, called or known as Champions Neck" and bounded on the North by a Branch called Butchers' Branch and on East by the Mill Swamp and on South and West by Christopher Atkinson, his land also cow, calf, gun and Bible. To Son, Aaron Atkinson, parcell of land lying in Isle of Wight County and between Butcher's Branch and a Branch called Reedy Branch, 100 acres of land. To my Son, Reuben Atkinson, a tract of land conveyed by patent, 150 acres called New Surrey, a cow, calf and a Bible. To Son, Amos Atkinson, live stock, Bible, etc. To Son, Daniel Atkinson, Bible, furniture, etc. To Son, Jacob Atkinson, feather bed, bolster, Bible, etc. If any son that was a bequest of land dies, his part to Son, Amos. If a second should die, his part to son, Daniel. If a third, his part to Son, Jacob. All rest of Estate of wife, Elizabeth, at her death divided among children. Son, Absolom, Exerx. Wit: William Little, John Waller, Thomas Atkinson. D.: 17 April, 1736. Probated: 18 May, 1737. Bk. 8, p. 686.

ATKINSON, Robert: Leg.- Son, Benjamin Atkinson, plantation he lives on & 100 acres on Hart's Branch. Son, Robert Atkinson, plantation in Southampton on Gregory's Branch by Mill Branch. Son, John Atkinson, 140 acres mouth of Reedy Branch. Sons, William and Benjamin Exers. Wit: Benjamin Bailey, Benjamin Gray. D.: 28 August, 1749. Prob.: 20 Mar., 1749. Book 9, p. 629.

ATKISON, Thomas: Leg.- Plantation I now live -- below mouth of Jones Hole Creek or Swamp - to Wife, Mary. My other plantation with all the land to my son, Thomas Atkison, and his heirs to be delivered when he is 21, horse, etc. To daughter, Mary, a negro, if no heirs to my daughter, Elizabeth and her heirs. Daughter, Lucy, a negro, if no heirs to daughter, Anges. Wife, Mary two negroes. Son, Wm., carpenters tools. Wife and Son, William Exers. Wit: John Weaver, Timothy Ezell, Henry Gauler. D.: 1 Feb., 1725. P.: 15 June, 1726. Book 7, p. 640.

ATKISSON, William: Est.- By Elizabeth Atkisson, Admr. Signed by James Washington, Augustine Hargrove, John Hancocke. 15 Oct., 1735. Book 8, p. 526.

ATTKINS, Thomas: Est.- By Elizabeth Attkins. Signed: William Short, Peter Bagley. Book 6, p. 70.

AVERY, George: Leg.- Body to be buried at descretion of "my loving Unckel, Thos. Flood". To Unckel, Richard Rose, wearing apparel. Brothers, Thos. Avery and John Avery, rest of my estate. Thomas to have choice of guns. Unckell Thomas Flood, Exer. Codicil makes bequests to Thomas, son

of Richard and Elizabeth Rose. Wit: Fra. Clements, John
Sowerby. D.: 22 May, 1692. P.: 5 July, 1692. Book 4,
p. 269.

AVERY, John: Wm. Rose, Guardian of John Avery acknowledges to
have received of Ed. Bookey who married the Relict and
Exrx. of Richard Avery, deceased -- the whole of John
Avery's part of his father's estate. Wit: Charles Holesworth, George Avery. 3 July, 1688. Book 4, p. 62.

AVERY, Richard: Leg.- Mentions Son, George, and Son, William
Avery, guns. Son, John Avery. Wife Jane one-third of
estate, other two-thirds to Sons, William Thos. and John
equally divided. Two brothers, Wm. Rose and Thomas Flood
to assist wife. Wife Exerx. D.: 12 7br, 1685. P.: 5
Jan., 1685. Wit: Wm. Brown, William Rose. Bk. 3, p. 45.

AVERY, Richard: Est.- Wit: John Moring, Owen Meyrich, Geo.
Foster. Jane Avery, Wife, made oath. 4 May, 1686. Book
3, p. 52.

BAGE, Thomas: Est.- Eliza Bage Admr. 2 July, 1700. Signed:
Jno. Watkins, Nicholas Witherington, William Foster.
Book 5, p. 205.

BAGE, Thomas: Est.- Eliza Bage admr. 30 Mar., 1742. P.: 17
Nov., 1742. Signed: Richard Andrews, Henry Watkins,
Robert Warren. Book 9, p. 417.

BAGLEY, Hugh: Est.- Estate appraised by Edward Greene and
Will. Harvey. 20 May, 1693. Book 4, p. 309.

BAGLEY, Hugh: Est.- Hugh Bagley, late of the colony, dead,
left an Estate, and Sarah Bagley, Relict, makes suit for
Com. of Admr. Thomas Wiggins married said Sarah and it is
ordered that Thomas Wiggins and wife, Sarah, make full inventory of Hugh Bagley's estate at next court. 21 April,
1695. Book 5, p. 42.

BAGLEY, John: Leg.- Son, Thomas Bagley, my plantation and half
the land that lies upon it. Son, Peter Bagley, all rest of
land. Wife, Elizabeth, all rest of estate and Exer. 11
Dec., 1736. P.: 16 Feb., 1736. Wit: Richard Bullock,
John Jones, Judah Jones. Book 8, p. 656.

BAGLEY, Peter: Leg.- Cousin, John Bagley, where John Bagley
lives 75 acres. Son, George Bagley, 75 acres where I live
and another 200 acres, a part of pat. of 400 acres. Son,
John Bagley, 73 acres where I live and 200 acres. "All
my children", bequests of slaves. Daughter, Sarah Tucker,
cow and calf, etc. Servant Simon Rowland set free at 21
and given three barrels of corn, and clothing. Son, George,
Exer. Made: 15 Nov., 1735. Probated: 17 Dec., 1735.
Wit: Wm. Short, Richard Bullock, Wm. Short, Jr. Book 8,
p. 547.

BAGLEY, Peter, Sr.: Est.- By Hue (Hugh) Bagley. 3 March,
1684. Appraised by Edward Greene, Adam Heath. Book 3,
p. 20.

BAGLEY, Peter: Est.- George Bagley, Exer. Wit: Wm. Harris,
Richard Jones, Richard Bullock. 17 Mar., 1735. Book 8,
p. 576.

BAGLEY (BAILEY), Robert: Est.- John Pasmore, admr. 19 Aug., 1719. Book 7, p. 208.

BAGLEY, Thos.: Est.- Wit: Richard Washington, Richard Jordan. 20 May, 1713. Book 6, p. 149.

BAILEY, Edward: Leg.- To Son, Thomas Bailey, all land of which he is possessed, divided from rest of my land by a lately marked line. Beginning at Cypress Swamp, northerly to a pine in my head line to a white marsh and Cypress Swamp to beginning. Also a Gold Ring, two new chairs, besides what he is possessed of. To my son, Edward Bailey, the remaining part of my land which lies above the lately marked line including the plantation where I now live with all the land belonging. If he die it is my desire that my three daughters, Elizabeth, Hannah and Jane inherit for their children, (if they please to) and possess my now dwelling and that part of my Son, Edward's land which lies between the dividing line and the slash between the two springs. To daughter, Mary, wife of Samuell Briggs, 40 shillings, or its value out of estate. To daughter, Hannah, a cow. To dau., Faith, widow of Joseph Blackburn, 'dec'd. besides what she already has, a cow. To dau., Sarah, wife of Benj. Andrews besides what she already has, a cow. Three friends Nicholas Maget, Robert Watkins, and John Chapman value estate and divide in three parts for three daughters, Elizabeth, Hannah and Jane. D.: 7 Sept., 1735. Prob.: 15 Dec., 1736. Wit: Nicholas Maget, William Newsum, John Chapman. Book 8, p. 648.

BAILEY, Robert: Leg.- "My mother Elizabeth Tarver", a horse at her death to Sister, Sarah Boyce, horse, chest, dishes, etc. Sister, Mary Tarver, dishes, etc. To Samuall Tarver a gun now at his house. To Benjamin Bailey, my brother Anselm's Son, to my brother Anselm Bailey clothes. To brother, Walter Bailey, horse, pistol and holster. To Sister Jane Laughter, corn and a bed and furniture. To John Inman, chest & clothes, Cozen, William Warren jackets. To Capt. Holt's Son, Thomas, 5 lbs. Capt. Holt owes for corn. Brothers Anselm and Walter Bailey, Exers. 4 Oct., 1712. P.: 18 Mar. 1714. Wit: John Tooke, Thos. Waller. Book 6, p. 134.

BAKER, Henry: Leg.- To Wife, Sarah Baker, half my land, orchards, etc. during her natural life, also household goods of various kinds, pewter dishes, brasses, one great chest, spinning wheel, spoons, Trencher, live stock, etc. To Son, Henry Baker, the other half of the land, orchard, etc. and all my wife's part at her death, provided he pay to his brother, Edward Baker, 2000 lbs. of good tobo. in five equal payments - 400 per annum. To Son, Henry Baker, loom, 6 spoons, etc., etc. I give to my son, John, one cow; I give my Son, William Baker, 2 shillings sterling. I give to My grandson, William Baker, one yearling. I give to my daughter, Mary, one gold ring, etc. and all the rest of my estate, my debts and legacies being paid. I give between my six daughters, Mary, Susannah, Elizabeth, Alice, Sarah & Anne, Appts. wife, Sarah Baker, Exrx. All the children now with her to have their shares of things in the house. 24 Feb., 1697. 2 July, 1700. Wit: Thomas Waller, Wm. Williams, Roger Squire. Book 5, p. 205.

BAKER, Henry: Est.- 27 Apr., 1701. Wit: Robt. Lancaster, Nicholas Sesome, Charles Savidge. Sarah Baker Exerx. of

Henry Baker. Book 5, p. 224.

BAKER, Lawrence: Leg.- To my wife, Elizabeth 2 negroes and one-third part of my estate. To daughter, Catherine, wife of Ar. Allen, all lands, etc. two-thirds of my estate. Wife, Elizabeth and Son, Arthur Allen, Exers. Wit: Robert Caulfield, Fra. Taylor, Nicholas Pasfield, Phillip Shelley. 18 March, 1681. 6 7br., 1681. Book 2, p. 290.

BALEE, Robert: Est.- John Pasmore, Admr. 19 Aug., 1719. Signed: Robt. Hawthorne, Matthew Sturdevant, Robt. Greene. Wm. Thomas. Book 6, p. __.

BALEY, Daniel: Est.- Wit: Richard Averis, Samuel Maget. 14 Jan., 1680. Book 2, p. 279.

BAMER, Francis: Leg.- Wife, Mary Bamer, whole estate if she die to go to my children, equally divided, between, Martha Garrett, daughter of George Garrett and Mary Bamer daughter of William Bamer. To Jane Francis 30 shillings. Makes wife Exer. 4 June, 1729. P.: 17 Sept., 1729. Wit: Robert Butler, Thos. Anderson, James Piland. Bk. 7, p. 966.

BAMER, John: Leg.- To Wife, Anne Bamer, 3 negroes, furniture, horse, and her saddle and bridle, pewter, Russia, one-half dozen leather chairs, warming pan, bed with corde, etc. for her life and at her death to be divided among my four children. To Son, William Bamer, one negro, carpenter's tools, horse, etc. when he is 21 years old. To daughter, Hannah Bamer, one negro, one horse and furniture at 21 years. To son, John Bamer, My Trupers Arms, new saddle and bridle and other half of my tools given to Son, William. To daughter, Mary Bamer, bed, furniture, etc. when 21 years old, some new pewter. All remainder of estate to be divided among sd. Exer. Friend John Chapman and wife Exers. (Rem. of will torn & mutilated). Wit: Wm. Edwards, Samuell Thompson, Wm. Marriott. The estate was appraised 20 Oct., 1731. Book 8, p. 128.

BARD (BEARD), David: Leg.- Bequest to Maj. Samuel Swann all lands, tenements, etc. To Sampson Swann, Son of sd. Samuell Swann live stock. To John Browne clothing and corn. D.: 3 Feb., 1687/8. Prob.: 29 May, 1688. Wit: Robt. Randall, Thos. Swann. Book 4, p. 43.

BAREFOOT, Noah: Est.- By Grace Bedingfield, Admrx. Appraised by John Tyas, Edward Scarbro. D.: 25 Nov., 1711. Book 6, p. 83.

BARKER, George: Est.- Agnes Barker, Admr. 16 May, 1744. Signed: James Andrews, John Averis, Thos. Beddingfield. Book 9, p. 472.

BARKER, Grace: Leg.- Daughter, Elizabeth Andrews, yard of goods, Daughter, Sarah Lanier, 5 shillings, Daughter, Hannah Lashley, warming pan, Son, Josie Barker cattle and Exer. Son, Richard Barker, household goods, Daughter, Grace Barker, my Gold ring and household furniture and have charge of funeral. D.: 30 June, 1724. Prob.: 18 Aug., 1725. Wit: John Johnson, Thomas Johnson. Bk. 7, p. 599.

BARKER, Grace: Leg.- Brother, Josiah Barker, what he hath in possession. To cousin, Richard Barker, my plantation with 300 acres of land if he let his brother, John Barker, have

10

100 acres of this when he comes of age. Cousin, Josiah
Barker, iron kettle. Cousin, Mary Bishop, gold ring posy.
If she has no daughter to go back to Elizabeth Barker, the
Daughter of Josiah Barker. To cousins, William, Joshua
and Joel Barker, 5 shillings each. To Mary Bishop's son,
James, pewter dish. To Faith Barker small trunk. To
Elizabeth Barker a trunk. D.: 19 Feb., 1741. Prob.: 15
May, 1750. Wit: Robert Lanier, Josiah Barker, Josiah C.
Barker. Richard Barker, Exer. Book 9, p. 637.

BARKER, Jethro: Leg.- Son, John Barker, plantation where he
now lives with all land adjoining. Son, Henry Barker, 3
lbs. Daughter, Jane Field, three pounds, Daughter, Mary
Andross, three pounds, Son, Jethro Barker, three pounds.
Three granddaughters, Son George's children, Agnes, Mary
Elizabeth 150 acres of land, on North Side of Otterdam
Swamp where my said Son, George Barker, lived and twenty
shillings. To granddaughter, Sarah, daughter of Jehu
Barker five pounds. Son, Jehu Barker, the plantation where
I live on with all land adjoining and the remainder of my
estate and make him Exer. 5 Jan. 1744. Prob.: 15 March,
1747. Wit: Nicholas Partridge, Hugh Ivie, Nicholas
Partridge, Jr. Book 9, p. 567.

BARKER, John: Leg.- Daughter, Elizabeth Andrews, five shillings, Daughter, Sarah Lanier, ten shillings, Daughter,
Hannah Lashley, twenty shillings. To Son, Robert Foster,
40 acres of land that lies between two branches joyning
to the land that his father Foster bought of Abraham Evans
where Thomas Hunt lived. To Son, John Barker, 400 acres of
land that he now lives on, cattle, etc. in his possession.
To Son, John Barker, my plantation at Nottoway River being
222 acres including all land between Robert Hunt and the
Indian Cabin Creek, after his mothers' death. To grandson,
John Barker, a cow. To my son, Josiah Barker, 400 acres
that he now lives on at the Second Branch below his
Brother including all the 400 acres from that branch to
Richard Barker's line. I give to my son, Josiah Barker,
222 acres at Nottoway River - down to Capt. Clements' line.
To wife, Grace Barker, my plantation that I live on for her
life, - at her decease the plantation, 300 acres lying
between John Barkers and Thomas Cotten to my daughter,
Grace Barker. To granddaughter, Grace Foster, corn and
tobacco. Orders Son, Josiah Barker to take possession of
the estates of Christopher, Grace, and Robert Foster, not
to appraise but pay them as they come of age. Wife,
Grace Barker, Exer. 9 Oct., 1713. P.: 19 May, 1714.
Wit: Thomas Cotton, John Johnson, Elizabeth Figures.
Book 6, p. 191.

BARKER, John: Leg.- Sister, Mary Barker, brother, Joshuay
Barker. Mary Bishop, Exerx. 11 April, 1736. P.: 17
Sept., 1740. Wit: Josiah Barker, Faith Barker. Book 9,
p. 211.

BARLOW, John: Leg.- To Son, William Barlow, the plantation
where I live including Land between the Otterdam Swamp and
a small branch that runs into Syars Branch at the Little
Field that Wm. Barlow first cleared then down Branch to
Richard Pace's corner -- to the three creeks. To Son,
John Barlow, the plantation where John White now lives,
after John White and his wife's decease - and rest of my
land that lyeth on both sides of Three Creeks. To my Son,
Nathaniel Barlow, all Land I bought of Daniel Hicks on

11

Poplar Creek in Brunswick County. If he die to go to John
Barlow. Plantation where I live to my wife for her life,
William to live there during her life at her death to be
his property. Desires all rest of estate divided between
wife and children. The men to divide are Richard Pace,
Richard More and Thos. Avent. Estate in wife's hands until
son, Wm. Barlow, comes of age unless wife marry, then estate be divided at once. Son, William Barlow and wife,
Sarah, Exers. D.: 7 July, 1727. P.: 16 Oct., 1728.
Wit: Thos. Avent, Richard More, Richard Pace. Book 7, p.
864.

BARLOW, John: Est.- Thomas Avent, admr. 17 Sept., 1729. Wit:
Richard Pace, Daniel Hix, Charles Steuart. Bk. 7, p. 969.

BARLOW, John: Est.- Thomas Avent, admr. 16 Aug., 1738. Book
8, p. 881.

BARNES, John: Leg.- What is due me from my kinsman, Robert
Barham, ye son of Charles Barham late of Merch. Hundred,
deceased, be paid Wife, Jane, and what I owe to any other
person. To my son, John Tooke my gun. Remainder of estate
to loving wife, Jane, and two daughters, Sarah and Susannah, to be equally divided between them. Makes wife Exerx.
D.: 2 March, 1690-91. Prob.: 2 June, 1691. Wit: Sam
Howlon, Arthur Allen, Thomas Binns. Book 4, p. 202.

BARNES, John: Est.- Inventory of appraisement of Est. of John
Barnes late of Lawnes Creek Parish, deceased, presented by
Relict and Exrx., Jane. Sworn to by Henry Tooker. 4 July,
1691. Sworn as true 6 Sept., 1692 by John Tooke. Book 4,
p. 277.

BARROW, Thomas: Est.- Year 1690. Signed: John Thompson,
George Williams. Book 4, p. 170.

BARTLETT, Walter: Leg.- To daughter, Ann Moreland, live stock.
Wife, Alice Bartlett, land where I now dwell and the plan-
tation where Bishop lives, at her death to my grandson,
Bartlett Moreland. If he die to his brother, Thomas More-
land, if he die to his brother, John Moreland. Makes wife
Exerx. 4 Feb., 1695. Probated: 5 Sept., 1699. Wit:
Joseph Seat, William Bruton, John Greene, John Hancocke,
Richard Morris. Book 5, p. 179.

BATTELL, John: Est.- John Battell acknowledged receipt of his
father, Mathew Battell's estate from Benjamin Harrison.
6 7br., 1681. Signed: Jos. Malden, Thos. Blunt. Book 2,
p. 290.

BATTELLE, John: Leg.- Daughter, Faith Battle place where
Thomas Emry lives. Makes her Exerx. Has formerly disposed
of property. 21 Oct., 1728. P.: 19 Feb., 1728. Wit:
John Phillips, John Bee. Book 7, p. 894.

BATTLE, John: Est.- By Faith Battle. 18 June, 1729. Book 7,
p. 949.

BATTS, William: Leg.- To wife the use of my plantation whereon I now live for her life, at her decease I give sd. plantation to my son, John, and his heirs. Gives wife negro
for her life, at her death to my daughter, Martha and her
heirs. Give wife household furniture and maintenance for
years after my death. To son, William, the plantation I

12

bought of Henry Taylor and negro and furniture, horse, etc.
To daughter, Mary, one negro and feather bed and furniture.
To daughter, Elizabeth, one negro and feather bed and
furniture. To daughter, Martha, one large Bible and skil-
let. I give to my grandson, William Batts, feather bed and
furniture and ten pounds cash when he is twenty one years
old. To grandson, William Bain, a violin and forty shillings for schooling. All rest of estate I desire to be
equally divided between my wife and son, William, Exers.
31 Dec., 1741. Probated: 17 Nov., 1742. Wit: Charles
Binns, Henry Holt, David Drew. Book 9, p. 419.

BEARD, Thomas: Leg.- William Rookings, gives him whole estate.
20 Sept., 1741. Probated: 17 Oct., 1749. Wit: John
Harper, Ann Williams, Eliza. Dugall. Book 9, p. 618.

BECKWITH, Elizabeth: Leg.- To goddaughter, Eliza Lucas, daughter to William Lucas a cow. 6 March, 1687. Bk. 4, p. 38.

BEDINGFIELD, Henry: Leg.- To wife, Isabel, use of my estate
for her life. To Son, Thomas, feather bed and furniture.
To Son, Nathaniel, rest of estate. Wife, Isabel and son,
Nathaniel, Exers. 30 Apr., 1747. Probated 15 Sept., 1747.
Wit: William Willis, Peter Hawthorne. Book 9, p. 560.

BELL, John: Est.- Estate appraised by Ann Bell. 17 June, 1713.
Signed: Henry Hart, James Bruton. Book 6, p. 150.

BELL, John: Leg.- All debts to be paid. I give to son, John
Bell, all my land lying south of Spring Swamp 135 acres,
with houses, orchards, etc. To son, Burrell Bell, five
pounds current money, To son, Benjamin Bell, five pounds
current money. To son, Balaam Bell, five pounds current
money. To son, James Bell, the plantation I now live on,
on North side of Spring Swamp 500 acres, with houses, orchards, etc. To my daughter, Ann Parham, five shillings.
To my Daughter, Hannah Thompson, five shillings. To my
daughter, Mary Bell, fifty shillings, cow, furniture to be
delivered to her when she is 21 years old or married. Rest
and remainder of estate to wife, Hannah Bell, if she marry
to go to children. Wife, Hannah, Exerx. 19 Apr., 1746.
Prob.: 18 June, 1746. Wit: Silvanus Stokes, Edward
Shelton, Charles Judkins. Book 9, p. 531.

BELL, John: Est.- Signed: Ephraim Parham, Thos. Moore, Robert
Wells. 19 June, 1750. Book 9, p. 649.

BELL, Joseph: Leg.- Cousin, Burrel, 250 acres North side
Spring Swamp. Brother, John, rest of estate and pay debts.
(This will badly mutilated and illegible, first part not
readable). John Bell names Exer. Wit: Gregory Panhup,
John Clark. Book 8, p. 311.

BELL, Richard: Leg.- Son, Wm. Bell, coopers and carpenters
tools. Daughter, Mary Bell, pot and dishes. Daughters,
Sarah Bell, Eliza. Bell, and Amy Bell, five shillings each.
Son, Richard Bell, forty shillings. Son, Joseph Bell,
forty shillings, Son, Benjamin Bell, forty shillings. Wife,
Sarah Bell, rem. of estate for her life and make her Exer.
8 Nov., 1734. Prob.: 19 Feb., 1734. Wit: Thomas Edmunds, Bartholomew Figures. Book 8, p. 462.

BELL, Richard: Est.- Bal. due to Richard Bell. Sarah Bell,
Exer. 21 Apr., 1736. Signed: Benjamin Cocke, Henry King.

13

Book 8, p. ___.

BELL, Wm.: Est.- John Bell, admr. 22 Apr., 1725. 18 Aug.,
1725. Signed: Robert Watkins, Henry Watkins, Robert Judkins. Book 7, p. 596.

BENNETT, Ann: Widow deed of gift to her son, William Rowland.
2 Mar., 1696/7. Book 5, p. 125.

BENNETT, Jonas: Leg.- Southwark Parish. To godson, David
Andrews, Jr., a yearling and a new Bible. To goddaughter,
Sarah Bage, the same. To wife, Ann Bennett, whole estate
and makes her Exerx. Wit: Richard Rose, Samuell Alsbrook,
David Andrews. 8 May, 1696. 15 7br., 1696. Bk. 5, p. 110.

BENNETT, Jonas: Est.- Appraised by George Foster, John Moring,
William Foreman. Signed: Ann Bennett. 2 Mar., 1697/7.
Book 5, p. 125.

BENNETT, Richard: Est.- Benjamin Chapman, admr. 16 Dec., 1719.
Signed: Wm. Foster, William Howell, Charles White.
Book 7, p. 230.

BENNETT, Richard: Est.- Benjamin Bennett, admr. 18 Feb.,
1735. Signed: Capt. John Chapman, James Washington,
William Evans, Thomas Bell. Book 8, p. 569.

BENTLEY, John: Est.- Elizabeth Cling signed in court. 4 July,
1710. Signed: William Rookings, William Blackburne.
Book 6, p. 27.

BENTLEY, Thomas: Leg.- Bequest to Mrs. Elizabeth Harrison,
wife of Capt. Henry Harrison, all my estate real and personal. Bequest to Elizabeth Simmons, daughter of Mr. John
Simmons, ten pounds current money. Bequest to Thomas Alsobrooke horse and furniture. Henry Harrison, Exer. and puts
wife in his care. 4 Dec., 1718. Prob.: 17 July, 1723.
Wit: E. Goodrich, William Wynne. Book 7, p. 455.

BERRY, Nathaniel: Est.- Signed by Eleanor Berry. 23 Aug.,
1710. Signed: Edward Moreland, Samuel Cornwell. Book 5,
p. 416.

BERRYMAN, Ann: Leg.- To son, John Berryman, four head cattle.
To two sons, John and Joseph Berryman, one-half of my
hoggs and hay, son, William Berryman, the other half. To
son, Joseph Berryman, four head cattle. To son, William
Berryman, all the remains of my cattle. To son, John
Berryman, large pewter dish, Tankard and five new plates.
To son, Joseph Berryman, the largest flat pewter dish and
small deep dishes, etc. To daughter, Lucy Berryman, to
daughter, Ann Berryman, to daughter, Margaret Berryman, all
rest of estate. Sons, William, John, and Joseph Berryman,
Exers. 11 Aug., 1748. Prob., 15 Nov. 1748. Wit: Joseph
Edwards, John Edwards. Book 9, p. 590.

BERRYMAN, Augustine: Leg.- To wife, Ann, household goods, etc.
To son, John, cattle. Son, Joseph, mare and gun. Son,
William, two cows and gun. Remainder of estate to wife and
children equally divided among three sons and three daughters. Wife and son, John, Exers. 23 Oct., 1735. Prob.:
21 Apr., 1736. Wit: Henry Mcdonnae, William Drew, John
Thompson. Book 8, p. 580.

14

BERRYMAN, John: Leg.- To wife, place we now live - then to son, John, Son, Robert, where David Rice lately lived. Daughter, Elizabeth, not married to stay, if she desires, with Robert. "My six children and wife" the rest of my estate. 23 Aug., 1711. Probated: 25 Nov., 1711. Wit: Katherine Peacocke, Ann Hunnicutt, Samuell Hargrove. Book 6, p. 82.

BERRYMAN, John: Est.- Katherine Berryman, Exerx. 19 Dec., 1711. Signed: John Bailey, Carter Crafford. Bk. 6, p. 89.

BINNS, Charles: Leg.- Son, Charles Binns, two small tracts of land, one bought of Thos. Moreland and the other of Joseph Delk and 100 lbs. current money and 15 lbs. per annum for schooling. Gives wife use of plantation for life then to son, Charles. After sale, at wife's death, proceeds to all children. Nephew, Thos. Binns, guardian to son Charles. If Thos. Binns die, then brother, Thos. Eldridge guardian to Charles. To daughter, Elizabeth Binns, one hundred pounds. Daughter, Martha, 100 lbs. Child in esse 100 lbs. if daughter but if boy 100 lbs. and land at wife's death in Blackwater in Nansemond Co. To nephew, Thos. Binns, wearing apparel. To Sally Binns, gold ring. To Sarah Lande, fifty shillings. To Jean Gwaltney brought up by me fifty shillings. To John Champion fifteen shillings. 16 Oct., 1749. Prob.: 20 Mar., 1749. Wit: William Batts, John Newsum, Jno. Harris, Jos. Newburn. Book 9, p. 626.

BINNS, Thomas: Est.- 4 July, 1699. James Mason, Exer. Signed: William Newsum, William Chambers, Matthew Swann. Book 5, p. 181.

BINNS, Thomas: Est.- 1 May, 1705. Ethelred Taylor, Eliza. Taylor, admr. William Gray, Robert Ruffin. Bk. 5, p. 331.

BINNS, Thomas: Leg.- To wife use of plantation I live on during her life, after which to my son, Thomas Binns--and for want of such heirs to my daughter, Sarah Binns-and for want of heirs to my brother, Charles Binns. To my brother, Charles Binns, all my clothes. To goddaughter, Mary Price, five pounds to be paid to her when she is 12 years old. After debts are paid and funeral expenses, estate to be divided between my wife and children, share and share alike. Wife and Charles Binns, Exerx. 18 Oct., 1722. Probated: 20 Nov., 1723. Will presented by Jane Binns & Charles Binns, Exers. Wit: Thos. Holt, Charles Binns. Book 7, p. 484.

BINNS, Thomas: Est.- Jane Binns, Exerx. and Charles Binns, Exer. 18 Mar., 1723. Signed: Wm. Drew, Arthur Allen, Benjamin Edwards. Book 7, p. 512.

BINUM, John: Est.- 28 Jan., 1716. By Robert Warren. Signed: Allen Warren, Wm. Foster, Zacharias Maddera. 20 Feb., 1716. Book 7, p. 44.

BIRD, Thomas: Leg.- He is of Upper Chippoakes Creek in Southwark Parish in Surry Co. I give unto son, Thomas, onehalf of my mill and 300 acres of land lying upon the Eastern most side of Southern Run when he comes of age, etc. and ye other half of my land, and the land and plantation belonging to it whereon I now live after the decease of his mother, go to him and his heirs, etc. and also I do give 2000 pounds of tobo. and caske and my silver bole and

Tankard and my scale ring and my large andirons and a fixed
gun. Secondly, I do give unto my three daughters 300 acres
of land lying upon the South Side of ye Southern Run to
them and their heirs, etc. to be equally divided between
them and 2000 pounds of tobacco and caskes. If Thomas die
in minority his share to his sisters. To son, William, one
shilling. To Mary, my wife, one halfe of my mill and the
land I now live on during her life. Fifthly, it is my will
that my son, Thos. and his heirs may have liberty to get
timber - for repair of mill upon any part of my severall
tracts of land. To Mary, my wife, all rest of estate and
make her Exerx. 21 Jan., 1687. Prob.: 5 Jan., 1688. Wit:
John King, John Rogers, Eliza Moss. (Relict, Mary, married George Nicholson.) Book 4, p. 99.

BIRD, Thomas: Est.- 20 April, 1689. Bacon, Nathaniel, Esq.,
Pres. of his Majestie's Councill, of Virginia, whereas
Thomas Bird, deceased, in his will appointed his Relict,
Mary, his Exrx. of his will, who being married to George
Nicholson be at a court 5 January, 1688, made suit that a
Probate on the will be granted to him, and this authority
was given in request of his said wife, and has now rendered
full account as required. Signed: Nathaniel Bacon. Book
4, p. 113.

BISHOP, John: Est.- Admr. granted to Francis Mason. Signed at
James Citty by the Governor, 14 June, 1676. Bk. 2, p. 117.

BLACKBURN, Joseph: Est.- By Faith Blackburn, admr. 15 Aug.,
1733. Book 8, p. 314.

BLACKBURN, William: Leg.- To Son, John 50 acres -- at mouth of
Spring Run, to Old Field-head of Deep Bottom - to Stony
Run - to land I hold on lower side of Stony Run. To son,
William, 50 acres adj. my now dwelling house - between my
plantation John Sharp now lives to - Son John's beginning
at head of Deep Bottom - divides me and Geo. Williams. Son,
Benjamin, remaining part of my land. Wife, Exerx. 10
July, 1710. Prob.: 20 Mar., 1711. Wit: Nathaniel Har-
rison, Eliza. Norwood. Book 6, p. 47.

BLACKBURN, William: Leg.- (For most part this document is
illegible from water stains). Brother, Joseph Blackburn,
Sister, Mary Brown. Mentions, Edward Greene. Brother,
Joseph Blackburn, Exer. 26 Jan., 1732. Prob.: 21 Mar.,
1732. Wit: Wm. Saunders, Wm. Dredge, Francis Smith. Book
8, p. 267.

BLACKGROVE, Samuel: Leg.- My executors to sine William Crips
the Sore? for that land if William Crips will take that for
the hose I bote of him if not my executors to take it and
sine it to how he wil. I give Wm. Crips a Turnel ? I give
Elizabeth Crips heifer, pote and puter dish. I give Sara
Strinkfeler, heifer and puter dish. I give my dame a litel
dish and skelet. I give Charles Briggs my hose and bidel
and sudel, etc. Makes John Phillips, Exer. 26 March, 1728.
Prob.: 19 June, 1728. Wit: Elizabeth Crips, Elizabeth
Crips, Jr., John Smith. Book 7, p. 824.

BLOW, George: Est.- 18 Jan., 1717. Presented by Benj. Chapman. Signed: Charles Savidge, Wm. Davidson, Lawrence
Smith. Book 7, p. ___.

BLOW, Richard: Dead, his Relict, Eliza. Blow, applies for

16

admr. of his estate. 21 Oct., 1687. Book 4, p. 23.

BLUNT, Richard: Leg.- I give to son, Richard Blunt, land and
plantation I now live on 800 acres also new survey adjoining Wm. Blunt and Samuel Maget's Land, also two negroes and
ten head cattle when he comes of age, except plantation and
land above devised which I desire my wife to have during
her life; but if son, Richard, die before he comes of age
then to be equally divided between my sons, John and Benjamin and their heirs. I give and bequeath to Mr. Nicholas Edmonds all the lands of mine on south side of Great
Creek adjoining his own land, provided the sd. Ni. Edmonds
make over to my son, John Blunt the like quantity adjoining my land on North side of sd. creek. I give to son,
John Blunt, all my land on Great Creek, Brunswick Co. 425
acres, two negroes and ten head cattle, etc. to be delivered to him when he comes of age. If he die then son, Benjamin inherit it and negroes divided between sons, Richard
and Benjamin, when they come of age. To son, Benjamin, all
land in Isle of Wight County on Blunt's Swamp 300 acres,
also land adjoining negroes, cattle - when he is 21 years
old. If he dies to son, John. To daughter, Mary Irby, two
negroes. To John Irby, mare and twenty pounds. To daughter, Elizabeth Blunt, negroes. To daughter, Lucy Blunt,
two negroes. To cousin, William Blunt, all the land below
Ready Branch that was taken up between his father and myself 150 acres, his share. To wife, Ann Blunt, six negroes
and residue of estate divided between wife and five children, Richard, John, Benjamin, Elizabeth, Lucy. Wife Exer.
12 April, 1747. Prob.: 10 June, 1747. Wit: Robt.
Nicholson, Wm. Browne, Benj. Ellis. Book 9, p. 555.

BLUNT, Thomas: Southwark Parish. Leg.- Desires that real estate be divided among my children according to my desire
& make Will and Testament, etc. To Howell Edmunds and to
Elizabeth his wife 100 acres of land adjoining ye land
where they now live on ye side next ye Cattail Branch up
sd. Branch - to ye Blackwater Swamp and five lbs. money.
To son, Thomas Blunt, all ye remaining part of land contained within that pat. Also - land at Seacocke Swamp and
whereas Henry Briggs gave my said son cattle, all cattle
on plantation be sd. sons'. To son, Richard Blunt, the
land I now live on beginning at Benj. Harrison's corner
tree on ye south side of Blackwater Swamp - to head lines -
to cor. tree in sd. Harrison's line, etc. except 100 acres
conveyed to Thoas. Figgers. To son, Wm. Blunt, all remaining part of ye land contained within both ye two patts,
also my old plantation with all ye land belonging which I
bought of Mr. Henry Briggs to son William and his heirs. I
give to my son, Henry Blunt, 210 acres north side Nottoway
River, beginning lower part of pat. already seated. I
give to my son, Benjamin Blunt, though unbaptized, the remaining part of ye Patt. of land at Nottoway River 200
acres but if either of my said sons, Henry or Benjamin, die
in minority the survivor is to enjoy the whole tract of
land. I give to John Flood and Mary his wife 100 acres of
land on South side Nottoway River - on Whitewood Swamp on
East side of sd. Swamp beginning at Indian line -- I give
unto Howell Edmunds and unto Joel Barker ye remaining part
of ye pat. of land which lyeth on ye side of sd. Swamp to
be equally divided between them and then Howell Edmunds to
have his first choice, etc. I give unto my sons, Thomas
Blunt and Richard Blunt, all ye remaining part of ye patt.
which lyeth on ye contrary side of sd. Swamp to be equally

divided between them, etc. To loving wife, Priscilla
Blunt, twenty-five pounds current money and two negroes.
My desire is that my personal estate be divided between my
wife and six youngest children only, my son, Thomas, to
have no part - his already given to him. Wife made Exer.
21 Sept., 1708. Probated: 7 March, 1709. Wit: Wm.
Killingsworth, Hinsha Gilliam, Samuel Briggs, Henry Floyd.
(Blunt, Thomas: Est.- Admr. by Priscilla Thomas and Wm.
Thomas in 1716). Book 5, p. 442.

BLUNT, Thomas: Est.- 6 Nov., 1709-1715. Signed: Priscilla
Blunt, Henry Harrison, John Simmons, Thos. Bentley.
2 May, 1710. Book 6, p. 4.

BLUNT, Thomas: Est.- 20 Mar., 1716. Signed: William Thomas,
Priscilla Thomas. Goods received from Benj. Bradly,
London Merchant. Book 7, p. 50.

BLUNT, Thomas: Leg.- To my couzen, Anne Edmunds, daughter of
Howell Edmunds, fifteen pounds current money. I give unto
my sister, Ann Blunt, one negro. I give unto my brother,
Richard Blunt, all my land on Seacocke Swamp and that land
at the Whitewood Swamp, but if my brother, Richard Blunt,
should die without issue - then land at Seacocke Swamp
shall fall to my cousin, Howell Edmunds. I also give to
my brother, Richard Blunt, this plantation where I now live
till he marries or dies and then to return to my sister,
Anne Blunt, for her disposing. I give to brother, Richard
Blunt, two negroes, if Richard die to sister, Anne Blunt.
To couzen, Jane Flood, all my right and title to that land
my father gave her Father and mother. To brother, Richard,
all my personal estate and allow my sister, Anne maintenance - if my brother and sister should ever part, then my
sister, Anne Blunt, have one-third part of all stock and
crop there is at that time. Appoint brother, Richard
Blunt, Exer. 9 Feb., 1718. Prob.: 15 April, 1719. Wit:
Howell Edmunds, John Gilliam, Hincha Gillom. Bk. 7, p. 177.

BLUNT, Thomas: Est.- By Richard Blunt. 16 Dec., 1719.

BLUNT, Thomas: Est.- 19 June, 1723. By (brother) Richard
Blunt, Exer. of Will. Book 8, p. 450.

BLUNT, Thos.: Est.- By Richard Blunt Exer. of Will. 18 Oct.,
1721. Book 7, p. 379.

BLUNT, William: Est.- 16 Mar., 1736. Elizabeth Blunt, admr.
Signed: William Simmons, John Adrews, Sam. Maggett. 20
Apr., 1737. Book 8, p. 669.

BOLLING, Stith: Leg.- I give to my son, Stith Bolling, and his
heirs forever the land I have joyning on Appamattox River
that I purchased of William Mitchell, and Robt. Mitchell
and Drury Bolling and the land my Father purchased of John
Howell containing between 500 and 600 acres upon the foot
of Nottoway. I give to my son, Alexander Bolling and his
heirs forever my plantation at Stony Creek, an entry at
Buckhorn joyning to Robt. Williams and Morgan Mackenny. I
give to my sons, John and Robert Bolling, a tract of land
on both sides Buckshod Creek. Robert to have the Upper
part and John the lower side with a survey adjoining the
old patent. All the rest of my entries and surveys to be
equally divided on quantity and quality between my four
sons, Stith Bolling, Alexander Bolling, John Bolling and

Robert Bolling. Rest of estate and negroes to be equally
divided between my loving wife and my four sons and two
daughters and appoint wife and brothers, Robert Bolling
Exers. Probated: 16 Aug., 1727. Wit: J. Bolling, Jr.,
John Chapman, John Barmer. Book 7, p. 751.

BOLLING, Stith, Capt.: Est.- 21 Sept., 1727. Signed: Eliza.
Bolling, Robert Bolling, Nich. Maget. Wm. Brown, Jr., John
Simmons. Book 7, p. 950.

BOOKEY, Edward: Est.- Probate is granted Nich. Maget, and
Fortune, the wife of Edward Bookey, Exrxs. of his Will,
these are now granted authority to dispose of the estate.
26 Oct., 1694. Book 5, p. 26.

BOOKEY, Edward: Leg.- I give to my wife where I now live and
personal estate at her death bequest to Faith Magget.
Makes wife Exerx. and Fortune Bookey, Exerx. 9 Oct., 1712.
Wit: Nicholas Maggett, John Owen, James Spittles. Book
6, p. 132.

BOWMAN, Jeane: Leg.- All debts to be paid. To son, John
Tooke, five shillings, to daughter, Jeane Newby, one cow.
To Elizabeth Ezell, my daughter, one bed. Son-in-law,
Michael Ezell, 500 pounds tobo. and his son, William, a
cow. Son, Wm. Tooke a cow. Granddaughter, Sarah Newby,
a cow, daughter, Sarah Cornell, a horse. To Isaac Cornell,
my grandson, a cow; Samuell Cornell, grandson, a horse;
daughter, Susannah Barnes, all rest of my good and cattle
and makes her Exrx. 5 Oct., 1702. Prob.: 4 Mar., 1706.
Wit: Wm. Price, Susannah Price, John Mills. Bk. 5, p. 358.

BOWMAN, Thomas: Est.- 3 Nov.m 1699. Jane Bowman, admr. of
Thomas Bowman (a Quaker) declares the inventory to be true.
Signed: Wm. Chambers, Thos. Walker, Mathew Swann. Book 5,
p. 186.

BRADDY, Edward: Est.- By Judith Wyche, administrator. 17 May,
1721. Signed: Curtis Land, John Hatty, Richard Poole.
Book 7, p. ___.

BRADY, John: Leg.- To son-in-law, George Williams, my plantation with all land, houses, etc. sword, gun and shot
bag. If he dies without issue my wife, Eleanor Brady,
shall have possession. All rest estate to wife and son-
in-law, Geo. Williams. Makes them Exers. 28 June, 1675.
Prob.: 28 March, 1676. Wit: Ni. Meriweather, George
Arnoll, Jno. Fawcett. Book 2, p. 107.

BRADY, John: Est.- Probate granted to Mrs. Eleanor Brady and
Mr. George Williams on the will of Mr. John Brady, dec'd.
Signed at Great Spring by Sir William Berkeley. 16 Mar.,
1676. Book 2, p. 117.

BRANTLEY, Hester: Leg.- Eldest daughter, Priscilla, clothes
and side saddle. To daughter, Elizabeth, clothes, Bible.
If they die, Sister, Elizabeth Joyner, to have Priscilla's
part and sister, Grace Warren to have Elizabeth's part.
My two sisters' children, Elizabeth Joyner and Grace
Warren. Makes James Willson and James Pyland Exers. of estate. 28 April 1727. Prob.: 17 May, 1727. Wit: Elizabeth Gray, Elizabeth Barlow. Book 7, p. 724.

BRANTLEY, Hester: Est.- Paid Elizabeth Barlow, Robt. Butler,

Eliza. Pyland, Sarah Glover, Eliza. Gray, bal. due James
Willson, Exer. 19 Mar., 1728-9. Book 7, p. 911.

BREWER, Nicholas: Est.- John Davis, Admr. 15 March, 1729-30.
Signed: Thomas Avent, Richard Pace, Charles Stewart,
Isaac House. Book 7, p. 1024.

BREWSTER, Mrs. Elizabeth: Est.- Presented by John Watkins,
admr. 27 May, 1675. An inventory of severall debts due to
the estate of my deceased mother, Mrs. Elizabeth Brewster.
Signed: John Moring, Jno. Whitson, Jno. Smith, Nicholas
Witherington. Book 2, p. 90.

BREWTON, William: Leg.- Sister, Mary, thirty shillings.
Sister, Anne, twenty shillings. Daughter, Martha, three
negroes. Daughter, Sarah, three negroes; daughter, Eliza-
beth, three negroes. Wife and friend, Charles Binns,
Exers. 18 July, 1737. Prob.: 16 May, 1739. Wit: Thos.
Binns, Jos. Bridger, Geo. Brewton. Book 9, p. 57.

BRIDGMAN, Edward: Est.- 3 April, 1679. Signed: Samuel Cornell, William Hancocke, Edward Taner. Book 2, p. 214.

BRIDGMAN, Edward: Est.- 1 July, 1679. John Barnes, admr.
Wit: Robert Caufield, Fra. Mason, Wm. Edwards. Book 2,
p. 17.

BRIGGS, Charles: Leg.- (Page mutilated and illegible in first
part of will). To son, George Briggs (portion gone). To
my daughter, wench Jane & negro, wench Tom and negro. To
daughter, Sarah Nicholson and her husband, Joshua Nicholson, 425 acres land on South side Three Creek in Isle of
Wight Co. and four negroes. To grandson, Henry Vaughn,
three tracts of land on second Swamp, ninety or 150 acres,
and one negro. To daughter, Eliza. Vaughn, one negro and
ten pounds. To daughter, Eliza. Nicholson, one negro. To
sons, George Briggs and Howell Briggs, and daughter,
Francis Rose, all the money I have in England and all my
store goods which is for sale to be equally divided amongst
them. To my (illegible) Howell Briggs the plantation
where I now live and one tract of land on ye Major's Branch
containing (illegible) slaves named (illegible) -- Howell
Briggs, Exer. Remainder illegible. Book 8, p. 14.
Codicil to Will: (Page on which this will is written is
partly gone) -- Vaughn one feather bed. ___ which I have
given to Henry Vaughnn. He dying without issue to his
sister, Elizabeth Vaughan (both under age). To sons,
George and Howell Briggs, equally divided. 20 Nov., 1729.
Probated: 20 May, 1730. Howell Briggs, Exer. Wit:
Joel Barker, Wm. Thomas, William Rose. Book 8, p. 15.

BRIGGS, George: Leg.- To brother, Henry Briggs, half of hogs
on Nottoway River. Brother, Samuel Briggs, admr. and
Exer., of all lands and chattels and at my death all that
belongs to me and pay all that I owe. D.: 26 May, 1698.
Probated: 7 March, 1698/9. Wit: Will. Killingsworth,
Howell Edmunds, John Case. Book 5, p. 166.

BRIGGS, Henry: Leg.- To Son, Henry Briggs, 150 acres upon
boiling spring continuing down Otterdam Swamp, a breadth
of 150 acres. To son, Charles Briggs, all land from the
150 acres before mentioned, unto my son-in-law, Thos.
Blunt, his line to him, the said Charles Briggs his heirs,
etc. My will is that the land laid out for my son-in-law,

Thos. Blunt, according to his bill of sale by me signed, be
acknowledged in Court by my Exer., to him, Thos. Blunt and
his heirs. I bequeath unto my two sons, George Briggs and
Samuel Briggs, after ye decease of my wife, Margery Briggs,
all ye rest of my land not before exprest, to be equally
divided betwixt them and that half my plantation I now live
on to my son, George Briggs, to them - said Geo. Briggs
and Samuel Briggs, etc. Daughter, Marie Briggs, dishes,
etc. Wife, Margery, after debts are satisfied, all estate
real and personall except what in the will is before
named. Makes her Exerx. 26 Sept., 1681. Probated: 6
July, 1686. Wit: Sylvester Joles, Daniell Sturdivant,
Lu. Longwell. Book 3, p. 58.

BRIGGS, Henry: Est.- In will appointed his Relict, Margery
Briggs, Exrx. as asked by said Margery of Court. Granted.
21 Oct., 1687. Book 4, p. 26.

BRIGGS, Henry: Est.- By William Briggs, admr. Signed:
Andrew Lester, James Anderson, Rueben Cash. 17 Jan., 1738.
Book 8, p. 903.

BRIGGS, Henry: Leg.- To Grandson, Henry Bedingfield, my plan-
tation on South side of Beaver Dam Swamp 170 acres of land.
To daughter, Mary Bedingfield, all she is possessed with.
To daughter, Ann Barton, all she is possessed with. To
daughter, Hannah Hill, all she is possessed with. To
daughter, Prisselah Barker, all she is possessed with. To
grandson, James Chappell, bed, etc. To grandson, Thos.
Chappell, my gun. To daughter, Rebecca Chappell, a cow.
To son-in-law, James Chappell, my daughter, Elizabeth
Chappell, all rest of my estate which they have in their
possession. Makes son-in-law, James, Exer. 22 Jan., 1738.
Pro.: 21 Nov., 1739. Wit: John Rosser, James Chappell,
Jr., John Jarrod. Book 9, p. 97.

BRIGGS, Samuel: Leg.- To son, William Briggs, one-half of
what land I have in Brunswick County upon a creek called
Wagua, I desire he may have the lower half and one negro
man. To son, Henry Briggs, one negro man. To daughter,
Sarah Gilliam, five pounds sterling. To daughter, Sarah
Collier, five pounds sterling. To daughter, Mary Edmunds,
one negro, which she has in possession and five pounds
sterling. I give to my son, Thomas Briggs, all my land in
Hunting Quarter and all the stock belonging - I give to
my son, Robert Briggs, one-half my land in Brunswick County on Wagua Creek, with the plantation and stock and one
negro, only my wife to have use of negro until Robert is
21 years old. Gives Robert one negro. To son, Nathaniel
Briggs, one plantation on Bly's Branch with all the stock
and nine hogs which were on Beaver Dam, one negro girl, one
negro man. My wife to have use of negroes until Son,
Nathaniel Briggs, is 21 years old. To son, Benjamin Briggs,
all the land where I now live. Gives son, one negro, but
wife to have use during her widowhood and desires son,
Benjamin, to receive his estate when 18 years old. To
Daughter, Ann Briggs, a negro girl. To Daughter, Lucy
Briggs, two negro girls. To Daughter, Hannah Briggs, two
negroes if Hannah die to daughter, Lucy; if Lucy die to
Hannah; if both die to son, Benjamin Briggs. Gives wife,
Mary Briggs, bed and furniture, side saddle, horse. Remainder of estate I desire to be equally divided betwixt
my wife and my four youngest children, and desire that
three youngest daughters receive their estate at 18 years

21

old or married. Wife Exerx. 26 Mar., 1736. 21 Sept.,
1737. Wit: Thos. Edmunds, Rich. Blunt, James Anderson.
Book 8, p. 730.

BRIGGS, William: Leg.- To brother, Thos. Briggs, all my land
in the fork of Meherin River. To Cousin, Hincha Gilliam,
50 acres land between old and new line of Hincha Gilliam,
deceased, also eleven pieces of silver. To son, John
Briggs, all my land in Surry County, one negro and furniture. To son, William Briggs, 335 acres of land in Brunswick County on a creek called, Waqua, and negro and furniture, etc. To son, Henry Briggs, 418 acres of land in
Brunswick County on head of Creek called, Sturgeon, one
negro and furniture. All my land that lies in Upper fork
of Crouches Creek to my two sons, William and Henry Briggs,
to be equally divided, when son, Henry is 21 years old.
If, William or Henry die without issue to go to survivor.
To daughter, Elizabeth Chappel, negro and furniture &
horses, which she already possessed of. To daughter, Mary
Chappell, negro, Prayer book, Furniture, etc. To daughter,
Amy Briggs, one negro, bed and furniture, etc. To daughter, Lucy Briggs, one negro, etc. To wife, Mary Briggs,
negroes. Remainder of estate to wife, Mary, if she marry
to go to children. Makes wife Exerx. 8 Feb., 1748. Prob.:
19 Apr., 1748. Wit: JOhn Hay, Edmund Ruffin, Willet
Roberts, John Irby. Book 9, p. 569.

BRIMINGTON, Bryan: Est.- William Cocke, Admr. 16 June, 1754.
Signed: John Tyus, Wm. Looshas (Lucas?), Sr. Book 6,
p. 194.

BROOKS, William: Est.- John Brooks, admr. 19 Aug., 1729.
Signed: Thos. Jones, Robert Mitchell, James Mitchell. 19
Nov., 1729. Book 7, p. 992.

BROWN, Edward: Leg.- (will illegible, but quite long at
least seven bequests.) Wife Exerx., Mary Brown. Wit:
Thomas Goldne (Gwaltney), Robert Lancaster. Probated:
15 Nov., 1732. Book 8, p. 241.

BROWN, Edward: Est.- By Mary Brown. 19 Sept. 1733. Book 8,
p. 331.

BROWN, Henry: Est.- 21 Apr., 1742. Pd. to Lemuel Cocke and
Jane his wife, to Henry Brown, to Ann Brown, to Rebecca
Brown. Book 9, p. 404.

BROWN, Mary: Leg.- Sister-in-law, Faith Blackburn, clothing.
To Anne Macsheden, clothing. To Elizabeth Cooper, clothing.
To Sarah Dugan, clothing, to Faith Blackburn, daughter to
my sister-in-law, clothing. To Mary Blackburn, daughter to
my sister-in-law, clothing. To Wm. Blackburn, son to my
sister-in-law, clothing, pistols and rem. of my husband's
estate, etc. Makes Thomas Hamlin, Exer. 22 Sept. 1736.
Prob.: 20 July, 1737. Wit: Robert Grimes, Eliza Cooper.
Book 8, p. 734.

BROWNE, Henry: Leg.- To wife, Elizabeth Browne, all the estate
which she possessed at any time before my marriage with
her, all negroes and other estate which she had from Mr.
Bolling and her own acquiring till the day of our marriage,
she paying all debts and legacies from Stith Bolling's
estate. I give to my son, Henry Browne, six negroes. To
my daughter, Jane Browne, six negroes. To my daughter,

22

Elizabeth Browne, six negroes. To my daughter, Ann Browne,
five negroes. To child in esse if it be a boy all my land
in Brunswick County and all my land in Surry County near
Burchen's Island on Black Water Swamp and five negroes, if
it is a girl, I give her five negroes but the land in
Brunswick and Surry Counties to my Son, Henry Browne. Son,
Henry Browne, all my tract of land in Surry Co., known as
Spring Swamp. To my wife three negroes at her death divide among my children. I forgive the following people the
debts they owe me, namely: John Bynam, Edward Harris,
Richard Bennett, Sr., John Bell, Thomas Bell and John
Andrews. I give William Rogers, Sr. ten pounds current
money and ten pounds credit in some store. I give to Edward Harris ten pounds current money ten pounds credit in
some store. I give to all persons hereafter named a Ring
to amount to 20 shillings sterling each that is to say to
my wife and each of her children, Jane, Ann, Alexander,
and John Bolling one and to each of my own children, Jane,
Elizabeth, Henry, and Anne Browne and to the Child to be
born, one apiece. To my brother, William Browne and his
wife and to all their children one apiece. To my brother,
Henry Edloe, and his wife and all their children. To my
sister, Anne Browne, one to Mr. William Simmons and his
wife. To Mr. John Simmons and his wife to Mr. Howel Briggs
and his wife. To Richard Cocke and his wife and his son,
Hartwell Cocke. To the Rev. Mr. Eelbeck and his wife and
to Rebecca Edloe. To the officers and each of the Troopers belonging to the Troopes which I have commanded a ring
apiece to the value of tenn shillings current money each.
To John Andrews his wife and all their children a ring to
value of tenn shillings. My will if any of my children die
before coming of age or marry, their part divided with
survivors except the land, which I would have descend as
the law directs. After all debts are paid remainder of estate to be divided among my children, Henry, Jane, Elizabeth, Ann, and the child to be born. Appts. father, Wm.
Browne, and Brother, William Browne, Jr., to be Exers. 23
Sept., 1734. Prob.: 19 Feb., 1734. Wit: Henry Eelbeck,
Chris. Clinch, Charles White, Richard Cocke. Book 8, p.
458.

BROWNE, John: Est.- Settled by Eliza Browne. 15 Apr., 1719.
Signed: John Tyus, William Edwards, Jr. Bk. 7, p. 175.

BROWNE, Samuel: Est.- By William Browne, admr. 16 May, 1749.
Signed: William Little, John Little, Robert Hart.

BROWNE, Thomas: Leg.- To Mary Browne, my wife a horse, saddle
and bridle and eight pistoles out of my estate and all my
other estate real and personal. To grandson, William
Butterell, a bequest. To my only daughter, Ann Mcexodon?
one shilling. All rest of my estate to Wife and Nath.
Harrison and John Cargill, and they to be Exers. If my
wife should marry I give one-half of my estate to be divided between wife and grandson, William Butterell. 4 Sept.,
1735. Prob.: 15 June, 1737. Wit: Thomas Hamlin,
Barnaby Tate. Book 8, p. 701.

BROWNE, Thos.: Est.- 20 Jan., 1737. John Cargill, Exer.
Signed: Robert Grimmer, John Griffith, John Moring. Book
8, p. 733.

BROWNE, William: On behalf of his daughter, Mary Ashe, for
admr. on her estate. Granted. 2 Apr., 1690. Bk. 4, p.294.

BROWNE, William: Est.- 9 Jan., 1705. Signed: Thos. Collier,
Charles Wyche, Wm. Browne. Book 5, p. 341.

BROWNE, William: Leg.- To my grandson Wm. Browne, the plantation where his mother now lives and all land belonging.
Main Run of Broad Swamp from its mouth on James River - to
include all my land below the said swamp. My daughter-in-
law, Mary Browne, shall have the full enjoyment of the a-
foresd. plantation so long as she continue a widow. I give
to my grandson, Henry Browne, the plantation where I now
live and rem. of tract belonging. To grandson, Henry
Browne, my tobo. plantation in Isle of Wight (one at Fishing Place, the other where Francis Mabry now lives, etc.
To grandson, William Browne, two plantations in Brunswick
Co.) one where Joseph Moody lives, the other on Rose's
Creek, all stock, etc. when he is 18 yrs. old. To grandson, Philip Edloe, one negro, bought and put in his father's
care. To grandson, William Edloe, one negro. To granddaughter, Jane Edloe, one negro and thirty pounds. To
granddaughter, Rebecca Edloe, one negro. To grandson, John
Edloe, one negro. To granddaughter, Mary Edloe, one negro.
To granddaughter, Ann Browne, Daughter of my son, Henry,
three negroes. To great-grandson, Henry, son of Lemuel
Cocke, 20 pounds. To granddaughter, Rebecca Browne, one
negro. To granddaughter, Elizabeth Browne, two negroes.
To granddaughter, Ann Browne, (dau. of my son, William) two
negroes and 40 lbs. To granddaughter, Martha Browne, one
negro. To granddaughter, Lucy Gray, daughter of William
Gray, 50 lbs. To grandson, Wm. Browne, two negroes and
100 lbs. Interest and principal to be paid him at 18 yrs.
old. If he die to my granddaughters, Mary Eaton, Elizabeth Browne, Anne Browne, Martha Browne, and Ann Browne,
My son Henry's daughters. To Grandson, Henry Browne, my
Grist Mill. Gives to grandson, Henry Browne, many negroes
and tract of land where his father did live at Blackwater
Swamp provided he make a good title to Thomas Bell, this
was not made at his father's death. If grandson, William,
die before of age 18 then to my grandson, Henry Browne.
Rest of estate to grandson, Henry Browne, and makes him
Exer. Patrick Adams. 3 July, 1746. Prob.: 19 Jan.,
1747. Wit: Patrick Adams, Richard Cocke, Peter Warren.
Book 9, p. 563.

BROWNE, William (Capt.), Jr.: Leg.- On his death bed desires
his children to walk uprightly, etc. if not wife may dis-
inherit them. Wife not to administer on estate, if possible not to do so -- desires Mr. Wm. Eaton should defer
building his house and help wife build hers then she help
him. The direction of his wife and family is left to
Capt. Richard Cocke and Mr. William Eaton. All of my fe-
male children to fare alike. I have directed that my
daughter, Mary, pay Mr. Wm. Eaton, part of 300 lbs. balance
to be paid him. Inform Capt. Cocke that Henry has his
father's watch, Pistols, and holsters and 6 pistoles cash
of his estate. I desire that Eliza. Cobbs's and Eliza.
Bage's debts to be forgiven them. Ledderdale's account in
the desk -- to be accounted with Mr. Prentice. Mary Brown,
widow and James Balfour, legetee. 18 Sept., 1744. Book
9, p. 44.

BROWNE, William, Sr.: Leg.- To granddaughter, Jane Jordan, negro girl and other bequests. To granddaughter, Mary Sowerby, the wife of Francis Sowerby, and to her children that
shall be born, negroes. If no heirs to Wm. Browne, son of

Wm. and Jane Browne. To daughter, Ann Flood, wife of
Walter Flood, fifty pounds. To daughter, Priscilla Blunt,
the wife of Thomas Blunt, five pounds. To son, Henry
Browne, 20 shillings. To grandson, John Flood five pounds.
To other grandchildren, Walter Flood, Fortune Flood, Mary
Flood, Wm. Browne, Henry Browne, Jane Browne, Mary Jordan,
the younger and William Blunt 40 shillings apiece. And
whereas I have made agreement with Robt. Grice for a plantation where he now lives containing about 270 acres for
which plantation I am to have 8000 pounds tobo. and Robt.
Grice to have 8 years to pay and hereafter named Exer. to
make acknowledgement of it to said Robt. Grice, paying
tobo. above mentioned. The land where Sion Hill lived and
hath built a mill contained in my patent of a tract of land
on the south side Blackwater. My wish that Exer. make a
new survey of said land to said Sion Hill-having already
made satisfaction for the same. Rest of estate to son,
William Browne, and make him Exer. and whereas my son,
William Browne, is now gone for England and it is uncer-
tain how it may please God to deal with him and that he
may die before he returns to possess estate which God for-
bid--if he should die to my son Wm. Browne all my land I
have at Blackwater. To grandson, Henry Brown, piece of
land in James Citty now in occupation of John Child. Daughter, Jane Browne, wife of William Browne, ten pounds. To
granddaughter, Jane Browne, daughter of William and Jane
Browne, eighty pounds when 18 or married. Grandsons
William and Henry Browne, sons of Wm. and Jane Browne.
Walter Flood, Nich. Maget, Thomas Blunt, Exrs. 4 Dec.,
1704. Prob.: 3 July, 1705. Wit: Francis Sowerby,
Charles White, Nich. Maget, Wm. Bruson. Book 5, p. 305.

BRUCE, James: Est.- Patrick Adams, admr. 18 Mar., 1746.
Signed: John Avary, Edward Bagley, John Jarrett. Book 9,
p. 550.

BRUTON, James: Leg.- Daughter, Elizabeth, 5 shillings. Daughter, Mary Kae, one negro, at her death to grandson, Bruton
Kae. Grandson, John Kae, negro, etc. Daughter, Ann
Jurden, one negro. Son, Wm. Bruton, two negroes. Grandson, James Bruton, three negroes. Wife two negroes for
life, at her death to son, Wm. Bruton, two daughters, Mary
and Ann, a cow apiece. Wife and son, Wm. Bruton, Exers.
5 Feb., 1734. Prob.: 17 Mar., 1735. Wit: Charles Binns,
Benjamin Bell. Book 8, p. 573.

BRUTON, Sarah: Leg.- Daughter, Mary, three youngest daughters,
Martha, Sarah and Elizabeth. Mentions James Dering and
two young daughters. James Dering, Exer. 10 March, 1744.
Prob.: 7 April, 1745. Wit: Charles Binns, John Seward.
Book 9, p. 500.

BRYAN, Frederick: Leg.- Wife, brother-in-law, John Ruffin, is
made Exer. Mentions wife and "each of my children." 23
Feb., 1747. Prob.: 17 May, 1748. Wit: James Baker,
John Ruffin. Book 9, p. 577.

BULLOCK, Richard: Leg.- To Henry Hollingsworth a calf. To
Godson, Richard Phelps, clothing and live stock. Son,
Richard Bullock, plantation where he now lives with all
land belonging to it, when 18 yrs. old. Mr. Henry Harrison
have charge of Richard's estate. Wife, Mary Bullock, rest
of estate real and personal. Wit: Daniel Parker, Adam
Heath, Wm. Short. 25 March, 1703. Prob.: 6 July, 1703.

25

Book 5, p. 287.

BUNNILL, Hezekiah: Leg.- Grandson, Thomas Anderson, livestock and dishes. Two youngest grandsons, George and Richard Williams, a heifer. To daughter, Jean, small chest. To granddaughter, Joanna Williams, all my land. To wife one-third of personal estate. George Williams and Joanna, his wife, Exers. Granddaughter, Joanna, all the rest, after debts and legacies paid. 27 June, 1709. Prob.: 5 Nov., 1709. Wit: Jeremiah Ellis, John Sharp, Thomas Sowerby. Book 5, p. 433.

BURGESS, Robert: Leg.- He of Surry Co., makes wife, Ann Burgess, Extrx. To Thos. Dunn, Son of Jno. Dunn, of Surry all my land after death to wife. If Thomas Dunn die, to go to John Dunn, Sr. paying to "my brother", Thomas Burgess, and his children 40 lbs. In case Dun never hears from the said Thomas Burgess and his children then Dunn to pay 5 lbs. sterling to the Chappel at Upper part of Surry Parish. To Richard Shoker (or Stokey). To John Rawlings. John Dunn not to mortgage land from his children, to be continued in name of Dunn. Wife all goods, etc., in Virginia. 6 Feb., 1682. Prob., 4 7br, 1683. Wit: John Rawlings, Launselett Bock. Book 2, p. 333.

BURTON, Anthony: Est.- Wm. Atkinson, admr. 20 March, 1733. Signed: John Weaver, Daniel Epps, Henry Mitchell. Book 8, p. 359.

BUTLER, William: Est.- Joyce Butler, widow and admr. 5 Oct., 1678. Signed: Robert Kae, Jno. White, Wm. Newsum, Wm. Seward. Book 2, p. 6.

BYNHAM, John: Est.- Son John Bynham, admr. 17 May, 1692. Book 4, p. 239. Acct. of estate in 1719, by Robert and Ann Warren. 20 May, 1719. Signed: Thos. Cocke, Wm. Cocke. Book 7, p. 187.

BYNTON, Richard: Est.- By Lucy Bynton. 4 May, 1708. Signed: Robert Flacke, John Thropp, Thos. Warde. Bk. 5, p. 393.

BYRD, John: Geo. Foster, aged 55, swore that being at the house of Wm. Foster in April last, where John Byrd, deceased lay lowe in bed and sd. Byrd told deponent he Byrd had given all his estate to Wm. Foster, that Wm. Foster took care of him, Byrd, as long as he lived. 4 Sept., 1694. Robert Warren 27 years old, swore to same. Book 5, p. 19.

CALLAHAM, Morris: Leg.- To daughter, Francis Callahan, hogs, cows, dishes, etc. Wife, Frances Callaham, rest of estate, and makes her Exerx. 19 Dec., 1720. Prob.: 18 Oct., 1721. Wit: Wm. Jones, Wm. Malone, Nich. Callaham. Book 7, p. 376.

CALLIHAN, Morris: Est.- By Nicholas Callihan, Exer. 20 June, 1722. Book 7, p. 401.

CANNON, John: Leg.- Wife, Joanna, use of all estate for life. Daughter, Joanna Justice, one negro for life. Granddaughter, Joanna Scarbrough, all my land and plantation where I live - 370 acres and one negro. To granddaughter, Jean Justice, one negro. To granddaughter, Mary Justice, one negro. To granddaughter, Elizabeth Justice, furniture, bed, etc. To granddaughter, Lydia Justice, one negro. To

To granddaughter, Sarah Justice, seven lbs. and furniture.
To great granddaughter, Joannah Scarbrough, 7 lbs. To
grandson, John Justice, Jr., one gun. To cousin Cannon,
son to Benj. Cooper, 20 shillings for schooling, three
grandchildren, John, Eliza. and Sarah Justice. Wm. Scarbrough have negro until Mary Justice is of age or married.
John Justice, Exer. 11 July, 1741. Prob.: 21 Oct., 1741.
Wit: John Nicholson, John Collier. Book 9, p. 388.

CAREN, Joseph: Est.- 25 May, 1703. Signed: Phillip Shelly,
John Drew. Book 5, p. 279.

CARGILL, John: Leg.- Wife (this page is illegible and torn.)
"Brother David" "my seven sisters" "property given to my
son's disposal" (not of age). Makes Son, John, Exer. Wit:
Wm. Phillips, Robert Wager, John Jarrett. Bk. 8, p. 182.

CARGILL, John: Est.- By Robert Gray, Joseph John Jackman,
John Nicholson, Eliza. Cargill, admr. 18 Apr., 1744.
Book 8, p. 469.

CARGILL, John: Est.- By Thos. Cocke guardian. 27 Jan., 1747/8.
June 21, 1748. Book 9, p. ___.

CARLILE, Robert: Est.- By Mr. John Nicholls. 3 Nov., 1711.
Elizabeth Carlile, admr. Signed: John Weaver, Daniel
Horton. Book 6, p. 83.

CARPENTER, Mary: Est.- Wm. Knott, John Wapple, Wm. Hunt, Ann
Avery, John Bentley made oath to inventory. 7 Nov., 1699.
Signed: Wm. Rookings, Robert Nicholson, John Good. Book
5, p. 1184.

CARPINDOR, William: Est.- Appoints his Relict, Mary Carpinter,
Exerx. of his estate. Book 5, p. 111.

CARR, John: Leg.- To Joseph Farloe a gun, Bible and rest of
est. Signed: Elizabeth Coggin, Wm. Welling. 5 Mar.,
1677. Book 2, p. 164.

CARR, John: Leg.- To friends, Matthew Current, of Prince
George Co. and Richard Ransom, of Brunswick all my whole
estate. The latter Exer. 9 Jan., 1737. Prob.: 15 Feb.,
1737. Wit: Ellen Rookings, Stephen Mercer, Richard
Steward, James Watts. Book 8, p. 796.

CARR, Thomas: Leg.- Bequest to John and Elizabeth Allen 1000
lbs. Tobacco, to Samuel Carrell 450 lbs. tobacco, to Edward
Rowell and makes him Exer. 4 Jan., 1693. Prob.: 6 Mar.,
1693. Wit: Samuell Carrell, Thomas Hart. Bk. 4, p. 346.

CARR, Thomas: Est.- Edward Rowell, Exer. and makes return
1 May, 1694. Book 3, p. 8.

CARRELL, Benj.: Est.- Appt. at Jno. Carrell's in Isle of
Wight County, Benj. Cocke, Wm. Drew, Dolphine Drew. 17
July, 1750. Book 9, p. 652.

CARRELL, Benjamin: Leg.- To wife profits of land leased in
Lawnes Creek Neck. To son, Joseph, 17 lbs.; to daughter,
Mary, 7 lbs.; four children, Katherine, Benj. Joseph, and
Mary to have rest of my estate. Wife, Joice Carrell, Exerx.
20 Nov., 1745. Prob.: 20 Mar., 1749. Wit: William
Seward, Jordan Thomas. Book 9, p. 625.

CARRILL, William: Est.- By Thos. Bedingfield. 19 Dec., 1711.
Signed: Robt. Ruffin, Wm. Hamlin. Book 6, p. 89.

CARROLL, John: Est.- 27 June, 1706. By Samuel Thompson.
Signed: Allen Warren, John Lather. Book 5, p. 353.

CARTER, George: Est.- Eliza, Carter, orphan of Geo. Carter.
Geo. Carter's widow married Wm. Hare. She received estate
for 40 yrs. and then half to Eliza. Carter. 8 7br., 1679.
Book 2, p. 220.

CARTER, Thomas: Est.- Bartholomew Figures, admr. 16 Jan.,
1739. Signed: John Andrews, Samuel Maget, Robert Judkins.
25 Feb., 1739. Book 9, p. 111.

CARTERIGHT, Robert: Leg.- To be buried under direction of
friend, Benj. Harrison. To brother, Richard Carteright,
clothing. To Hezekiah Bunnel, razor, etc. To eldest
daughter of Eliza. Carteright wedding ring and great Bible
and the gift she had from Jno. Orchard, Rich. Carteright
and Jane Bunnell cutglass and gun. To son, Robert Carteright all my land in Va. and a gun. Rest of estate to be
divided among his three children, Wm. Carpinder have
tuition and keeping of son, Hezekiah and daughter, Elizabeth and Richard Carteright, My daughter, Mary. 19 Feb.,
1675/6. Prob.: 24 Mar., 1676. Wit: Benj. Harrison,
John Orchard. Nuncupative Will. Book 2, p. 107.

CARTRIGHT, Robt.: Est.- 1675-1676. Goods delivered for orphans. Thos. Hux for coffin. Orphant children claims from
estate. Book 2, p. ___.

CARTWRIGH, Robert: Est.- 6 Jan., 1679. Signed: Hezekiah Burnell, Water Flood, Richard Avery, sec. to orphan, Elizabeth.
Wit: Wm. Thompson, Wm. Edwards. Book 2, p. 9.

CARTWRIGHT, Robert: Est.- 10 Nov., 1676. Signed: Mr. Nath.
Knight, Mr. Wm. Norwood, Geo. Jordan. 12 Nov., 1677.
Book 2, p. 178.

CARTWRIGHT, Robert: Gave his estate to his sister, Elizabeth
Rogers and her sister, Mary and to Goddaughter, Sarah
Rogers. To "old Man" Wm. Rogers. 7 Nov., 1699. Wit:
George Middleton, Nath. Harrison. Book 5, p. 186.

CASELY, Michell: Leg.- Son, Mickel Casely, 10 lbs. & horse.
To dau., Mary, 8 lbs. and horse, etc.; to daughter, Sarah,
cows. To dau., Martha, cows. If son, Mickel die, dau.
Mary, have land purchased of Coll. Thos. Cocke. To father-
in-law, Wm. Moss. Gives my girl, Elizabeth, her freedom
and cow. Wife, Elizabeth, Exerx. Makes Charles Lucas and
Joshua Nicholson overseers of will. 23 July, 1739. Prob.:
21 Nov., 1739. Wit: Jos. Nicholson, William More. Book
9, p. 105.

CAUFIELD, Robert: Leg.- Neece, Eliza, wife of Wm. Holt, land
purchased of Wm. Gray, for want of heirs to go to Wm. Holt.
To neece, Mary, wife of Ja. Bruton, land purchased of
Joseph Rogers. If no heirs to James Bruton. To nephew,
John Seward "land left me by my father" on Hog Island. To
Wm. Cockerham, land purchased of Richard Jordan. To Mrs.
Mary White to be paid her by Thomas Binns out of his debt
to me. To Francis, daughter of Francis Mason; To Eliza,
dau. of Arthur Allen; Katherine, dau. of Arthur Allen; To

James, Son of Arthur Allen; to Arthur Allen and "my sister,
his wife". To Mrs. Eliza. Holt; To Mr. Fra. Mason, To Wm.
Hancocke and his wife. To Mr. Samuel Newton, To John
Collins, To Chas. Williams. To Mary, his daughter, where
John Sugars lives. To wife, Elizabeth all est. in Va. and
England and makes her Exerx. 2 Jan., 1691. Prob.: 19
Jan., 1691. Wit: Robert Lancaster, Phillip Shelley, John
Coker, Rich. Morris, John Page, Fra. Taylor. Book 4,
p. 240.

CHAMBERS, John: Est.- By Wm. Drew, admr. 21 June, 1727.
Signed: Carter Crafford, John Newsum, Aug. Hunnicutt.
Book 7, p. ___.

CHAMBERS, Jonathan: Est.- Israel Dickins, admr. 17 Sept.,
1735. Signed: Henry Freeman, John Wilbourne, Wm. Greene.
Book 8, p. 520.

CHAMBERS, Olive: Est.- 6 Aug., 1720. John Chambers, admr.
Signed: Wm. Edwards, Augustine Hunnicutt, Martin Johnson.
21 Sept., 1720. Book 7, p. 279.

CHAMBERS, William: Nuncupative Will. His whole estate to be
divided equally betwixt his wife and his two children. A
bequest to Charles Jarrett, a cow. 18 May, 1677. Book 2,
p. 123. Com. of Administration granted Margery Chambers
on Est. of Wm. Chambers. 12 May, 1677. Bk. 2, p. 129.

CHAMBERS, William: Est.- 26 May, 1679. Orphans William and
Mary Chambers. Wit: John Price, Fra. Mason, Wm. Edwards,
Wm. Gray, Robert Ruffin, Wm. Newsum. Book 2, p. 14.

CHAMBERS, William: Leg.- To son, John, 2 negroes, money and
tobacco due from estate of Richard Byton. Gives 20,000
nailes suitable for buldg., a horse, hooks and hinges and
glass, one-half the hoggs and cattle, furniture and goods
belonging to the plantation. Son, William, all the land I
now possess, but if he die without issue, to give the
plantation I live on to my daughter, Martha, and tract at
Blackwater to daus. Mary and Olive equally divided. Gives
Wm. negroes when 18 yrs. old. Four daughters, Elizabeth,
Mary, Olive and Martha, all rest of personal estate to
wife, Olive, and makes wife Exerx. 16 July, 1718. Book
7, p. 137.

CHAMPION, Eliza.: Est.- Charles Champion, admr. 16 June,
1736. Signed: Robert Lancaster, Samuel Lancaster, Thos.
Bell. Book 8, p. 600.

CHAMPTON, Benjamin: Leg.- To Son, John, my plantation, where
I now live after my wife's decease and Syder Mill. To son,
Charles, all my sypress timber, above ye main swamp, Troop-
er's saddle, arms and camblet coates. To son, Benjamin,
wearing clothes, etc. Dau., Elizabeth, bed, pewter dishes
& plates, etc. Dau., Anne, pewter dishes & plates, etc.
Dau., Mary, pewter dishes & plates, etc. Wife all rest of
estate and makes her Exerx. 6 April, 1735. Prob.: 17
Sept., 1735. Wit: Chas. Binne, Samuel Lancaster, John
Wall. Book 8, p. 514.

CHAPMAN, Benjamin: Est.- By Mary Chapman, admr. Negroes -
Tom, Frank, Jack, Jacob, Isaac, Will, Abraham, Jamey, Joe,
Judy, Beck, Dina, Nanny. 19 Oct., 1720. Bk. 7, p. 285.

CHAPMAN, Mary: Leg.- To daus. Mary Pierce & Sarah Barrow, in
N. C. all goods and chattel in their possession. To
daughter, Mary Donaldson, negro and to each of her children
a Bible. To dau., Ann Foster, 5 lbs. To grandchildren,
Hannah and Mary Bamer, to each 10 lbs. when 21 yrs. old or
married. If either die, to dau., Ann Foster. Son, John
Chapman, all rem. of estate after above legacies and debts
are paid and 4 negroes and to send some handsome token to
my son William Taylor of the Kingdom of Ireland. Makes
son, John Chapman, Exer. 29 Aug., 1730. Prob.: 15 Dec.,
1736. Wit: Sarah Fort, Deborah King. Bk. 8, p. 648.

CHAPPELL, Samuel: Leg.- To Son, Samuel Chappell, 5 shillings.
To dau., Eliza., 5 shillings. To son, Thomas, 125 acres
part of my land on Occhineachy Neck in North Carolina. To
son, James, 125 acres in Occhineachy Neck, North Carolina.
To son, John, part of tract I now live on - to Deep Bottom,
between me and Robert Jones, 130 acres. To my son, Benjamin, 150 acres adjoyning where I now live, patented in my
own name. To son, Robert, all the remainder of my land I
live on, after my wife, Elizabeth's decease. To son, Drury,
40 shillings. To dau., Sarah, 5 shillings, to dau.,
Bethiah, 5 shillings, to dau., Mary, feather bed, to Emelie,
5 shillings. Makes wife Exerx. Made 1740. Prob.: 21
Nov., 1749. Wit: Samuel Peete, Robert Jones, James
Chappell. Book 9, p. 620.

CHARLETON, _____: Est.- By Jno. Rutherford and Hen. Francis.
Samuell Swann appt. High Sheriff for Surry Co. 8 br, 1675.
Signed: Wm. Berkeley. Book ___, p. 115.

CHESSETT, Thomas: Est.- James Chissett, admr. 13 Dec., 1700.
Signed: Nicholas Witherington, Wm. Lyle. 4 Mar., 1701.
Book 5, p. 222.

CHESSUTT, James: Leg.- Wife, Elizabeth Chessutt, bed and fur-
niture, etc. Daughter, Phebe Chessutt, chest. Son, John
Chessutt, tools. Grandson, James Nelson, cow. Son, John
Nelson, clothing. Son John Parr, clothing. Four daughters,
Elizabeth, Sarah, Phebe, Annie. Wife Exerx. 25 Sept.,
1710. Prob.: 7 Nov., 1710. Wit: Mich. Harris, Edward
Bockey. Book 6, p. 37.

CHINGE, Walter: Est.- By Thomas Allvirs. 4 Jan., 1720. 15
Feb., 1720. Signed: Wm. Pulley, James Cooper, William
Knott. Book 7, p. 300.

CLANTON, William: Leg.- Son, Richard, bed, etc. Daughter,
Agnes Clanton, cow; daughter, Joanah Clanton, chest; son,
Nathaniel Clanton, clothing; son, Richard Clanton, rest of
clothing. Wife, Mary, rest of estate real and personal
and Exerx. 15 Sept., 1725. Prob.: 21 Sept., 1726. Wit:
John Gilliam, Edward Clanton. Book 7, p. 649.

CLARK, Jane: She gives to son, John Tanner a gift. 22 Oct.,
1693. Book 4, p. 351.

CLARK, John: Leg.- Devises that daughter and her husband have
plantation they live on for life then to "my grandson",
John Barham. If he have no heirs, to granddaughter, Eliza-
beth Barham. Grandson, Robert Barham, land bought of
James Briggs, if no heirs to granddaughter, Mary, Grandson,
Charles Barham, daughter, Eliza. Barham. To Edward Harris,
Wife Mary and makes her Exer. 2 Oct., 1715. Prob.: 15

May, 1717. Wit: Thos. Lane, Wm. Holt. Bk. 7, p. 65.

CLARK, Robert, Sr.: Leg.- To son, Samuell, 200 acres of land where he now lives. Daughter, Mary Sledge, one cow. To Daughter, Elizabeth Muzelwhite, one cow. Son, Samuel Clark is to keep and maintain his mother that is, Robert Clark's lawful wife. Son, Samuel Clark, Exer. 17 Feb., 1723. Prob.: 18 Mar., 1723. Wit: James Jones, Alex. Chestnutt, Samuel Clark. Book 7, p. 522.

CLARK, Thomas: Leg.- To daughter, Hannah, household goods & live stock; to daughter, Mary, household goods and live stock; To son, Thomas, all my lands in general. (Thos. not of age.) After decease of wife, Mary, who is to have rest of estate. Brother-in-law, Wm. Knott. Makes wife, Mary, Exerx. 8 May, 1688. Prob.: 4 7br, 1688. Wit: John King, John Wapple. Book 4, p. 81.

CLARK, William: Est.- Signed: Nicholas Cocke, Sheriff. 21 Aug., 1734. Book 8, p. 411.

CLARKE, Benjamin: Est.- Elizabeth Clarke, admr. 16 May, 1744. Book 9, p. 471.

CLARKE, Edward: Est.- Arthur Kavenaugh, admr. 17 Feb., 1713. Signed: George Wyche, Thomas Avent. Book 6, p. 175.

CLARKE, Henry: Nuncupative Will. Wm. Edwards, Jr. gent. aged 31 years made oath that he wrote the will of Henry Clarke late of Surry Co. by request and on his instruction. Will dated ___ day of Feb., 1720. Went to Henry Clarke's house to read it to him but due to illness of his son, Benjamin, he would not have it read. Said if his son, Benjamin, died he would make another will. Mentioned son, Henry Clarke, Son, John Clarke, Son, Wm. Clarke, Banjamin Clarke, and makes him Exer. Made: Feb., 1720. Prob., 19 July, 1721. Book 7, p. 349.

CLARKE, Henry, Sr.: Leg.- To son, Henry Clarke, gun, chest & bed. To daughter, Elizabeth Essell, iron pot. Wife, Jane Clarke, whole est. To child in Esse. Makes wife Exerx. 14 Jan., 1676/7. Prob.: 7 Jan., 1678. Wit: Rand. Holt, Thos. Edwards. Book 2, p. 195.

CLARKE, John: Acknowledge from Wm. Newsum receipt in full. 6 May, 1673, of estate left him by his father, Richard Clarke. Book 2, p. 27.

CLARKE, Richard: Est.- 1 May, 1686. Signed: Wm. Carpenter, John Tayler. Sworn to by John King. Book 3, p. 65.

CLARY, Benjamin: Est.- Lewis Deloney, admr. 18 Feb., 1735. Book 8, p. 564.

CLARY, Thomas: Leg.- Niece, Judith, wife of Robert Lancaster, Jr., pewter dishes. To Charles Pitt, 20 shillings. To Charles Williams, 530 lbs. tobacco. All rest of estate to Brother, Wm. Clary and sister, Ann Pitt. Nephew, Edward Brown, Exer. 25 Sept., 1707. Prob.: 4 Nov., 1707. Wit: Thomas Holt, Joseph John Jackman. Book 5, p. 378.

CLARY, Thomas: Est.- 6 Dec., 1707. Signed: Edward Moreland, Wm. Harris, Edward Brown. Book 5, p. 384.

31

CLARY, William: Leg.- To son, Thomas Clary, one-half the tract
of land he now lives on; to Benjamin Clary, the other one-
half of land and six silver spoons; to William Clary, one
silver head cane; to son, Joseph Clary, a gun; to daughter,
Catherine Morley, a cow; to son, Charles Clary, 15 pence;
to daughter, Elizabeth Morley, 15 pence; to daughter, Mary
Williams, 15 pence; to daughter, Martha, 15 pence. Wife
and son, William, Exers. 26 Dec., 1724. Prob.: 21 July,
1726. (Wife, Elizabeth Clary, filed will) Bk. 7, p. 590.

CLAYE, Thomas: Leg.- To wife, Elizabeth Claye, and her heirs
my whole estate and makes her Exerx. 10 April, 1679.
Prob.: 6 May, 1679. Wit: Nicholas Pasfield, John Greene,
Robert Caufield. Book 2, p. 204.

CLEMENS (CLEMENTS), Samuel: Leg.- To Wm. Clements gun and
sword. To Mary Adams, daughter of Peter Adams, one cow.
To "my mother" my whole estate and makes her Exerx. (Mary
Boston qualified as Exerx.) 28 Apr., 1727. Prob.: 21
Aug., 1728. Wit: Michael Harris, Geo. Piland. Book 7,
p. 854.

CLEMENTS, Bartholomew: Leg.- To William Rookings all effects
in Col. Water's hands and wescoat at Mr. Throuston's in
Elizabeth River. William Rookings made Exer. 15 Sept.,
1713. Prob.: 25 Oct., 1731. Wit: Richard Lewis, George
Haywood, John Dawson. Book 6, p. 161.

CLEMENTS, Bartholomew: Est.- By John Wapple and William Knott.
16 Dec., 1713. Amt. due from Coll. William Walters of
Accomack. P. 189. Book 6, p. 173.

CLEMENTS, Francis: Leg.- Land for a glebe to churchwardens and
Vestry of Southwark Parish bought of Maj. Nich. Meriweather
by my father, Francis Clements, dec'd., provided churchwardens pay my uncle, Capt. Wm. Browne, ten pounds. Uncle,
Maj. Nich. Meriweather, and Capt. Wm. Browne, a gold ring.
Cozens, Wm., David, Eliza, Jane, Sarah and Mary Meriweather, children of Maj. Nich. Meriweather and to Ann
Johnson, wife of Thomas Johnson, Jane Walker, Mary, Elizabeth and Anne Browne a gold ring each. To brother, Benjamin Clements, 50 acres on Spring Swamp and 116 acres.
Mother-in-law, Lydia Clements. Brother, Thos. Clements,
my plantation. Mentions couzen, Henry Browne, couzen Wm.
Browne, Jr. and makes latter Exer. 8 April, 1721. Prob.:
21 June, 1721. Wit: Nich. Maget, Henry Browne, Edward
Harris. Book 7, p. 346.

CLEMENTS, John: Leg.- Son, John Clements, 100 acres adjoining
John Twy's?. Two daughters, Ann and Mary Clements. To
Thos. Foster, son of George Foster, decd. 175 acres ad-
joining Ogburn and Allen Warren and Major Marriott. To
son, Samuell, my now dwelling plantation and all rem. of my
land. If no issue to daughter, Ann and Mary Clements.
Elizabeth Warren, wife of Allen Warren, one shilling.
Elizabeth Warren, daughter to Allen Warren, gold ring.
Jane Warren, daughter of Robert Warren, gold ring. Wife
Mary and her three children all rem. of estate. Samuell,
Ann and Mary Clements. Makes wife Exerx. Friends Mr.
Samuell Thompson and Capt. Wm. Browne and Capt. Thos. Holt
overseers of will. 12 May, 1704. Prob.: 2 May, 1710.
Wit: Bray Hargrave, John Kitching. Book 6, p. 9.

CLEMENTS, William: Leg.- Wife Ales Clements to five children,

Lucy, Elizabeth, Samuell, Wm., and Henry, all of my estate
divided equally. To Samuell Thompson 100 acres of land on
Pideon Swamp. Makes wife Ales, Exerx. 26 April, 1741.
Prob.: 20 May, 1741. Wit: Mary Davis, Samuel Thompson.
Book 9, p. 326.

CLERK, John: Est.- By Thos. Edmunds. 14 Sept., 1729. Book
7, p. 970.

CLINCH, Christopher: Leg.- To daughter, Eliza. Clinch, (not
16 yrs. old) seven cattle, household furniture, her
mother's Bible, chest, etc. To Child in esse, if such
there be, a bequest. Wife, Ann Clinch, Exerx. William
Seward and William Hancocke overseers of Will. 27 Apr.,
1679. Prob.: 16 June, 1679. Book 2, p. 210.

CLINCH, Christopher: Leg.- To wife, Hannah Clinch, the plantation where I now live and all that land below Beaver Dam
Swamp while single, if she marry only one-half the tract
with the house, etc. for her life, also'one negro. To
son, Joseph John Clinch, the plantation where he now lives
and another on the road from James River to Mangum's
Bridge. To son, James Clinch, the rem. of that tract where
son, Jos. now lives on the James River to Mangum Bridge.
To Wm. Clinch, all that part of land which I now live on
which lies above Beaver Dam Swamp and after wife's death
this tract to son William. After debts are paid rest of
estate to my wife's children, William, James, Mary and
Margaret. Makes wife and son, William Exers. To daughter,
Elizabeth Holt, 5 lbs.; to daughter, Mary Clinch, 2 negroes;
to daughter, Margaret Clinch, 2 negroes. Son, William,
my desk. 13 Dec., 1736. Prob.: 20 Apr., 1737. Wit:
Robert Warren, Richard Rowell. Book 8, p. 675.

CLINCH, Hannah: Leg.- To daughter, Margaret Clinch, furniture,
etc. To daughter, Mary Clinch, bed, furniture, etc. To
son, James Clinch, bed, furniture. To son, Jos. Clinch,
a desk and makes him Exer. The rest of the estate to be
divided among all the children. 10 Apr., 1739. Prob.: 16
Jan., 1739. Wit: Richard Cocke, John Holt, Thomas Holt.
Book 9, p. 106.

CLINCH, James: Inv.- 4 Feb., 1748/9. By Jane Clinch, admr.
Signed: Zach Madders, Wm. Smith, James Davis. Book 9, p.
566.

COATES, John: Leg.- To wife, Mary Coates, the use of the plantation and land for life, then to be sold and divided between sons John and Joseph (neither 21 yrs. old). __ Apr.,
1744. Prob.: 18 July, 1744. Wit: Wm. Willie, Henry
Mitchell, Henry Mitchell, Jr. Book 9, p. 480.

COCKE, John: Est.- By Robert Wynne, sheriff. 17 Aug., 1743.
Book 9, p. 449.

COCKE, Nicholas: Leg., To son, William, the lands and plantation on North side of Birchen Swamp, cattle, etc. but
reserving land -- below Wiggin's house -- next to David
Hide's, also negroes. To son, John Cocke, the plantation
where I live, all stock, etc. and Land Hook up at John
Shehawcon Swamp -- 230 acres, horse, negro, etc. To daughter, Frances Simmons, what is in her possession and 2
negroes, To daughter, Ann Woddrop, what is in her possession
and 2 negroes. To daughter, Elizabeth Cocke, 2 negroes and

33

gold ring. To daughter, Martha Cocke, 2 negroes, gold ring and bed. To daughter, Catherine Cocke, 2 negroes, gold ring, bed, etc. To granddaughter, Susannah Cocke, one negro. To granddaughter, Elizabeth Woddrop, one negro. To granddaughter, Lucy Simmons, ten lbs. to be paid by my son, William Cocke. To granddaughter, Sarah Simmons, ten lbs. to be paid by son, John Cocke. All the rest of my estate to be divided between my seven children, William, John, Frances, Ann, Elizabeth, Martha and Catherine, and appoints Col. Thos. Cocke, and William Cocke, Exers. 4 Apr., 1748. Prob.: 19 Apr., 1748. Wit: James Roe, Howell Briggs, Joseph Mumford, Robert Woobank. Book 9, p. 517.

COCKE, Thomas: Leg.- Daughter, Elizabeth Cocke, 400 lbs., 3 negroes, bed, etc. To son, Lemuel Cocke, negroes at decease of his mother. To son, Thomas Cocke, all my land at Wintico and Mecherrin in Brunswick Co., stock, cattle, negroes, etc. If my son, John die before he comes of age then the land at Wintico to son, Lemuel Cocke, and son, Thomas, land where I live. To son, John, where I now live with several tracts adjoining same. Wife, Hannah Cocke. 7 June, 1750. Prob.: 18 Dec., 1750. Wit: Wm. Short, Richard Jones. Book 9, p. 672.

COCKE, Walter Flood: Leg.- To son, Thomas Cocke, the plantation where I live also land on Otterdam -- 700 acres. To son, John Cocke, five shillings, to daughter, Ann Hamlin, 5 lbs. The rest of my estate to son, Thomas Cocke. 1 Aug., 1735. Prob.: 21 Mar., 1738. Wit: Henry Berry, John Wage, Francis Hagood. Book 9, p. 34.

COCKE, William: Leg.- To son, Nicholas Cocke, all land that I hold on southwest side of Birchen Swamp and that purchased of Richard Hide, Sr., also land purchased of Mr. John Brashare and all bookbinding tools. To son, Richard Cocke, land bought of William Halso and also from Richard Hide over the county road, 150 acres reserving one-half acre for my son William Cocke's warehouse and one-half to Thomas Cocke to build a warehouse. To son, Thomas Cocke, land on Nottoway River -- 400 acres where Lemon Murfrey now dwelleth. To son, William Cocke, the plantation where I now live on and the land bought of Richard Wiggins and John Wiggins after the decease of my wife, Mary Cocke, and to son, Nicholas Cocke, to be free and have land bought from Wiggins. To daughter, Mary Spratley, 30 lbs., to son, Thomas, a quarter part of my sloop and cargo discounting his wages for the last voyage and the present voyage. To granddaughter, Frances Cocker, 5 lbs. To granddaughter, Eliza. Spratley, 5 lbs. All other estate to my wife. 29 Apr., 1720. Prob.: 19 Oct., 1720. Wit: Walter Cocke, John Dawson, Mary Dawson. Book 7, p. 282.

COCKE, William: Est.- Ann Cocke, admr. 26 Sept., 1732. Signed: Nich. Maget, Samuell Thompson, Benjamin Chapman Donaldson. Book 8, p. 232.

COCKER, William: Est.- 12 7br, 1678. By Nicholas Wilson. The estate paid to widow and five orphans. Col. Nicholas Wilson who married Relict of above said decease made oath to above. 12 7br, 1678. Book 2, p. 184.

COCKER, William: Est.- Wm. Cocker and John Little and John Dunford are bound to the court to pay unto Isabella, orphan of William Cocke, dec'd. her portion of his estate,

her education, etc. Signed: J. I. Rodwell. 12 Mar.,
1686/7. Book 3, p. ___.

COCKERHAM, ____ (Capt.): Est.- Presented by Charles Barham and
Robert Caufield. 29 Oct., 1672. Book 2, p. 20.

COCKERHAM, Thomas: Leg.- To son, Timothy, my wearing clothes,
to grandson, Samuel Benson, cows, pewter, etc. when he is
21 yrs. old. To daughter, Elizabeth, one shilling, to
daughter, Ann, one cow. To wife, Elizabeth, all the rest
of my estate after debts and legacies are paid for her
life, at her decease to be divided equally between my two
daughters, Ann and Priscilla. Makes wife, Exerx. (Wife's
name Elizabeth). 17 Jan., 1709/10. Prob.: 15 May, 1717.
Wit: Michael Harris, John Cocke. Book 7, p. 60.

COCKERHAM, William: Leg.- To brother, Thomas Cockerham, my
clothes, remainder of my estate to my wife, Mary. Mentions
son, William Cockerham and makes him Exer. 22 Jan., 1706.
Prob.: 4 March, 1706. Wit: Nathan. Harrison, John
Griffin, John Bentley. Book 5, p. 361.

COCKIN, William: Est.- By Capt. Samuell Swann. 9 Mar., 1677/8.
Signed: Elizabeth Wilson, James Riddick, Richard Drew.
Book 2, p. 176.

COGGEN, William: Est.- By Elizabeth Coggin. 20 Mar., 1716.
Signed: Thomas Davee (or Dovell), Charles Farrell,
Patrick Braddy. Book 7, p. 49.

COGGIN, Thomas: Est.- By Elizabeth Coggin, admr. 26 July,
1737. Signed: Roger Delk, Newitt Edwards, John Glover.
Book 8, p. 711.

COGGIN, William: Leg.- To son, William, my house and lands
after my Wife's decease and the rem. of my estate to be
equally divided with the rest of my children. Makes wife,
Elizabeth and Robert Holmes, Exers. Desires that children
be educated. 25 July, 1677. Prob.: 5 March, 1677. Wit:
Robert Parke, Joseph Farlow, William Coockins. Book 2,
p. 164.

COKER, John: Leg.- To son, William Coker, 100 acres at upper
old plantation and at his death to his son, John Cocker.
To wife, Margarette, and her heirs all the rest of my
estate. 22 May, 1711. Prob.: 19 Oct., 1720. Wit: John
Allen, James Allen, Arthur Allen. Book 7, p. 281.

COKER, Margaret: Leg.- To my grandson, John Coker, 50 acres
of land where he now lives, beginning at James Bennett's
line -- easterly to the Pocoson Spring Branch to Samuel
Baser's line. To John Coker, Jr., that is the son of my
grandson, John Coker, 230 acres of land on the west side
of Cypress Swamp adj. John Phillips' land on the south
side of Cypress Swamp, on east side and Samuel Vaser's
land on the north and Wm. Coker's land on west. If he die
to his brother, Thomas Coker, and appoints John Coker,
father of the said child and Anthony Evans to hold his land
in their possession until said John Coker is 18 yrs. old.
To grandson, John Coker, a Bible, trunk, etc., at my son's
William's house and all rest of estate at William Coker's
to him. To grandson, John Coker, all the rest of my estate
in general. Makes grandson, John Coker, Jr., Exer. 21
Sept., 1721. Prob.: 20 Dec., 1721. Wit: Thomas

Atkinson, John Phillips, Priscilla Coker. Bk. 7, p. 384.

COLEMAN, Stephen: Est.- 11 April, 1693. Signed: Adam Heath, Edward Greene, William Harvey. Book 4, p. 291.

COLLIER, Benjamin: Est.- Elizabeth Collier, admr. 21 April, 1736. Signed: Joseph Nicholson, Charles Lucas, Marmaduke Cheetam. Book 8, p. 581.

COLLIER, John: Est.- By John King. 15 9br, 1677. There appeared in Court Mary Rawlin, ye relict of above, and certified to the inventory as being correct. Bk. 2, p. 15.

COLLIER, John: Est.- 1 July, 1679. John Rawlings Bond. Roger Potter and John King were surety for orphans. Book 2, p. 4.

COLLIER, John: Est.- 18 July, 1716. By Jane Collier, in 1718. Signed: Jane Lather and John Lather, admrs. Wit: Thomas Flood, Michael Harris, Nicholas Maggett. Book 7, p. 22.

COLLIER, John: Leg.- To daughter, Mary, one guinea, and to Moses Johnson, one guinea, to son, William, bequest. To son, Thomas, land. To daughter, Grace, (illegible), to son, Benjamin. To son, Charles, houses and plantation. To son, Henry, all the rem. of my land. (this will is partly obliterated from water stains and not decipherable). All remainder of my money and pewter to be divided between my sons, Benjamin, Henry and the remainder of estate after debts are paid to be divided between the same three, Charles, Henry and Benjamin by lot. Give son, Henry, to son, William, until he is 21 yrs. old. Gives son, Charles, to Moses Johnson, until he is 21 yrs. old. Makes, Moses Johnson, son, John, and son, Thomas, Exers. 3 July, 1732. Prob.: 15 Nov., 1732. Wit: Wm. Hux, Solomon Hawkins, Charles Lucas.

COLLIER, Joseph: Leg.- To son, John Collier, a tract of land where he now lives, part of the tract where I now dwell -- the land runs to a tree in Caleb Ellis' line and contains 100 acres, also gives him household goods, after the de- cease of my wife. To son, Joseph Collier, a tract of land part of where I live beg. at Bowling Alley line - to Miry Branch, 100 acres. To son, William Collier, tract of land - at horse-going Branch - to Joseph's line, 100 acres. To son, Thomas Collier, all the rem. of my plantation and land where I now live. If any die their part to survivors. To daughters, Mary, Jeane, Elizabeth and Sarah, each a cow. Mentions his wife, Jeane, Exrx. 10 Dec., 1726. Prob.: 19 Apr., 1726. Wit: Nich. Cocke, Richard Wigins, Wm. Barton. Book 7, p. 698.

COLLIER, Thomas: Leg.- To grandsons, Thomas Collier and John Collier. To daughter-in-law, Jane Lather, to daughter, Sarah Marriott, wife of William Marriott, to granddaughter, Mary Marriott, to grandsons, William and Thomas Marriott. Makes son-in-law, William Marriott and grandson, Thomas Collier, Exrs. 15 Feb., 1727/28. Prob.: 20 March, 1727. Wit: John Cargill, Robert Watkins, Henry Barnes. Book 7, p. 794.

COLLINS, John: Leg.- To son, John Collins, all my goods and chattel when he is 21 yrs. old. It is my will that Sarah Sanburne, wife of Samuel Sanburne, shall have the bringing up of the said child. To William Goodman, 1000 lbs. of tobacco to keep my child this year. The rest of my estate to the children of Rebecca Goodman, Jean Nuby and Elizabeth Izzard. Friends Arthur Allen and Samuel Newton, Exers. Wit: John Coker, Henry Wiggs, Joseph Thorpe, Thomas Thorne. 20 9br, 1683. 2 Jan., 1693. Book 4, p. 342.

COLLINS, John: Est.- 8 Jan., 1694. Inventory of goods in the presence of William Goodman and Robert Hinman, Joseph Thorp, Timothy Thorp, Joseph Tooke, Michael Izzard at the house of John Collins. Book 5, p. 12.

COLLINS, John: Est.- James Rookings, admr. 18 Dec., 1750. Signed: Robert Lanier, Charles Lucas, Thomas Sowerby. Book 9, p. 678.

COOK, Avis: Leg.- To daughter-in-law, Elizabeth Cook, my clothing. To daughter, Lucy Guillidge, clothing. Bequest to sons, William Killingsworth and John Killingsworth. Wit: John Barker, Joseph Harris, Mary Underwood. 9 June, 1711. Prob.: 15 Aug., 1711. Book 6, p. 75.

COOK, John: Leg.- To son, John Cook, my Indian woman, hogs, etc. To Henry Cook, my Indian boy, etc. Mentions daughter, Joanna Cook. To wife what was her former husband's. Wife, Avis Cook, Admr. 10 April, 1711. Prob.: 20 June, 1711. Wit: Geo. Rochell, William Heath, Joshua Harris. Book 6, p. 61.

COOK, William: Leg.- To son, William Cook, beds, furniture, etc. To son, Rubin Cook, 175 acres of land, one negro, etc. To son, James, 3 negroes, bed, pewter, etc. To daughter, Elizabeth, wife of Thomas Tomlinson, one negro. To daughter, Rebeccah, wife of James Anderson, one negro. To daughter, Sarah, wife of Henry Mitchell, one negro. To daughter, Mary, wife of Wm. Briggs, one negro. To daughter, Susannah, wife of Miel Hill, one negro. To daughter, Hannah, wife of Richard Gary, one negro. To daughter, Amy, wife of John Maclin, one negro. Son, James Cook, Exer. 1 May, 1740. Prob.: 19 Nov., 1740. Wit: John Barker, Wm. Brewer, Thomas Lanier. Book 9, p. 248.

COOKE, James: Leg.- To wife, Elizabeth, my estate. Wit: Thomas Pittman, Robert Littleboy. 3 March, 1701/2. Book 5, p. 245.

COOPER, James: Leg.- Mentions wife, Elizabeth Cooper and four children, John, William, Thomas and Martha. To daughter, Johanna Gilbert, 20 shillings. The plantation where I now live should be at the disposal of my wife, Elizabeth Cooper, unless she marry, then if sold the value to be divided between her and my four children now living with me, named above. Makes wife Exerx. 28 Feb., 1729/30. Prob.: 20 Nov., 1734. Wit: Wm. Saunders, Richard Stewart. Book 8, p. 425.

COOPER, John: Est.- Appraised by Francis Mason. Signed: John Phillips. 3 July, 1677. Margaret Hodge, the Relict of John Cooper, deceased, swore this to be a true inventory. (Relict married John Hodge). Book 2, p. 132.

COOPER, Thomas: Est.- 29 May, 1688. Sworn by Elizabeth, Relict of Deceased. Book 4, p. 51.

COREN, Joseph: Leg.- Bequests to Mary Baker, Maj. Tooker and

and Henry Baker, equally divided. Bequest to Mary Groves. 6 March, 1701/2. Wit: Ludwick Crawford, Daniel Mack-daniell, Mary Grouse? Book 5, p. 247.

CORKER, William (Capt.): Nuncupative Will. Made at the house of his daughter, Judith Clay, widow in Isle of Wight Co. where he lay sick. 25 Feb., 1675. To wife, estate on the north side of the James River, she paying debts and to pay her orphan children, and debts to Richard Holder and Richard Lynsey. Ni. Meriweather. To Eldest daughter, Susannah Corker, estate on the south side of the James River and Watch that was her mother's. Mentions "three daughters". Mentions daughter, Lucy. Confirms a sale of land to Elizabeth White and her sister, Mary. Gives 50 acres to John Vincent. Daughters, Susannah, Judith and Lucy. To Robert Spencer, who married Elizabeth White, land. 4 Sept., 1677. Wit: John Vincent, Robert Spencer. Book 2, p. 140. (Mr. George Branch married Susannah, eldest daughter of sd. Corker).

CORNELL, Samuell: Est.- Wife, Katherine Cornell. 24 July, 1680. Signed: John Barnes, Wm. Gray, Wm. Hancocke. Book 2, p. 262.

CORNELL, Samuell: Est.- To be divided into five parts. To Catherine, Relict of sd. Cornell and 4 children viz: Elizabeth, Mary, Samuell, and Susanna. 4 7br, 1683. Wit: Edward Rowell, Katherine Rowell. Book 2, p. 333.

CORNWELL, Isaac: Leg.- Estate to wife and children equally divided. Presented by Eliza. Cornwell, his wife, Exerx. Samuel Alexander, witness. 19 July, 1727. Book 8, p. 746. (Eliz. Taylor in 1734.)

CORNWELL, Samuell: Leg.- Wife, Sarah, to live on sd. plan-tation for life. Eldest son to take the plantation where Charles Pitt now lives in my place and stead and continue there for life where my brother-in-law, Samuell Hargrove liveth. My son, Jacob, to have the management if he does not stay and to son-in-law, Samuel Sebrell, that land known as Billisen's Field. To son, Aaron, a place on that Creek and 300 acres. Also, if needed 100 acres put to my hands by Robert Lacey I give my son, John. To wife, ten lbs. To son, Moses, the plantation known as Dikeses, 400 acres not to be sold out of the family. Has plantation at Bindonokeeck Swamp. Appoints friends, Benjamin Chapman and Samuel Sebrell, trustees. Mentions Eldest daughter. Eldest son, Samuel, and wife made Exers. 14 March, 1717/18. Prob.: 20 Aug., 1718. Wit: John Hancocke, John Bruce, Nathan Marlow. Book 7, p. 140.

CORNWELL, Samuell: Est.- 20 Oct., 1731. Estate of Samuell Cornwell, the Younger. Samuell and Jacob Cornwell, Exers. Book 8, p. 137.

COTTEN, Mary: Leg.- To grandson, David Hide, round table, four Russia chairs, linens, Church Bible and prayer book was his fathers'. To granddaughter, Mary Cotten, chest, a Bible, etc. To son, Thomas Cotten and daughter, Jane Cotten, the remainder of my estate. Makes Thomas Cotten, Exer. 7 March, 1728/9. Prob.: 21 May, 1729. Wit: John Paynter, Alex. Hay. Book 7, p. 928.

COTTON, Thomas: Leg.- To wife, Mary Cotten, my plantation and

38

land for life, at her decease to Cousin Thomas Cotten, son
of Walter Cotten and Elizabeth, his wife. To Mary Smith,
daughter of John Smith and Elizabeth his wife, bed, dishes,
etc. Bequest to Richard Hide and cousin William Cotten.
To Kinswoman, Ann Mylone, one shilling. Wife, Mary, Exerx.
26 Feb., 1718. Prob.: 18 March, 1718. Wit: Jethro
Barker, Sr., John Johnson, Grace Barker. Book 7, p. 168.

CRAFFORD, Carter: Leg.- To son, John, the plantation where
I now dwell on Sunken Marsh at John Ruffin's line. To
Son, Carter, where John lately lived -- adj. where Catherine Peacocke lived in procession of John Drew. Mentions
daughter, Constance, daughter, Faith Hart, and wife. Makes
wife and sons Exers. 5 Aug., 1743. Prob.: 15 Feb., 1743.
Wit: John Ruffin, Daniel Hudson. Book 9, p. 458.

CRAFFORD, Robert: Est.- By Margaret Crafford. 16 March, 1714.
Book 6, p. 226.

CRAFFORD, Robert: Leg.- To Carter Crafford, Jr., a tract of
land on South side of Blackwater Swamp 200 acres, and 2
negroes for his life. Then negroes to Cousin Carter. To
couzen, Mary Crafford, my brother Carter's daughter, a
riding horse, etc. To couzen Carter, the rest of my
estate. I desire a sermon to be preached at my funeral and
to be buried by my father and mother. Brother Carter and
Couzen Carter Exers. 9 Oct., 1735. Prob.: 19 Nov.,
1735. Wit: Henry Mcdonnae, James Worden, John Brown.
Book 8, p. 537.

CREED, William: Leg.- Makes Noah Barefoot and David Andrews
Exers. and bequests to both, and inheritance not yet received by Wm. Creed coming from Col. Brown to be equally
divided between Barefoot and Andrews. Prob.: 6 Mar.,
1687/8. Wit: Bluitt Beaumont, Robert Judkins, Rich.
Moonk, Thos. Lane. Book 4, p. 35.

CREWES, Thomas: Leg.- Son, Thomas Crewes, land and plantation.
Mentions three daughters, Elizabeth, Catherine and Feeby.
The estate to be divided between wife, Phoeby, and children. 12 Feb., 1696/7. Prob.: 1 March, 1697/8. Wit:
David Andrews, William Foster. (In appraisement of this
estate, 15 May, 1698, Phebe Kiggin is Exerx.) Book 5,
p. 152.

CREWES, William: Est.- Signed: John Mooring and George
Foster. 29 Aug., 1691. Book 4, p. 227.

CREWS, Thomas: Leg.- To son, William Crews - tract of land of
80 acres where I live. To son, Thomas Crews - a tract of
land called Haystack - 120 acres. To son, John Crews, a
tract of land called Gray's (which I bought of Henry and
Catherine Jones and Wm. Dennis and Samuel Jenkins) - 100
acres. If my wife continue a widow until my children come
to 21 yrs. the children may stay with her; if she marry
they have children to have their inheritance at 16 and free
from her. The children to have good education and money
out of estate. If the child, in esse, be a boy he is to
have one-half of a tract of land on the north side of
Cypress Swamp (part I bought of Ann Warren) 300 acres. If
a girl, then the land to remain in common. To daughter,
Elizabeth Crews, blue and white curtains, and vallance,
soup plates, 6 new spoons, etc. My desire is that when the
pewter which I send for to England comes in that the 6

dishes be equally divided between my three sons, also my
saddle, Briddle, Pistols and Holsters. A new Bibel to
sons, William and to Thomas Williams and to John Hunnicutt. Wife, Mary, Exrx. 21 Jan., 1727/8. 17 July, 1728.
Wit: Wm. Williams, Walter White, John Chapman. Book 7,
p. 832.

CRIPPS, Marriott: Est.- William Cripps, admr. 21 Feb., 1738.
Book 9, p. 18.

CRIPPS, William: Leg.- To Richard Fealds, the plantation where
he dwells with 100 acres of land. To William Ward, Son of
Benj. Ward, 50 acres to Feald's line. To grandson, Thomas
Tyas? the plantation where I now live when he is 21 yrs.
old. To my nephew, Mary Cripps, 40 shillings. To my
nephew, Ann Fealds, two cows and pewter dishes. To Green
Fields, Son of Richard Fields, two cows when he is 21.
Elizabeth Cripps, widow of my brother, John Cripps, Exerx.
and have maintenance out of my estate. Anselm Bailey, Jr.
and Thomas Bell, Exers. Wit: Samuell Thompson, Benjamin
Clerk, Benjamin Bailey. 8 Aug., 1749. Prob.: 20 March,
1749. Book 9, p. 627.

DANIELL, Thomas: Leg.- To Joan Hogwood, 20 shillings. To
William Hogwood, clothing. To Wm. Duell, clothing. To
Elizabeth Hogwood, 20 shillings. To George Hogwood,
clothing and remainder of estate. 29 Feb., 1720. Prob:
21 Sept., 1720. George Hogwood, Exer. Wit: Harry Floyd,
William Williams. Book 7, p. 281.

DAVIDSON, Mary: Legatees- sons John and William; grandson
William Clements; granddaughter, Elizabeth Boykin. Sons
John and William Davidson, Exers. 2 May, 1737. Prob.:
21 Sept., 1737. Wit: Edward Wesson, Joseph Clarke. Book
8, p. 725.

DAVIDSON, William: Leg.- To son, William, a plantation at the
head of Peacock Swamp, 200 acres. To daughters, Mary,
100 acres of land upon Two Forks of Three Branches, also
bed, chest, clock and key, etc. To William Clements, my
youngest mare. To son, Thomas, a new Bible. Rem. of estate, after debts and legacies, to all my children. Makes
wife, Exerx. Wit: Michael Harris, Samuell Clemmons,
Henry Sikes. 12 April, 1727. Prob.: 16 Nov., 1727.
Book 7, p. 771.

DAVIES, Mary: Est.- 16 June, 1679. Sion Hill, admr. Signed:
Geo. Williams, Geo. Foster, Robt. Ruffin, Wm. Edwards.
Book 2, p. 17.

DAVIS, Arthur: Leg.- Mentions son, John Davis. Grandson,
John Davis; daughter-in-law, Elizabeth Davis; daughter,
Margaret; daughter, Mary Davis; son, Arthur Davis; son
Peter Davis; son Robert Davis; Son John Davis, and makes
him Exer. 27 Jan., 1718. Prob.: 15 July, 1719. Wit:
Nicholas Dering, John Barler, John Grizzard. Bk. 7, p. 203.

DAVIS, Edward: Leg.- Daughter, Frances, not of age. Wife,
Elizabeth. Makes Mr. Fra. Mason and Mr. Wm. Edwards overseers of will. Wit: Wm. Blunt, Jno. Phillips, Alice Phillips. 4 May, 1679. Prob.: 1 July, 1679. Bk. 2, p. 212.

DAVIS, Edward: Leg.- To friend, Richard Curby (Kirby) clothing.
To wife, Elizabeth Davis, land bought of John Ingram and

also to her the rem. of my estate. Makes wife Exerx. Wit:
Robert Nicholson, Richard Curby. 3 June, 1735. Prob.:
17 Sept., 1735. Book 8, p. 513.

DAVIS, James, Sr.: Leg.- To son, James Davis, 80 acres of
land. To sons, Henry and Robert Davis, land where I live,
lower part to Henry, to son, Thomas Davis, land on John's
Branch in Isle of Wight Co. and one negro. To two sons
Thomas and Nathaniel, a bill bond from James Shivers. To
sons, John, Henry, James, Nathaniel and Robert, one negro
each. To daughters, Ann Nicholson and Jane Warren, one
negro each. Wife, Elizabeth Davis, Exerx. 4 Sept., 1746.
Prob.: 21 Jan., 1746. Wit: Thomas Warren, John Warren,
John Slate. Book 9, p. 546.

DAVIS, Nicholas: Leg.- Gives wife whole estate. Signed: Mary
Davis, Exerx. Wit: Carter Croifford, John Davis. 15 May,
1717. Book 7, p. 67.

DAVIS, Nicholas: Leg.- To son, William Davis, all the estate
he is posses of. To son, John, my gun. To wife, Elizabeth
Davis a bed. To daughters, Mary and Elizabeth, a cow each.
The rem. of my estate to my wife and John, Mary, and Eliza-
beth Davis. ___ ___, 1728/9. (date of probate torn off.)
Wit: Ed. Bailey, John Simmons, Jr. Book 8, p. 41.

DAVIS, Richard: Est.- 17 Jan., 1748. Signed: John Thompson,
John Moring, James Davis. Book 9, p. 599.

DAVIS, Sollomon: Est.- 8 Xber, 1680. Lt. Col. Wm. Browne,
Arthur Allen, Justice of the Peace, grant the request of
John Gutheridge, the elder of ye Isle of Wight, to administer on the estate of Sollomon Davis, deceased. Book
2, p. 270.

DAVIS, Thomas: Thomas Davis makes deed of gift to his grandson,
Mathew Ellis, the son of James and Elizabeth Ellis. 11
Mar., 1703/4. Wit: Allen Warren, Thomas Warren. Book 5,
p. 297.

DAVIS, Thomas: To son, James Davis, all the land and houses
I possess. To Mathew Ellis, son of James Ellis, clothing
and a cow. To granddaughter, Elizabeth Ellis, 500 lbs. of
tobacco and a cow. To granddaughter, Isabella Ellis, 500
lbs. of tobacco and a cow. To grandson, Thomas Ellis, 500
lbs. of Tobacco and a cow. To grandson, Thomas Davis, a
negro. Granddaughter, Jane Davis, a negro. To grandsons,
John, James Henry and son, James Davis, each a negro. To
daughter, Elizabeth Ellis, a Good Bible. All the rest of
estate to wife and James Davis. Friend Samuel Thompson,
wife and son, James, Exers. 27 Sept., 1716. Prob.: 21
Dec., 1720. Wit: Samuell Thompson, Thomas King, Zachariah
Maddera. Book 7, p. 287.

DAVIS, Thomas: Leg.- To son, Thomas Davis, a cow, clothing,
etc. Son-in-law, Wm. Bird, pistols, holsters, breast
plate, etc. To daughter, Elizabeth Ellis, 5 shillings.
To wife, Rebecca Davis, all the rest of my estate and makes
her Exerx. 25 Aug., 1748. Pr.: 18 Oct., 1748. Wit:
John Bennett, Peter Hawthorne. (Rebecca Hawthorne, admr.
21 Mar., 1748.) Book 9, p. 589.

DEAN, Samuel: Est.- Wm. Epps, admr. Signed: John Mason, Wm.
Cook, Wm. Shands, David Jones. 21 July, 1742. Book 9,

DEESOMORE, Robert: Est.- Attachment made by Capt. Lawrence
Baker. 4 April, 1679. Book 2, p. 207.

DELK, Roger: Leg.- To Eldest son, John Delk, the land and
plantation where I now live after wife's decease. To
daughter, Rebecca, a large silver cup, 2 gold rings, and
silver bodkin. To two younger sons, Roger and Joseph Delk,
my land at Blackwater - 490 acres to be equally divided.
All the rest of my estate to my wife, Rebecca, and my
children. Makes wife, Rebecca, Exerx. 24 Oct., 1692.
Prob.: 4 July, 1693. Wit: Joseph Seale, Wm. Hancocke,
Fra. Taylor. Book 4, p. 309. (In 1694, John Greene
having married Relict, Rebecca, asks for probate.) (In
1699, George Ezell having married, Rebecca, daughter of
Roger Delk asks for admr. on Roger Delk's estate.)

DENNIS, Robert: Est.- Nathaniel Dennis asks for administration.
21 Oct., 1687. Book 4, p. 24.

DENTON, Pollard: (illegible for most part) Wife, Elizabeth
Denton, Exerx. 10 Apr., 1727. Prob.: 19 July, 1732.
Wit: Wm. Hulme, Chris. Tatum, Henry Tatum. Bk. 8, p. 203.

DEWELL, James: Leg.- To brother, Thomas Dewell, my wearing
apparel. To friend, Ellen Rookings all of my estate and
makes her Exerx. 27 Oct., 1750. Prob.: 20 Nov., 1750.
Wit: William Pulley, Jr., Richard Stewart. Bk. 9, p. 667.

DEWELL, John: Est.- Benjamin Cocke, admr. 19 Sept., 1749.
Signed: William Cocke, William Rookings, James Rookings.
Book 9, p. 618.

DICKENS, Thomas: Leg.- To sons, James and Binford Dickens, 136
acres of land equally divided. To daughter, Sary Dickens,
a cow, horse, etc. To Hildy Dickens, a cow, horse, etc.
To son, Jarns, one mare. Wife, Elizabeth. Prob.: 15 Nov.,
1727. Wit: Thomas Binford. Book 7, p. 770.

DICKESON, Edward: Est.- By Ni. Witherington. 1 May, 1677.
Signed: Thos. Ironmonger, Thos. Crews, Thos. Foscroft.
Book 2, p. 132. In a deposition make Katherine Surcutt,
age 30 years, it was stated that Edward Dickeson living at
Mr. Edwards said if he die before Ni. Witherington, the said
Witherington should have all he had. That they came over
in this country together, Dickeson was very sick on board
shippe and Ni. Witherington was helpful to him. He was
advised to make a will and replied, "Katherine, you have
often heard me say that Ni. Witherington should have all I
have when I dye", etc. 14 Nov., 1677. John Phillips, aged
45 years testified to the same. Book 2, p. 153.

DIGBY, Charles: Est.- 19 Sept., 1711. Signed: Thos. Davis,
Wm. Judkins. Book 6, p. 77.

DILL, John (Capt.): Est.- 21 Aug., 1734. Thomas Avent,
Sheriff. Book 8, p. 415.

DINKINGS, Thomas: Est.- Elizabeth Dickens, Admr. Signed:
David Poythras, Wm. Petteway, Wm. Parham. Bk. 8, p. 784.

DINKINS, Thomas: Leg.- To sons, Thomas, James, Charles, each
one shilling. To daughters, Mary Vandinan, Ann Sesshings,

and Margaret Perry, each one shilling. To wife, Margaret, the plantation I live on for life, and then to son, William Dinkins, being one-half of the upper part adj. Thomas Dinkins, Jr. To son, Sanders Dinkins, one-half of my land-lower half. To wife, Margaret, the rest of my estate. 30 Oct., 1717. Prob.: 21 May, 1718. Wit: David Poythras, Jos. Fowler, Robert Wynn. Book 7, p. 118.

DOBE, John, Sr.: Leg.- To my granddaughter, Mary Vinsen, and her child, Thomas a mare and colt. "To loving grandchild-ren in general" one shilling each. To son, John Dobe, Jr., the land he now lives on for life, on the south side of Myery Meddow, 200 acres, at his death to his elder son, John Dobe. To son, Robert, the land I live on, on the north side of Myery Meddow, 200 acres, all the rest of my estate not given to be possessed by my son, Robert Dobe, and makes him Exer. 19 Mar., 1716/17. Prob.: 15 Aug., 1722. Wit: John Scott, Sr., Bethyer Scott, John Scott, Jr. Book 7, p. 415.

DOBY, John: Leg.- To my wife, Ann, all that Plantation and land where I dwell - containing 533 acres with houses, etc. for her life. At her decease to my two sons, Peter Doby and Robert Doby, to be equally divided. To my wife, I give an entry of 200 acres of same which I have in the county of Prince George during the term of her life, at her decease I devise it to my two sons, Peter and Robert Doby. To my wife, I give all my slaves, goods, chattels, personal estate, etc. and make her my Exerx. 3 July, 1735. Prob.: 15 June, 1737. Wit: Thomas Eldridge, Sr., Thomas Eldridge, Jr. Book 8, p. 700.

DOLE, Peter: Est.- Mary Dole, admr. Signed at James Citty by the Governor. 14 June, 1676. Book 2, p. 117. Mary Parke appeared in Court and made oath as to the administration of Peter Dole, by Richard Drew, James Reddick, Wm. Newsum and John Dunford. In 1677, the estate of Peter Dole, was administered by Robt. Parke and found correct. p. 118.

DOLES, Catherine: Of Isle of Wight Co. To my grandson, Peter Doles, son of Rachel Doles, my daughter, bed and furniture. Makes daughter, Rachel, Exerx. 24 Feb., 1749. Wit: Laurence Lancaster, John Stephenson. Memorandum: If my grandson should die, if my daughter die, to go to children Martha and Benjamin Stephenson, children of my daughter. Ann and Peter Stephenson, her husband. 19 Mar., 1750. Presented by John Alsobrook, who married the widow. Book 9, p. 683.

DORCH, Walter: Est.- 2 June, 1684. Signed: Geo. Foster, Jno. Watkins. Book 4, p. 4.

DREW, John: Leg.- To wife, Elizabeth, son, John Drew. Daugh-ters, Elizabeth, Mary, Sarah. Makes wife, Exerx. 24 Jan., 1702/3. Prob.: 2 Mar., 1702. Wit: Thomas Drew, Rich. Taylor, Will, Drew. Book 5, p. 263.

DREW, John: Est.- Debtor to John Shugars and Elizabeth his wife, Exers. of sd. Drew. Signed: John Shugars, Elizabeth Shugars. Wit: Arthur Davis, William Cockin. 16 July, 1711. Book 6, p. 93.

DREW, Richard: Est.- Mabell Drew, Exerx. for her husband. Wit: Nathaniel Braxup, Thomas Jarrett, Robt. Caufield, Wm.

Seward. __ _____, 1676. Book 2, p. 117.

DREW, Richard: Leg.- To my son, Edward Drew, 400 acres of
land bounding upon Richard Harris and Captain Baker. To
son, John Drew, a parcell of land binding on a cob of
meadow at a fallen white oak to Blunt's corner tree. To
son, Richard Drew, the Plantation I live on. The rest of
my estate to my wife with plantation and housing for her
life. At her decease to my daughter, Mabell Drew. If any
son die the survivor to inherit. To daughter, Mabell Drew,
her deceased sister's wearing apparel. Robt. Caufield,
and son, Thomas Drew, Exers. 4 April, 1679. Prob.: 6
May, 1679. Wit: Nicholas Willson, Joseph Ford. Book 2,
p. 204.

DREW, Sarah: Est.- By John Sugar. 19 March, 1711. Signed:
Thos. Holt, Wm. Gray, Jr. Book 6, p. 98.

DREW, Thomas: Est.- 17 Oct., 1739. Judith Drew, admr. with
the will annexed of Wm. Drew, Exer. of sd. Thomas Drew.
Signed: John Thompson, John Crafford, John Berryman. Book
9, p. 94.

DREW, Thomas: Leg.- Son, David Drew, son Thomas Drew, son,
John Drew. Mentions daughters, Mary and Faith. Friends
Charles Binns and Benjamin Bailey. 13 Feb., 1737/38.
Prob.: 21 Apr., 1742. Wit: Charles Binns, Wm. Hart,
Benjamin Bell, Thomas Binns. Book 9, p. 408.

DREW, Thomas: Est.- David Drew and John Drew, Exers. 17 Mar.,
1745. Book 9, p. 524.

DREW, Thomas, Sr.: Leg.- To son, John Drew, 5 shillings. To
son, Thomas Drew, my plantation he now lives on and my
Plantation Called Bokatinke which I bought of Joseph Rogers,
also negroes. To my grandson, Wm. Drew, my Plantation he
now lives on and my Plantation that James Ealy formerly
lived on and two negroes. To granddaughter, Martha Drew, 2
negroes. To granddaughter, Elizabeth Drew, 2 negroes.
Friend, James Ransom, 5 lbs. To my wife, Faith Drew, the
use of my Plantation and negroes for her life. To son,
William, the rest of my estate. 17 March, 1733/34. Prob.:
26 Nov., 1734. Wit: John Wills, Frances Litel, Robert
Little. Wm. Drew, Exer. Book 8, p. 431.

DUCE, John: Est.- 20 Oct., 1691. Phyllis asks for admr. on
estate. Book 4, p. 238.

DUCHEE, Melchisadeck: Est.- 5 Mar., 1708. By Ann Duchee.
Signed: Edward Moreland, Benj. Champion. Bk. 5, p. 410.

DUES ?, John: Est.- Inv. by Phyllis, Relict and admr. of deceased. 19 Jan., 1691. Signed: Richard Jordan, Thomas
Mathews. Book 4, p. 243.

DUNCAN, David: Leg.- Wife, Elizabeth Duncan, household good,
horses, etc. To son, Nathaniel, all my slaves. Son,
David Duncan, one negro. Son, John, two negroes, bed, etc.
Son, Peter, 2 negroes, son, Daniel, 2 negroes, son Nathaniel, the land and plantation where I live, household good,
etc. Daughter, Jennett. __ _____, 1744. Prob.: 17 July,
1744. Wit: Hugh Ivey, John Hays. Book 9, p. 508.

DUNFORD, John: Est.- Mary Dunford, Relict. 13 March, 1688.

Prob.: 29 May, 1688. Wit: Henry Tooker, Jos. Ford, Thos. Drew, Walter Taylor. Book 4, p. 43.

EDMUNDS, Howell: Leg.- To my eldest son, Thomas Edmunds, the Plantation where I now live and the land I lately had as a Patent, on the Wild Catt and an entry on Nottoway River, adj. Benjamin Clements and Thomas Butts, also 200 acres at Great Creek after Nicholas Edmunds, has made his choice. If no issue, to surviving brother or his heirs, to my son, Howell Edmunds, a tract of land on Blunt's Swamp in Isle of Wight County, and the stock belonging thereto and debts due to me from Abraham Saul and George Wood and 300 acres at the Great Creek, if no issue to surviving brother's heirs. To son, Nicholas Edmunds, 500 acres of land upon Great Creek in Brunswick Co. and choice of stock and 3 negroes. To daughter, Sarah Jones, one Pistole to buy a ring and one negro. To daughter, Elizabeth Edmunds, 3 negroes and her choice (after son, Thomas) of certain furniture, cattle, etc. To daughter, Ann Edmunds, 2 negroes, furniture, catt.e, etc. The rem. of my estate, after debts and legacies are paid to son, Thomas Edmunds, and makes him Exer. 24 Dec., 1728. Prob.: 20 Aug., 1739. Wit: Andrew Lester, Wm. Briggs, Doelong. Book 7, p. 962.

EDMUNDS, Thomas: Est.- Edmund Ruffin. Ann Ruffin, admr. 19 Oct., 1743. Book 9, p. 453.

EDMUNDS, Thomas (Capt.): Est.- Ann Edmunds, admr. Signed: Howell Briggs, Rich. Blunt, Samuell Maget. 12 May, 1737. Book 8, p. 697.

EDMUNDS, William: Leg.- To son, Wm. Edmunds, all my land on east side of Nottoway River, patent of 830 acres, part ajjoining on Coll. Ludwell's line 250 acres more or less. To son, David Edmund, a tract of land binding on John Hunt, westerly - to the road and tract adj. 170 acres. To my seven daughters, a neck of land between Branches, Nanny Towny Branch and Great Spring Branch, while single or widows, and afterwards to John Edmondgrey Edmunds. I give to my son, John Edmundgrey Edmunds, all the remainder part, namely, my Plantation, and all my land joining him. To two daughters, Mary and Sarah Edmunds, 280 acres on Parker's line, Clement Land and Indian Land equally divided. Sons, Wm., David, and John 200 acres equally divided adj. Coll. Wall's land. I bought of Thomas Peters towards Nottoway Bridge. Wife, Mary Edmunds, one slave. Daughters, Susannah, Elizabeth, Faith, and Christian, one slave each. Son David, and daughter, Phyllis, one slave each. 19 Feb., 1730. Prob.: 16 July, 1740. Wit: Rich. Parker, Nath. Moss. Book 9, p. 197.

EDWARDS, Benj.: Est.- 17 July, 1750. Signed: Wm. Seward, Jr., Wm. Seward, Wm. Drew. Book 9, p. 649.

EDWARDS, Benjamin: Leg.- To my brother, William Edwards, my tract of land given me by my father. If there is any further estate belonging to me after my debts and funeral are paid I give to my brother, Nath. Edwards. To brother, John Edwards and sister. Sarah Edwards, one negro. If sister die or marry to brother, Wm. Edwards. To sister, Mary Edwards, two negroes. Brothers John and Wm. Edwards, Exers. 6 Nov., 1721. Prob.: 21 Nov., 1722. Wit: Ann Cary, Arch. Blair, Henry Cary. Book 7, p. 472.

EDWARDS, John: Leg.- To son, John, where he lives between Mr. Thompson and myself path from son, John's to Wm. Twet's south to the College Line. If son, John, die without heirs to son, William. To son, William land near Hound Island Swamp - if he die to son, Benjamin. To son Benj., all the rest of the tract. To son, Nathaniel, after my wife's death the plantation where I live. To couzen, Thos. Edwards, the Plantation where he now lives if he die to my daughter, Sarah. To cozen, Wm. Edwards, the North end of the land on West side of Round Island Swamp - if no heirs to my daughter, Mary. To cozen, John Edwards, the rem. of land on West side of Round Island Swamp, if he die to my daughter, Mary. To daughter, Ann, 20 shillings for ring. All rest of personal estate to wife, Ann, and makes her Exerx. 12 July, 1712. Prob.: 20 Nov., 1713. Wit: William Edwards, Wm. Holt, Elli Taylor. Book 5, p. 147.

EDWARDS, Thomas: Leg.- Wife, Elizabeth; Son, Thomas; Son, William; Son, John; Daughter, Sarah; Daughter, Elizabeth. Wit: Jno. Edwards, Eth. Taylor, Tho. Lane. 4 Feb., 1702/3. Prob.: 2 March, 1702. Book 5, p. 262.

EDWARDS, Thomas: Est.- By Eliza. Edwards, Relict. 30 Apr., 1703. Signed: Edward Drew, Thomas Garroll, Jno. Clarke. Book 5, p. 279.

EDWARDS, William: Leg.- To son, Benjamin Edwards, the Plantation where I now live with all land belonging and my mill, also Tract of land on Green Swamp, also where Richard Rose lives, all my land at the Round Hill and a half acre at James Town and two negroes - To son, William Edwards, all that tract of land known as My Old Plantation on Crouche's Creek, also tract on Pigeon Swamp near where Thomas Warren lately lived -- 1100 acres and also a tract on the South side of Nottoway River called New Spain - also that Land I purchased of. Joseph Lane and Thomas Jarrell at the upper end of the place called the String. To my son, Micajah Edwards, all these Tracts--lyeing on South side of Blackwater Swamp known as Cippahawk and Tarrapin - three surveys and two entrys - all the land I have on Cippahawk branch, Tarrapin and main Swamp and Plantation on Nottoway River where my negro, Frank, now lives and tract in low ground, of that river and one back of that. To John Cargill, Clerk, the Land that lies back of Creeds. To Francis Regan one Dividend of Land lying at the mouth of Susquehannah branch, where his Plantation now is. To Thos. Jarrell one small Tract on the lower End of his line and the great Swamp below his house not exceeding 10 acres, formerly promised to Samuel Kindred. To my daughter, Mary Edwards, a cabinet in my Inner Room 70 lbs. To daughter, Elizabeth Edwards, one negro. To daughter, Ann Edwards, one negro and 70 lbs. money. To daughter, Sarah Edwards, one negro and 70 lbs. Rest of my estate to all my children, if death of either of my sons, before 21 yrs. old or married to descend to surviving brother and pay to their sisters 50 lbs., and personal estate divided among all children. My rings and other jewells to be distributed among my children as directed in the paper where they are sealed up. To Cozen, Sarah Edwards, 15 lbs. It is my will that Micajah Perry and Comp. pay my son, Benjamin Edwards, 100 lbs. sterling I sent them, bequeathed to my said son by his Grandfather, Benjamin Harrison, Esq. and interest. Makes son, Banjamin, Exer. and friends Phillip Ludwell, Esq. and Nathaniel Harrison, Esq. and Doctor

Archibald Blair, Trustees. 9 Jan., 1721/22. Prob.: 21
Feb., 1724. Wit: John Cargill, William Edwards, Jr.,
John Edwards, Nathaniel Edwards. Book 7, p. 389.

EDWARDS, William: Leg.- Wife, Sarah Edwards, one negro.
Daughter, Mary, one negro. Daughter, Elizabeth, one negro.
Daughter, Hannah, one negro. Daughter, Sarah, one negro.
Daughter, Rebecca (not of age) have 20 lbs. when 21. Re-
mainder of estate to be equally divided between wife and
five daughters. 10 Feb., 1744/45. Prob.: 20 Mar., 1744.
Wit: Wm. Holt, Thos. Warren, Saml. Thompson. Bk. __,
p. ___.

ELDRIDGE, Thomas: Leg.- Wife, Judith, Land and Plantation
where I now live at her decease rem. to son, William, and
his heirs. To wife use of land at a place called Blackwater, in Prince George Co. until son, Wm., is 21 yrs. old,
then to him. To wife all land in Brunswick Co., at her
death to sons, Wm. and Richard. To wife, use of land on
North side of Waughrick Branch in Prince George County
turned out by my son, Thomas, for her life, this said land
and an entry I made with Col. Robert Bolling - to sd. son,
Thomas. Gives son, Thomas, my law books, silver tankard,
1 doz. silver spoons. To daughter, Judith, 4 slaves. To
daughter, Elizabeth, 4 slaves. To daughter, Mary, 4
slaves. To daughter, Anne, 4 slaves. To daughter,
Martha, 4 slaves. To sons, Richard and William, slaves.
To son, Richard, land at Roxdale in County of Henrico. To
son, Richard, land I purchased of James Dickens and Bindlord Dickens on South side of Nottoway River in Surry
County. To wife, land at Hunting Quarter, at her death to
all my daughters. I give to my Grandson, Thomas Eldridge,
and my granddaughter, Jane Eldridge, 15 lbs. each, when 21
years old. Tuition, care, etc. of all children, under
age, to my wife & all rest of estate. 17 Aug., 1739.
Prob.: 20 May, 1741. (No witnesses) Book 9, p. 317.

ELLES, Jeremier: By Elizabeth Elles. 17 May, 1738. Signed:
Holan Sturdyvaut, Wm. Jones, Wm. Pelling. Bk. 8, p. 847.

ELLIS, James: Leg.- To John Hill, two negroes, pots, kettles,
live stock, new nailes - money due me in England, etc.
To Sarah Hill, daughter of John Hill, to William Rowland,
great bed, furniture, puter dishes, pewter tankard and
stick. To Wm. Reade, bed and furniture, pewter dishes,
cattle, gun, etc. To Samuell Read, the son of William
Reade, one cow and to Mary, daughter of William Reade, one
cow. To William, the son and Mary the daughter of William
Rowland to each a cow. Rest of household goods to John
Hill, William Rowland, and William Reade to be divided. To
friend, Samuell Thompson, appoints him my sole Exer. 26
June, 1714. Prob.: 25 July, 1714. Wit: Thos. Collier,
Edward Clarke. Book 6, p. 207.

ELLIS, John: Leg.- Whole estate to be sold and money to be
divided as follows: Child in esse, if it lives, one-third
part of estate. To daughter, Mildred Ellis, one-third of
estate at 18 yrs. To wife, Mary Ellis, one-third part of
estate. If any die, surviving child to inherit. Wife
Exerx. 10 Jan., 1739. Prob.: 20 Feb., 1739. Wit:
Andrew Lester, Morris Pritchett, Richard Blunt. Book 9,
p. 117.

ELMES, Matthew: Est.- Deceased, 1694. Judah Elmes affirms

this inventory as true. Signed: Wm. Harvey, Adam Heath. 2 March, 1694. Book 5, p. 39.

ELTON, Robert: Est.- Signed: Joseph Seale, Will. Hancocke, Edward Morland, John Page. Book 4, p. 308.

EMERY, John: The wife of John Emery was Susannah Green, daughter of Richard Green, latter died intestate. Shown in deed to George Tortt, of Isle of Wight County. 16 Dec., 1713. Book 6, p. 169.

EMERY, Thomas: Leg.- To son, Benj. Emery, 150 acres of land on Western Run. To son, Green Emery, my first levy of land 100 acres, rugs, etc. cow and pewter, etc. To rest of children each a cow and calf when 21 yrs. old. To son, Thomas Emery, a gun, soward and cartouch box. Rest of estate to wife, Susannah. Makes wife Exerx. 6 May, 1734. Prob.: 17 July, 1734. Wit: Thos. Eppes, Jeremiah Ellis, Rebecker Ezelle. Book 8, p. 391.

EMMERSON, John: Leg.- To Joan Seldon, when she is free a westcoate. To Wm. Browne, son of Major Browne, my Scimiter. To Lt. Coll. Geo. Jordan, Mr. Ben. Harrison, Mr. Arthur Jordan, Mr. Nath. Knight, Maj. Wm. Browne, Mr. Thos. Jordan, Mr. Walter Flood, Fra. Hagwood, Mr. Ni. Meriweather, Mr. James Jordan, Mr. Edward Baly, Mr. Robert Lee and Mr. Jno. Moring, to each one pair of gloves. Makes Mr. Christopher Foster, Exer. Bequest to Ann Sowerby. 25 Sept., 1676. Prob.: 18 May, 1677. Wit: John Moring, Jone Willson, John Emmerson. (Indexed "John Emerson") (Wife was Faith Emerson, p. 167.) Book 2, p. 123.

EPPES, Daniel, Jr.: Est.- Mary Epps, administrator. 30 Mar., 1733. Signed: Wm. Shands, Thos. Hood, Robt. Doby. (In 1737 Francis Mabry and Mary Mabry, admrs.) Bk. 8, p. 358.

EVANS, Abraham: Lkg.- To son, John Evans, my Plantation whereon I now live with a certain parcell of land adjacent – being all from ye Upper End of that Tract of land - near ye Horse Bridge over ye Swamp - 100 acres after decease to my wife, Elizabeth Evans, also my Plantation on Nottoway River and 130 acres belonging to it. To son, William Evans, land, part of land I live on -- Line near Horse Bridge - to lower part - 50 acres. I give to Abraham Macklemore - land at Nottoway River - 70 acres and adjoining the Plantation given to son, John, if he die without issue, to go to son, John Evans. To son, certain cows, etc. and to his two sons. To my wife, Elizabeth Evans, my Plantation and with houses, with privileges of 100 acres belonging for life, goods, chattels, etc. Son, John Evans, Exer. 4 August, 1708. Prob.: 18 June, 1712. Wit: Tho. Smith, Barthol. Andrews, Thos. Smith, Jr. Book 6, p. 105.

EVANS, Anthony: Leg.- To wife, Ann Evans, for her life my Plantation where I now dwell. 100 acres and the other half of said land, to my son, John Evans, at his mother's decease to have the other half. To son, William, the same in manner and form as his Brothers. If son, William, have no heirs then to son, Anthony Evans. If he have no heirs to son, Benjamin Evans. Gives Son, John, gun and sword with E. E. upon the barrell. Rest of estate to wife, Ann. If wife marry children to be free at 17 years old. Wife, Ann, Exerx. 12 July, 1707. Prob.: 25 Feb., 1710. Wit: Thos. Waller, Alice Waller, Mary Waller. Bk. 6, p. 42.

EVANS, Benjamin: Leg.- To brother, John Smith, ye plantation
I bought of my sister, Mary Evans, the sd. Plantation and
Land thereto belonging and one negro at the death of my
mother and everything else. 16 Apr., 1729. ·Wit: Jos.
Washyer, Wm. Cripps. Book 7, p. 921.

EVANS, John: Est.- Thos. and Mary Gwaltney, Exers. 15 Aug.,
1733. Book 8, p. 315.

EVANS, Robert: Nuncupative Will. Gave his whole estate to
Elinor Vahan and her child. Will proven 11 July, 1679,
by oaths of James Ellis and Mary Skinner. 30 July, 1679.
James Ellis, aged 27, deposed to this, Mary Skinner deposed the same. Book 2, p. 215.

EVANS, Robert: Est.- By Elinor Nichollson, 2 May, 1681.
Stephen Vahan claims his part of estate of Robert Evans.
If Stephen die, this estate to return to Elinor Nichollson.
Book 2, p. 283.

EVENS, John: Leg.- Land and Plantation on the South Side of
Seacocke Swamp to be sold by my Exer. as Personall estate.
To wife, Mary Evens, best bed and furniture. To son,
John Evens, small gun with letters I. E. and same on back
of Sword. Makes wife, Exrx. and after debts and legacies
paid my estate to be divided between my wife and three
children. 24 March, 1726/7. Prob.: 19 July, 1727. Wit:
John Phillips, John Smith. Book 7, p. 747.

EVIND, John: Est.- By Mary Evins. 18 Oct., 1727. Signed:
Chas. Binns, Wm. Hart, Hugh Hunniford. Book __, p. 758.

EWART, James: Est.- 18 June, 1735. Thos. Avent, Sheriff.
Book 8, p. 504.

EZEL, George: Leg.- To Eldest son, George, my land leased to
me by Adam Heath, lying and being in Charles Citty County
near the head of Upper Chipoakes Creek, and horses, cows,
etc., when he is 21 yrs. old. To Eldest daughter, Elizabeth, bed, blankets, etc., 3 pewter dishes and 3 plates to
be given to her at 16 years or married. To daughter, Mary,
pewter dishes, plates, etc. cows when 16 years old or
married. To daughter, Lucy, cows, horses, pewter dishes,
etc. when 16 years old or married. To daughter, Sarah,
the same. To son, Timothy, furniture, beds, etc. when he
is 16 years old. Wife, Elizabeth, Exerx. 24 Dec., 1692.
Prob.: 11 Apr., 1693. Wit: John Pestell, John James.
Book 4, p. 293.

EZEL, George: Leg.- Son, George Ezel, ye Tract of land where
he now lives and 10 shillings. To son, William Ezel, land
I now live on and my Trooper's arms. To son, John Ezel,
tract of Land on Meheria River in Brunswick County. To
son, Edward Ezell, Tract of land on Reedy Branch. To
daughter, Mary Ezell, side saddle and Bridle -- Rest of
will mutilated. 20 Jan., 1730. Presented by Rebeckah
Ezell. Proved by Thos. Cock and Jeremiah Ellis, Jr. Wit:
Wm. Thorp. Book 8, p. 70.

EZELL, Michaell: Leg.- To son, Wm. Ezell, feather bed, mare,
saddle and bridle and all rest of goods and chattels. I
give one-half of aforesd. to my son, William; and the other
half to my daughter, Elizabeth, and my son-in-law, John
Atkinson, whom I nominate my Exer. 6 Feb., 1713/14. Prob.:

18 Dec., 1717. Wit: Wm. Hurdle, Samuell Cornwell. Book 7, p. 83.

EZELL, Timothy: Est.- 4 Mar., 1696. Wife, Mary. Signed: N. Harrison, Jere. Ellis. Book 5, p. 126.

FARMER, Thomas: Est.- 2 Nov., 1723. By Agnes Farmer. Signed: Samuell Magot, Joell Barker, John Andrews. Book 7, p. 496. 18 June, 1729, p. 955, Est. Thos. Farmer was administered by Agnes Bynum, James Bynum.)

FATHERBE, Ann: Leg.- To son, William Evins, bed, furniture, etc. To son, Anthony Evins, pewter dishes, one negro. To grandson, John Evins, pewter dishes and two plates and cow. To daughter, Mary, one negro. Three daughters, Elizabeth, Martha, Anne. Son, William, Exer. 17 May, 1734. Prob.: 19 Nov., 1735. Wit: Chas. Binns, Samuel Warren. Book 8, p. 537.

FAULCON, Abraham: Leg.- To brother, Jacob Faulcon, stock of hogs and cattle and corn, furniture, all money in John Bamer's hands and all I have in Benjamin Evans hands and he to pay all my debts in this country, my mare. To brother, Nicholas Faulcon, all my tract of land, my negro, my goods which came in this year and two bhos. of lot and he to pay Capt. Randolph and Company, Merchants in London, also all the Troopers arms I have and my table. Makes Jacob and Nicholas my sole Exers. 16 Mar., 1726. Prob.: 18 Oct., 1727. Wit: Wm. Edwards, Wm. Holt, John Judkins. Book 7, p. 764.

FAULCON, Isaac: Leg.- Wife have and enjoy the Plantation where I live for her life, her dower, at her decease to son, Nicholas Faulcon -- Gives wife negroes. To son, Abraham, 2 negroes and plantation where he lives at Reedy Swamp and land on West side. To son, Jacob, 2 negroes and Plantation where he now dwells on the East side of Spring Branch. To son, Nich. Faulcon, 2 negroes, household goods, some personal estate. Wife, Jane, Exerx. 12 Mar., 1726/7. Prob.: 18 Oct., 1727. Wit: Geo. Piland, Wm. Holt, John Ruffin. Book 7, p. 761.

FAULCON, Jacob: Leg.- To Sarah Edwards, Daughter to Thomas Edwards, deceased, 19 lbs. Sterling, 4 lbs. current money, a gold ring and 1 hhd. of tobacco and two cows. To brother, Nicholas Faulcon, all the rem. of my estate and makes him Exer. 3 Feb., 1727. Prob.: 16 ___, 1727. Wit: Wm. Edwards, John Friday, Edward Pettway. Book 7, p. 770.

FEDDER, John: Est.- Henry Rose, Mary Rose, 17 May, 1721. Signed: John Sowerby, Wm. Ray, Elias Fort. Book 7, p. 332.

FELPS, Humphrey: Leg.- Wife Eleanor Felps. To three sons that are gone from me, namely: William, Humphrey and Richard, all the estate of mine they have in their hands. To son, Callepe Felps, one cow and to my Three sons, John, Thomas & Nathaiel. 50 pounds of Tobacco apiece, when they are 21 and to my Daughter, Mary, one Large Bible. Same to wife Eleanor, and son, Francis Felps, to be equally divided between and makes them Exers. of estate. 19 Sept., 1713. Prob.: 20 July, 1715. Wit: Jestes Willison, John Lanier. Book 6, p. 251.

FERRABY, Benjamin: Leg.- To James Badcock all my money. To

Benjamin Nichols, a Bible. To Stith Bolling, Jr., 20
shillings. To wife, Ann, household goods and one negro and
negro to Benjamin Evans. If he die before her then to John
Evans and if she have a child, that child to be given to
William Evans. Wants funerall sermon preached. Makes
wife, Ann, Exerx. 30 May, 1723. Prob.: 20 July, 1726.
Wit: Edward Brown, John Worden. Book 7, p. 646.

FIELDS, John: Leg.- To wife, Jean Fields, all estate. 20
Oct., 1735. Prob.: 21 Jan., 1735. Wit: Thos. Edmunds,
Anne Edmunds. Book 8, p. ___.

FIGURES, Bartholomew: Est.- By Robert Owen, Hannah Owen. 12
Feb., 1699/1700. Signed: Thos. Blunt, Wm. Hunt, Sam'll.
Briggs. Hannah, wife to Bartholomew Figures swore to
Inventory above. Book 5, p. 198.

FIGURES, Thomas: Leg.- To brother, Bartholomew Figures, all
estate, real and personall. 20 March, 1710. Wit: Thos.
Bullifant, Jno. Doois. Book 6, p. 47.

FITCHETT, John: Est.- Signed: William Browne, Admr. 20 July,
1720. Signed: Nich. Maget, Rich. Andrews, Will. Marriott.
Book 7, p. 274.

FITCHIT, William: Est.- 19 Nov., 1740. Mary Fitchit, admrx.
Signed: John Tynes, John Moring, Jos. Witherington. Book
7, p. 239.

FIVEASH, John: Leg.- Makes wife, Exerx. To son, Francis
Fiveash, one cow and gun when of age. Daughter, Mary, one
cow. Brother, Peter Fiveash, overseer of will. 27 Jan.,
1687. Prob.: 20 May, 1688. Wit: Charles Judkin,
Robert Judkin, Thos. Harebottle. Book 4, p. 41.

FLAKE, Robert: Leg.- To daughter, Elizabeth Flake, bed and
furniture, pewter and 600 acres of land on West side of the
Second Swamp, all the rest to be equally divided between
the rest of my children. Appoints son-in-law, William
Gwaltney, Exer. 18 Aug., 1722. Prob.: 15 Apr., 1724.
Wit: Charles Binns, Hugh Hunniford. Will presented by
William Braddy and Katherine his wife, next of kin to sd.
deceased. Book 7, p. 528.

FLEMING, Lawrence: Leg.- To Robert Watkins my plantation I
live on with all the land thereto belonging. To James
Davis the use of the Plantation John Revell now liveth on
untill ye said Revell's youngest Son that now is, shall
come to ye age of 21 years, then I give sd. Plantation to
son of sd. Revelle. To John Revelle the debt he now oweth
me and to be disposed to schooling of his youngest son to
whom I likewise give a cow. To Daniell Macdaniell the
debt he oweth me to be disposed of as schooling his son,
John Macdaniell, and give him a cow. The rest of estate I
give to be equally divided between Mr. JOhn Watkins, his
six children, wife, four sons and two daughters. Appoints
Mr. Robert Watkins, Exer. To Phillis Fort my riding
horse. 8 Dec., 1710. Prob.: 25 Feb., 1710. Wit: Edward
Bayley, Sam'l. Williams, Elias Fort. Book 6, p. 44.

FLOOD, Ann: Leg.- To grandson, John Flood, deceased husband's
gun and cane. Husband's wearing apparel to be equally
divided amongst my sister Thomas' three sons, William,
Henry and Benjamin. Residue of estate, real and personal,

to be equally divided between my two daughters, Mary and
Ann Flood and appoints Nathaniel Harrison, Esq. Exer. 26
Mar., 1723. Prob.: 21 Aug., 1723. Wit: Mich. Harris,
Joseph Witherington, Robert Smith Woobank. Book 7, p. 469.

FLOOD, Ann: Leg.- To daughter, Faith Phillips, for life a side
saddle and is to return to my granddaughter, Elizabeth
Collier. To my granddaughter, Eliz. Watkins, a ring and
Mustard Pot, given me by Mrs. Potter. To my granddaughter,
Jean Reeks, bed and bedding, pewter dishes and plates, cow
and hogs. To grandson, Thos. Reeks, some hogs. To
granddaughter, Mary Phillips, gown, petticoat and some
cotton bought of Mrs. Jacquelin. To granddaughter, Elizabeth Collier, all the remainder of my estate, whose husband, Thomas Collier, I make Exer. 25 9br, 1728. Prob.:
19 Mar., 1728. Wit: John Cargill, Benj. Chapman, Rch.
Rose. Book 7, p. 915.

FLOOD, Harry: Leg.- To daughter, Ann Flood, in England (If
she is living) I give 20 shillings sterling. What remains
to be equally divided between my Daughter, Elizabeth
Nicholson and her six children (to witt) Henry, Robert,
Mary, George, James and Ann Nicholson, or to the survivors
of them and I appoint my son-in-law Robert Nicholson my
sole Exer. (Under the direction of Col. John Allen) of
this my Will and Test. 18 Dec., 1739. Prob.: 15 Oct.,
1740. Wit: Thomas Hamlin, Ldelong, Elizabeth Rookings.
Book 9, p. 228.

FLOOD, Johannah Joice: Leg.- To Robert Nicholson, 15 lbs.
current money. To daughter, Joice Nicholson, 10 lbs.
current money. To daughter, Ann Nicholson, 10 lbs. current
money. To daughter, Elizabeth, my Gold Ring and 15 lbs.
current money. If son, Robert, dies under age or without
heirs - his part to be equally divided between my two
Daughters, Joice and Ann Nicholson, if either daughter die
under age or without heirs their part to be divided between my son, Robert and the surviving daughter. My desire is that Capt. Henry Harrison may have my daughters,
Joice and Elizabeth with their portion in full which belongs to them and deliver the same to them when of age or
married. To Capt. Thos. Cocke, son of William Walter
Cocke, my daughter, Ann Nicholson, with her portion given
her when of age or married. 21 Oct., 1720. Prob.: 18
May, 1743. Wit: Nich. Cocke, Mary Dawson, Mary Allstin.
Book 9, p. 433.

FLOOD, John: He late of the Colony, dying left an estate,
whereof David Andrews, Jr. who married the Relict made suit
to the Court for administration, 1 July, 1679, was granted.
Book 2, p. 219.

FLOOD, John: Est.- By David Andrews and Mary Andrews. 4 Aug.,
1679. Signed: Jno. Watkins, Nich. Witherington. Book 2,
p. 234.

FLOOD, John: Leg.- To daughter, Jane Flood, a negro boy. To
wife, Mary Flood, a negro woman. To daughter, Mary Flood,
one negro, bed, etc. when she is 18 years old or married.
I having sent 5 HHds. of Tobacco for England, my will is
that what come back to be valued in money and one-half to
daughter and one-half to my wife. If daughter die before
18 years old then her part to my wife and my Brothers and
Sisters. Wife, Mary Flood, Exerx. 6 Mar., 1709. Prob.:

20 June, 1715. Wit: Nath. Harrison, Thos. Flood. Book 6, p. 63.

FLOOD, John: Nuncupative Will. 4 Oct., 1739. To sister, Fortune Flood, a sufficient maintenance. To Nicholas Edmunds all my estate. Presented by Wm. Simmons, Rich. Davis, Charles Summons, John Davis, Anne Hamlin. 21 Nov., 1739. Book 9, p. 104.

FLOOD, Mary: Est.- 20 Feb., 1724/25. Legatees Brother and sister, William and Anne Cocke. Book 8, p. 282.

FLOOD, Walter: Leg.- To daughter, Ann Flood, Plantation where I now live and all the land thereto belonging, beg. at mouth of Ware Swamp Run -- to Tussach's -- to George Norwoods -- to Sunken Marsh -- to James River -- to bounds between Coll. Harrison and me, to river side to Ware Swamp, if daughter, Ann, have no heirs then land go to my grandson, John Flood, if he have none, to be equally divided between my two granddaughters, Fortune and Elizabeth Flood, if either die to survivor. Wife have Plantation for her life. Rest of land to my grandson, John Flood, only from Tussuch's Strait across to Jarrod's line up to Jordan's land, including Plantation called Chareeby's and all my land therein to head line. If give to my son, Walter's widow for her life, if she do not marry, if so then to grandson at 21 years old. To granddaughter, Jane Flood, 20 shillings, to buy a ring. To granddaughter Fortune Flood, a negro. To grandson, John Flood, one negro. To granddaughter, Eliza Flood, one negro. To daughter, Ann Flood, 4 negroes. To wife, negroes and to maintain daughter, Mary, if wife die slaves to Mary. Friend, Nath. Harrison, Exq. and Wm. Browne, Gentlemen, Exerx. and gives each a mourning ring. 14 Oct., 1722. Prob.: 25 Nov., 1722. Wit: Nich. Maget, R. Smith Woobank, Nath. Edwards. Book 7, p. 422.

FLOWERS, David: Est.- 19 Apr., 1748. Signed: John Moring, Richard Proctor, Joshua Proctor. Book __, p. 576.

FORBUSH, George: Est.- To Thos. Smith and Eliza, his wife, admr. of Forbush. Pd. Wm. Edwards for funeral. Pd. Jno. Boyce and Mary, his wife in Rt. of sd. Daughter. Due to Eliza, daughter of Theo. Forbush. 28 May, 1695. Book __, p. 49.

FORBUSH, James: Est.- To Eliza. Forbush, admr. and Exer. of Theophilus Forbush, Dr. to Exer. of aforsd. James Forbush. 1 July, 1694. Book __, p. 39.

FORBUSH (FORBES), James: Leg.- To son, John, Boy, Cattle, all that he owes me in tobacco and a gun. To daughter, Elizabeth Forbush, cows, and a gold ring that her mother left her. To two sons, Theophilus Furbross and George Furbush all rest of my estate between them. 28 Dec., 1687. Prob.: 6 March, 1687/8. Wit: Nich. Witherington, Katherine Witherington. Book 4, p. 36.

FORBUSH, Theo.: Est.- To Tho. Smith and Eliza, his wife, admr. of sd. Theophilus. 28 May, 1695. Book __, p. 48.

FORD, Joseph: Leg.- To wife, Mary, bed with curtains and vallance, cupboard and round table, truck, a flaggon, lookingglass, 4 pewter dishes, 4 plaits, etc. To son-in-law, William Dickson, feather bed, rugs, blankets, chest,

Great Bibel, pewter, etc. To daughter-in-law, Mary Dickson, her mother's feather bed and bed which she brought to my house with its furniture at ye day of her marriage, or ye death of her mother which first happeneth. One Oxford Bible, cows, etc. To Mrs. Baker, 3 books, viz: "Smith's Sermons", "Sir Richard Bakon Meditations" and "Cabbott's Discourse". To Rebeckah White, one cow, two Pewter dishes, etc. when 18 years old or married. To Joseph Phillips, son to Thos. Phillips, one Oxford Bibel Claspt and to Tho. Phillips my great Hatt. To Mary and Sarah Baker each a faggon as they are marked. To Joseph Ford, son of Edward Ford, my gun and London Bibel, one cow. To Joseph Richardson, Junior, Joseph were and Thos. Parker each Bibel Claspt. To Robert Sutpork one cow. Rest of estate to be equally divided between wife, Mary, and her son and daughter, William and Mary. Wife Exerx. 30 Apr., 1702. Prob.: 6 July, 1703. Wit: Hen. Baker, Thomas Drew. Book 6, p. 286.

FOREMAN, William: Est.- 3 Nov., 1703. Robert Warren, Joseph Proctor, William Browne, Jr. Book 5, p. 295.

FORMAN, William: Leg.- To Benjamin Foreman 50 acres of land I bought of Luke Meazle att Blackwater, if no heirs to the College of William and Mary -- forever. Gives to trust in his friend Capt. Wm. Browne the care of my wife, Hester, for maintenance and at her death estate, personal and real to him. Capt. Wm. Browne and wife Exers. 2 Jan., 1701/2. Prob.: 5 Jan., 1702. Wit: John Hatch, Ben. Ferribee, Sion Hill. Book 5, p. 262.

FORT, Elias: Est.- Elizabeth Fortt, admrx. Signed: Wm. Rose, John Sowerby, Nicholas Prockter. 20 May, 1724. Book 7, p. 535.

FORT, Elias: Est.- By Eliza. Bynam. 21 July, 1725. Book __, p. 593.

FORT, Elias: Leg.- To son, John Fort, the tract of Land and Plantation which he now possesses with one negro. To Holiday Fort all that Tract of land and Plantation where I live and one negro, and at his decease to his Eldest daughter and her heirs, also grind stone and stilyard. To my grandson, John Fort, all my land lying upon John Shehawkin Swamp where William Fitchett now lives. To my Daughter, Phillis Pennington and her heirs negro boy, and then to her eldest daughter. To daughter, Mary Foster, negro girl and to her Eldest daughter. To daughter, Alice Foster, negro boy for her life then to eldest daughter. To daughter, Faith King, negro boy. To wife, Sarah Fort, all goods and chattels. 30 Sept., 1732. Prob.: 19 Mar., 1739. Wit: Jno. Chapman, John Bynum, Jos. Andrews. Book 9, p. 135.

FORT, John: Leg.- To son, Thomas Fort, my land belonging to my Plantation and the remainder to my son, Richard Fort. My house I now live in I give to my son, Thomas Fort, and the land about it and the remainder of my land I give to son, Richard Fort, to be equally divided. To my son George Fort, bed and furniture. To son, Elias Fort, a cow. To daughter, Hannah Phillips, a cow. To daughter, Mary, 5 shillings. To daughter, Sarah, 5 shillings. To son, John Fort, 5 shillings. To son, William) 5 shillings. To son-in-law, John Phillips, the care of my two sons, Richard and Thomas Fort, until they are of age. Remainder of estate to

sons, George, Richard and Thomas Fort. 21 Oct., 1725.
Prob.: 10 Mar., 1725. Wit: William Bynum, William Hancock. Book 7, p. 632.

FOSCROFT, Thos.: Est.- By Jno. Moring. 16 June, 1679, on
Oath of Capt. Roger Potter. Book 2, p. 210.

FOSTER, Ann: Leg.- Two youngest sons, Robert and Thomas Newsume, all my estate except clothes. Two daughters, Eliza.
and Ann, clothes. Sons, Exers. 22 Mar., 1707. Prob.:
20 Mar., 1711. Wit: Thos. Lane, Jr., Jean Lane. Book 6,
p. 48.

FOSTER, Christopher: Leg.- To my Eldest son, John Foster, my
Plantation which I now live one, with all land thereto belonging. To my youngest son, Christopher Foster, my Plantation which I bought of Abraham Evans near the Blackwater
Swamp. All the rest of my estate in general to be divided
between and among my wife and four children, Jno. Foster,
Christopher Foster, Faith Foster, and Eliza Foster. Wife,
Elizabeth Foster, and her Father, Mr. John Barker, Exers.,
jointly of my Will and Test. Whereas the Upper part of
this Will hath been long made and it hath pleased God to
Bless me with three children, more or less: Grace, Robert,
and Fortune Foster. They to have equal part with my wife
and four children above named for personall estate and gives
Robert Foster all that part of land above given to son,
Christopher, which lyeth on East side of the Branch Called
Cattail Branch to Robert Foster, it having been given to
son, Christopher, not with standing. To Wife, Elizabeth
Foster, bed I die on and rest of will as written. Son,
John, have all rest of land on Nottoway River and he pay
charges out of his own part. 27 Mar., 1710/11. Prob.:
18 July, 1718. Wit: Edward Bagley, Thos. Andrews. Book
6, p. 72.

FOSTER, George: Leg.- To wife, Ann, all that part of estate
now in her possession. To son, William and his heirs, all
my housing and land, and all other part and parcell of my
estate and my debts and ye rent of my mill only exceped and
it is my Will and Desier ye my son, Thomas, be Religiously
brought up in the feare of the Lord by my son, William, and
that learn him to right and read and cast up account and
to give him at 21 a feather bed and bonester, my cows,
horses, etc. Debts due him be divided between wife and
sons, William and Thomas and two daughters, Eliza. and
Mary. Son, William, Exer. 16 Dec., 1697. Prob.: 4 Jan.,
1697. Wit: Thos. Crus, William Gray, John Fitchett.
Book 5, p. 148.

FOSTER, William (Capt.): Leg.- To son, Henry Foster, my Plantation where I now live with all land thereto belonging
and three negroes, bed, furniture, cows and carbine. To
daughter, Mary Foster, bed and furniture and two negroes,
cows. All rest of estate to be divided between my two
children, Henry and Mary, when of lawfull age or married.
My wearing clothes to my brother, Thomas Foster and makes
him Exer. 13 Feb., 1720/21. Prob.: 19 Apr., 1721. Wit:
Nich. Maget, Thos. Cruse, Sam. Alsobrook. Book 7, p. 327.

FOX, George: Est.- Francis Maybury. 19 Aug., 1719. Signed:
Nich. Maget, John Tyus. Book 7, p. 208.

FRANCIS, Henry: Petition of Henry Francis to the Rt. Hon. Sr.

William Berkeley Knt. Governor and Capt. General of Virginia saying that ten years ago Henry Francis purchased of John Legrand land in Surry - about 150 acres - held in quiet possession, but learn land is <u>esclicatable</u>, begs to have some released. Petition is granted. 17 Nov., 1674. Book 2, p. 80.

FRANCIS, Henry: Will of Henry Francis Southwarke Parish. To Francis Ostin all my land, etc. - when of age. Rest of estate to Robert Ostin, father of sd. Francis and makes him Exer. 17 Feb., 1689/90. Prob.: 19 Jan., 1691. Wit: Benja. Harrison, of Henry, John Rawlings. Bk. 4, p. 242.

FRANCIS, Henry: Est.- __ Jan., 1691/92. Fra. Swann make return. Thos. Clements. 1 May, 1694. Book __, p. 7.

FREEMAN, John, Sr.: Leg.- To son, William Freeman, 300 acres of land at head of Caraneaks and all rest of my estate, real and personal, bonds, goods and chattels and makes him Exer. 17 Oct., 1724. Prob.: 16 Feb., 1725. Wit: Wm. Bridger, Henry Bedingfield. Book 7, p. 623.

FRENCH, Samuell: Est.- 27 Oct., 1730. Maj. John Simmons. By Richard Lewis, admr. of estate. Book 8, p. 74.

FUTERELL, Thomas: Thomas Futerell, dead, left estate and Gilian Futerell, his Relict, asks for Com. of admr. be granted to her. Granted. 29 Apr., 1693.

GARDNER, Tepaniah: Est.- 16 July, 1701. Signed: John Wapool, Wm. Knott, Nath. Harrison. Book 5, p. 249.

GEE, Charles: Est.- 5 July, 1709. Signed: Hanah Gee, John Cooke, William Cooke, William Heath. Book 5, p. 414.

GEORGE, William: Est.- William Batts, who married Sarah George, admr. 18 April, 1733. Signed: William Gray, William Edwards. Book 8, p. 284.

GILBERT, Elinor: Leg.- To Eldest daughter, Elinor -- <u>Eaves</u>? given her by her Godfather, Nicho. Williams. To daughter, Mary, to son, Roger, the whole dividend of land, but if he die under age to go to my two daughters. Household stuff to the two girls by Mrs. Plow and Margery Heath. Part of Tobacco due me from Mr. Proctor (1600 lbs.) to build a house on the Plantation - Two daughters, Exerxs. Mr. Proctor and Mathias Marriott, advisors. Wit: Samuel Plow, Geo. Proctor. 19 May, 1673. Prob.: 20 9br, 1673. Book 2, p. 35a.

GILBERT, Mary: Est.- By Elinor and Mary Gilbert. 7 Apr., 1674. Book 2, p. 50.

GILBERT, Roger: Leg.- To son, Thomas Gilbert, my land and Plantation where I live. To son, William Gilbert and daughter, Mary Gilbert, rest of plantation. Friend, Nich. Maget, Exer. 4 Jan., 1725/6. Prob.: 16 Mar., 1725. Wit: Matthew Metcalf, Thos. Howell, Robt. Judkins. Book 7, p. 632.

GILBERT, William: Leg.- To wife, Joanah Gilbert, all my Land in Brunswick County, joining upon Thomas Allston, also Land and Plantation where I live for her life, then sold and equally divided among my children. To son, John

Gilbert, a gun, sword and cartouch box, stock, cattle, etc.
To son, James Gilbert, cows, etc. To son, William Gilbert,
gun, sword and cartouch box. To daughter, Mary Gilbert,
bed, cows, etc. To daughter, Elizabeth Gilbert, bed, cows,
etc. To daughter, Martha Gilbert, Gold ring, cows, furniture, etc. To daughter, Hannah Gilbert, bed, cows, gold
ring. To daughter, Anne Gilbert, gold ring, cows, etc.
Makes wife Exerx. 3 Feb., 1739. Prob.: 19 Nov., 1740.
Book 9, p. 257.

GILLIAM, Hincha: Leg.- To my wife the use of my whole estate
during her widowhood, if she marry before the children become of age the remaining part of my estate to be equally
divided between my wife and children. To my daughter,
Elizabeth Gilliam and my son Hincha Gilliam, one negro each.
To Hincha this Plantation all the land belonging and my
gun. I give to my son, John Gilliam, my land adj. Myrick
on Wayea and one negro. To my daughter, Ann Gilliam, one
negro. To my son, Samuell, my entry upon Crouches Creek.
To O'se Tapley my land on Roanoke River adj. on Siril
Welche's land -- provided he pay my brother, John Gilliam,
20 lbs. 16 shilling, and brother, John, to keep the money
for my three sons to be divided equally among them when
they become of age. Makes wife Exerx. 3 Jan., 1736/7.
Prob.: 20 Apr., 1737. Wit: Rich. Blunt, John Gilliam,
Wm. Briggs. Book 8, p. 607.

GILLIAM, Hinshea: Leg.- To my son, Hinshea Gilliam, the Plantation where he now lives with all land adjoining. To son,
Walter Gilliam, the Plantation where he now lives with 200
acres to be taken of my land next to Rockon Swamp. If he
die without issue to go to my son, Thomas Gilliam. To son,
Charles Gilliam, the Plantation where he now lives and 100
acres on the North side of a Branch between his Plantation
and mine for his life, at his death to his son, Charles
Gilliam. The remainder of my land 340 acres to my wife,
Fortain Gilliam, for her life and at her death to my son,
Thomas Gilliam. To my three sons, Charles, Walter and
Thomas Gilliam, 40 acres on the North side of Nottoway
River a fishing place and not to molest or deprive each
other of privileges. To son, Charles Gilliam, 200 acres
adj. Benj. Harrison and Nath. Fillips. Mentions daughters,
Priscilla and Lydia Gilliam, and gives Thomas 200 A.
13 Jan., 1733. 20 Nov., 1734. Makes Thomas Exer. Wit:
Benj. Clements, John Gilliam, Edward Clanton. Book 8, p.
432.

GILLIAM, John: Leg.- To my son, John, my Plantation in Carolina and Roanoke River with land belonging and two negroes.
To my son, Hinche, all the land on the North side of the
branch that my mill stands on, 150 acres and one negro. To
son, Burrell, all the land I hold on the South side of the
Great Branch next to Charles Brebray, 150 A. and one negro.
To my son, Levy, one negro. To my wife, Sarah, the use of
my Plantation for her life then to son, John. To daughters, Sarah, Amy, Mary and Millie, each one negro. At
death of my wife the rem. of my estate to sons, Isom and
Hansille, and my daughters, Tibatha and Ledea, makes wife
and son, John, Exers. 9 Aug., 1738. Prob.: 20 Sept.,
1738. Wit: John Dunn, Thomas Dunn, Moses Johnson. Book
8, p. 902.

GLOVER, Richard: Leg.- To my wife, Sarah Glover, half of my
estate to the bringing up of my two youngest sons, and the

other half to be equally divided among my six children.
Makes wife Exerx. 16 July, 1715. Prob.: 15 Feb., 1715.
Wit: Nicholas Thomson, Elener Thomson, James Piland. Book
6, p. 203.

GOOD, Robert: Est.- 16 Apr., 1746. Admr. Joseph Mason, Thos.
Atkins, John May, John Freele. Book 9, p. 528.

GOODMAN, Thomas: Est.- Elizabeth, his wife. 20 Dec., 1748.
Signed: Peter Warren, John Watkins, John Colleck. Book
9, p. 596.

GOODMAN, William: He announced his intention of Departing out
of the colony. 22 May, 1695. Book 5, p. 49.

GOODWIN, Thomas: Est.- William Jones, admr. 15 Mar., 1731.
Book 8, p. 172.

GOODWIN, Thomas (Capt.): Est.- 16 Apr., 1746. Signed: Thomas
Allstin, Peter Warren, John Allstin. Book 9, p. 526.

GOODWYN, Thomas: Leg.- Son, John Goodwyn, porringer marked
T.G.M. Wife, Mary, Son, Thomas? Prince George Co. (Page
torn, mutilated and illegible) Grandson, Thomas Goodwyn.
Daughter, Pennellope Taylor rest of estate when she is 19
years old. Son, Francis Goodwyn. (Son, William Goodwyn
and Francis not of age). Sons, John and Francis, Exerx.
7 Feb., 1730. Prob.: 25 Aug., 1731. Wit: William Shands,
Charles Gee, Nazareth Shands. Book 8, p. 135.

GORD, Henry: Leg.- To son, Harry Gord, land on Blackwater
River in Surry County that I purchased of Philip Huniford.
If he die before of age to go to my son, William Gord, and
if he die before 21 years old, to go to son, Nathaniel
Gord. To son, Harry, my gun. After debts are paid, re-
mainder of estate to the three sons. 20 Aug., 1677. Prob.:
15 9br, 1677. Wit: Henry Clarke, Robert Shaw, Rebecca
Shaw. Book 2, p. 152.

GORDIN, John: Est.- By John Weaver and Giles Underbill. 17
March, 1713. Signed: Mary Gordon, admrx. Bk. 6, p. 179.

GORING, John: Leg.- To son, Charles Goring (not 21) if he die
to William Holt, son of Mr. Randall Holt, late of this
county, deceased and Rem. divided between sd. William Holt
and his brother, Thomas Holt. Loving kinsman Coll. Charles
Morrison to take into his tuition and care my sd. son,
Charles, educate him and with friend, Robert Caufield sole
Executors. 15 May, 1679. Prob.: 4 9b, 1679. Wit:
John Moyel (or Moyee), Elizabeth Holt. Book 2, p. 233.

GOURD, Henry: Est.- John Goring, admr. Signed: Charles Amry,
Martin Thorne. 7 May, 1678. Book 2, p. 171.

GOURD, Richard: Est.- By Mary Gourd. Signed: John Freeman,
James Samon. 18 July, 1711. Book 6, p. 69.

GRANTHAM, Edward: Leg.- To son, Edward Grantham, my Plantation
and land 100 acres. To son, Thomas Grantham, 100 acres
adj. Edward. To son, John Grantham, the rest of my land.
To daughter, Elizabeth Grantham, one shilling. To Daughter, Joanne Grantham, bed and household goods. Wife,
Elizabeth Grantham, and my five children, John, Joane, Edward, Thomas and Eloner Grantham, the rest of my estate

equally divided. Makes wife, Exerx. 1 May, 1700. Prob.:
5 Sept., 1704. Wit: Edward Bayley, Wm. Johnson, Robert
Andrews. Book 5, p. 321.

GRANTHAM, Edward: Est.- By Elizabeth Avery. 2 Jan., 1704.
Signed: William Johnson, Thomas Andrews, Robert Andrews.
Book 5, p. 329.

GRANTHAM, John: Leg.- To son, Thomas Grantham, my now dwelling
Plantation, 150 acres, beg. at John Griffin's corner tree -
to horse meadow branch. To my son, Steven Grantham, a
parcell of land -- 150 acres. To wife for her life and at
her death to my daughter, Sarah Grantham, and the rest of
my estate divided between my wife and three children,
Thomas, Steven, and Sarah Grantham. Wife and son, Thomas,
Exerx. 16 Jan., 1737/38. Prob.: 19 Mar., 1739. Wit:
Christopher Moring, Jr., Robt. Snipes, Haner Fichett.
(Wife, Sarah, probated Will). Book 9, p. 129.

GRAVES, John (Capt.): Est.- 23 Mar., 1673. Coll. Thomas
Swann, Exer. Book 2, p. 24.

GRAY, Fransis: Est.- Mary Gray, admrx. 16 June, 1679. Signed:
Roger Potter, George Foster, Thos. Jordan, Wm. Edwards.
Book 2, p. 16.

GRAY, John: Leg.- To my wife one-third of my estate and my
daughter the rest. Bequest to "cousin" John Gray, Will.
Gray's son. If daughter die estate to my Brother, William
Gray's children. Bequest to Fra. Gray, son of "my couzen",
Will. Gray. Brother Wm. Gray and Cozen Wm. Gray see after
my will. Makes wife Exerx. 16 May, 1683. Prob.: 3 July,
1683. Wit: George Foster, Thomas Bage. (Mary Nicholson
signed on estate 3 Mar., 1684.) (Robert Nicholson signed
on estate in 1685) Book 2, p. 331.

GRAY, John: Leg.- To sister, Lidie, household goods. To
brothers, Thomas and Gilbert, cattle hogs, and rest of
estate. Mentions Father, gives him clothing and makes him
Exer.: 23 June, 1708. Prob.: 9 Nov., 1708. Wit: Michael
Harris, John Hicks. Book 5, p. 403.

GRAY, Patrick: Est.- Elizabeth Gray, admr. 18 May, 1726.
Wit: John Chambers, John Newsum, Thos. Edwards. Book 7,
p. 636.

GRAY, Thomas: Leg.- Mentions brother Francis Gray 3 daus. To
my sister, wife of Francis Gray, my clothing. To brothers,
John and William Gray, all of my Plantation and land. Rest
of my estate to my three brothers, Francis, John and William Gray. 16 Apr., 1676. Prob.: 1 May, 1676. Wit:
Nate. Knight, John Ironmonger. Book 2, p. 113.

GRAY, William: Leg.- To Charles Tucker and Henry Clark, each
a cow. The rest of my estate to my wife, Mary, and my son,
Thomas, to be equally divided. Wife, Mary, Exerx. Friends
Wm. Foster, and David Andrews, overseers of Will. 8 Feb.,
1710. Prob.: 20 Oct., 1714. Wit: Wm. Foster, David
Andros. Book 5, p. 212.

GRAY, William: Leg.- To my son, William Gray, land where
Thomas Cockerham lived and where Thos. Mathews lived and
John Cocks now lives -- To Robert Snipes, to Mr. Samuell
Thompson's and land formerly Babb's. To son, Gilbert Gray-

where Thos. Rose lives called Regon's - To Wm. Gray's
four sons, Wm. Gray, Robt. Gray, Jos. Gray and Thomas Gray.
To daughters, Mary Gray, Faith Ruffin, Priscilla Gray. To
grandson, William Andrews, granddaughter, Elizabeth Ed-
wards, to grandson, Wm. Gray, to grandson, Wm. Ruffin. Son
Wm. overseer of Will. Son, Gilbert, Exer. 3 June, 1719.
Prob.: 18 Nov., 1719. Wit: Nich. Maget, Robt. Judkins,
Samuell Maget. Book 7, p. 226.

GRAY, William: Leg.- To my son, Wm. Gray, all my Plantation
and land where he now lives and negroes and stock, etc. on
the Plantation and 30 lbs. money. To son, Robert Gray, all
my land and Plantation where he now lives and all my land
adj. to it left me by my father called Babb's land and land
purchased by me of my brother, Gilbert Gray, also 6 negroes,
stock, cattle, etc. and 20 lbs. To my son, Joseph Gray,
all my plantation and land where he now lives and land
purchased by me of Charles Jones and his wife adj. to it,
7 negroes, stock, cattle, etc. and 20 lbs. To my son,
Thomas Gray, all my land and plantation where he now lives,
7 negroes, stock, cattle, etc. and 20 lbs. To son, Edmund
Gray, my land purchased of Robt. Scott, lying in Isle of
Wight Co. If my son die before 21 years old to my son,
James Gray. To son, Charles Gray, one negro and 420 lbs.
To son, James Gray, 470 lbs. cur. money. To my daughter,
Lucy Briggs, wife of Howell Briggs, 20 shillings. To my
wife, 3 negroes for life then to all my children. The rem.
of my estate to be divided between my wife and my children,
Wm. Gray, Robt. Gray, Jos. Gray, Thos. Gray, Lucy Briggs,
wife of Howell Briggs. Son, William to have care of son,
Edmund, until he is 21, have educated, etc. Son, Robert,
to have care of son, James, until he is 21 yrs. old. Four
sons, Exer. 10 Mar., 1731. Prob.: 16 June, 1736. Wit:
Timothy Thorpe, Sampson Willson, Nath. Gibbs. Bk. 8, p.
604.

GREEN, Burwell: Est.- Ann Green, admr. 19 Sept., 1733.
Signed: Henry Mitchell, John Weaver and Christopher Tatum.
Book 8, p. 330.

GREEN, Edward: Leg.- To kinsman, John Nichoss, all my life.
Bequest to Wm. Peoples, to Wm. Killinsworth, to John, a
Frenchman, a loop that Wm. Killinsworth is building. 25
Dec., 1705. Prob.: 7 May, 1706. Wit: John River, Rich.
Moore, Wm. Harrison. Book 5, p. 352.

GREEN, John: Leg.- He now in the service of his country against
the Indians desires in case of his mortality or accident
that Capt. Lawrence Baker receive his wages and a debt due
from Thos. Hux, Sr., etc. 19 Aug., 1679. Wit: Francis
Taylor, Wm. Crudge? Book 2, p. 242.

GREEN, John: Est.- Signed: Roger Delk. 4 May, 1703. Signed:
Edward Moreland, Jos. Seat, John Sugars. Bk. 5, p. 276.

GREEN, Nathaniel: Leg.- To wife, Faith, my plantation where I
lived for her life then to my son, Nathaniel. To son,
Nathaniel Green, my Troopers Arms, etc. To child in Esse
my land and Reedy Branch. Mentions brother, William Green.
Makes brother, Peter Green. Makes brother, Peter Green,
heir is children die. Brother, William Green, and wife
Exers. 23 Jan., 1736. Prob.: 20 Nov., 1738. Wit: Wm.
Richardson, Henry Gauler, Simon Gale, Mary Epes. Book 7,
p. 878.

GREEN, Nathaniel, Sr.: Leg.- To Benjamin Hunt all my land of
the North side of Nottoway River. To William Hunt one
negro. To John Hunt Jr. 20 lbs. cash. To Benj. Hunt all
the other estate not disposed of and appoints him Exer.
30 Nov., 1749. Prob.: 20 Nov., 1750. Wit: Robt. Farrington, Burrell Green, Densie Knight. Book 9, p. 669.

GREEN, Peter: Leg.- To my son, Nathaniel Green, 180 acres on
the North side of Woodyard Swamp and a parcel of land sur-
veyed with Wm. Wynne also stock. To my daughter, Elizabeth Green, one negro and pewter dishes. To sons, Frederick and Peter Green, 1100 acres at the head of South-
western Swamp to be equally divided. To daughter, Jane
Green, one negro. To son, Mildend Green, the Plantation
where I now live and 50 acres in the fork of Woodyard
Swamp. To my wife, Mary Green, 2 negroes and the use of my
plantation for life at her death to my three children,
Mary, Olive and Mildend, when 21 years old or married.
Makes wife and son, Nathaniel, Exers. 17 Dec., 1745.
Prob.: 19 Mar., 1745. Wit: Nathaniel Green, Robt. Far-
rington, Rebecca Epps. Book 9, p. 521.

GREEN, Richard: Est.- By Mary Green. 18 Apr., 1711. Signed:
Jeremiah Ellis, Geo. Ezell, Geo. Rochell. Bk. 6, p. 51.

GREEN, Robert: Leg.- To my Cozen, Thomas Bobbitt, my Plantation and land, 150 acres where I live and one negro. To
my cozen, Mary Sturdivant, 5 lbs. To my Cozen, Ann Threewitts 2 negroes, great chest, etc. To my Cozen, John Mercer, one negro and the rem. of my estate to John Mercey and
Thomas Bobbitt. 9 Aug., 1750. Prob.: 18 Sept., 1750.
Wit: Edward Pettaway, Wm. Green, Ann Threewitts. Book
9, p. 661.

GREEN, William, Sr.: Leg.- To son, Burrell Green, and son,
Benj. Green the land where I now live and equally divided,
Benjamin to have along the River side -- to sons, Wm.,
Burrell, Benj. each a negro. To my daughter, Mary Randall,
widow, and my daughter, Elizabeth Hunt, all my ready money
in the hands of Lewis Parham and Burrell Green and James
Green. Son, Burrell Green and daughter, Mary Randall,
Exers. 8 Nov., 1749. Prob.: 15 May, 1750. Wit: Robt.
Forrington, Daniel Knight, Wm. Wynne. Book 9, p. 635.

GREGORY, John: Leg.- All of my estate to wife, Barbara Gregory. 14 7br, 1667. 4 Mar., 1678. Wit: Roland Davis,
Wm. Prosser. (Rowland Davis swore that the date year 1667
should be 1676.) Book 2, p. 197.

GRICE, Robert: Leg.- To son, Francis Grice, land called Old
Tom's on Blackwater Swamp beg. at the Swamp and so to the
skull house and to a path that comes from my dwelling house
and all cattle, hogs upon the Plantation, beds, etc. To
daughter, Ann Grice, bed, furniture, cow. To daughter, Ann
and Faithy Grice, all my land on the East side of Long
Branch to be equally divided. To Cozen, John Bynum, land
on the Swamp to Burchen Island Bridge. To son, John Grice,
my plantation I live on and all the remainder of my land.
To granddaughter, Mary Horn, Cow, pewter dishes, etc. 19
Dec., 1720. Prob.: 15 Feb., 1720. Wit: Wm. Byrum,
Harmon Horn, John Bynum. Book 7, p. 307.

GRIFFIN, James: Leg.- To son, James Griffin, all my land. To
wife, Mary, all my personal estate. To daughter-in-law,

Mary Spane, a cow. 16 Jan., 1711. Wit: John King, Robert Marler. Book 5, p. 94.

GRIFFIN, James: Est.- By Elizabeth Griffin. 6 Sept., 1709. Signed: Edward Moreland, Sam. Cornwell. Bk. 5, p. 426.

GRIFFIS, Thomas: Leg.- To wife, Mary, the Land and Plantation where I live extending to Frenchman's Branch, and land on other side of Branch to my son, Thomas. Gives wife one negro for life then to son, Edward. To son, one negro, also my Trooping Saddle and Trooping Armes, 2 cows, pigs, etc. To my son, John, All the land I have a Right to in the County of Prince George and gives him one negro, 2 cows, one gun. To my sons, Travis and Edward, 100 acres of land which I have on Three Creeks in the County of Isle of Wight to be equally divided between them, the upper half to son, Travis, and one negro boy, 2 cows, etc. To son, Edward, 2 cows, etc. To daughter, Jane, one feather bed and furniture, sheets, blankets, pr. curtains and valline, 4 pewter dishes, 6 pewter plates, 2 cows, etc. To daughter, Mary, feather bed and bolster, etc. same as Jane. To daughter, Elizabeth, the same. To wife, tuition and care of all my children -- until they are 21 years old. To wife, Mary, residue of personal estate. Wife and brother-in-law, Travis Morris, Exers. 8 April, 1726. Prob.: 21 Sept., 1726. Wit: Edward Holloway, Tho. Eldridge. Book 7, p. 649.

GRIFFIS, Thomas: Est.- Presented by Mary Hay, Exerx. 19 Oct., 1726. Book 7, p. 650.

GRISWITT, Marmaduke: Leg.- To Walter Griswitt the Plantation where I live and 100 acres on Jeremy Swamp. To son, George, 100 acres on Henry Sorrows' line. To Daniel Guttre, 100 acres on the meadow, paying my wife, Ann Griswitt, 5 lbs. 10 shillings. To son, Thomas Griswitt, the remainder of my land. Remainder of estate to be equally divided between wife and three sons. Wife Exerx. 3 Jan., 1741/42. Prob: 18 Aug., 1742. Wit: Nath. Briggs, Stephen Hamlin, James Jones. Book 9, p. 414.

GROVES, John: Est.- John Groves, admr. 16 July, 1740. Signed: Saml. Maget, Bartho. Figures, Robt. Judkins. Book 9, p. 178.

GROVES, John: Est.- 20 Mar., 1749. Signed: Benj. Ellis, Saml. Maget, John Andrews. Book 9, p. 630.

GROVES, Thomas: Appointed his wife, Phoebe, to be his admrx. Probate is granted her in his will. 5 May, 1698. Book 5, p. 156.

GULLEY, Robert: Leg.- To wife, Lucey, my land for her life then to son, Robert Gulley. Friends, Edward Bookey and William Foreman to assist wife to administer estate. 15 Aug., 1695. Prob.: 2 Mar., 1696/7. Wit: Edward Bookey, Nicholas Maget. Book 5, p. 118.

GULLY, Lucety: Leg.- Son, Robert Gully, Daughter, Elizabeth Gully, Daughter Lucety Gully. Friends, William Foreman and William Browne, Jr. Exers. 18 Oct., 1700. Prob.: 4 Mar., 1700/01. Wit: Wm. Lyle, Judy Lyle. Book 5, p. 221.

GULLY, Lucy: Est.- William Foreman, Exer. 6 May, 1701. John
    Moring, Thos. Collier. Book 5, p. ___.

GWALTNEY, John: Est.- 20 Dec., 1748. Mary Gwaltney, admrx.
    Signed: Wm. Little, John Little, Jos. Sampson Clark,
    Mary Gwaltney, admrx. Book 9, p. 598.

GWALTNEY, Joseph: Leg.- To Aunt Martha Gwaltney my Plantation
    for life then to my brother, Thomas Gwaltney. To brother,
    William Gwaltney, pewter dishes. To brother, Benj. Gwalt-
    ney, pewter dishes. To brother, James Gwaltney, pewter
    dishes. All rest to my brother, Thomas Gwaltney, and makes
    him Exer. 24 Oct., 1750. Prob.: 20 Nov., 1750. Wit:
    Jacob Atkinson, Daniel Atkinson, Robert Hart. Bk. 9, p.
    668.

GWALTNEY, Martha: Leg.- To James Gwaltney, son of John Gwalt-
    ney, bed, pewter, etc. To Thomas Gwaltney, son of John
    Gwaltney, all rest of my estate. 15 Nov., 1750. Prob.:
    16 Apr., 1751. Wit: Benj. Gwaltney, Wm. Gwaltney. Thomas
    Gwaltney, Exer. Book 9, p. 686.

GWALTNEY, Thomas: Est.- Thomas Gwaltney, admr. 15 May, 1728.
    Signed: Sam. Taylor, Charles Binns, Wm. Hart. Book 7,
    p. 806.

GWALTNEY, Thomas: Est.- Paid John Gwaltney. John Gwaltney,
    admr. 19 Nov., 1729. Signed: Will Cockes, Chas. Binns,
    Book 7, p. 993.

GWALTNEY, William: Leg.- To daughter, Ruth, wife of Robert
    Petway, one weather. To my son, William, 2 deep puter
    dishes. To my son, John, two deep dishes, gun and pott.
    To my grandson, Thomas, deep dishes, brass kettle. My two
    daughters, Mary and Martha, to have it while he is single.
    To grandson, Edward Boykin, one cow. To two daughters,
    Mary and Martha, the Plantation so long as they live single,
    also cattle, sheep, etc. to be equally divided between them
    and all household goods and makes them Exerx. 20 Mar.
    1728. Prob.: 2 Mar., 1732. Wit: Thos. Holleman, Ed.
    Brown, Jno. Brown. Book 8, p. 257.

HALE, Edward: Leg.- Makes Mr. William Thompson, minister in
    Surry County, sole Exer. and gives him all estate.
    ____, 1675. Prob.: 2 May, 1676, by oaths of Mrs. Jane
    Plow. The other witness being gone to New England. Book
    2, p. 114.

HALIDON, Edward: Probate granted William Thompson on Will of
    Edward Halidon. Signed: at James Citty by the Governor
    in 14 June, 1676. Book 2, p. 117.

HALL, Isaac: Leg.- To Sons, Lewis and George Hall, the Plan-
    tation where I live divided between them by a line beg.
    at the River brink also land adj. from Lewis Green to Henry
    Gaul's line to be equally divided, Lewis the Upper Half and
    George the lower half. To son, William Hall, the land adj.
    Benjamin Harrison (from here on Will is illegible from
    water stain) except son, (Isaac Hall) Remainder of estate
    to my wife and children. 2 ___, 1728. Prob.: 19 Aug.,
    1730. (Presented in Court by Judith Hall, Exerx. and
    oaths of John Spain and Peter Green.) Book 8, p. 40.

HALLOMAN, Richard: Leg.- All my land to my four sons, Richard,

William, Thomas and Samuell, equally divided. To my wife,
Margarett, to have the use of my Manor Plantation for life.
Daughter, Ann Halloman, one cow. Makes wife Exerx. 6 Jan.,
1710. Prob.: 20 June, 1711. Wit: Thos. Halloman,
Charles Bass, Wm. Pittman, Thos. Pittman. Book 6, p. 62.

HAMLIN, Charles: Est.- Timothy Bridges and Susannah, his wife,
Henry Floyd, Thomas Clarke. 16 Aug., 1721. Bk. 7, p. 355.

HAMLIN, Charles: Est.- By William Hamlin, Admr. of Timothy
Bridges, dec'd. who was administrator of Charles Hamlin.
20 Nov., 1723. Book 7, p. 488.

HAMLIN, Thomas: Est.- By William Clinch. 19 Feb., 1750.
Signed: John Jarrett, Geo. Berrick, Thos. Collier. Book
9, p. 684.

HANCOCK, Jane: Leg.- To son, William Hancock, leather couch, 2
Russia Leather chairs, small chest, etc. Son, John Hancock, black leather truck, 2 Russia leather chairs, warming pan, chafing dish, 9 cattle, etc. Son, Joseph Hancock,
live stock, etc. Daughter, Eliza. Ogburn, large bed, furniture, etc. Daughter, Mary, wife of Thos. Clary, one
rundle bed and clothing. Daughter, Duejates, wife of Wm.
Raines, one large looking glass, linen, etc. Daughter,
Martha Hancock, 5 pewter dishes, etc. After my debts and
funeral expenses are paid all my estate in Virginia or
England be divided equally between my son Joseph Hancock
and Elizabeth Ogburn, and makes them Exers. 2 May, 1733.
Prob.: 15 Jan., 1734. Wit: Wm. Carroll, Charles Holt.
Book 8, p. 443.

HANCOCK, John: Leg.- (first part totally illegible by large
water stain)--wife, Jane, Son, John Hancock, Trooper's
Arms. Son, Joseph,--Daughters--to four daughters. Daugh-
ter, Martha Hancock, daughter, Duegates ?. 24 Nov., 1731.
Prob.: 17 May, 1732. Wit: John Brittle, John Price.
Book 8, p. 191.

HANCOCK, Joseph: Est.- 11 Aug., 1750. Signed: Wm. Drew,
Dolphin Davis and Thomas Davidson. Book 9, p. 663.

HANCOCK, Susannah: Lkg.- To son, James, a gold ring. To
Fanny Hancock, estate of 25 lbs. current money. To two
youngest son, Wm. and Henry Hancock, the remainder of my
estate and to each a ring. To son, Nath. Sebriel, one case
of bottles, bed, etc. To granddaughter, Mary Sebriel, a
gold ring, and makes Nathaniel Sebriel, Exer. 5 Nov.,
1750. Prob.: 20 Nov., 1750. Wit: Jacob Bruce, Michael
Smalley. Book 9, p. 666.

HANCOCKE, William: Leg.- To my only son, John Hancocke, the
Plantation where he lives on the North side of the Swamp
adj. myself. To my wife, Elizabeth, the Plantation where
I now live at her death to my son. 22 Oct., 1693. Prob.:
2 Jan., 1693. Wit: Jos. Seale, John Sugar. Book 4, p.
343.

HANCOCKE, William: Est.- By Elizabeth Hancocke. 26 Oct., 1694.
Book 5, p. 25.

HARDIN, Banjamin: Leg.- To my daughter, Martha Hardin, 4 head
of cattle, pewter dishes, etc. To my wife, Sarah Hardin,
bed, horse, saddle, briddle, etc. (Next bequest illegible)

I give to Elizabeth--one cow. Son, Benjamin Hardin, Exer.
6 Feb., 1732. 9 Jan., 1734. Wit: Wm. Stanly, Henry Gray,
James Baker. Book 8, p. 382.

HARE, William: Leg.- Sworn to by Wm. Newit and Thos. Williams.
His estate to go to Robert Crafford after debts and funeral
expenses are paid. Desires that Crafford divide equally
the land between his two youngest sisters. 4 July, 1693.
Book 4, p. 308.

HARGRAVE, Bray: Est.- Mary Hargrave, admr. Signed: By Robert
Lancaster, Benj. Champion, John Halleman. 17 Apr., 1728.
Book 8, p. 797.

HARGRAVE, Lemuel: Leg.- To grandson, Jesse Hargrave, that
plantation where his mother now lives and all land on the
East side of Great Branch 100 A. and a mill then to Samuel
Hargrave when he is 21 yrs. old. Son, Jesse, in possession
of decease son, Benj's land on the South side of Roanoke
River in North Carolina. To grandson, Samuel Hargrave,
the Plantation where I lately lived and on the west side of
Great Branch, 100 acres. Bequest to son, Joseph Hargrave.
Also to son-in-law Anselm Bailey, Jr. 2 May, 1740. Prob.:
15 Sept., 1742. Wit: Arthur Pollard, Jos. Handcocke,
Sarah Borreman. Book 9, p. 415.

HARGRAVE, Richard: Leg.- To daughter, Judeth Lowery, bed,
furniture and my box. To son-in-law, James Lowery, 2
chests. To son, Bray Hargrave, one gun. To son, Lemeull,
one gun. Samuell Thompson, Exer. 19 May, 1704. Prob.:
4 July, 1704. Wit: Wm. Thompson, John Lather. Book 5,
p. 313.

HARNY, William: Leg.- To wife, Sara, my land and Plantation
for life and then to William Scogging ye son of Richard
Scogging of Prince George. To John Scogging of Surry for
life then to Frances Scogging his daughter, a chest that
was her grandmothers. Bequest to Joan Adkins of Surry Co.
10 Jan., 1703. Prob.: 5 Sept., 1704. Wit: Wm. Killingsworth, Nath. Phillips, Thos. Adkins. Book 5, p. 320.

HARNY, William: Est.- By Sara Ellis. 2 Nov., 1704. Signed:
Wm. Short, Adam Heath. Book 5, p. 329.

HARRIS, Eliza.: Est.- Widow. By Henry Harris. 16 June, 1711.
Signed: John Barker, Thos. Cotton. Book 6, p. 62.

HARRIS, Elizabeth: Leg.- Son, Joseph Harris, cow, pewter
dishes, etc. and daughter, Mary Horne, pewter dishes, etc.
Daughter, Jane Harris, 300 lbs. of tobacco at John Nicholson's, pewter, chest, etc. To daughter, Elizabeth Harris,
all the remaining part of my estate and makes her Exerx.
23 Mar., 1710. Prob.: 16 May, 1711. Wit: Jethro Barker,
John Cooke, John Averiss. Book 6, p. 55.

HARRIS, John: Est.- By Unity Harris, widow and admrx. of
John Harris. 3 May, 1687. Signed: Wm. Newsums, John
Clarke, Wm. Newitt. Book 3, p. 82.

HARRIS, John: Est.- By Mr. John Barker and Patrick Lashley.
11 Feb., 1698/99. Mary Harris, admrx. to John Harris made
oath to same. Book 5, p. 165.

HARRIS, John: Leg.- To wife, Sarah, the feather bed that I

lie on and the furniture that belongs to it. To daughter,
Mary, the rest of my estate. 19 Jan., 1719. Prob.: 15
June, 1720. Wit: John Kitchen, Robt. Ruffin. Book 7,
p. 273.

HARRIS, Joseph: Est.- 5 Sept., 1719. Signed: John Mason.
Giles Underhill, John Wilkason. Book 7, p. 218.

HARRIS, Margarett: Leg.- To son, John Taylor, 20 shillings.
To daughter-in-law, Ann, wife of John Taylor, one pair of
white gloves. To daughter, Hannah, wife of Christopher
Clinch, 20 shillings and a crepe gown. To son, Edward
Taylor, 20 shillings. To daughter-in-law, wife of Edward
Taylor, one pair of white gloves. To daughter, Margarett,
wife of Bartlett Moreland, a callico gown, petticoat and
20 shillings. To son, Thomas Taylor, 20 shillings. To
daughter-in-law, Mary, wife of Thomas Taylor, a pair of
white gloves. To granddaughters, Elizabeth Judkins,
Elizabeth Clinch, and Margarett Taylor, to each a black
silk hood. To daughter, Mary, wife of James Vaughan, my
camblett hood and cloak and black silk hood, all my estate
in Virginia, England or elsewhere to my daughter, wife of
James Vaughan. Makes son-in-law, James Vaughan, Exer. 7
June, 1721. Prob.: 20 Sept., 1721. Wit: Wm. Gray, Wm.
Seward, Thos. Edwards. Book 7, p. 366.

HARRIS, Michael: Leg.- Bequest to son, John, daughter, Mary
and wife. Makes John, Exer. 7 Jan., 1739/40. 21 Mar.,
1743. Wit: Sam. Thompson, John Davis, Wm. Marriott.
Book 9, p. 462.

HARRIS, Richard: Leg.- To son-in-law, Walter Taylor, my land
and my daughter, Jane Stringfellow. To son, Walter Taylor,
a black horse. To wife, Jane Harris, the rest of my estate.
Wife, Jane Harris, Exerx. 18 Apr., 1679. Prob.: 16 June,
1679. Wit: Thos. Waller, Walter Taylor. Book 2, p. 209.

HARRIS, Thomas: Est.- William Edwards, admr. 4 7br, 1688.
Book 4, p. 82.

HARRIS, William: Est.- 4 Aug., 1693. Signed: John Phillips,
Wm. Newett, John Clarke. Book 4, p. 324.

HARRIS, William: Leg.- Wife, Margarette, grandson, Harris
Taylor, granddaughter, Mary, wife of Thomas Taylor. Land
purchased of Robert Girly to go to grandson, Harris Taylor.
To granddaughter, Mary, land at her death to her husband,
Thomas Taylor. At their death to their son, Thomas Taylor.
Friends, Capt. Thos. Holt and Wm. Gray to divide property
and overseers of Will. Thomas Taylor, Exer. 1 May, 1720.
Prob.: 19 Apr., 1721. Wit: Wm. Gray, Wm. Gray, Jr.
Book 7, p. 325.

HARRIS, William Mr.: Est.- Estate in England. Thomas Taylor,
Exer. 18 July, 1722. Book 7, p. 402.

HARRISON, Benjamin: Leg.- To son, Nathaniel, 100 acres of
land where his mill stands, one-half of land in ye Towne
of Flowerty Hundred and all my land in Martin's Brandon in
Prince George County. To son, Henry, ye Plantation whereon
I now live remaining part of land I bought of John Barker
not already conveyed to him, also 450 acres in one patent,
950 acres in another, and all my land at Cabbin Point. All
joining my Plantation with several parcels or tracts and

all negroes belonging to Plantations. Also all plate,
household goods, new sloop Henry with all my boats and
sails-please God it come safe in. If Henry die without
heirs all real estate to son, Nathaniel. He paying my
grandson, Benjamin Harrison, 100 lbs. To William Stringer,
350 acres of land on the South side of Blackwater Swamp,
if he remove out of the county to my son, Henry. To Joell
Barker my land at Wildcatt on the South side of the branch
where he now lives. (I give 20 lbs. sterling to buy Orna-
ments for ye Chappell, that Exers. take care to provide so
soon as maybe after ye Chappell is built and my will is
that 5 acres of my land be laid out where Ye Old Chappell
now stands, and be held for that use forever.) To my
daughter, Sarah, 400 lbs. To daughter, Hannah, 400 lbs.
To my grandson, Benjamin Harrison, 400 lbs. when of age.
To my grandchildren 100 lbs. each when of age or married.
After debts and funeral expenses estate to Nathaniel Harrison and makes him Exer. wether money in England,
Barbadoes, Debts here in ye Country, goods, store or what-
soever. 6 April, 1711. Prob.: 6 Feb., 1712. Wit: Thos.
Cocke, Wm. Short, Geo. Rochell, John Tyus. Bk. 6, p. 131.

HARRISON, Mary: Leg.- (Five Bequests are illegible), then
daughters, Ann Harrison, Mary. Mentions five daughters.
Hannah Churchill, Elizabeth Cargill, Sarah Bradby, Ann and
Mary Harrison. 25 Feb., 1732. Prob.: 21 Mar., 1732.
Wit: LDelony, Thos. Browne. Book 8, p. 263.

HARRISON, Nathaniel: Leg.- To wife, Mary, all the houses and
land where I live and all my other land adj. thereto and
the use and labor of all my slaves now settled and belonging on the said lands and use and occupation of all my
household goods which I am possessed of at the places
aforesd. for her natural life - I direct that until my son,
Nathaniel Harrison, arrive at the age of 21 or married that
all the profits from slaves and land (except those slaves
on the plantation adj. where I live) shall be for the sole
benefit of all my daughters, except my daughter, Hannah
Churchill, who has already received as much of my estate as
I could then conveniently spare to be equally divided. If
not sufficient then each daughter to have 500 lbs, sterling a share. To son, Nathaniel, all my land -- in the counties of Charles Citty and Prince George. To my son, Benjamin, after the decease of my wife, the remainder of all
land, houses, etc. and all land at a place called Joseph
Swamp in the county of Surry. The remainder of sd. land
to sons, Nath. and Banj. If no issue to my brother, Henry
Harrison, gentlemen -- on condition that he pay Hannah
Churchill, my daughter, and to my other daughters when 21
years old or married 1000 lbs. sterling apiece. If he
fails to do this then -- to my nephew, Benjamin Harrison,
of the county of Charles Citty, gentleman and sd. nephew
pay 1000 lbs. each to daughter, Hannah, and other daughters
when 21 years old or married, if he fails to do this --
to go to my daughter, Hannah, first choice in the division.
To son, Nathaniel, 4240 acres at a place called New Hope
in the county of New Brunswick, and all slaves, stock, etc.,
when he is 21 years old or married. If he dies leaving
a son, the son to inherit. But if he leaves only daughters,
to go to my son, Benjamin. He paying the daughters 2000
lbs. sterling when 21 years old or married and giving them
a handsome education, etc. - To wife and brother, Henry
Harrison, all the lands I have in ye county of Henrico, to
be sold and the money equally divided among all my daugh-

67

ters. To son, Benjamin, all my land at Cypress Swamp, 750 acres, and mills and remaining land in Surry County and land in Brunswick which was devised to me by will of David Crawley late of Prince George County, deceased, and land at place called Brandy Quarter in Brunswick County and two lots and an acre of land in the Citty of Williamsburgh with houses, etc. and the remainder of slaves and household goods, which I have before given to my wife for her life -- when 21 years old. Provisions are made as to whether his issue be daughters or sons. To each daughter now not married one negro ten years old. To Mary Edwards now residing with me one negro. To John Simmons of Surry Co. land called Bolton's in Isle of Wight on condition that John Simmons build a corn mill on my land at a place called Rocky Creek in Brunswick Co. with dam, floodgates, etc. All the rest of my estate to wife and appoints wife and brother, Henry Harrison, and son, Nath. Harrison, Exers. 15 Dec., 1726. Prob.: 24 Feb., 1727. Wit: James Baker, Thos. Eldridge, Nath. Edwards. Book 7, p. 736.

HARRISON, Solomon: Leg.- To son, John Harrison, all my land in general. Mentions "all my children". To wife, Mary Harrison, several negroes and use of all land for life then to my children. Sons, William, Benjamin and Henry Harrison to be free when 21 yrs. old or married. Mentions daughter, Martha. 11 Mar., 1736. Prob.: 18 July, 1739. Wit: Wm. Rookings, Wm. Dewell. Book 9, p. 71.

HART, Henry: Leg.- To two sons, in N. C., Thomas Hart and John Hart, one negro. To my son, Joseph Hart, my Plantation at my wife's death. To son, Henry Hart, land on Lightwood Swamp. To six eldest daughters, 40 shillings each. Mentions daughter, Lucy. To daughter, Lydia, the Plantation called Kate's, to four sons, John, Joseph, Thomas, Henry all the rest of my estate and makes them Exers. 8 Nov., 1734. Prob.: 21 Nov., 1739. Wit: Charles Binns, Henry Hart, Wm. Jordan. Book 9, p. 96.

HART, Robert: Leg.- To son, William, all my land and Plantation on the main Blackwater Swamp excepting one, also a negro. The first child of sd. negro to go to my grandson, Robert Hart, also two other negroes. Son William to bring up son, Thomas to as much learning as he has himself and give him half a gross of bottles, 2 stone jugs, and a fifth part of all linen in the house. To son, Robert, all my land and plantation on the other side of ye Middle Branch in ye Isle of Wight Co. a negro, a big brass kettle, one doz. bottles, and 60 yds. of Ozenburg, if Robert have no heir then to go to his youngest brother. To my daughter Ann, one piece of Dowlas, 20 or 30 ells, and to each of her sons a cow and calf, to my sd. daughter, Ann, one negro girl and a dozen bottles. To daughter, Elizabeth, 25 lbs. current money of Va. to buy a negro, and the cattle on my plantation called here, one doz. bottles, etc. and one new Tankard. To daughter, Sarah, one negro, but if she have no heir to her two youngest sisters, and all the cattle on the plantation called hers, and one dozen bottles, etc. To daughters, Mary and Priscilla, one negro each. To son, Thomas, one negro and my Plantation I live on with all the land belonging in the county of Surry, and my Plantation on the other side of the main Swamp whereon Richard Mizel now dwells, bounded by the Spring Branch and Gwaltney's line and the main Swamp, also a steer, bed, furniture, etc. to be equally divided between him and my

grandson, Robert Hart, and son Thomas pay him 10 lbs. at
18 and also his whole estate at 18 years old. Wife,
Priscilla, one negro for her life. All the remainder of
estate to be divided. 23 June, 1720. Prob.: 20 July,
1720. Wit: Thos. Penneton, Wm. Knott. Book 7, p. 277.

HART, William: Leg.- To son, Robert, my grist mill--and the
Plantation called Griffin's beg. at the mouth of Mill
Branch--to main Swamp - 250 acres, household good, etc.
To son, William, land on the South side of Nottoway River
that he now lives on beg. at the River Bank -- 200 acres.
To son, John, 200 acres of land on the South side of the
Nottoway River beg. at Wittie's Branch--negro, stock, etc.
To son, Moses, all the rest of my land on the Nottoway
River, 240 acres, Negro, Pewter, etc. To son, Thomas, the
Plantation called Mosley's. To wife 4 slaves and at death
one to daughter, Mary, rest to be sold and money divided.
Daughter, Lucy, one negro. Daughter, Sarah, one negro.
Four youngest children, Lucy, Mary, Sarah and Thomas. To
wife the Plantation where I now live. Wife and son,
Robert, Exers. 27 Apr., 1744. Prob.: 18 July, 1744.
Wit: Charles Binns, John Evans, Thomas Hart. Bk. 9, p.
475.

HARTE, Thomas: Est.- __ 7br, 1673. Paid wife's third part.
Rest due to three orphans of Thomas Harte, dec'd. viz:
Henry, Thomas, and Robert Hart. Signed: William Newsum.
Book 2, p. 62.

HARTWELL, John: Leg. - Mentions wife. To daughter, Elizabeth,
5 negroes. To my mother, Elizabeth Eggleston, wife of
Mr. Benj. Eggleston, negro. To my uncle, Thomas Rogers, 10
lbs. To my friend, Mr. Benj. Howard, my pistol, sword,
etc. To my daughter, Elizabeth, one-third on my personal
estate. To my cozens, John Drumond, Geo. Marable, Jr. and
Henry Hartwell Marable, children to my loving sister, Mary
Marable. To daughter, Elizabeth, all land in Surry County
at wife's death. Geo. Marable and wife, Elizabeth, Exerx.
9 Feb., 1710. Prob.: 19 May, 1714. Wit: James Deans,
Benj. Wheler. Book 6, p. 184.

HARTWELL, John: Est.- Stith Bolling and Elizabeth Bolling,
admrs. 15 Xbr, 1725. Book 7, p. 618.

HATLY, Shard: Leg.- To John Hatly and makes him Exer. Estate
to be equally divided by three men. 1 Dec., 1720. Prob.:
15 Feb., 1720. Wit: Rich. Parker, Jr., Geo. Wyche, Custis Land. Book 7, p. 301.

HAVILAND, Anthony: Leg.- To daughter, Mary Haviland, all my
estate. Friend, Wm. Simmons, made bargain for daughter
and at her death the whole estate to William Simmons and
makes him Exer. 23 Feb., 1687/8. Prob.: 6 Mar., 1687/8.
Wit: Thos. Middleton, John Middleton. Book 4, p. 35.

HAWTHORNE, John: Leg.- Son, John, Son, Peter, land that was
James Simmons. Son, Nathaniel, land adj. Daniel Eppes.
Son, Joshua, John Hicks, Francis Maybury, John Weaver, and
Geo. Reives to lay off the land. John Hicks to sell the
slaves and to wife and all my children. Wants land at
Maratick River and now called North Carolina to be sold.
Wife and John Hicks, Exers. 5 Apr., 1720. Prob.: 19
Oct., 1720. Wit: Robt. Jeffry's, Geo. Rives, Francis May-
bury. Book 7, p. 285. (Estate of John Hawthorne by

Rebecca Hawthorne. 15 Feb., 1720)

HAWTHORNE, John: Est.- 17 Mar., 1724. By Thomas Davis who
married the Exerx of sd. deceased. Signed: Christopher
Tatum, Daniel Epes, John Davis. Book 7, p. 573.

HAWTHORNE, John: Est.- 20 July, 1743. Francis Maybury, Henry
Mithcell, John Newsum. Book 9, p. 446.

HAWTHORNE, Robert: Est.- By Elizabeth, his wife, 21 May, 1729.
Signed: Wm. Parham, John Threewitt, Solomon Wynne. Book
7, p. 944.

HEATH, Adam: Leg.- Daughter, Elizabeth, shall have her time
in the plantation where I live and the lands and crops from
Wm. Short's line to -- the Swamp named Thatch House Spring
Branch, if she marry she is to have 7 yrs. to provide her-
self in. To son, William Heath, the plantation where he
lived and 150 acres belonging lying in Prince George Coun-
ty. To daughter, Elizabeth, 100 adj. Wm. Heath in Prince
George County. Makes wife, Sarah, Exerx. 9 Nov., 1716.
Prob.: 20 May, 1719. Wit: James Fleacher, Thos. Coullop,
John Flefelce. Book 7, p. 366.

HEATH, Elizabeth: Leg.- To Thomas Jones and Richard Jones a
bequest. (remainder of will torn and illegible) 10 May,
1729. Prob.: 16 June, 1731. Wit: John Hanersly, Rich.
Jones, John Jones. Book 8, p. 112.

HEATH, William: Leg.- To eldest son, Abraham Heath, 350 acres
in Charles Citty Co. To youngest son, Adam Heath, 300
acres part in Surry Co. and part in Charles Citty Co. and
all bills due from James Watkins and John Minard. To
Sarah and Elizabeth, daughters of sd. sons 50 acres
bought of Edmond Howell. 20 Sept., 1680. Prob.: _____,
1681. Wit: Thos. Pittman, Sr., Jos. Malden, Wm. Heath.
Wife, Margery Heath, Exerx. Book 2, p. 284.

HEATH, William: Leg.- To grandson, John Heath, son of Abraham
Heath dec'd.

HEIDON, Mary: Nuncupative Will. Ann Clarke age 32 years deposed that she was at the house of Charles Williams and
heard Mary Heiden say that Charles Williams should have all
her estate, paying a certain amount to Edward Napkin, 12
years old, Elinor Evans, and William Gordone. 6 July,
1680. Edward Napkin, aged 42 years deposed the same.
Prob. granted to Charles Williams on above said will of
Mary Heydon. 6 July, 1680. Book 2, p. 260.

HICKS, John: Leg.- To son, Thomas Hicks, one shilling. To
grandson, William Hicks, son of William Hicks, one shilling. To son, Joseph Hicks, my Plantation after his mother's death if no issue to my daughter, Christiana. To
wife, Denias Christiana Hicks, remainder of my estate and
makes her Exerx. 25 Mar., 1721. Prob.: 15 Nov., 1722.
Wit: Wm. Rose, James Mersingale, Thos. Buryber. (Probated by Isodenias Christiana Hicks) Exerx. Bk. 8, p. 247.

HICKS, John: Leg.- To son, Robert, a tract of land I now live
on and requests that son, Robert Hicks, go live with son-
in-law, Robert Tatum, until he comes to age of 18 years.
To two sons, John Hicks and Daniell Hicks, my tract of land
which I took up on Stevens Branch in Brunswick Co. to be

equally divided between them and that son, John, live with
my son-in-law, John Rose, until he is 21 yrs. old. To son,
Joshua Hicks, a copper kettle, all the rest of estate to
wife, Rebeckah Hicks and makes her Exer. 30 Sept., 1728.
Prob.: 20 Aug., 1729. Wit: Arsilla Rieves, Eliz. Reives,
Christopher Tatum. Book 8, p. 963.

HIDE, Richard: Leg.- To son, Richard Hide, half on my Plantation, livestock, etc. To daughters, Elizabeth Smith,
and Jean Hide, each a cow, etc. To granddaughter, Ann
Smith, a pewter tumbler. To grandson, John Smith, a gun
(his Father living). To wife, Mary Hide, half of my land
and plantation. 13 Oct., 1710. Prob.: 25 Feb., 1710.
Wit: John Tyus, Edward Scarbro. Book 6, p. 40.

HIDE, Richard: Leg.- To Eldest son, David Hide, plantation
where I now live when he is 18 yrs. old also one negro.
To son, Banj. Hide, one negro. Son, Richard Hide. Wife,
Mary Hide. Friend, John Smith, overseer of Will. 2 May,
1719. Prob.: 17 June, 1719. Wit: John Tyus, Mary
Cotten. Book 7, p. 191.

HIDE, Richard: Est.- By Charles Lucas. 10 Apr., 1725.
Signed: Nich. Maget, Wm. Browne. Book 7, p. 910.

HIGH, Thomas: Leg.- To two sons, John and Joseph, my land to
be equally divided. Wife, Hannah, rest of my estate and
makes her Exerx. Friends, Robert Ruffin, Wm. Edwards, Fra.
Mason, overseers of Will. 2 Mar., 1687. Prob.: 3 July,
1688. Wit: Rich. Hargrave, Eliz. Harton. Book 4, p. 59.
(Hannah High married George Foster who asks for administration on the estate of Thomas High 20 Oct., 1688.) Book
4, p. 85.

HILL, Benjamin: Est.- William Harris, admr. 15 July, 1719.
Wit: Thos. Holt, Timothy Tharpe, Wm. Judkins. Book 7,
p. 202.

HILL, Harmon: Est.- Capt. Lawrence Baker, admr. 10 July,
1679. On behalf of decedants orphans. Signed: James
Riddick, Walter Taylor, Thos. Drew. Book 2, p. 235.

HILL, Richard: Est.- Hannah Hill, admr. 19 July, 1727.
Signed: Wm. Gray and John Newsum. Book 7, p. 746.

HILL, Thomas (Capt.): Est.- Priscilla Hill, admrx. 15 June,
1737. Signed: Wm. Seward, Sampson Willson, John Holt.
Book 8, p.___.

HILL, William: Nuncupative Will. Gives all he has to Mr. Edwards. George Hasty and his child to have a coat. 1 Feb.,
1675. Signed: Mary Skinner, Wm. Clarke. Book 2, p. 102.

HIX, William: Est.- By Elizabeth Hix. 16 May, 1711. Signed:
James Stanton, John Brown, John Blewer. Bk. 6, p. 59.

HODG, John: Leg.- Mentions wife, Margott, and desires that his
debts be paid out of his estate and the remainder to his
wife and his two children, James and Mary Hodg, equally
divided. To my wife's daughter, Elizabeth Cooper, a yer-
ling. My son, to have his estate at 18 and my daughter at
15 years old. Makes wife Exerx. 17 May, 1679. Prob.:
1 July, 1679. Wit: Wm. Newett, John Phillips, Wm. Liles.
Book 2, p. 212.

71

(Margaret Hunnicutt Relict of John Hodge dec'd made oath
that his Inventory was correct.)

HODGE, John: Est.- 7 7br, 1680. Signed by Augustine Hunnicutt, Jr. Book 2, p. 263.

HODGE, John: Est.- James Hodge acknowledges receipt to John
Clarke for his full share of his dec'd. Father's John
Hodge's estate. 15 July, 1696. Book 5, p. 113.

HODGOOD, Francis: Leg.- Mentions four children, Richard,
William, George, and Daughter, Frances. Gives them his
personal estate. Mentions sister Mary Crede, gives her
silver bodkin, to his daughter a gold ring. Friend, Lt.
Coll. Jorden to take son, George, into his care and care
of his Godmother, Mary Rome?. 3 Jan., 1676. Prob.: 18
May, 1677. Wit: George Jordan, Thos. Flood. Book 2,
p. 122.

HOGOOD, George: Leg.- Wife, Ann Hogood, Sons, Francis and
Richard Hogood, estate to children equally divided. Sons,
George and John Hogood, Exers. 20 Dec., 1727. Prob.:
17 Jan., 1727. Wit: Wm. Rookings, Thos. Clarke. Book 7,
p. 781.

HOGWOOD, Richard: Est.- 21 June, 1679. Signed: Wm. Browne,
Benj. Harrison. Book 2, p. 222.

HOLLEMAN, John: Leg.- To my three sons, Henry, Robert and John
Holleman, the tract of land and I now live on, 368 acres,
to be divided by three Neighbors whom they may select. To
my youngest son, Mathew Holleman, about seventeen pounds of
cash money. To my four sons each a cow & calf. To my
daughter, Martha Holleman a cow. The remainder of my estate to my wife, Mary Holleman, and makes her Exer. Made
18 Sept., 1736. Prob.: 20 Oct., 1736. Wit: Absalom
Atkinson, Wm. Pittman, Benj. Pittman. This will presented
by Josias John Holleman, next of kin, admr. Bk. 8, p. 634.

HOLLEMAN, Joseph: Est.- By Unity Messer, formerly Holliman,
Robt. Messer. 18 Oct., 1732. Signed: Jas. Washington,
Ed. Bailey. Book 8, p. 239.

HOLLEMAN, Mary: Leg.- To my son, John Holleman my still, horse,
saddle, bridle & all the Horse Arms I leave to my son,
John Holleman, and make him my Exer. The residue of my estate to be equally divided amongst my children, John,
Robert & Martha Holleman. Wit: Absalom Atkinson, Wm. Pittman. 7 Oct., 1730. Prob.: 20 Oct., 1730. Bk. 8, p. 635.

HOLLEMAN, William: Est.- By Marie Holliman. 2 Jan., 1704.
Signed: Joseph Lane, Robert Hill, Joseph Wall. Book 5,
p. 328.

HOLLEMAN, William: Leg.- To my Brother, Thomas Holleman, the
land and Plantation where Joseph Hargrave now lives, if no
heirs then to my Brother, Samuell Holleman. To my Brother,
Richard Holleman the rem. of my estate, and my gun, sword,
etc. Makes Thos. Holleman, Exer. Wit: Nich. Maget, Wm.
Browne, Jr., Nath. Davis. 26 Dec., 1728. Prob.: 19 Mar.,
1728. Book 7, p. 911.

HOLT, Elizabeth: Leg.- To Charles Holt, son of my son John
Holt, deceased, 2 cows. To Joseph Holt, son of above

mentioned John Holt, bed and bedding, etc. To Benjamin
Holt, son of said John Holt, cows. To my granddaughter,
Mary Seward; son, Thomas Holt and daughter-in-law, Frances
Holt, a bequest. To Thomas Edwards, a debt. Mentions,
sons, Wm. and Thos. Holt, daughters Jane Hancocke, wife of
john Hancocke and Lucy, wife of Joseph Mountfortt. Makes
sons, Wm. & Thos. Exers. Wit: Robt. Bayley, Margret
Taylor. 4 March, 1708/9. Prob.: 3 May, 1709. Book 5,
p. 411.

HOLT, Elizabeth: Leg.- To daughter, Tapphenas Newsom a
gound, and petticoat. To daughter, Ann Holt, 2 cows. Dau.
Mary Holt, 10 pounds money, chest, pewter dishes, bed, etc.
To son, Charles Holt one negro, and all the rest of my est.
and makes him Exer. 13 June, 1737. Prob.: 21 Sept.,
1737. Wit: Wm. Edwards, Mary Piland. Book 8, p. 729.

HOLT, John: Leg.- To son, Thomas Holt, my Land on the South
side of Nottoway River & 100 pounds money, 21 years old.
To my daughters, Mary & Elizabeth, when 21 years old, or
married. Rest of my est. to my son; John. Brothers,
Joseph Holt & Charles Binns to assist the Exer. Son, John,
Exer. Wit: Thos. Holt, Edwards Taylor, Rob. Martiall,
Christ Clinch. Made: 19 July, 1723. Prob.: 18 Dec.,
1723. Book 7, p. 491.

HOLT, Randall: Leg.- To my eldest son, John Holt, all my land,
if he die under age, to go to my son, William Holt. If he
die, to my son, Thomas Holt. Mentions wife and six children (does not name them). Makes wife & son, John Exers.
2 7br, 1679. Wit: John Moyer, Jno. Goring. Bk. 2, p.
223.

HOLT, Thomas: Leg.- To Daughter, Elizabeth Cocke, wife of
Nicholas Cocke, ten shillings. To daughter, Mary, wife of
Wm. Hansford, one negro. To granddaughter, Martha Hans-
ford, one negro. To daughter, Katherine, wife of Thos.
Cocke, 5 shillings. To Martha, wife of Mr. John Newsum,
one negro. Daughter, Lucy Holt, horse, saddle, bridle,
etc. Sons, Henry & James, each one negro. To wife --
(Remainder of will illegible). Prob.: 17 Mar., 1730.
Wit: Timothy Tharp, Charles Barham, Samson Wilson. Will
presented in Court by wife, mary Holt. Book 8, p. 86.

HOLT, Thomas (Capt.): Est.- 20 Oct., 1736. Mary Holt, Exer.
Signed: James Ingles. Book 8, p. ___ .

HOLT, William: Leg.- p To son, William Holt my Troopers Arms.
To son, Thomas Holt all of my land on the South side of
Nottoway River where he now lives. To dau. Sarah 5 shill-
ings. To daughters, Tapphanas Newsum, Elizabeth, Ann &
Mary and son Charles the rem. of est. to be equally
divided. Makes wife Exer. (Wife was Elizabeth Holt.) Wit:
John Ruffin, John Friday. 28 Sept., 1725. Prob.: 18
May, 1726. Book 7, p. 637.

HORTON, Daniel: Est.- By Martha Horton. 18 June, 1718.
Signed: John Weaver, Nich. Partridge, Giles Underhill,
Wm. Thomas, Jno. Simmons. Book 7, p. 125.

HORTON, Thomas: Leg.- To daughter, Elizabeth Barrow 5 shillings. To daughter, Mary Proctor, 5 shillings. To daughter, Ann Rose, my plantation & all Land thereto belonging
and all goods and chattels, and makes her Exerx. Wit:

John Phillips, James Binum, Agnes Binum. 8 Nov., 1727.
Prob.: 21 Aug., 1728. Book 7, p. 839.

HOSKINS, Ann: Nuncupative Will. She ill at Coll. Swanns'
house, asked Robt. Randall to make her will. She gave
Margery Davis a bed and the rest to Robert Randall. Ann
Burd testified to the same. 4 9br, 1679. Bk. 2, p. 236.

HOSKINS, Edward: Est.- By Elizabeth Hoskins. 19 Apr., 1727.
Signed: Richard Blunt, Henry Briggs, Samuel Briggs. Book
7, p. 689.

HOSWORTH, Ann: Est.- Commission of administration granted to
William Scarbro on her est. Signed at James Citty by the
Governor, 18 June, 1675. Book 2, p. 82.

HOUSE, Samuel: Est.- Jean Avery, John Avery. 17 July, 1723.
Signed: Ed. Bayley, Nich. Davis, Chris. Morning. Book 7,
p. 458.

HOUSE, Thomas: Est.- 25 Jan., 1718. Signed: Silvanus Stokes,
John Evans, Cornelius Loftin. Book 7, p. 158.

HOUSLWORTH, Ann: Leg.- Desires to be buried at the discretion
of her father, William Scarbro. Bequest to brother,
Walter Houlsworth, and to sister, Ann Houlsworth, Sister
Mary, cows in possession of Mr. Tatum. Wit: John Ruther-
ford, William Simons. 6 March, 1673. Prob.: 4 May, 1675.
Book 2, p. 81.

HOWARD, John: Est.- 5 March, 1705. Signed: George Blow,
Rich. Holleman. Book 5, p. 345.

HOWELL, Edmond: Est.- 2 Oct., 1747, by Olive Howell. Signed:
John Newsum, John Crafford, Carter Craffoed. Book 9, p.
563.

HOWELL, Edmund: Leg.- To my only son, William Howell my whole
est. with some exceptions. To my godson Gibson, son of
Thos. Gibson, to godson Henry Baker. Makes George Foster
Exer. and gives him the care of son until he is 21 years
old. If son die, his inheritance to Henry Baker, George
Foster & Thos. Ironmonger & his children. 9 Oct., 1679.
Prob.: 23 Dec., 1679. Wit: Thos. Pittman, Sr., John
Moring. Book 2, p. 240.

HOWELL, John: Leg.- To daughter, Ann Gibbs one cow. To daughter Mary Hood (Flood?) one cow and a seal skin trunk. To
two sons, Nathaniel Howell & John Howell all of my land to
be equally divided. If son, John never return again, then
to my son, Nathaniel. Makes Nathaniel Exer. Wit: Christopher Tatum, Elizabeth Youron ? 13 Aug., 1716. Prob.:
19 Feb., 1717. Book 7, p. 93

HOWELL, Nathaniel: Leg.- To son John household goods. To
daughter, Mary Chambers two leather chairs etc. To son,
William Howell a gun. To wife, Susannah Howell all of my
estate, but if she marry to be divided among wife and my
three children, Nathaniel, Thomas and Ann Howell. Makes
son, John, Exer. Wit: Christ. Tatum, Henry Mitchell.
1 April, 1741. Prob.: 16 June, 1742. Book 9, p. 410.

HOWELL, William: Leg.- To son, William Howell my plantation
with all the Land thereto belonging, looking glass, live-

stock of all kinds, etc., he to pay to Capt. Wm. Browne 13
pounds cur. money. To son, Edmond Howell household goods,
livestock, one silver seal of his own name, dishes, etc.
To son, Thomas Howell household goods, livestock, etc. To
son, Joseph Howell, the same. To daughter Joan Alsobrooke,
wife of Samuel Alsobrooke, one large pewter dish, livestock, etc. To daughter, Elizabeth Fitchett, one deep pewter dish, livestock, etc. All the rest of est. to son
William after debts and funeral expenses are paid. Friends
Wm. Browne and Nich. Maget overseers of will. 9 May, 1718.
Prob.: 15 June, 1720. Wit: Wm. Brown, Nich. Maget, Mary
Heigh. Book 7, p. 272.

HOWELL, William: Leg.- Bequest to two children, Joannah &
    Elizabeth, and child in esse. 28 March, 1732. Prob.:   17
    May, 1732. Book 8, p. 195.

HOWELL, William: Est.- 20 May, 1741. By Jos. John Snipes.
    Book 9, p. 335.

HOWES, Robert: Est.- 11 March, 1698/9. Margarett Howes, Admrx.
    Signed: George Williams, John Bineham. Book 5, p. 173.

HOWSON, George: Est.- 9 May, 1696. John Pulitson, admr.
    Signed: Thos. Binns, John Clarke. Book 5, p. 105.

HUMPHREYS, Robert: Est.- By Mary Humphrey, admrx. 15 June,
    1714. Signed: Robert Hix, David Crawley. Book 6, p. 196.

HUNNICUTT, Augustin: Leg.- My wife Margaret to have my Plan-
    tation for life, then to my son Augustine Hunnicutt. To
    daughter, Katherine cattle, etc. To daughter, Ann bed,
    etc. Makes wife, Exerx. 10 Mar., 1708. Prob.:   2 May,
    1710. Wit: Charles Pitt, Augustine Berriman, Samuell
    Cornwell. Book 6, p. 6.

HUNNICUTT, Augustine: Leg.- To my wife the use of my plantation
    until my son Robert is 21 years old. Gives wife use of
    household goods etc. To son, Augustine 800 lbs. tobacco
    & negro. To son, John, household goods, etc. To son,
    Robert the plantation where I now live and where John
    Berriman and John Drew now live, negroes etc. To daughter,
    Martha, negro, furniture, etc. To daughter, Mary, furni-
    ture etc. Rest of est. to be divided between sons John &
    Robert and daughters Martha & Mary. John & Robert Exers.
    Wit: Wm. Seward. 14 July, 1743. Prob.: 19 Oct., 1743.
    Book 9, p. 451.

HUNNICUTT, Augustine, Senior: Leg.- To son, Augustine Hunni-
    cutt, 40 acres of land added to what I have given him for
    the time of my lease from Mr. George Carter, deceased. To
    son, Robert all land near the plantation where I live to
    Warrinock. To wife, Mary, the plantation where I now live
    for life, at her death to my daughter, Katherine. Wife,
    Mary & son Augustine, exers. Made 30 May, 1682. Prob.:
    6 March, 1682. Wit: Rob. Caufield, Robt. Fellows. Book
    2, p. 325.

HUNNICUTT, John: Est.- Elizabeth Hunnicutt, admrx. 4 July,
    1699. Signed: John Clarke, Thomas Horton. Bk. 5, p. 173.

HUNNICUTT, Margaret: Leg.- To daughter, Elizabeth wife of Ed-
    ward Rowell beds, blankets etc. and to her son Richard
    Rowell one cow. To daughter, Mary, wife of Bray Hargrave

one ewe. To Margaret Haregrave a cow and pewter dishes.
To daughter Katherine, wife of Charles Pitt one cow and to
her daughter, Ann, one cow. To my daughter Ann, wife of
Augustin Berryman a bed tables etc. To Martha, daughter of
my son Augustin Hunnicutt and her daughter, Martha, a bequest. 23 Aug., 1717. Prob.: 16 July, 1718. Wit: Robert Berryman, Thomas Waller. Book 7, p. 132.

HUNNICUTT, William: Est.- 6 Oct., 1718. Elizabeth Hunnicutt
admr. Signed: Wm. Thompson, John Beberry, James Nicholson.
Book 7, p. 173.

HUNNIFORD, Hugh: Leg.- Wife Jane all my estate, and makes her
Exrx. Charles Binns, Thos. Binns. 18 Mar., 1746. Book 9,
p. 551.

HUNNIFORD, Philip: Est.- 31 May, 1687. By Elizabeth Hanniford.
Signed: Anthony Evans, Nich. Sessums, Henry Norton. Book
4, p. 10.

HUNNIFORD, Phillip: Est.- 21 Oct., 1687. Admr. granted to
Elizabeth Hunniford to admr. on her husband's est. Book
4, p. 23.

HUNNIFORD, Phillip: Leg.- To two daughters-in-law, Mary Judgson, and Elizabeth Judgson, my estate, if they die to Elizabeth Huniford, their mother. 2 April, 1677. Prob.: 18
May, 1677. Wit: Richard Jordan, Sr., Edward Napkin.
Book 2, p. 124.

HUNNIFORD, William: Leg.- To my wife, Katherine, all my personal estate. To my son, William Hunniford my Plantation
and Land that Robert Bland lives on in the Lower Parish,
and to wife and son all land bought of Nich. Maget. Son,
William to be free at eighteen years old. To my brother
Hugh Hunniford my cane. To Sarah Judkin 5 shillings. Makes
wife and brother Exers. 28 Dec., 1710. Prob.: 25 Feb.,
1710. Wit: Wm. Browne, Harry Floyd, Nich. Maget, Francis
Price. Book 6, p. 41.

HUNT, Thomas: Est.- By Elizabeth Hunt. 6 July, 1711. Signed:
Wm. Edmunds, Henry Bedingfield. Book 6, p. 65.

HUNT, Thomas: Est.- Paid James Ellico his wife's part. 5 Apr.,
1713. John Jones and Elizabeth Jones, admr. Bk. 6, p. 140.

HUNT, Thomas: Leg.- To wife the use of my plantation for her
life then to my granddaughter, Mary Horn, 100 acres of
land. To my son, Thos. Hunt 5 shillings. To my son, John
hunt 5 shillings. To Dau. Elizabeth 5 shillings. If my
granddaughter, Mary Horn die without heirs, to go to my
granddaughter Mary Hunt. Makes wife, Exerx. 3 April,
1724. Prob.: 21 Dec., 1726. Wit: Sam. Maget, Mary Byrum,
James Byrum. Book 7, p. 671.

HUNT, William: Leg.- To son, William Hunt 200 acres of land
ad. where he now lives and one negro. To son, Thomas Hunt
400 acres ad. his now dwelling Plantation, Troopers Arms,
Trooper's saddle and bridle. To son, John Hunt my now
dwelling Plantation and all Land between Tanyard Branch
and Ostin's Branch. To son, George, the Plantation where
John Wapple formerly lived. To daughter, Sarah Hunt where
Katherine Middleton formerly dwelt, with 100 acres adjoining. To daughters, Elizabeth and Mary Hunt to each 100

76

acres, on Hunting Quarter Swamp. Mentions wife and all my children. Maj. Nathaniel Harrison and Capt. Henry Harrison and Mr. John Simmons overseers of will. 20 March, 1711. Prob.: 20 June, 1715. Wit: Ja. Stanton, Curtis Land. (Wife was named Sarah). Book 6, p. 64.

HUNT, William: Est.- John Goodwin and Sarah Goodwin, admrs. 15 May, 1728. Book 7, p. 811.

HURDLE, Elizabeth: Leg.- To daughter, Joanna Madra 20 shillings. To Grandson, John Madra the rest of my estate, To daughter, Christian Hurdle "some few particulars". Grandson, John Madra, Exer. 6 May, 1747. Prob.: 15 Sept., 1747. Wit: James Bridges, Thos. Davidson. Bk. 7, p. 752.

HURDLE, William, Sr.: Leg.- To daughter, Joanna Maddery two negroes. To wife, Elizabeth Hurdle two negroes for her life. To daughter Elizabeth Hurdle one negro. To sons, Martin Hurdle and Wm. Hurdle one negro each. Son, Benjamin one negro. To wife the rest of est. Wit: Francis Camer, Francis Littel. 12 April, 1727. Prob.: 16 Aug., 1727. (Wife was Elizabeth).

HUSKEY, John: Est.- Thos. Threewitt, admr. 17 Sept., 1740. Signed: Thos. Wynne, Stephen Houseman, Ed. Ackles. Book 9, p. 207.

HUTCHINGS, John: Est.- Sarah Hutchings, admr. 19 Aug., 1719. Book 7, p. 204.

HUX, William: Leg.- To Sam Thompson a gun. To the daughter of William Forman a cow. To two daughters of my brother, Ironmonger all my land, That land Thomas Ironmonger lives on to Susannah Ironmonger and land I live on to Mary Ironmonger. All the rest to my brother, Thomas Ironmonger and with his brother John Ironmonger my Exers. and after my debts are paid to his two daughters. 31 Oct., 1676. Prob.: 1 May, 1677. Wit: Wm. Thompson, Sr., Samuell Thomson. Book 2, p. 122.

INMAN, Robert: Leg.- If wife, Mary Inman live a widow, then son, Robert to remain with her. If she marry, Robert to be at age at sixteen years and the est. to be divided. If Mary Inman, wife of Robert Inman marry against his wish to sons, John & Robert and Daughter, Sarah. 6th of the first month, 1698/9. Prob.: 3 March, 1701/2. Wit: Thos. Tavor, Phillis Carroll, Samuel Cornell. Book 5, p. 237.

IRONMONGER, John: Nuncupative Will. 19 Jan., 1691. John Ironmonger, dying, told Mary Ironmonger of bequests to his Brother's daughter, and his brother's son, also to cousin Samuell Argebrook's two children.

IRONMONGER, Thomas: Est.- 7 July, 1691. Mary Ironmonger admr. made oath to same. Book 4, p. 213.

IRONMONGER, Thomas: Est.- 18 April, 1711. Signed: Thos. Collier, Edward Bookey. Book 6, p. 53.

JACKSON, William: (Verbal Will) Leg.- Mentions his son, John Jackson, son, George Jackson, son, William Jackson, son, Samuel Jackson. Mentions wife. Made 16 Jan., 1710. Prob.: 25 Feb., 1710. Wit: Wm. Nichols, Robert Nichols. Book 6, p. 46.

JARRARD, Nicholas: Leg.- Mentions wife, Elizabeth, and gives
her the Plantation he lives on for her life, then to go to
his eldest son, Nicholas, also negro to wife. To eldest
son, Nicholas, one negro and 400 acres of land, joining
the plantation where he lives. To son, John, 350 acres of
land on the west side of Parker's Branch, beg. at the Great
Spring-- To son, Thomas plantation called Winkeleses with
350 acres of land joining to it. To daughter, Sarah, 350
acres of land lying on the northward side of Reedy Branch.
To child in esse 350 acres on the east side of Reedy Branch.
The rem. of est. to be divided among all of the children.
Makes wife, Elizabeth Exerx. 1 June, 1718. Prob.: 16
July, 1718. Wit: Wm. Rose, Geo. Walker, Thos. Burk.
Book 7, p. 131.

JARRELL, Thomas: Leg.- Son, Thomas Jarrell. To wife, Jean,
all my Plantation where I live for her life, and at her
death to my son, Thomas, also my walking cane. To daughters, Julian and Catherine one cow each. Makes wife Exerx.
17 July, 1713. Prob.: 17 Feb., 1713. Wit: Robert Newton, Elizabeth Onails, Samuel Cornwell. Book 6, p. 174.

JARRETT, Charles: Leg.- To son, Richard Jarrett, all that part
of land on the upper side of Reedy Branch above my plantation where I now live. If he die without issue, the land
to my son, George Jarrett. To son, George Jarrett that land
& Plantation where said George now lives at Blackwater for
his life, at his death to my daughter Martha Jarrett. To
wife the Plantation where I live for her life then to son,
Richard; if no issue, to son, George; and at his death to
the two daughters. The remainder of the estate to wife,
Mary, and the children equally divided. Wit: John Glover,
George Glover, Patrick Brady, James Willson. Made 9 June,
1719. Prob.: 16 Sept., 1719. Book 7, p. 217.

JARRETT, Ferdinand: Leg.- To son, John Jarrett the Plantation
where I now live with all land from the river up the Broad
Swamp to Joe's Point...To Mr. Walter Flood's up the race
field called Charity's...to the river. If no heirs to go
to daughter, Elizabeth Witherington, wife of Joseph Witherington. To daughter Hannah Jarrett, and my son Henry Jarrett all the rest of that 230 acres of land that Capt.
Francis Clements bought of Godfrey Lee, of London, to be
equally divided, if Henry recovers from the sickness he is
now afflicted with. If he die, to my daughter Hannah, if
no heirs to daughter, Jane, also daughter Hannah and son,
Henry 225 acres of Land, the half of 450 acres I bought of
Capt. Francis Clements by patent dated 20 April, 1689. If
Henry die to Hannah, and for want of heirs to dau. Jane.
To son, John Jarrett, 225 acres, the uppermost part of 450
acres, for want of heirs to dau. Elizabeth Witherington.
To dau. Mary a bed, etc. To son, John, my silver shoe
buckles. To dau. Faith a silver dram cup. Bequest to
granddaughters, Jane and Elizabeth Witherington. Son-in-
law Joseph Witherington, Exer. Wit: Nich. Magett, Mich.
Harris, Thos. Penington. 26 Mar., 1720. Prob.: 15 June,
1720. Book 7, p. 268.

JARRETT, Ferdinand: Est.- 17 Oct., 1722. Joseph Witherington,
Exer. The est. paid Jane and Elizabeth Witherington,
daughters of Jos. Witherington, Jno. Jarrett, Hannah Jarrett, Mary & Jane Jarrett, Faith Jarrett, Mary Jarrett &
others. Wit: Isaac Johnson, Thos. Cocke, Coll. Harrison,
Wm. Sharp, Wm. Pulley. Book 7, p. 418.

JARRETT, George: Leg.- To dau. Martha, all my Land upon the upper side of Reedy Branch, part of the tract where my father lives, also pewter dishes, etc. To wife, Elizabeth all the rest of the estate, and makes her Exerx. Wit: James Willson, Samuel Parks. Prob.: 19 April, 1721. Book 7, p. 328. (Book 7, p. 352. Elizabeth Humphrey, Exerx. signs Inventory of Geo. Jarrett's Est.)

JARRETT, Henry: Leg.- All that I have, I give to my father, Ferdinando Jarrett after my death. 19 Mar., 1719/20. Prob.: 20 July, 1720. Wit: Thos. Pennenton, Wm. Knott. Book 7, p. 278.

JARRETT, Mary: Leg.- All of my estate in Virginia and England to my two daughters, Martha Jarrett, and Mary Jarrett. Makes Martha Exrx. 23 Nov., 1720. Prob.: 20 Sept., 1721. Wit: John Chambers, Wm. Gray, James Elley. Book 7, p. 369.

JARRETT, Mary (widdow): Est.- 6 Oct., 1721. Thomas Shelly and Mary Shelly, Exers. Wit: Roger Delk, Wm. Ezell, Wm. Drew. Book 7, p. 382.

JARRETT, Nicholas: Est.- 16 Jan., 1733. By Sarah Jarrett. Signed: Robt. Jones, Samuel Chappell, James Chappell. Book 8, p. 345.

JARRETT, Richard: Leg.- To son, Charles Jarrett all my land (Charles not 21 years old). To dau., Elizabeth, for her dowry, the dwelling house on the upper plantation and as much ground as can be cleared for five years. To wife, Margery, the dwelling on the plantation to enjoy it as long as she is a widow; after marriage, half the Plantation for life. Makes wife, Exerx. Overseers of will are friends, Richard Drew, Mr. Robt. Caufield. If son die in non age, his part to my brothers in England equally divided, but if they are dead to my daughter's children. If no heirs one-half my est. to my cousin, Richard Wyat. Capt. Law. Baker to have use of tobacco house, friends Mr. Richard Drew & Mr. Robt. Caufield. Wit: Richard Drew, Hen. Baker. 13 July, 1672. Prob.: 7 Jan., 1672/3. Book 2, p. 22.

JARRETT, Richard: Inv. 2 Dec., 1673. Appraised by James R. Reddick, Walter Bartlett, Richard Briggs and Wm. Butler. Pd. Charles Jarrett his part of his father's est. Book 2, p. 33.

JEFFRES, John: Leg.- To my son, Joseph Jeffres all my Land on the N. E. side of the Clift & tar Kiln branches and my gray horse. Son Joseph, I commit to the care and command of my son, Richard, till he comes to the age of 21 years. Son, Joseph, to have peaceable possession of the College Plantation whereon I live, and a long square muzzle gun, giving his brother Richard a gun & 20 shillings when he is 21 years old. Desires that his father have use of the Plantation and the Land belonging to it that he now lives on, for his life, at his death, to my son John Jeffres. To daughter, Lucy Jeffres, the bed I lie on etc. To dau. Rebecca Jeffres household articles. Rest to be equally divided with all my children, and makes son, Joseph, Exer. 24 Dec., 1745. Prob.: 19 Mar., 1745. Wit: Samuel Maget, Arthur Richardson, Wm. Owen. Book 9, p. 523.

JELKS, Richard: Leg.- To son, William all such worldly goods as it hath pleased God to endow me with. (Wm. not 21 years old). Makes Fra. Mason his Exer. If son die, the est. to go to Francis Mason. Wit: Richard Hargrave, John hunnicutt. 31 Jan., 1687. Prob.: 28 May, 1695. Book 5, p. 49.

JOHNSON, John: Est.- By Thos. Collier, Sheriff. 15 Aug., 1722. Book 7, p. 414.

JOHNSON, John: Leg.- To son, John Johnson, the Plantation that he lives on in Surry Co., with all the cattle he can raise in five years, the chist in Brunswick County, and all my carpenter's tools. To son, Peter Johnson, all the coopers tools, round table, dishes, etc. To son, Richard Johnson, all my turner's tools, sword, sheep, etc. To daughter, Hannah Woodward, cow, etc. To Daughter, Rosemond Underwood, a cow, etc. To dau. Betty Sollowman, one cow. To son, Leveton Johnson, the manner plantation where I formerly lived, if he have a son, if not, to my son, Peter's son, John Johnson, and if he dies before he comes of age, to my grandson, John Johnson, the son of Thomas Johnson, deceased, all the rest of my goods and chattels, but to maintain their mother. Makes sons, Peter & Leveton, Exers. Wit: Wm. Renn, Wm. Minton. 11 June, 1742. Prob.: 20 April, 1743. Book 9, p. 431.

JOHNSON, John: Est.- By Mary Johnson, admr. 7 Apr., 1750. Signed: Wm. Clinch, John Harris. Book 9, p. 645.

JOHNSON, Martin: Leg.- To son, Martin Johnson, riding horse, cattle, etc. To daughter, Elizabeth, one negro, cows, etc. To daughter, Grace, cows, etc. To son, Thomas, feather bed, pewter plates, etc. To son, William, tankard, pewter plates, etc. To son, John, cows, etc. To godson, John Andrews, one cow. To godson, William Howell, a cow. Makes son, Martin Exer. Wit: David Andrews, Michael Harris. 12 Mar., 1702/3. Prob.: 4 May, 1703. Bk. 5, p. 275.

JOHNSON, Martin: Leg.- To Elizabeth Clark a chest, chair, table & form, etc. To Benjamin Clark whole crop of corn & tobacco, he paying rent. To Cousin, Mary Johnson, bed, etc. To son of John Johnson, William Johnson by name; and John Johnson, the son of Thomas Johnson, all of my pewter, beds, etc. between them. To Elizabeth Holt 20 shillings. To my godson, Benjamin Holt, a cow. To my brother, Thomas Johnson a cow & makes him Exer. Wit: Thos. Bedingfield, Wm. Holt. 4 Aug., 1724. Prob.: 19 Aug., 1724. Book 7, p. 547.

JOHNSON, Richare: Est.- 15 June, 1743.

JOHNSON, William: Leg.- To sons, William & Richard Johnson small bequests, and son, Aaron Johnson to be with Thomas Bentley & wife until he is sixteen. To son, Moses Johnson, my now dwelling Plantation with 200 acres of land. If he die to his brother, Aaron Johnson. Mentions wife, Elizabeth Johnson and gives her tobacco in Isle of Wight County. Mentions daughters, Martha and Mary Johnson. Land on Nottoway River to be sold to pay debts, and rem. to wife and daughters, Martha & Mary, and son, Moses Johnson. Wife & dau., Martha, Exers. Wit: Fra. Sowerby, Chris. Moring, Samuel House. 4 Nov., 1709. Prob.: 4 July, 1710.

Book 6, p. 28.

JONES, Arthur: Leg.- To son, Arthur Jones, guns, tools, and
bill of Thomas Lisbon's for 600 lbs. tob., bill of Phillyp Luper for 600 lbs. tob. To daughter, Mary Hook, one
sheep. To daughter, Sarah, land upon Joseph's Swamp &
Nottoway River at Dob's lower field., to Nottoway River.
To Daughter, Jane, land at corner pine..to the river. To
daughter, Mary, all the rest of the land at her mother's
death. To daughter, Prudence, a negro boy provided old
John Freeman will acknowledge the land to his son, Henry,
where he now liveth. To daughter, Elizabeth Jones, pewter
dishes, etc. Wife, Prudence all rest of est. and negro.
Makes her Exerx. James Sammon and Giles Underhill overseers of will. 22 Jan., 1715/16. Prob.: 16 May, 1716.
Wit: Jones Williams, Wm. Bridges, Wm. Beech. Book 7,
p. 16.

JONES, Elizabeth: Leg.- To Catern Jones, wife to Henry Jones
a chest & clothing. To son, Henry Jones, all the rest of
est. real & personal, cattle hogs etc. Wit: Henry Freeman, James Ray. 22 Nov., 1723. Prob.: 15 Apr., 1724.
Book 7, p. 526.

JONES, James: Est.- By Mary Jones, Admrx. 17 June, 1713.
Signed: Thomas Davis, Edward Rowell. Book 6, p. 150.

JONES: James: Leg.- To my son, James Jones, lands in Prince
George County, four negroes, half dozen leather chairs sent
for to London, and money due from John Barnes for rent of
my plantation in Prince George County and a mare brought
from Brunswick County, until such time as my son, Howell,
shall attain the age of 21 years, then the labor of certain
slaves to return to wife, Sarah, for her life, or she
marry. James to act at 20 years of age & be paid his legacies. To son, James a silver-headed cane and best sword.
To son, Howell, Land & Plantation bought of Wm. Kelly on
N. E. side Arsemoosak Swamp when son, John is 20 years old
etc. To son, Howell, one Horseman's Sword in the possession of David Jones. To daughter, Elizabeth three negroes
(Brunswick County) household goods, mourning ring, etc.
To son, John, Lands & right of Lands in Isle of Wight County, also negroes, beds, etc. and to receive legacies at
20 years of age, but if no issue to son, Howell. To son,
Thomas, Land & Plantation where I now live and 75 acres...
on Atamoosank Swamp, household goods etc. and to receive
legacies at 20 years old. If he have no heir to my son
James. Child in esse to have land in Brunswick County. If
it die land to son, Howell. To brother, Robert, the other
75 acres of new survey...next to John Stegall's..from
Jarratt's line...to Capt. Mason's line. To my cousin Robert Jones one pistole and all ready money after debts
& funeral expenses are paid. To wife, Sarah, negroes for
her life, and she to bequeath in what manner she likes.
Wife, sons, James & Howell Exers. Wit: Robert Jones,
Robert Jones, Jr., Richard Jones. Made: 22 Aug., 1742.
Prob.: 16 Feb., 1742. Book 9, p. 427.

JONES, John: Leg.- To daughter, Mary Jones all my land in
Surry Co., provided she have issue; if not, the land to my
daughter, Betty Jones. To my daughter, Rebecca Jones, all
my land in Isle of Wight, provided she has issue, if not
to Daughter Betty Jones, gives her three negroes, etc.
Wife to have Plantation where I now live for her life, and

three negroes. Appoints his wife's father, William Betts, my brother Richard Jones and Holmes Boyseau my Exers. 9 March, 1742/3. Prob.: 17 Aug., 1743. Wit: David Jones, John Goodwyn, --Wife, Sarah, negroes. Bk. 9, p. 447.

JONES, John: Est.- 21 Dec., 1743. Sarah Bard, admr. Book 9, p. 456.

JONES, Mary: Est.- 19 May, 1747. Signed: James Anderson, Thomas Bedingfield, Josiah Barker. Book 9, p. 554.

JONES, Susannah: Est.- Henry Baker, admr. of est. Due to said Jones, estate other things from Robert Ruffin, Martin Johnson, Wm. Clarke, Jno. Hodges, Lewis Williams, Wm. Sweet, John Whitson, Jno. Amry, Wm. Alderson, Wm. Newsums, Peter Addams. 29 May, 1677. Book 2, p. 159.

JONES, Thomas: Est.- By Sarah Jones, admrx. 21 June, 1748. Signed: James Chappell, James Chappell, Jr., Robert Jones. Book 9, p. 579.

JONES, William, Sr.: Leg.- Mentions wife, Elizabeth. To sons, Henry, William and John Jones, small bequests. To son, Robert Jones all my land and all the rest of my est. __ February, 1714. Prob.: 16 Mar., 1714. Wit: Thomas Wynne, Robert Wynne. Book 6, p. 132.

JORDAN, Anna: Leg.- To John Rawlings, I give a servant boy. To Eliza. Rawlings clothing. To John Shorsby, Thos. Shorsby and Richard Rose their wives (blot)...to be divided equally. To my son, Edward Evans a bequest. If he die to my husband Thomas Shorsby's brothers' children. Jeremiah Ellis, Se., and Robert Cortrock to be Exers. 2 Oct., 1697. 22 July, 1697. Wit: Edward Scarbroo, Mary Rawlings. Book 5, p. 147.

JORDAN, Arthur: Leg.- To son, George Jordan all land I now possess, also one negro, bed blankets, etc. To son, River Jordan, a feather bed, two negroes, blankets, etc. To my son and daughter, Washington, one good feather bed, negroes, etc. To granddaughter Elizabeth Jordan one cow. To grandson, Arthur Washington one cow. Other estate in Virginia and elsewhere to sons, George and River Jordan to be equally divided. Desires that negro Charity, be given her freedom. As law directs that she must leave the country if freed, then arrange to have her transportation out of the country, and bring her back again. Made: 24 Sept., 1698. Prob.: 3 Jan., 1698/9. Wit: Nath. Harrison, Tho. Flood, Water Flood. Book 5, p. 160.

JORDAN, George: Leg.- Body to be buried by wife & children in Maj. Browne's orchard...Has tobacco in hand due to children of Wm. Jordan, long since deceased, which children I could never find; learned they lived in Yorkshire, now to be sent them. To two goddaughters, Col. Swanns' children, a piece of plate each. To Sarah Sowerby, George Norwood, George Briggs, Also godchildren, each a silver spoon..to George Norwood not ten years old. To friend Thomas Sowerby, To James Sowerby, to Wm. Arnall, to Mary Browne, godchild & to Mr. Cary..On 15th day of every Oct. a sermon of Mortality to be had at my house, the day my daughter Fortune Hunt died. If the day come on Sunday, Holy Communion to be given. Whoever shall enjoy the land, be it one thousand generations, who possess the Land shall perform both

82

Sermon & Prayer. To the Church a Baptismal Bason of Silver.
Mentions cousin Edward Bayly, Chris. Foster, Walter Flood,
George Jordan, James Jordan, River Jordan, Eliza. Jordan,
Thomas Flood. Exers. Coll. Swann & Major Browne. Nephew,
Thomas Jordan. Brother, Arthur Jordan, Seven nephews and
niece, Elizabeth Jordan. God bless the Colony where I
have lived forty-three years. Codicil. -- Has given
nephew Edward Bayly land, revokes the bequest of 600 lbs.
of tobacco and gives it to Chris. Foster & Water Flood.
Gives to Daniel Roome 500 lbs. of tob. Gives to Thomas
Andrews & wife, Dorothy, 600 lbs. of tobacco. 8 May, 1678.
Prob.: 5 9br, 1678. Wit: Will. Browne, Wm. Thompson.
Book 2, p. 191.

JORDAN, George: Leg.- Son, George Jordan land at Tuskahora
Branch. Son, Arthur Jordan, Land where I live, after his
mother's death. Son, Thomas Jordan, land at Sunken Marsh
called Stony Run. Son, James & River Jordan, the rem. part
of land on Sunken Marsh & Stony Run. Son, Charles Jordan,
all land on Reedy Marsh & two negroes. Wife to have until
her death. Wife, Mary Jordan to maintain "my three youngest children". Daughter, Mary Anderson a large Bible.
Daughter, Elizabeth Baley ten shillings. Wife and seven
youngest children. Makes wife, Exerx. Wit: Howell Edmunds, George Walker, James Masongall. 18 May, 1718.
20 Aug., 1718. Book 7, p. 145.

JORDAN, George Lt. Coll.: Deceased. 27 9br, 1682. Book 2,
p. 322.

JORDAN, James: Est.- Richard Washington, River Jordan, admrs.
of James Jordan, deceased, made oath. 9 July, 1699.
Book 5, p. 169.

JORDAN, Richard: Est.- 3 May, 1687. July 5th, Richard Jordan
appeared in Court and made oath to the Inventory of Richard
Jordan. Anthony Evans, Henry Norton, Nicholas Sessoms,
Joseph Wall. Book 3, p. 86.

JORDAN, Richard: Leg.- To son, Richard Jordan, the Land and
Est. that I have to bestow on him. To my son, Charles the
Land which was formerly Mr. Owens, being part of a tract
where I now live.. and all working tools. To son, Robert
that Plantation I do now live on that is to say the upper
end of that land, after the death of my wife. If either
son, Charles or Robert die without issue the land shall go
to the longest liver; if both die without issue to be e-
qually divided between my three youngest daughters, or the
longest liver of the three. To daughter Rachel, loom,
wheels, etc. To daughter, Elizabeth Fort a hog. To daughter Margaret Howse a hog. Daughter, Hannah ewe. Daughter
Mary ewe. Daughter, Sarah ewe. Makes wife and Josiah
Proctor & John Fort Exerx. Probate granted to Elizabeth
Jordan admrx. 24 Sept., 1695. Probated: 7 Nov., 1699.
Wit: Joshua Procktor, Rob. Owing, Richard Ham. Book 5,
p. 183.

JORDAN, River: Leg.- To wife, Priscilla Jordan my Plantation,
for her life, and at her decease to return to my child in
esse, to be it's forever. If child die in minority, then
after wife's decease, to George Jordan, eldest son of
George Jordan & the plantation where I live with all adjoining. To Arthur Jordan, son of George Jordan, a neck of
Land ad. said father's land up the swamp..to the Spring

Branch. To Thomas Jordan, son of George Jordan land adjoining John Gulledge and a servant mulatto boy to my wife
until the children are twenty-one years old. To Wm.
Browne, son of Wm. Browne, Jr. a cow. Rest of est. to
wife, Priscilla, and child in esse. George Washington to
be paid ten shillings, put of my child's part. To Mary &
Elizabeth Jordan, daughters of George Jordan. Wife
Priscilla Exerx. Wit: William Browne, Grace Barker, Patrick Lashley. 2 Dec., 1699. Prob.: 4 March, 1700/01.
Book 5, p. 220.

JORDAN, Robert: Est.- By Martha Jordan. 25 Feb., 1710.
Signed: Joshua Proctor, William Rose. Book 6, p. 42.

JORDAN, Thomas: Est.- By Coll. Wm. Browne, Mr. Ja. Jordan.
6 July, 1686. John Moring, Will. Foreman, Samuell Thompson.

JUDKINS, Charles: Leg.- To wife, Jane, bed, etc. To son,
James my long gun. To son, Charles a short gun and sword.
Sons, Thomas & William. Makes wife, Exerx. Mr. Samuel
Thompson and Mr. Wm. Foster overseers of will. Wit:
Michael Harris, William Foster. 13 Mar., 1709/10. 2 May,
170_. Book 6, p. 81. (Jean Judkins, widow of Charles
Judkins married William Williams). Book 6, p. 9.

JUDKINS, Robert: Leg.- To son, William Judkins all housing
and Land, gun, rapier, live stock, etc. To son, Robert
Judkins pewter dish and tankard, livestock, etc. To daughter, Elizabeth Judkins, two pewter dishes, chest called her
mother's and other things after her mother's decease. To
daughter, Sarah Judkins livestock, chest etc. Rest of
estate to wife, Elizabeth and makes her Exrx. Friends,
Fra. Mason, Capt. Thos. Swann & John Thompson. Wit: Wm.
Potway, Wm. Rivers, Samuel Cocke. 19 May, 1693. Prob.:
2 Jan., 1693. Book 4, p. 344.

JUDKINS, Samuel: Leg.- To son, Samuel Judkins, the Plantation
where I now live and all land I have, also negroes, furniture, leather chairs, rush chairs, oval table, gun,
scimiter, sword, books, bottles, etc. To daughter, Anne
Champion, the labor of one negro for life then to my granddaughter, Lucy Champion, also to daughter five pounds. To
daughter, Sarah Holt one negro, and at her death to my
granddaughter, Lucy Holt and five pounds. To granddaughter
Lucy Champion bed, furniture, etc. at eighteen years, or
married. To wife, Anne, the labor of negroes for her life,
and all the rest of my estate. Makes wife, Ann, and son,
Samuel Exers. Made 13 April, 1740. Prob.: 15 Oct., 1740.
Wit: Wm. Edwards, Chas. Holt, Nich. Judkins. Bk. 9, p.
219.

JUDKINS, Samuell: Leg.- Mentions three sons, Samuel, the eld-
est, Robert, and Charles. Wife, Lidia. Wit: Gerardt
Gronswolt, John Honeycutt. 13 Feb., 1671. 7 May, 1672.
Book 2, p. 13.

JUDKINS, Samuell: Est.- 18 May, 1705. By Samuell Judkins.
Signed: James Jones, James Ellis. Book 5, p. 339.

JUDKINS, Thomas: Leg.- To my brother William Judkins one
feather bed, etc. and half of the ezenburg in my chest. To
brother, James Judkins six pounds credit and my horse,
saddle & bridle, and rem. of ezenburg in my chest. To

brother, Charles Judkins, one negro and makes him Exer. Wit: Howell Briggs, John Owen, Thos. Alsobrook. 26 Jan., 1731/2. 19 July, 1732. Book 8, p. 205.

JUDKINS, William: Est.- Bartlett Moreland & Margaret Moreland, wife and administrator. 16 Aug., 1721. Signed: Wm. Seward, John Bruce, Thos. Edwards. (Bartlett Moreland died and James Vaughan married the Exrx. of Bartlett Moreland. Book 7, p. 394.

KATE, Robert: Est.- By Ann Kate. 15 April, 1730. Signed: Chris. Tatum, Wm. Tomlinson, Edward Davis. Book 8, p. 6.

KERNEY, James: Leg.- To son, Micajah land purchased of Benjamin Rogers lying on Chinkapin Swamp, if he have no heirs to daughter, Elizabeth and her heirs. If she die without issue, to daughter, Joannah. If she die to be equally divided between my two sons-in-law Benjamin Carrell and John Carrell. To my son, Micajah, my pewter tankard and pair of bellows, my miolin chest and long gun, etc. To dau. Elizabeth three pewter plates & two pewter dishes. To daughter, Joannah a spice mortar. Makes wife, Phillis Exerx. 24 Oct., 1711. Prob.: 18 July, 1716. 24 Oct., 1711. Prob.: 18 July, 1716. Wit: Samuell Johnson, John Judkins. Book 7, p. 23.

KERNEY, James: Est.- By Phillis Johnson. 18 July, 1716. Signed: Thos. Davis, Robt. Pettway, Edward Pettway. Book 7, p. 25.

KIGGIN, Terence: Est.- Phebe Kiggin, admrx. of Terence Kiggin. 4 July, 1699. Signed: Nicholas Witherington, William Foster. Book 5, p. 170.

KILLINGSWORTH, William: Leg.- To son, William Killingsworth my old Plantation and Land bounding thereto and a neck of land lying between my two Plantations. To daughter, Lucy Gulledge one hog. To son, John Killingsworth the remaining part of Land, beginning at the Plantation where I now live. Makes wife, Avis, Exerx. 29 Nov., 1709. Prob.: 7 Mar., 1709. Wit: Jno. Cooke, Sarah Bullivant, Mary Underwood. Book 5, p. 447.

KILPATRICK, James: Est.- Robert Caufield, admr. 15 June, 1677. Book 2, p. 129.

KILPATRICK, James: Est.- Lydia Kilpatrick swore to Inventory. 4 July, 1693. Signed: Arthur Jordan, Thomas Flood. Book 4, p. 307.

KILPATRICK, John: Est.- 21 May, 1677. Signed: John Basse, Wm. Newsum. Book 2, p. 139.

KIMBALL, Joseph: Est.- By John Simmons, Frances Mallory, admr. Signed: Arthur Kavenaugh, Thos. Avent. 17 June, 1713. Book 6, p. 180.

KINDRED, John: Est.- By Mary Kindred, Relict & admr. __ Jan., 1677. Signed: Wm. Newsum, Mathew Swann. Book 2, p. 164.

KINDRED, John: Est.- Paid to widow and three orphants, bed given by Sam. Mason to Sam. Kindred. 15 June, 1681. Book 2, p. 286.

KINDRED, John: Leg.- Wife to have Plantation where I now live, at her death to son, Samuel Kindred. The remaining part of my estate to be equally divided between my wife and children. Son to have his est. at 18 years. Wit: Augustus Hunnicutt, David Price, Carter Crafford. 29 Jan., 1702. Prob.: 4 May, 1703. Book 5, p. 278.

KINDRED, John: Est.- By Katherine Kindred. 6 July, 1703. Signed: Robert Crafford, Augustine Hunnicutt, Wm. Chambers. (In 1704, Katherine Peacock was Exerx. of her husband, John Kindred's Est. Book 5, p. 330) Book 5, p. 283.

KING, John: Leg.- To George Rochell, my Library of Books in Nansemond County. Book of Divinity by Tobias Christ, to Wm. Knott, Jr. Makes wife, Sarah, Exerx. 12 Aug., 1704. Prob.: 1 May, 1705. Wit: Wm. Knott, Sr., Wm. Phillips, Mary Williams, Jr. Book 5, p. 332.

KING, John: Est.- Faith King, Admr. 16 Nov., 1737. Signed: Jos. Clinch, Blanks Moody, Zacharias Maderna. Book 8, p. 761.

KING, Thomas: Est.- By Elizabeth Smith. 2 9br, 1680. Signed: Samuel Plow, Sion Hill, Elizabeth, the wife of Nicholas Smith, ye Relict of Thos. King, made oath that the Inventory is correct. Book 2, p. 276.

KING, Thomas: Leg.- (Much of this will is illegible) To son, John King the Plantation where he now lives. To wife, Deborah King, the Plantation where I now live. Son, Thomas King, my son, have enough timber to build him a house on a piece of land adjoining. Mentions three daughters, Elizabeth, Mary and Jane. to son, Thomas, Land purchased of John Chapman in Rest Park Meadow and a small parcel - 40 acres - adjoining. Land to be laid out in presence of Thos. Baley. To son, Joseph King four sheep. Mentions four sons, William King, Thomas King, James King, and Benjamin King, and gives them one-half of the estate; rem. divided equally. Wife, Deborah, Exerx. Wit: Wm. Baldwin, Wm. Newsum, Philip Newsum. 23 Aug., 1731. Prob.: 19 July, 1732. Book 8, p. 206.

KITCHEN, John: Leg.- To son, Benjamin Kitchen six pewter plates, gun, sword, etc. All rem. of est. to wife, Sarah, and makes her Exerx. Wit: John Edwards, Martin Johnson, Robert Ruffin. 12 Mar., 1719. 15 June, 1720. Book 7, p. 270.

KNIGHT, Jeremiah: Est.- 15 May, 1678. Signed: John Moring, Ar. Jordan, Thos. Sowerby, Wm. Newsum. Book 2, p. 170.

KNIGHT, Nathaniel: Leg.- Nathaniel Knight, Chirugeon, makes the following bequests: To Goddaughter, Mary Proctor, daughter of Mr. Geo. Proctor, a piece of plate. To godson, Nathaniel Phillips one cow. To Sam. Briggs, son to Henry Briggs, one cow. To Mary Browne 20 shillings to buy a ring. To Hannah Harrison money for a ring. To Ann Hoskins bed etc. To Samuel Magget, Sr., one cow. To Nathaniel Harrison, son of Benjamin Harrison a piece of plate. To Jno. Allen 400 lbs. After funeral expenses and debts are paid, the whole est. to be sold and money remitted to England for uses hereafter mentioned. To sister, Abigail Brooks one-half my estate. To father, Mr. Samuel Knight, in Stroodwater, in Glosister shire the other one-half. If father is dead, to go to eldest brother, Mr. Daniel Knight. Friends Maj. Wm. Browne and Mr. Benj. Harrison Exerx. 18 Feb., 1677/8. Probated: 5 Mar., 1677. Wit: Berkeley Browne, John Baily, Judith Parker. Book 2, p. 169.

KNOTT, Christian: Est.- Gregory Rawlings, Admr. 15 July, 1741. Signed: Thos. Allstin, Jas. Rookings. Book 9, p. 338.

KNOTT, Mary Mrs.: Est.- Alex. Finnie, Admr. 16 June, 1742. Signed: Wm. Rookings, Thos. Allstin, Robt. Grimes. Book 9, p. 411.

KNOTT, William: Leg.- To wife, the Plantation I live on being by Great Swamp below ye house of Mr. Rookings...to Tann fatts..between sd. Plant. and Robert Tucker's..to yellow bottom where Mr. Phillips' line crosses over, except the oldest orchard, that to go to son, and wife. To gr. dau. Mary Rawlings, bed, etc. Daughter, Christian. To son, Wm. Knott, all Land except bequest to wife, and to be possessed of at wife's death. Gr. son, Wm. Rawlings land ad. Thos. Clarke & Wm. Rookings. To dau. Christian, land adjoining Jas. Cooper and Thos. Piddington. To gr. son, son of James Bozeman, not yet baptized. Mentions wife and four children. Wife and Wm. Knott, Exers. 10 Feb., 1717. Prob.: 19 Feb., 1717. Wit: Nathaniel Harrison, Henry Smith. Bk. 7, p. 92.

KNOTT, William: Est.- Wm. Knott, admr. 19 Mar., 1717. Book 7, p. 111.

KNOTT, William: Nuncupative will. Leg.- To wife, Mary Knott. To Mary Lewis, daughter of Richard Lewis a sum for education for one year. To James Bowman's eldest son. To sister, Christian. 9 Sept., 1726. Wit: Nath. Harrison, Wm. Saunders. Book 7, p. 706.

LACEY, Mary: Leg.- To husband, Robert Lacey's couzens in England, the amount due me from the estate of Joseph John Jackman. Gives tobacco for repairs of meeting house in Surry. Bequests to Mary Bayley, Sarah Griffin, Francis Parsons, Ann Edwards, and to Elizabeth Griffin, daughter of john Griffin. Friends, Samuell Cornwell, and makes him Exer. Wit: James Griffin, Rob. Griffin. 3 day 7th month called Sept., 1715. Prob.: 19 Dec., 1716. Book 7, p. 37.

LACEY, Robert: Est.- By Sam. Cornwell. 20 Feb., 1716. Signed: Wm. Chambers, John Hancocke, Charles Jarrett. Bk. 7, p. 14.

LACIE, Robert: Leg.- To wife, Mary Lacie, my Land with houses, etc. for her life and two negroes. At her death the land and servants to my brother, George Lacie and his children to be equally divided with those then living. To wife, Mary, household good and chattels, and appoints Samuell Cornwell, Lawne's Creek Par., weaver and Samuell Hargrewe, planter, trustees. Wit: John Green, Melchisideck Duche, Roger Delke. Made 12 March, 1701/2. Prob.: 1 Sept., 1702. Book 5, p. 246.

LANCASTER, Robert: Leg.- To son, Samuel, the Plantation where he now lives with tools, etc. To son, William, razor, hone, etc. To son, Joseph, the Plantation where he now lives. 150 acres - with 13 pounds cash, bed and 4000 cypress boards, 3000 garden pails, and 50 gals. of brandy I have all ready for market. All rem. of est. to be divided among the three children, Elizabeth, Mary and Joseph. Mentions three daughters, Ann, Elizabeth and Mary. Makes son, Samuel, Exer. 12 Nov., 1738. 18 April, 1739. Wit: John Little, Wm. Hart. Book 9, p. 53.

LANCASTER, William: Est.- Mary Lancaster, admr. 21 Jan., 1740. Signed: Barth. Figures, Sam. Maget, Wm. Rose. Bk. 9, p. 264.

LAND, Curtis: Leg.- To son, Curtis, Plantation with 150 acres, I bought of Robert Inman. To son, Thomas my plantation I live on & 200 acres. To son, William a mare & colt. To daughter, Rebeckah two horses, and two cows. To son, John, two horses & two cows. To son, Robert two horses & two cows. Wife and son, William Land Exers. Wife, Mary one cow. 15 Dec., 1729. Prob.: 18 Mar., 1729. Book 7, p. 1015.

LANE, Richard: Leg.- Gives to wife his whole est. (Does not name her). If wife marry the estate to go to two sons (not named). 18 Mar., 1687/7. Book 3, p. 83.

LANE, Thomas: Leg.- Desires that land be divided between two sons, Thomas & Joseph Lane and makes them Exers., with procession by the neighbors. 5 Jan., 1708. Prob.: 3 Jan., 1709. Wit: William Holt, William Benson, Edward Pettway. Book 5, p. 440.

LANE, Thomas: Est.- Mary Lane, admr. 12 May, 1721. Signed: Wm. Ruffin, John Newsum, Wm. Holt. Book 7, p. 333.

LANE, Thomas: Lkg.- To grandson, Thomas Lane the Plantation his father lived on. Mentions grandsons, John Lane & Joseph Lane. Mentions Rebekah White. Daughter, Mary Hart. Mentions three grandsons and Rebekah Hart. 8 Oct., 1733. 20 Nov., 1734. Wit: Richard Ricks, Thos. Lanier, Wm. Barker. Book 8, p. 428.

LASHLEY, Patrick: Est.- By Walter Lashley. 18 April, 1711. Signed: Howell Edmunds, Samuell Briggs. Bk. 6, p. 51.

LATHER, John: Est.- By Jane Lather. 15 Feb., 1720. Signed: Nich. Maget, Rob. Judkins, Mich. Harris. Book 7, p. 319.

LATHER, John: Est.- Jane Lather, admr. 19 Apr., 1727. The est. paid Thomas & John Collier, orphans of John Collier, deceased. Book 7, p. 688.

LAWTHER, Henry: Est.- Admr. was granted to Wm. Thompson, deceased. Signed at James Citty by the Governor. 14 June, 1676. Book 2, p. 117.

LEATH, Peter: Leg.- (This was a verbal will) Mentions son, John, dau. Elizabeth, and wife. Probated by Sarah Leath. 13 Feb., 1737. Prob.: 19 Apr., 1738. Wit: John Jackson, John Parham. Book 8, p. 812.

LEWIS, Christopher: Leg.- To ye church at Southwarke Parish a silver flagon of two qt. measure. To William Thompson, minister, 1500 lbs. of tobacco, to be paid in 1675. To four godchildren, Solomon Davis, in Isle of Wight County, Luke Measell, Katherine Owen, Christopher Moring. Bequest to Jno. Carr. To Roger Williams, his son young Roger, Cattle, to Roger Williams, ye father, Christopher, tools, to Mary Jones, daughter of James Jones, cooper, tobacco, to the orphan of Mr. Thos. Harris..Sunken Marsh Mill, he now living with David Williams, at ye mouth of Chipeaks Creek.. lot & casks when of age. To ye chyrurgian that hath..cured Samuell Magget's daughter, 1000 lbs. of tobacco. To Wm. Thompson, son of Mr. Wm. Thompson, 500 lbs. tob. and to sister, Katherine Thompson 500 lbs. tob. To Charles Beckett, clothing to cost 500 lbs. tob. Desires to be buried in ye Chancell & Exers. to lay a tombstone over me & a funeral sermon, for which Exers. are to pay. Makes James Jones Exer. 1 Sept., 1673. Prob.: 7 April, 1674. Wit: Will. Foorman, Jno. Charles, Jno. Corker. Book 2, p. 35.

LEWIS, Morgan: Est.- By Patrick Maygaratery. 18 Feb., 1718. Signed: Sam Judkins, Jno. Judkins, Wm. Thompson. Book 7, p. 162.

LEWIS, Richard: Leg.- To Sarah Tyas, daughter of John Tyas, and Ann Tyas, one negro. To William Simmons the Plantation where I now dwell. To Wm. Simmons & Capt. Thomas Edmunds all my other Land, and makes them Exers. 18 March, 1732/3. Prob.: 17 Sept., 1735. Wit: Charles Lucas, Sam. Sowerby, Geo. Branch. Book 8, p. 512.

LILE, John: Est.- By Hannah Lile. 16 May, 1711. Signed: Thos. Bentley, Ben. Ellis. Book 6, p. 58.

LITTLE, Francis: Leg.- To son, Robert, the Plantation where he now lives, on the north west side of the marked trees..To son, Francis the Plantation where I now dwell and all Land lying on the South west side of the small branch, dividing him and Robert. To son, Francis livestock, household goods, etc. To son, Beaz, a cow. To wife all rest of est. for her life, then to be divided equally among the four children; Robert, Beaz, Francis and Sarah, the wife of Philip Jones, Robert & Francis Exerx. Wit: John Ruffin, Wm. Seward, Jr., James Wilson, Jr. 14 Aug., 1745. Prob.: 20 Nov., 1750. Book 9, p. ___ .

LITTLE, John: Leg.- To wife, Elizabeth, my whole estate. To son, John, a colt. Makes wife Exerx. The Est. to be divided among "my children". Wit: Phillip Shelley, James Griffin. 20 Feb., 1703/4. Prob.: 7 Nov., 1704. Book 5, p. 323.

LITTLE, William: Leg.- To my first son, Wm. Little, my Plantation and one-half of a tract of Land where he lives - 200 acres - after my wife's decease. To second son, John Little, the other half - 100 acres. To third son, Benjamin Little this Plantation & Land where I live, after my wife's decease. To my second daughter, Katherine Little an iron pott etc. To third daughter, Patience Little a cow etc. To wife, all rem. of movable estate. Sets negro slave free. Makes Wm. & Benj. Exers. 29 Sept., 1740. 19 Nov., 1740. Wit: Thos. Pretlow, Jr., John Atkinson, Martha Price. Book 9, p. 254.

LITTLEBOY, Elizabeth: Leg.- To Edward Mathias my whole est. and makes him Exer. 2 Dec., 1731. Book 8, p. 230.

LITTLEBOY, Robert: Leg.- (Will is torn and mutilated) godson, Edward Matthews. Wife, Elizabeth. 6 Feb., 1720/1. Prob.: 21 Oct., 1730. Book 8, p. 63.

LOFTIN, Cornelius: Leg.- To son, Wm. Loftin the Plantation

where I live on the south side of little Swamp & my Land
on the north side of sd. Swamp to Miry Branch to a bridge
that Silvanus Stokes & Robert Web made over swamp, to land
I bought of Walter Lashley. To daughters, Rebekah, Clee,
Mary, Elizabeth, and Sarah, each one shilling. To son,
Cornelius the personal est. after death of wife, Mary. Wit:
John Bell, Jonas Stokes. 5 April, 1735. Prob.: 21 Apr.,
1736. Book 8, p. 585.

LONG, Arthur: Est.- Mary Long, admrx. 22 Nov., 1700. Signed:
Thos. Tarver, Mich. Isell, Jno. Bayley. Book 5, p. 218.

LONG, Edward: Leg.- To son, Edward Long all my goods and
chattels, and all moveables and makes him Exer. To sons,
William, George, Thomas, Lewis, each a shilling. To Francis
Moore, daughter of Edward Long. Dau., Mary Long & Dau.
Mary Ann Long to live with brother until twenty-one or
married, and have part with brother. Prob.: 15 Aug., 1749.
Wit: Henry Savidge, Mercy Long.

LONG, Mary: Widdow of Arthur Long, and admr. of Est.- Makes
distribution of est. among other things a gold ring at
Carolina. So son, Arthur Long, a gun, formerly given him
by his grandfather. To daus. Eliza Long, Mary Long, and
to son, George Long. The six children to divide the remainder. 18 9br, 1679. Book 2, p. 241.

LONGBOTTOM, William: Leg.- To son, Jones the Plantation where
I live with 200 acres of land. To son, Samuel bed & furniture etc. To son, John, one negro. To son, Thomas a
bed etc. To child in esse a bequest. Mentions wife. The
rest of the est. to sons, Samuell & Thomas. Wit: Robert
Webb, Jr., John Hassell, Gregory Rawlings, Robert Weeks,
Sr. Made 20 Feb., 1733. Prob.: 18 July, 1733. Book 8,
p. 310.

LONGBOTTOM, William: Est.- Francis Hutchins & Jane Hutchins
Exers. Wit: Robert Gray, Howell Briggs. 18 April, 1735.
Book 8, p. 470.

LOTHER, Jane: Leg.- To granddaughter, Rebecca Andrews, one
large table, one half-dozen leather chairs-English leather-
bed, etc. To granddaughter, Priscilla Andrews three chists,
four cattle, etc. to be equally divided among her four
granddaughters. To daughter Martha Andrews, a side saddle.
Makes two sons, Thomas & John Collier Exers. To dau.
Martha Andrews all rest of Est. 28 Jan., 1740/1. Prob.:
20 May, 1741. Wit: Nicholas Maget, Peter Warren, Benj.
King. Book 9, p. 332.

LOTHER, John: Leg.- To wife, Jane and children. To wife Jane
bed with English tick. To son, John a bed, Bible etc. To
son, Henry, bed etc. To Daughter, Hannah Avery, cow. The
est. to be equally divided between wife, and children.
28 Jan., 1709/10. 7 Mar., 1709. Wit: Nicholas Smith,
David Burnett, Wm. Warren. Book 5, p. 443.

LUCAS, Grace: Leg.- To dau., Hannah, bed & chest. To daughter,
Martha, wearing clothes. Daughter, Ann, geese. To Vallen-
tine Williamson, sheep. To son, Charles Lucas one shilling.
Son, William, rest of est. Daus., Ann, Grace, Hannah,
Elizabeth, the latter very sick. If she die, Henry Briggs
to have no part of my estate. Son, Wm. Lucas & John
Collier Exers. Made: 22 Dec., 1719. Prob.: 17 Feb.,

1719. Wit: Thomas Cocke, James Anderson. Bk. 7, p. 249.

LUCAS, William: Leg.- To my son, William, the Plantation where now lives..To Ed. Ellis line-300 acres and two negroes, clothing, 1000 nails, goods when they come from England. To son, Charles all the rest of the Land three negroes bed etc. also goods sent for to England etc. To Daniel Eel-bank all that he is indebted to me and bed where he lodges at my new dwelling house until he is married. To grandson William Lucas 6 ells of dowlas. To daughters, Ann & Eliza-beth one shilling. To Daughter, Grace, pewter dishes, etc. To daughter, Hannah, one negro. To Daughter, Mary, pewter dishes. Makes wife, Grace Lucas, and son Charles, Exers. 1 Oct., 1716. Prob.: 18 Dec., 1717. Wit: Daniel Bel-bank, Henry Harrison, Thos. Bentley. Book 7, p. 79.

LUKELASCO, John: Est.- 18 Oct., 1721. By Martha Lukelasco. 18 Oct., 1721. Signed: Nich. Cocke, Wm. Moss. Book 7, p. 378.

LYLE, William: Leg.- To son, George, scimeter, plates, dishes etc. If he die, to son Thomas. If Thomas die then to fall to one child to the other. To wife rest of est. for life, or until she marry. If she marry to be equally divided with my wife and children, those living at my death. Makes wife, Exerx. 4 Jan., 1713. Prob.: 15 Apr., 1713. Wit: Michael Harris, Thos. Merrill. Will presented by Judith Lyle, admrx. Book 6, p. 139.

MACHAM, Joshua: Est.- By Elizabeth Macham. 15 Dec., 1709. Signed: Robert Clarke, John Jones. Book 5, p. 427.

MAGEE, Robert: Est.- By Henry Harrison, admr. 20 Jan., 1730. Signed: Richard Parker, Thos. Peters, Amos Sims. Book 8, p. 75.

MAGET, Nicholas: Leg.- To wife, Ann, the labor of six negroes for life then to son, Nicholas. Bequests to sons, Nicholas & Samuel Maget. To --- Wager, son of Robert Wager one negro. To Nicholas, son of Samuel Maget one negro. Bequest to Charity Pemlum Moody, daughter of Blanks Moody. To son-in-law, Robert Judkins one negro. To son-in-law, Blanks Moody one negro until John Spratley, son of John Spratley, late of James Citty, come to age of 21 years old. To wife, Ann Maget. To daughter, Fortune Watkins. To daughter, ⌐ane Sowerby. To Benj. King. Makes son, Exer. 18 Nov., 1743. Prob.: 15 May, 1745. Wit: Deborak King, Wm. Browne, Jr., Benjamin King. Book 9, p. 503.

MAGET, Samuel: Leg.- Mentions son, Nicholas Maget. Bequest to two children, Nicholas Maget and Fortune, the wife of Edward Booky of all estate in Virginia & what is due from the Orphan's Court in Middleborough in Ireland to be di-vided. 5 May, 1692. Prob.: 3 Jan., 1692. Wit: Will. Browne, John Moring. Book 4, p. 302.

MAIN, John: Est.- 20 Jan., 1724. Signed: Sam. Chappell, Robert Jones, Charles Sledge. Book 7, p. 552.

MALDEN, Joseph Mr.: Est.- By Eliza. Thompson, Relict & Admrx. of Mr. Jos. Malsen. 26 March, 1688. Signed: John Clemons, Thos. Warren, Sam'll Judkins. Book 4, p. 62.

MALLONE, Nathaniel: Leg.- (Much of this will is illegible from water stain) Sons, Nathaniel, Drury, Thomas, William, Daniel. Son-in-law, Jos. Harper. Son, Drury, Exer. Prob.: 21 Mar., 1732. Wit: Robert Wynne, John Gilliam, Jr., Wm. Harper. Book 8, p. 268.

MALONE, William: Leg.- To son, William 97½ acres of Land at Gawler's Meadow..to south west swamp..To Nath. Robertson, deceased, line..to my line. To son, John the Plantation I live on and land 97½ acres, beg. at Lawler's meadow to son, William's line, and to my son, John, to s. w. swamp after my wife's decease, and some household goods. To Daughter, Elizabeth, bed, cows etc. To daughters, Sarah, Anne, Amey, Hannah, Agnes and Milly, each a cow. Makes wife, Exerx. 3 May, 1736. Prob.: 16 Oct., 1745. Book 9, p. 513.

MANARD, John: Est.- By John Maynard. 7 March, 1698/9. Signed: Charles Judkins, John Smith. Book 5, p. 167.

MANGUM, John: Est.- By Olive Mangum, admrx. 20 Dec., 1744. Signed: Samuel Maget, Robert Judkins, Barth. Figures. Book 9, p. 486.

MARGARETY, Patrick: Est.- By Mary Magarety. 17 May, 1721. Signed: John Bamer, John Judkins, Samuel Judkins. Book 7, p. 333.

MARRIOTT, Mathias: Leg.- Wife, Allice, to have and enjoy the Land I live on for her widdowhood; after her death or marriage to return to my son, William Marriott; if he die without issue to go to my grandson, Thomas Flake, son of Robert Flake. The rest of my estate to my wife Allice, and my son, William. To daughter, Margaret Flake and daughter Elizabeth Hill and daughter, Marriott Crips to each a book of Divinity. Makes wife, Exerx. Made: 12 June, 1705. Prob.: 2 Sept., 1707. Wit: James Thompson, Wm. Hunniford, Roger Williams. Book 5, p. 374.

MARRIOTT, William: Est.- 11 July, 1673. This estate is indebted to George Proctor, who married the Relict and Exerx. for debts and legacies. Paid Wm. Atkinson, by will to his wife's legacy. Paid Mr. Salway, who married Elizabeth Peck, due by will. By debts in Henrico Co., Isle of Wight County, Charles Citty Co., and James Citty Co., Dr. King's bill etc. etc. Book 2, p. 37.

MARRIOTT, William: Est.- 7 9br, 1682. Paid to Mr. Proctor in right of his wife, one-third of est. Amt. to orphans which is due Mr. Sam. Thompson as marrying ye surviving of ye two orphans. Deduction for funeral, and other expenses. Book 2, p. 323.

MARSHALL, Robert: Est.- Wm. Gray, Admr. 19 July, 1727. Signed: Joseph Delk, John Bruce, Thos. Edwards. Book 7, p. 743.

MARTIN, Peter: Est.- 9 June, 1688. Signed: Chris. Foster, John Vinson. Book 4, p. 60.

MARTIN, William: Est.- By Sarah Martin, Admrx. 18 May, 1736. Signed: Solomon Wynne, John Wynne, Hollum Sturdivant. Book 8, p. 695.

MASON, Elizabeth: Leg.- To friend, John Allen 20 shillings.

The rem. of the estate to seven grandchildren: Eliza,
Mary, Katherine, Martha, Lucy, Frances and Thomas Holt, Jr.
Makes John Allen, Exer. To granddaughter Katherine Holt
one negro. To granddaughter, Mary Holt, one negro. To
Granddaughter, Martha Holt, one negro. Wit: Wm. Edwards,
Thos. Binns, John Allen. Prob.: 17 Feb., 1713. Book 6,
p. 173.

MASON, Francis: Leg.- To son, James Mason one-half of 300 acres
of Land formerly belonging to John Bushup, late of this
county, deceased. To daughter, Frances Holt..proper acres.
To Frances, wife of Thos. Holt, negroes, etc. To granddaughter, Eliza Holt one negro. To Grandchild, youngest
of Daughter, Holt. To friends, Mr. Wm. Edwards, Arthur
Allen, Thos. Binns, Mrs. Eliza. Caufield & Mrs. Mary White
20 shillings each, to buy a ring. To my wife all the land
where I live for her life, then to son James Mason. If
orphan Francis Price remain with wife, until he comes of
age, to have two cows etc. and taught to improve reading
and writing. Desires that William, son of Richard Jelks,
continue with my son-in-law, Thos. Holt until 21 years old,
and pay him what belongs to him of his father's estate.
Wife Elizabeth. 4 Oct., 1696. Prob.: 2 Mar., 1696/7.
Wit: Ar. Allen, Joseph Coron, Richard Hargrave. Book 5,
p. 116.

MASON, James: Est.- By Elizabeth, his wife, admrx. 18 July,
1701. Book 6, p. 73.

MASON, Joseph: Est.- By Phebe Mason, admrx. 20 Mar., 1749.
Signed: Robert Jones, Howell Jones, Nich. Partridge. Book
9, p. 642.

MAYBRY, Charles: Leg.- To son, Charles, 340 acres of Land between Raccoon Swamp and Spring Swamp. To son, Francis,
119 acres of Land on the South side of Hornet Swamp. To
son, William, the Land beginning at Little Swamp, and extending to New Branch, joining to Charles Battles..to Old
Field..to Racoon Swamp. To son, Ebrill, the Plantation
where I live and the remainder of Land, in which my wife is
to have a life right. To son, Cornelius, 119 acres of Land
on the south side of Plowman's and 100 acres between
Charles Battles & Roberts land. To daughters, Elizabeth,
Rebecca, Emidia, and Mary Battle, and daughter--(no name)
each a bed etc. Son, William, wife, Rebeccak, and son
Charles, Exers. Made - 16 March, 1749. Prob.: 15 Aug.,
1749. Wit: Charles Maybry, Rebeccak Maybry, John Hargrave,
Nathaniel Clanton. Book 9, p. 615.

MAYBRY, William: Leg.- Gives 250 acres of land at New River
to Robert Eacolls, also clothing, horse, saddle etc. Makes
him Exer., but must pay Abraham Green and John Edwards.
Made: 13 Jan., 1749. Prob.: 15 May, 1750. Wit: John
Jackson, Robert Jackson. Book 9, p. 637.

MAYBURY, Elizabeth: Leg.- (Widow, Relict of Francis Maybury)
To son, Charles Maybury the Indian slave, Robbin, bed,
riding horse & gun. To son, Hinshaw Maybury, the Indian
slave, Jack, gray mare & gun. To son, George Maybury, bed
& furniture and gun. To daughter, Judith, bed and furniture. Mentions brothers, John and Hinshaw Gilliam. Daughter, Eliza Paine, widdow. Son, Francis West, Daughter,
Mary, Daughter Ann, son, John West. Estate to be divided
by my two brothers, John and Hinshaw. Wit: Henry Walthall,

John Dolling, Susan Featherstone. Made: 6 June, 1713.
Prob.: 15 Feb., 1715. Book 6, p. 260.

MAYBURY, Francis: Leg.- To son, Francis Maybury, land bought
of John Freeman and recorded in Charles Citty County, and
land bought of Thos. Busby, and recorded in said county.
To son, George Maybury, 125 acres of land on Horn Branch of
Three Creeks. To sons, Charles and Hanchey Maybury, 400
acres of land on Fountain Creek, to be equally divided. To
daughter, Ann Peoples, one ewe. To daughter, Mary Fox, one
ewe. To daughter, Judith Maybury one ewe. To wife, Elizabeth, the Indian slaves Robbin and Jack, and the rest of my
estate, and makes her Exerx. Wit: Thos. Wynne, Henry
Bedingfield, Robert Wynne. Made: 22 March, 1711/12.
Prob.: 18 June, 1714. Book 6, p. 106.

MAYBURY, Francis: Leg.- Wife, Eleanor, Exerx. Mentions sons,
William and Francis. Wife to have Plantation for life, then
to son Francis. William to have land on Three Creeks, Isle
of Wight Co., and 250 acres in Surry Co. 12 Jan., 1728.
Prob.: 19 Feb., 1728. Wit: Chris Tatum, Hancha Maybury.
Book ___, p. 892.

MAYO, James: Est.- By Henry Harrison. 14 Feb., 1725. Signed:
Robt. Hicks, Arthur Kavenaugh, Thos. Avent. Bk. 7, p. 395.

MEADE, William: Est.- Honour Meade (wife) and John Pulister,
& Wm. Jackson, administrators of Est. of William Meade.
6 June, 1696. Signed: John Edwards, Ann Edwards. Book 5,
p. 95.

MEAZEL, Luke: Est.- On back of the Inventory.was written that
Elizabeth, wife to Robert Hill, appeared in Court and swore
to Inventory. 6 Oct., 1694. Signed: Robert Hill, Eliza.
Hill. Book 5, p. 7.

MEAZLE, Luke: Nuncupative Will. Bequest to daughter Elizabeth,
after decease of wife. Mentions daughter, Sarah. 4 July,
1693. Wit: Thos. Smith, John Greene, Eliza. Binam. Book
4, p. 308.

MEEDS, Honour: Est.- 12 May, 1711. By John Bruce. Signed:
John Hancocke, Jonathan Cocke. Book 6, p. 57.

MEGARETY, Patrick: Est.- Mary Megarety, admrx. 16 Feb., 1725.
Signed: Nicholas Maget, John Newsum. Book 7, p. 625.

MERIWEATHER, Francis: Est.- Nicholas Meriweather was granted
administration on the estate of his brother, Fra. Meriweather. Signed: at James Citty by the Governor. 14 June,
1676. Book 2, p. 117.

MERIWEATHER, William: Est.- Capt. Francis Clements and Elizabeth, his wife, and Nicholas Meriweather applied for administration on the estate. Elizabeth and Nicholas, sister
and brother of said deceased. 21 April, 1695.

MIDDLETON, George: Est.- By Katherine Middleton. 4 July, 1710.
Signed: Robert Ruffin, John Simmons. Book 6, p. 19.

MIDDLETON, Thomas: Est.- Wm. Edwards, Sheriff. 13 Sept., 1725.
Signed: Richard Lewis, Charles Lucas, Jos. Nicholson.
Book 7, p. 604.

MILES, John: Est.- Alice Miles, admrx. of John Miles, deceased.
4 Jan., 1697. Signed: Hart. Ellis, Thos. Tynes. Book 5,
p. 154.

MITCHELL, Robert: Est.- Mary Mitchell, admrx. 21 Dec., 1726.
Signed: John Brown, John Davis, Thomas Sessom. Book 7,
p. 670.

MIZELL, Luke: Est.- 21 9br, 1673. John Smith, who married
Deborah, relict and Exerx. of Luke Mizell, makes account
of estate. Account allowed by Court for Skilltimber's
child. Balance of estate divided between John Smith and
Luke Mizell, orphant. Book 2, p. 39.

MONK, Richard: Leg.- Mentions wife, and son-in-law, Robert
Hunnicutt. Appoints Oysteen? Hunnicutt and Robert Crafford
overseers of will. Made 1 March, 1687/8. 29 May, 1688.
Wit: Nicholas Smith, Robert Crafford. Book 4, p. 42.

MOORE, Richard: Est.- By Alice Moore. 23 Nov., 1720. Signed:
John Davis, Thomas Davis. Book 7, p. 348.

MOORE, Richard: Est.- By Charles Kimball and Alice Kimball
admr. and admrx. 16 Aug., 1727. Signed: Wm. Gray,
LDeloney. Book 7, p. 751.

MOORE, Tristam: Est.- Late of Isle of Wight County. Boaz
Little, and Ann Little, admr. 16 Feb., 1742. Bk. 9, p.
426.

MOORE, William: Leg.- To son, William Moore all the Land from
the upper side of Old Field, where Capt. Thos. Wynne former-
ly lived, to Capt. Robert Wynne's, and John Robards, etc.
Mentions grandsons, William, Francis, Daniel, Richard Eppes
and gives each a cow, and same to granddaughter, Sarah
Eppes. To Grandsons, Robert Pettaway, Wm. Pettaway, John
Pettaway, each a cow. To granddaughters, Ann & Selah
Pettaway each a cow, also Granddaughter Phebe Pettaway.
Daughter, Mary Pettaway & daughter, Elizabeth Pettaway.
Daughter, Susannah Eppes. Mentions wife, Elizabeth Moore,
and wife's seven children. Son, William & wife, exers. 4
April, 1744. 18 July, 1744. Wit: Chris. Tatum, Geo.
Rives, Richard Rives. Book 9, p. 476.

MORELAND, Bartlett: Leg.- To daughter, Mary Moreland, the
land in York County that came to me by marriage with my
first wife, and to be in care of Jane Hunniford, wife of
Hugh Hunniford, untill eighteen years old. Mentions wife,
Elizabeth, and two daughters, Mary and Lucy Moreland. Wit:
Thos. Holt, Wm. Gray, Wm. Hurdle. Made: 9 July, 1725.
Prob.: 18 Aug., 1725. Book 7, p. 595.

MORELAND, Bartlett: Est.- Returned by James Vaughan, who married ye Exrx. of Bartlett Moreland's estate. 17 Sept.,
1729. Signed: Henry Brown, Thomas Edmunds. Book 9, p.
971.

MORELAND, Edward: Leg.- To eldest son, Bartlett Moreland 20
shillings. To wife, one negro. Bequests to son, Edward
and Daughter, Mary. To daughters, Ann & Elizabeth a ring
each. Mentions seven children: Thomas, Elizabeth, Mary,
Ann, Edward, Martha and Katherine. Makes wife, Exerx. and
gives to her and to the seven children all the estate in
Virginia and elsewhere. Friends, Robert Ruffin and William

Gray, Jr., trustees. Made 15 Dec., 1712. Prob.: 17 Mar.,
1713. Wit: Roger Delk, Wm. Tanner. Book 6, p. 181.

MORELAND, Edward: Est.- Geo. Reddick and Mary Reddick admrs.
19 Mar., 1717. Signed: Nich. Maget, Thos. Cocke. Book
7, p. 106.

MORGAN, Elizabeth: Relict of Richard Morgan, deceased, she
lately found dead in the house of Edward Napkin. 4 May,
1686. Signed: Jos. Wall, Thos. Pittman, Jr. Bk. 3, p. 55.

MORRELL, Thomas: Leg.- To wife, Elizabeth, the Plantation and
Land where I live, south by the swamp, where Capt. William
Browne's Mill stands..to Roger Gilbert's..north to Capt.
Browne's, to Robert Judkins and Robert Watkins. After my
wife's death, to son, William. To son, George, the Land
called Runaway - 40 acres. To son, Thomas, the remaining
part of the land. To son, John a horse when 21 years old.
To two daughters, Mary & Elizabeth, each five shillings.
Made 5 May, 1719. Prob.: 17 June, 1719. Wit: Nich.
Maget, Mich. Harris, Wm. Allen. Book 7, p. 190.

MOSS, John: Leg.- To wife, Martha one negro, to John Moss at
wife's death. To son, Henry Moss, pistolls, holsters, and
Breast plate. To son, Thomas, my gun and sword. To son,
John one horse. My whole estate to my wife and children.
Makes wife, Exrx. Made: 11 Oct., 1734. Prob.: 19 Feb.,
1734. Wit: John Mason, Wm. Moss. Book 8, p. 463.

MUGGETT, Ann: Leg.- Bequest to Phillip Shelley, Jr., and if he
die to his youngest brother, John Shelley. Bequests to
Elizabeth Sugar, and to granddaughter, Ann Shelley. Bequest to Phillip Shelley, Senior. Wit: Geo. Long, Thos.
Partridge, Thos. Cooke. 4 Sept., 1689. Prob.: 1 July,
1690. Book 4, p. 144.

MUNGER, John: Est.- Brother, Spenser, admr. and Thos. Taberer.
17 May, 1672. Book 2, p. 14.

MUNGER, Nathaniel: Leg.- To Mary Benitt 40 shillings etc. To
Mary Roberts, clothing etc. To William Drew four pounds to
educate godchildren two of Will Coging, one of Newitt Ed-
wards, one of Ethill Stanley. Rest of estate to Priscilla
Harrison, daughter of Will. Drew, and makes him Exer. Wit:
Wm. Coging. Made: 26 May, 1731. Prob.: 21 July, 1731.
Book 8, p. 119.

MURRER, William: Est.- By Robert Jones, Exer. 20 June, 1716.
Book 7, p. 20.

NASH, William: Est.- Appraised by Jno. Clements and James
Jones. 2 Mar., 1691/2.

NASH, William: Inventory Est.- Jno. Thompson, admr. 3 Oct.,
1696. Wit: John Clements, James Jones, James Ellis.

NEWITT, Elizabeth: Leg.- To daughter, Elizabeth Price for life,
the plantation I live on, containing 86½ acres, to be kept
in good repair, and at her death to my grandson, Wm. Edwards; if no heir, to my granddaughter, Eliza. Edwards;
if no issue to my grandson, Newitt Edwards. To Grandson,
Newitt Edwards the plantation where Martin Johnson lives,
86½ acres; if no issue, to go to my granddaughter, Elizabeth Edwards. To Wm. Newitt Edwards, son of Newitt Edwards

96

one negro. To Griffin Windum, 630 lbs. of tobacco. To my
two daughters Elizabeth and Frances 21 lbs. 11s. to be e-
qually divided, and they give a discharge to my grandson,
Thomas Edwards that they never will trouble my Exer. for a
legacy left them by my husband, Wm. Newitt, being for the
same sum in Mr. Ball's hands, in England and that they enjoy the legacy left them by my husband, if they can recover
it of Mr. Ball. To grandson, Wm. Edwards, after funeral &
debts paid, one-half of my estate to be equally divided
between my daughter, Elizabeth and her children; Daughter,
Eliza. and her children. Daughter, Frances and her children. Son-in-law, Edward Drew, and Grandson, Thos. Edwards Exer. 2 Aug., 1717. Prob.: 18 Nov., 1719. Wit:
Wm. Edwards, Martin Johnson, Wm. Price. Bk. 7, p. 225.

NEWITT, William: Leg.- To grandson, Newitt Edwards, the Land
bought of Robert Warren, when Robert Foons' lease is out;
if he die, to his brother, John Edwards; if he die, to
William. Daughter, Frances. To Newitt Drew, land bought
of James Briggs; if no heir, to go to another son that
might be born to daughter, Frances; if not to Thomas Drew.
To two daughters, property in England. Mentions wife,
Elizabeth, and makes her Exerx. Wit: Thomas Lane, Edward
Drew, John Clark. 18 Aug., 1710. Prob.: 25 Oct., 1713.
Book 6, p. 161.

NEWSUM, George: Est.- 6 July, 1697. Signed: Thos. Binns,
James Mason. Book 5, p. 129.

NEWSUM, John: Leg.- To son, William Newsum my Land and Plantation where I now live. To son, Joel Newsum, two negroes
when he comes to 18 years old. To wife, Sarah, two negroes
and remainder of my estate to my wife, and all my children.
Sons, William & Joel to be of age at 18 years and to receive
their est. Brother, William Newsum to sell one negro, and
divide the amount between my wife and children. Wm. Newsum and Carter Crafford overseers of will. 15 Dec., 1723.
Prob.: 15 July, 1724. Wit: Wm. Newsum, Wm. Holt. Book
7, p. 545.

NEWSUM, John: Est.- By Sarah Ruffin, Exerx. 16 Feb., 1725.
Signed: Joseph Allen, John Newsum.

NEWSUM, William: Leg.- To my son, William, my Plantation and
Land in Rich Neck, provided that said land be never assigned
or sold for 21 years, etc. To son, John, my Land and Plantation that I bought of Mr. Harris, where I now dwell. To
my two sonnes, Robert and Thomas all my Tract and Dividend
of Land called Hopewell, to be equally divided- Robert to
have choice, and my wish is that my three sons, last named,
if one die to decend to the other. Gives negroes to son,
Wm.; son, Thomas; daughters, Elizabeth and Ann, and to two
eldest sons. Remainder of the estate to be divided between my wife and children. Sons, William and John, and
wife, Anne, Exers. Friends, Mr. Fra. Mason and Mr. Robert
Ruffin overseers of will. Wit: Matthew Swann, Henry Hart,
Bray Hargrave. 10 June, 1691. Prob.: 5 Sept., 1691.

NEWSUM, William: Est.- Due to George Foster, and Ann, his wife,
and of ye Exers, of said deceased. 4 Mar., 1694. Fra.
Mason, Jno. Thompson. Book 5, p. 48.

NEWTON, Samuel: Leg.- 23 of the 3rd month called May, 1702.
To Mary Lucie, my grate Bible. To Arthur Allen, cows,

History of the Primitive Fathers. Samuell Cornhill to be
guardian of John Collins, orphant, until he comes of age,
then pay him his estate, and the remaining two thirds part
to Edman Hosier, in Talbot Court in grate Church Street,
in London, the other third part, I bequeath to Mary Hart,
widow, at the Sign of the Hart in Denmarke St., in Rat-
cliff, near London. Appoints Samuel Cornhill of Lawnes
Creek Parish, weaver, sole Exer. Wit: Michael Ezell, John
Greene. __ March, 1703. Book 5, p. 298.

NICHOLLS, Roger: Est.- __ July, 1708. By Sarah Nicholls, Wm.
Chambers. Book 5, p. 395.

NICHOLSON, Ann: Leg.- To daughter, Mary Allstin a gold ring.
To daughter, Ann Rookings, gilded trunk, bodice etc. To my
four children my money, to be equally divided - 17 lbs. 10
shillings, that I have liberty to dispose of by my marriage
contract. Makes Thomas Allstin, Exer. Son, William Rookings, not of age. 28 Feb., 1719. Prob.: 15 Feb., 1720.
Wit: Nath. Harrison, Elizabeth Pardon, Eliz. Harrison.
Book 7, p. 299.

NICHOLSON, George: Leg.- To daughter, Agnes Farmer, one cow.
To daughter, Jane, the land I gave to my grandson, Isaac
Farmer. To son, Robert Nicholson, that 50 acres of Land
which I bought of Thomas Collier for 99 years, and one
cow. To my wife, Mary Nicholson, my Plantation where I
live for her life and at her death to son, George with 15
acres I bought of Richard Jones, Jr., where my lot house
and orchard now stand..down to the bridge, also cows,
horses, etc. To wife, Household goods, and one-third of
est.; the other two-thirds to three sons, George, Robert,
and Parks Nicholson. The heirs to confirm a sale of land
to James Binham land between Nottoway and Mahern Rivers,
taken up with John Battwell. Wife, Mary and son, George,
Exers. Wit: Maj. Francis Rea, Wm. Savage, R. Hall.
13 Feb., 1712/13. Prob.: 21 Nov., 1716. Book 7, p. 35.

NICHOLSON, George: Leg.- To brother, Parks Nicholson, the Land
where I live, bed, cows etc. To brother, Robert Nicholson.
To Richard Jones Jrs. eldest daughter, one cow. Makes
Mother, Mary Nicholson, my Exerx. Wit: Henry Harrison,
Thomas Clare, Robert Lanier. 6 Mar., 1719/20. 17 May,
1721. Book 7, p. 332.

NICHOLSON, James: Leg.- To wife, Elizabeth for life my Plan-
tation extending to Wm. Gray's line. To son, James the
rest of the Plantation. To son, Benjamin Nicholson, the
Plantation after my wife's death. Makes wife, Exerx. 6
Dec., 1722. Prob.: 17 July, 1723. Wit: Nich. Maget,
Zacharias Maddera, Roger Gilbert. Book 7, p. 457.

NICHOLSON, Robert: Leg.- To granddaughter, Hannah, five pounds
for her schooling. To son, Joshua, land purchased of
Francis Oysten - 180 acres - also negroes, and 15 pounds
for a gold ring. To son, John, three tracts of land; one
purchased of Mr. George Lee; one purchased of my brother,
George Nicholson; one tract purchased of Thomas Dunn - 235
acres, also one negro and a gold ring. To son, Robert, the
tract of land purchased of Robert Rivers - 200 acres - and
negroes and gold ring. To daughter, Joyce, one negro and
gold ring. Daughter, Elizabeth, one negro, forty pounds,
money to buy each of my two youngest children gold rings.
All of the remainder of money in America and England to

wife and three sons, Joshua, John and Robert, equally divided. Makes wife, Exerx. Friends, Nicholas Cocke, Sampson Lanier, overseers of will. Wit: Gregory Rawlings, John Rawlings, Mary Rawlings. 29 Sept., 1719. Prob.: 17 Feb., 1719. Book 7, p. 244.

NICHOLSON, Robert: Est.- Joanna Joyce Flood Exerx. 18 Aug., 1725. Book 7, p. 597.

NORRIS, Mary: Est.- Mary Norris, late of this colony, died and left an estate. Madan Mary Swann has made suit for administratrix. Coll. Wm. Browns, Arthur Allen, Justices of the Peace, grant this. 5 July, 1681. Book 2, p. 287.

NORTH, John: Leg.- Wife, Katherine North. ___ Oct., 1673. Signed: Wm. Thomson, Fra. Mason. Book 2, p. 34.

NORWOOD, William: Leg.- To son, Edward Norwood, one shilling. To son, George, my now dwelling house and 100 acres of Land, horse, hoggs etc., on condition that son, George, comply with my request to my daughter, Sarah Norwood and not else. To son, Richard Norwood, a neck of Land called the Barren Track, with 80 acres of Land, to be separated from my other Land, to be run by Mr. Waller and Mr. Thos. Flood, also to Richard, horses, negroes, etc. To daughter, Elizabeth Branch, one large Pewter dish. To daughter, Lydia Sowerby, a flat handled silver spoon, and large pewter dish. To daughter, Sarah Norwood, one negro and a small silver cup, but her mother to have use of them for her life. To granddaughter, Elizabeth Branch one silver spoon she now hath. To daughter, Mary Norwood, one silver spoon, negro, and horse. All the rem. of est. to wife and four children, George, Richard, Sarah and Mary Norwood. Wife, Lydia, and son, George Exers. 6 June, 1702. Prob.: 7 March, 1703. Wit: John Shelton.

OGBOURNE, John: Est.- Presented by Elizabeth Ogbourne, admrx. 16 Feb., 1719. Signed: Will. Harris, Joseph Delk, John Bruce. Book 7, p. 254.

OLDESS, Wm.: Est.- Abate granted Tho. Edwards as marrying the Relict of Wm. Oldess, deceased. 15 June, 1677, on Oldess' Will. Book 2, p. 129.

OLISS, Will: Leg.- To Roger Nicholas all my wearing apparel. To Edward Amry, the son of Thos. Amry, deceased, a horse. To wife, Elizabeth Oliss, the rest of my estate in and out, bills, bonds etc. of every kind. Wit: Alex. Richardson, Timo. Issiell. Book 2, p. 123.

OLIVER, Edward: Est.- 26 Aug., 1676. Signed: Arthur Jordan, Wm. Carpinter. On back was written, Mandlin Oliver, Relict of Edward Oliver, certifies to the Inventory, 2 May, 1677. The above contents were presented by Jno. Warren, Husband of above Maudlin. 15 June, 1677. Book 2, p. 126.

OLIVER, John: Est.- By Mary Oliver, his wife. 15 Dec., 1725. Book 7, p. 616.

OWEN, Bartholomew: Est.- Signed Inventory by Jane Owen. 14 Feb., 1677. Wit: Wm. Fordman, Jno. Moring. Book 2, p. 163.

OWEN, John: Est.- Roger Delk, admr. 6 Aug., 1740. Signed:

John Hancock, Thos. Davidson, Newitt Edwards. Book 9, p. 215.

OWEN, Robert: Leg.- Son, Robert, gun and Sword. Daughter, Elizabeth one shilling. Daughter, Catherine one shilling. Son, William a gun. Son, John, a gun. To wife all the rest of my estate for life, then to be equally divided with the rest of my children, which she and I had together. Wit: Thos. Harris, Charles Briggs. Made: 6 Sept., 1715. Prob.: 19 Feb., 1717. Book 7, p. 92.

PACK, John: Will.- Late of London, now of Lawnes Creek Parish, Surry County, Made a will at his departure out of England in which he made John Blandford his Exer. This will to stand for estate in England; but not to have any Concern with property in Virginia, which he now disposes of Viz: To oldest brother, Christopher Pack, Orgin, Base Veyall, and Spinet, To Friend Capt. John Allen, a case of tea spoons, tongs, china etc. To brother, Graves Pack, the goods brought in with us etc., and all else in Virginia. Makes friend, Capt. John Allen, Exer. 9 Aug., 1716. Prob.: 20 Mar., 1716. Wit: John Shelley, Thomas Shelley, Jno. Wilson. Book 7, p. 48.

PARHAM, Edward: Leg.- To daughter, Phebe Parham, when of age or married one Indian girl, cows etc. To daughter, Ann Parham, bed, mare, pewter dishes and spoons etc. To son, Edward Parham, the Plantation where I live, with all land belonging thereto and cows, horses etc. To son, Gower Parham, 100 acres of land where Robert Marlow now lives, small chest, gun, livestock etc. To daughter, Elizabeth Parke, pewter dishes and plates, bed, cows etc. To daughter, Lina Parham, bed, cows, pewter basons, dishes, plates etc. and the rest of est. to be equally divided. Lewis Green to have son, Gower, to bring him up, and use his est. until he is 21 years old. Thos. Sessoms to have son, Edward Parham, until he is 21 years old, to use his est. etc., and take care of the rest of my children. Appoints Thos. Sessoms, Ephraim Parham, and Lewis Green, Jr. overseers of will, and Exers. of same. Wit: Lewis Green, Sr., John Guillum, Jr. 12 Mar., 1709. Prob.: 5 July, 1709.

PARHAM, Ephraim: Leg.- To son, Ephraim Parham, 150 acres of Land on the South side of Nottoway River to Flatt Swamp, bed, Troopers Arms etc., if no heir to his brother, Lewis Parham. To son, Lewis Parham, a Plantation on the North side of Meherrin River, 180 acres, also cows, etc and Land upon Reedy Branch, the upper half, when 20 years old. To wife, Frances, negroes, household good, etc. To daughter, Frances, wife of Hinchey Maybury, 10 pounds cur. money of Va. To granddaughter, Elizabeth Maybury, six leather chairs after the death of her grandmother. To grandson, James Parham, one cow. All grandchildren to have equal part of movable estate. Sons, Matthew and Ephraim Parham, Exers. 7 April, 1726. Prob.: 15 June, 1726. Wit: Peter Green, John Whittington, Richard Raines. Book 7, p. _41.

PARHAM, William: Est.- 25 July, 1733. Signed: Thomas Wynne, John Freeman, John Jackson. Book 8, p. 313.

PARKER, Richard: Est.- Judith Parker, Relict, admrx. 4 7br, 1677. Book 2, p. 141.

PARKER, Judah: Est.- William Hunt asked the Court for right to administer on the estate of Judah Parker, late of the Colony, who died and left an Est. 1 July, 1679. Thos. Pittman, Wm. Carpinter, Wm. Nance. Book 2, p. 218.

PARKER, Judith: Est.- 25 March, 1682. "Half her thirds is dew to Richard Parker, orphant". Signed: Benj. Harrison, Wm. Simmons. Book 2, p. 307.

PARKER, Richard: Leg.- Daughters, Ann Phillips, Faith Hunt, Judith Clements, Hannah Sisson. Son, Richard Parker, grandson, Frederick Parker, son, William Parker. Benjamin Clements, husband of Judith Clements. Wife, Mary Parker. Son, William Exer. 3 April, 1744. Prob.: 19 Feb., 1750. Wit: Elizabeth Jones, Jr., Elizabeth Jones, Robert Jones, Jr. Book 9, p. 680.

PARKER, Richard, Jr.: Leg.- To son, Richard Parker the Plantation where I live with 950 acres thereto belonging, provided that if child in esse be a male, he will return to said child 350 acres of the Indian Land on Reedy Branch, also to Richard Parker three negroes, pewter plates, horse & saddle, when 18 years old. To son, Thomas Parker, three negroes, horse and saddle, livestock, etc. when 18 years old. To son, Peter Parker a tract of land in North Carolina, in Northampton County, purchased of Joseph Riggon, deceased, date, 1742/3, 260 acres, and two negroes, pewter, live stock etc. when 18 years old. To son, William, a tract of land in Brunswick County, 350 acres, on Little Creek, said land purchased of Wm. Smith, deed date 1737, also stock etc. To daughter, Sarah Parker, negro, bed, horse, etc. To daughters, Martha, Mary, and Ann bequests of negroes, furniture etc. To son, Drury Parker, one negro. To son, Frederick Parker, one negro. Wife, Exerx. 27 Jan., 1750/1. Prob.: 16 Apr., 1751. Wit: Geo. Hamilton, Samuel Peete, Wm. Parker. Book 9, p. 689.

PARR, William: Est.- 18 March, 1737. Wm. Eppes, admr. Book 8, p. 862.

PARTIN, Elizabeth: Est.- Robert Partin, admr. 22 Jan., 1732/33. Signed: Wm. Rookings, Solomon Harrison, Thomas Allstin. Book 8, p. 284.

PARTIN, Robert: Est.- 16 May, 1744. Book 9, p. 474.

PASFIELD, Nicholas: Leg.- The plantation where John Case lives with all the appurtenances, to Henry Baker & his heirs forever. To Son, Nicholas Pasfield, a heifer etc. when ___ years old. To daughter, Mary, pewter dish and a plate when of age. Wife, Jeane, Exerx. 9 Jan., 1700. 4 Nov., 1701. Book 5, p. 227.

PATTISON, Dennis: Leg.- Bequest to John Cargill for funeral expenses and to his heirs. Makes him Exer. 12 Jan., 1712/13. 20 May, 1713. Wit: Edward Bailey, Richard Bennet. Book 6, p. 142.

PEACH, Mathias: Est.- William Reade, Admr. 1 July, 1679. Wit: Wm. Ruffin, Wm. Edwards, Sec. Jno. Moring. Book 2, p. 4.

PEACOCK, William: Leg.- To wife, whole estate, and makes her Exerx. Thos. Waller, Edward Rowell. Presented by Katherine Peacock. 9 Oct., 1722. Prob.: 15 July, 1722. Book

7, p. 546.

PEARIE, Richard: Est.- By John Taylor. 21 May, 1712. Signed: John Holt, Hugh Hunniford, William Seward, Wm. Harris. Book 6, p. 100.

PEEBELES, Thomas: Est.- Sarah Peebles, admrx. Signed: Nicholas Partridge, Jno. Tomlinson, Edward Weaver. 15 Feb., 1743. Book 9, p. 460.

PENENTON, Edward: Est.- John New & Tabitha New, Exers. 17 Sept., 1729. Signed: Geo. Vick, Richard Woodard, John Hadly. Book 7, p. 969.

PENENTON, Thomas: Leg.- To Thomas Penenton, my eldest son, 150 acres of land, with new house built on part of it lying on Mr. Stockes' Mill Swamp, near Hamlin's line, with a horse on Nottoway River, gun, sword and cartouch box. To son, William Penenton, 100 acres, adjoining the above, this being part of a survey of 250 acres. To Edward Penenton, my third son, the Plantation I live on after the death of my wife, Mary Penenton. To youngest children - John, George Penenton, daughter Mary Penenton, son, James Penenton, each a Bible. Wife to have all rem. est. 4 Feb., 1726/7. Prob.: 20 Dec., 1727. Wit: Wm. Saunders, LDeloney, Wm. Gilbert, Thomas Allstin. Book 7, p. 772.

PEPPER, Stephen: Leg.- To son, Stephen Pepper two guns and colt at 18 years old. To wife, Jane Pepper, all my estate, and at her death to be equally divided with all children then living. Makes wife Exerx. To daughter, Elizabeth a book called "Beveridge". To son, Stephen, "The Whole Duty of Man". To daughter, Sarah, "Sure Guide To Heaven". To daughter, Rebeccah, "Thoughts and Providence". To daughter, Jussy, "Best Experience". 1 March, 1739/4. Prob.: 16 April, 1746. Wit: Wm. Rose, Arthur Richardson. Book 9, p. 527.

PERRY, Micajah: Est.- 21 April, 1736. By Mr. John Cargill. Book 8, p. 588.

PERSON, John: Leg.- To son, John Person land where he lives, and land where my mother now lives, 156 acres. To son, Thomas, land at Fountain Creek. To son, Francis, ye Plantation in Isle of Wight. To son, Joseph, 100 acres on east side of second swamp, ad. Main Blackwater at Dykesses. To son, Benjamin, 250 acres south side of Fountain Creek. To son, Samuel, 150 acres at Meherin below John's land. To Son, William, 180 acres, part of where I live. To son, Jacob, where I live, 560 acres. To grandson, Joseph Tuke 40 shillings when 21 years old. To sister, Averelah Tuke. To daughters, Mary & Elizabeth. Mentions, Sarah, my wife and eight of my children; Thomas, Francis, Joseph, Benjamin, Samueal, William, Jacob and Elizabeth Person. Son, Thomas, Exer. 8 Aug., 1721. Prob.: 21 Mar., 1738. Wit: Wm. Cripps, John Glover, Sampson Lanser. Book 9, p. 51.

PERSON, John: Est.- Thos. Person, Exer. 21 Nov., 1730. Book 9, p. 102.

PESTELL (PESTLE), John: Est.- Susannah Holt (Formerly Sussannah Pestell) and John Holt, to pay to Ann, orphan of John Pestel, deceased, her portion of her father's estate. 23 Jan., 1695. John Edwards, Dorothea Gilbird. Book 5, p. 81.

PETTAWAY, William: Leg.- To son, Robert, the Plantation where I live, beg. at Crouches' Creek..to Judson's Spring.. to Land my father gave me..to tree standing at the head of a Valley called Thunderbolt Valley etc..and not to molest his brother, Edward, from enjoying a piece of Land my father gave to me..and my will that Edward, my son, enjoy this that I now live on. To Edward Pettaway, all the rest of that Land belonging to it, that my father gave me, I give to him. If either die without issue, the other to inherit both lands. To son, William Pettaway, a parcell of Land, 400 acres -- on the east side of Western Branch of Crouches Creek ad John Clemons. If there be a child in esse, it to have half of this. Other bequests of household goods, etc. to wife, and children. To wife, and two youngest sons, Edwards and William. John Thompson and Thomas Lane Exers. 15 Dec., 1696. Prob.: 5 Mar., 1699/1700. Probate granted to Elizabeth Pettaway, admrx. Wit: James Stanton, Jannett Wilson, Joyce Brittle. Book 5, p. 197.

PETTWAY, Edward: Leg.- To daughter, Eliza., wife to Samuel Judkins, twenty shilling. To daughter, Joyce, wife of Bartholomew Brittle, ten shillings. To daughter, Fortune Pettway, certain household goods, if she do not marry Will. Huggins; if she do, only 10 shillings. To Sarah, daughter of Robert Judkins, a hog. To son, Wm. Pettway, all my estate, and make him Exer. 27 Oct., 1690. Prob.: 6 Jan., 1690. Wit: Wm. Iles, Theoph. Forbush, Honor Blake. Book 4, p. 182.

PETTWAY, Joseph: Leg.- To daughter, Jane, five pounds, cash and negro. To son, Wm. Pettway, my Plantation in Brunswick County and one negro. To son, Joseph Pettway, 50 pounds cash and one negro. To son, Micajah, all land in Surry County, hot still, two negroes etc. The rest of money goods etc. to be equally divided Joseph, William and Micajah. Made 1745. Prob.: 19 Mar., 1745. Wit: Thos. Wrenn, John Hancell. Book 9, p. 522.

PETTWAY, Robert: Leg.- To son, Robert, the Plantation where I live, 50 acres, it being a track I purchase fo Wm. Brittle & track I bought of Henry Hart, 150 acres, and one negro; to have the est. at 18 years old. To sons, Edward and John bequests of money and negroes, and to have est. at 18 years old. To daughters, Mary and Elizabeth the same. Wife, Ruth, and son, Robert the rest of est., and makes them Exers. 26 Dec., 1728. Prob.: 19 March, 1728. Wit: Wm. Edwards, Wm. Edwards, Jr., George Mosely. Book 7, p. 902.

PHARLOW, Joseph: Leg.- Gives wife, Eliza Pharlow all worldly estate, and makes her Exerx. Child in esse provided for; if it die to Nicholas Willson, 12 April, 1679. Prob.: 6 May, 1679. Wit: Francis Taylor, Jno. Davis, Rich. Miller. Book 2, p. 206.

PHILLIPS, David: Est.- 5 June, 1696. Eliza. Phillips made oath to Inventory. Hezekiah Bunnell, John Sharp. Book 5, p. 108.

PHILLIPS, John: Est.- Ruth Phillips, Exerx. of John Phillips. Signed: Wm. Holt, Jno. Clark, William Newitt. 8 Apr., 1699. Book 5, p. 180.

PHILLIPS, John: Est.- By Thomas Phillips. 20 Oct., 1714.

Signed: Wm. Pulley, Thos. Middleton, John Griffin. Book
6, p. 213.

PHILLIPS, Joel: Est.- 30 May, 1691. Alis Phillips made oath
to Inventory. James Elis, Nicho. Witherington. Book 4,
p. 204.

PHILLIPS, John: Est.- 20 May, 1749. Geo. Cryer, Robt. Wager.
Book 9, p. 631.

PHILLIPS, Mary: Leg.- To daughter, Mary Edwards, wife of John
Edwards, my Plantation where I live for her life, then to
my daughter, Ann Phillips. To daughter, Ann, one negro,
and at her death said negro to my granddaughter, Ann Edwards. Gives daughter, Ann Phillips, 25 lbs. current money,
8 new pewter dishes, falling table, 6 Russia chairs,
tankard, riding horse etc.; if no issue to go to granddaughters, Mary Hancocke and Ann Edwards. Bequest to niece
Mary Crafford, daughter of Carter Crafford, of 40 shillings.
To sons, William and Swann Phillips; dau. Eliza. Hancocke
and Mary Edwards, each six pounds cur. money. To John Edwards, my son-in-law, four bbls. corn. To son, Wm. Phillips and Wm. Harrison the same. Rest of est. to be equally
divided among my five children; Wm., and Swann Phillips,
Eliza. Hancocke, Mary Edwards, and Ann Phillips. Friend,
Carter Crafford, Exer. 28 Mar., 1727. 19 Apr., 1727. Wit:
Wm. Newsum, Samuel Tayler, John Ruffin. Bk. 7, p. 697.

PHILLIPS, Nathaniel: Leg.- To Nathaniel Clanton all my estate.
22 Feb., 1729/30. Prob.: 21 Feb., 1738. Wit: Edward
Clanton, Thomas Don ?, Sarey Clanton. Book 9, p. 15.

PHILLIPS, William: Leg.- To my son, John, the Plantation given
to my wife by her father, Mathew Swann, and plantation
where Simon Murphy lately lived, purchased of James Briggs.
Son, Mathew Phillips. Daughter, Anne. Son, William Phillips the Plantation purchased of Wm. Hooker. Son, Swann
Phillips the Plantation in Isle of Wight County, purchased
of William Edwards. To Mathew Phillips land Mathew Swann
gave to his daughter, Sarah, now wife of Carter Crafford.
Daughter, Elizabeth, Daughter, Anne. Made 14 Feb., 1720.
Prob.: 19 April, 1721. Wit: Joseph Wattel, Wm. Newsum,
Carter Crafford. Book 7, p. 323.

PHILLIPS, William: Est.- By Mary Phillips. 16 Aug., 1721.
Signed: Wm. Drew, Martin Johnson, John Price. Book 7,
p. 359.

PHILLIPS, William: Leg.- To daughter, Mary 23 shillings, bed,
round table, gray horse, etc. To son, John, Trooper's Arms,
etc. To daughter, Sarah, chest, lock and key, cows, etc.
To daughter, Faith, silver beaker, pewter plates, etc.
Puts daughter, Sarah, under the care of Mrs. Ann Hamlin until she is eighteen years old. Makes son, John, and dau.,
Mary Exers. Wit: Nicholas Maget, Thos. Rooks, Jane Rooks.
5 Dec., 1734. Prob.: 15 Jan., 1734. Book 8, p. 437.

PICKERILL, William: Leg.- To Hanah Pickerill, my wife, my estate and makes her Exerx. Made: 31 Aug., 1701. Prob.:
3 March, 1701/2. Book 5, p. 237.

PIDINGTON, Thomas: Leg.- To eldest son, Thomas Piddington, my
house and land after my wife's death. To my three sons,
three guns, ye eldest to have his choice, and so to young-

est. The rest of my estate to my wife, Abigail and my
three children. Made: 13 Feb., 1701/2. Prob.: __ __,
1702. Wit: Wm. Rookings. Book 5, p. 246.

PILAND, George: Leg.- To wife, Mary, household goods, livestock, negroes, etc. to be sold and money equally divided
among three daughters, Mary, Martha and Priscilla. Makes
son, Richard and my wife Exers. Give wife Plantation for
life, then to son, Richard. Wit: Will Edwards, Samuel
Judkins. Made: 13 Dec., 1743. Prob.: 17 July, 1745.
Book 9, p. 506.

PINGINTON, Edward: Leg.- To son, Edward Pinginton, the Land
and Plantation where I now live, 230 acres, beg. at mouth
of Pasture Branch..to mouth of Wyche's Swamp Branch, the
mother of said lessee to have for her widowhood, on Land
and Plantation. To son, John Pingington, 230 akers of
land beg. at mouth of Ingen Branch..to Wyche's Branch...
to Hunting Quarter Swamp..to Hogpen Branch. To son, Edmond Pingington, all the remaining part of land between Edwards and John, 230 akers. To wife, a negro, and the remainder of the estate to wife and children. Wit: Wm.
Andrus, John Hatly, Nich. Bush. Made: 20 Nov., 1727.
Prob.: 17 April, 1728. Presented in Court by Tabitha
Pingington. Book 7, p. 799.

PITT, Charles: Leg.- To wife, two cows. To daughter, Milea,
dishes & plates. Son, Joseph Pitt. Daughter, Lucy, dishes
etc. To son, Joseph Pitt all the rest of the estate, and
makes him Exer. Made: 3 Jan., 1748. Prob.: 16 Oct.,
1750. Wit: Wm. Edwards, Jos. Clark. Book 9, p. 664.

POAKE, John: Leg.- To Laurence House my gun, sword and bolt.
To Wm. Macklin, bed, rugs, etc. To Mary Belinsbe all that
I possess within and without doors. Makes Wm. Macklin,
Exer. 9 Mar., 1724. Prob.: 19 May, 1725. Wit: John
Rainer, Henry Bailes, Thos. House. Book 7, p. 582.

POKE, John: Est.- Appraised by John Davis, John Brown and
Adam Tapley. Mary Belinsbe, Exerx. 21 July, 1725. Book
7, p. 590.

PORCHE, James: Leg.- (Illegible in first part) Son, Henry
Porche the place he lives on. Wife, where I live for her
life. Son, James Porch, 115 acres. To grandson, Alex.
Hay a bed rug etc. after my wife's death. To wife, Margery Porch, the rest of the est. Makes son, Henry Porch,
Exer. Wit: John Paynton, Wm. Bridges, Alex. Hay. Made:
6 Feb., 1732/3. Prob.: 21 Mar., 1732. Book 8, p. 264.

PORTIS, Edward: Leg.- Confirms to John Drew a sale of land
and to Christopher Clinch. Est. to be divided between
wife, Elizabeth, and four children (not named). Made: 11
March, 1719. Prob.: 18 July, 1722. Wit: Joseph Delk,
Robert Griffin, Thos. Holt, Wm. Judkins. Book 7, p. 407.

PORTIS, Edward: Estate- Elizabeth Portis Exerx. A servant
called James Eustace listed. 17 Oct., 1722. Wit: Thos.
Edwards, Jas. Seward, Thso. Taylor. Book 7, p. 419.

POTTER, Roger: Leg.- Makes wife, Ann, Exerx. and gives to her
his whole estate. Makes friends, Coll. Wm. Browne and his
son, Mr. Wm. Browne, overseers of the will. Made: 19
Sept., 1695. Prob.: 7 Jan., 1695. Book 5, p. 84.

PRETLOW, Joseph: Est.- By Wm. Drew. 18 Dec., 1740. Signed: Newitt Edwards, John Glover. Book 9, p. 416.

PRICE, Francis: Leg.- Mentions wife, and "All my children". Makes wife, Exerx. Wit: Thos. Binns, Charles Binns. Made 16 March, 1721. Prob.: 21 June, 1721. Book 7, p. 348.

PRICE, Francis: Est.- John Price, admr. 21 Nov., 1722. Signed: Nich. Maget, Thos. Cocke. Book 7, p. 425.

PRICE, John: Leg.- To my wife the use of my Plantation for her life, then to my son-in-law, Stephen Simmons, also negroes etc. Makes Stephen Simmons Exer. Made: 10 June, 1747. Prob.: 21 June, 1748. Wit: Nicholas Thompson, John Drew, Daniell Sebrell. Book 9, p. 579.

PRICE, Richard: Est.- Wm. Drummond, admr. Sworn to by Capt. John Ruffin. Signed: Wm. Edwards, John Newsum, Thos. Edwards. 18 Feb., 1735. Book 8, p. 568.

PRITCHARD, Morris: Leg.- To son, John 120 acres on Roanoke River, part of Land I bought of Wm. Lashley, with all buildings etc. To son, Richard, 100 acres of the above tract. To John Watts a water course through my land for convenience of a mill. To son, Casey, 100 acres of the first mentioned tract of land. To wife, Elizabeth, the use of my Plantation for her life, then to be divided between my children. Wit: Samuel Peete, Ann Prescott, Rachel Prescott. Made: 9 Nov., 1748. Prob.: 20 Dec., 1748. Book 9, p. 594.

PROCTOR, George: Est.- Jno. Moring, admr. 1 July, 1679. Sec. Robert Ruffin, Wm. Brown. Wit: Sam. Swann, Wm. Edwards. Book 2, p. 3.

PROCTOR, George: Est.- By Jno. Moring, admr. 6 March, 1682. Paid Mr. Sam. Thompson his part of Maj. Marriott's Est. in right of his wife. Book 2, p. 326.

PROCTOR, Joshua: Leg.- To sons, Robert and Richard Proctor 566 acres of Land adjoining to Spring Branch..Mr. Richard Washington, and Henry Watkins on west side of son, Richard's house. To son, Nicholas Proctor, 160 acres, where I now live. To daughter, Elizabeth Rowland, 10 sheep. To daughter, Katherine, 40 shillings. To daughter, Sarah, five pounds. Daughters, Mary and Hannah. Makes son, Robert, Exer. Wit: Nich. Smith, Allen Warren, Wm. Warren, Thos. Smith. Made: 22 March, 1717/18. Prob.: 20 Jan., 1719. Book 7, p. 235.

PULISTONE, John: Leg.- Bequest to wife, Ann. Assigns to wife, Ann, Power of Attorney from Mrs. Alice Stransford, widow, of London and Administration of Mr. Anthony Stranford, of London, merchant.. 12 Sept., 1669. Wit: Thos. Waller, Alice Waller, Mary Waller. Made 15 May, 1704. Prob.: 2 Sept., 1704. Book 5, p. 374.

PULLY, William: Leg.- To son, William Pulley, one shilling. To daughter, Martha Moss, a mare. To daughter, Hanah Clark, bed furniture etc. To Grandson, William Pully, all of my Land after my wife's decease. To wife, Mary, the remainder of my estate, and makes her Exerx. Wit: Wm. Rookings, Wm. Speed, Mathew Hubard. Made: 29 Mar., 1738. Prob.: 19 April, 1738. Book 8, p. 812.

RAINE, Simon: Est.- 16 Aug., 1738. Book 8, p. 887.

RAINES, John: Leg.- (This will is for most part illegible.)
"unto Richard Raines. Mentions child in esse. Makes wife
Exerx. Made: 18 Aug., 1731. Prob.: 19 Jan., 1731. Wit:
James Maclin, Jno. Denton, Edmond Denton, John Maclin.
Book 8, p. 151.

RANDAL, George: Est.- By James Sammon. Signed: Eliza Randal.
26 Feb., 1711/12. John Hathorn, John Hicks. Book 6, p.
103.

RANDALL, George: Leg.- To son, Peter, gun, sword, livestock
and furniture from his mother when 21 years old. William
Ramey to have my son, Peter and his estate, to keep till
said Peter comes to age of 21 years, but have part of his
time to 18 years old. To my youngest son (not named) two
cows, hogs, my flock bed etc. To daughter, Mary, the remainder of the estate. Wit: Mary Samon, Francis Maybury,
Robert Wynne. Made: 10 Feb., 1710. Prob.: 25 Nov., 1711.
Book 6, p. 81.

RANDALL, George: By Mary Randall. 17 Jan., 1742. Robert Farrington, Edward Farrington. Book 9, p. 422.

RANDOL, Peter: Est.- Mary Randol, admr. 21 Oct., 1741. Thos.
Vines, Thos. Mathis. Book 9, p. 386.

RANSOM, James: Leg.- To daughters, Catherine, Elizabeth and
Mary, negroes etc. To father and mother, five pounds, 20
shillings a year. To Elizabeth Smith two cows when of
age or married. To wife the use of the Plantation and a
negro for life, then to son, James, and gives James 25
pounds to purchase land. Gives to son, Gwathmey 25 pounds
to purchase land. Makes wife, James Baker, Charles Binns,
and John Ruffin Exers. Rest of estate to two sons. Made:
19 May, 1710. Prob.: 15 Oct., 1740. Wit: Arthur Smith,
James Carrell. Book 9, p. 227.

RAWLINGS, Elizabeth: Granted probate on the estate of her husband, Roger Rawlings. 21 April, 1695. Book 5, p. 47.

RAWLINGS, John: Leg.- To daughter, Elizabeth Rawlings four
pewter dishes, livestock etc. To wife, Elinor Rawlings
all the rest of my estate, and to my two children, Mary and
John when of age. Makes wife Exerx. Wit: George Lee,
John Legrand. Made: 6 March, 1673. Prob.: 1 July, 1674.
Book 2, p. 59.

RAWLINGS, John: Leg.- To son, Jno. Rawlings all my Land at
Blackwater in fee simple, and appurtenances thereto belonging, cattle, horses, hogs, a sword and musket etc. To son,
Gregory Rawlings, the house and land where I now live, 126
acres of land, and appurtenances belonging, also coopers
tools etc. and books. Son, Gregory to be of age on
Christmas day before he is 18 years old, and have ye Plantation. Daughter, Eliza. Partin to have cattle, hogs, etc.
together with other things in her possession. All the rest
of estate to wife, after debts are paid. Wife, Mary,
Exerx. Made: __ Aug., 1702. Prob.: 25 May, 1703. Wit:
Robert Nicholson, Hannah Nicholson, Sampson Lainer. Book
5, p. 279.

RAWLINGS, Roger: Leg.- To daughter, Elizabeth Petway, one

lamb. Small bequests to Wm. Petway's four sons, daughter,
Mary; dau. Eliza. To Sarah Hickman, one lamb. Makes wife
Eliza. Rawlings, Exerx. Wit: Richard Harding, Mary Hick-
man, Mary Phillips. Made: 19 Sept., 1694. Prob.: 5
Mar., 1694.

RAY, Francis: Leg.- To son, William Ray the tract of Land
where I live, 50 acres on north side of Blackwater. To
wife, Affiah, rem. of est. for life, then to two children
to be equally divided. Mentions child in esse, and gives
it an iron wedge, if a boy. William not 21 years old.
Makes wife, Exerx. Wit: Wm. Cooper, Fra. Ray, Benj. Reeks.
Made: 29 Apr., 1738. Prob.: 19 Mar., 1739. Book 9, p.
142.

RAY, Joseph: Leg.- To brother, Francis Ray, and to Harry
Floyd all estate in the hands of Thomas Farmer, and makes
them Exers. Wit: Wm. Kinchen, Wm. Barlow, Eliza. Partin.
Made: 10 June, 1721. Prob.: 21 June, 1721. Book 7, p.
342.

RAY, William: Leg.- To wife, Marthy, ye Plantation at Coper-
honk, for her life, and at her death to my son, Lenard Ray.
Rest of est. to wife, and makes her Exerx. Made: 9 Dec.,
1735. Prob.: 21 July, 1736. Wit: Henry Sowerby, Benjamin Sowerby. Book 8, p. 613.

RAYE, William: Leg.- (Too illegible and torn to read) Eldest
son...William Ray...Wife...Makes brother-in-law Wm. Pitman,
Exer. William Ray, one of the Exrs., presents will in
Court. Wit: Howell Briggs, Wm. Clary, Rich. Parker.
Made: 1 June, 1731. Prob.: 20 Oct., 1731.

READE, Margaret: Est.- Wm. Edwards, admr. Debtor to Wm.
Reade's estate. 28 Feb., 1693/4. John Moring, Will. Frowman. Book 4, p. 351.

READE, William: Est.- Wife, Margaret Reade appeared in Court,
and swore to the correct Inventory. 27 July, 1687. John
Malden, James Forbush, James Ellis. Book 4, p. 9.

READYHOT, Richard: Est.- 2 Sept., 1707. Geo. Blow, Richard
Holleman. Book 5, p. __.

REDDICK, James: Est.- Com. of admr. granted to Alice Reddick,
Relict, on the estate. 21 April, 1695. Bk. 5, p. 44.

REDING, Thos.: Est.- Mary Reding, widow of Thos. Reding, petitions the Court, her husband dying without a will is not
able to pay for administration; desires to pay off debt as
convenient to herself, will pay from her own labor, not
enough of estate. 12 May, 1676. Book 2, p. 117.

REDYHOOS, Richard: Est.- 3 Jan., 1709. Wm. Browne, John
Simmons. Book 5, p. 438.

REEKS, Richard: Leg.- To son, Thomas Reeks, cow, gun, sword
etc. when 21 years old. To daughter, Elizabeth Reeks, a
cow at 18 years old. To daughter, Jane, the same. To wife,
Faith, all the rest of the estate. Wit: Francis Sowerby,
Richard Resbe, Nich. Maget. Made: 10 Jan., 1708. Prob.:
6 July, 1709. Book 5, p. 417.

REEKS, Thomas: Leg.- To sister, Elizabeth Collier, cattle, bed

furniture, etc. To sister, Mary Dawson one cow. To
sister, Sarah Howser one cow. To sister, Faith Dudley one
cow. To William Collier, son of my sister, Elizabeth Collier, a gun. Makes brother, John Phillips, Exer. and gives
him all movable property and all land. If John Phillips
die, to Wm. Collier. Wit: John Jarrett, Anne Jarrett,
Geo. Barrick. Made: 15 Feb., 1744. Prob.: 20 Feb.,
1744. Book 9, p. 491.

REGAN, Daniel: Leg.- To eldest son, Francis, 70 acres of Land
after ye decease of his mother, adjoining my plantation;
but they must agree to live together; if not, to be equally
divided between them, but wife to have choice. To son,
Daniel, 50 acres of Land adjoining to son, Francis, when
18 years old. Thirdly, to son, Jeremiah, 50 acres of land
next adjoining son, Daniel's land. Fourthly, gives to
sonne, John, 50 acres next adjoining Francis. Rest of estate to wife, and children. Land lately purchased in
Charles Citty County from James Mumford, 50 acres, Francis
to sell and pay all my debts. Wife and Francis Exers.
Prob.: 2 Nov., 1686. Wit: John King, Nich. Meriweather,
Jeremiah Sowerby. Book 3, p. 88.

REGAN, Daniell: Est.- 6 Oct., 1687. Francis Regan and Eliza.
Regan appeared in Court and swore that the Inventory was
correct. Jno. Moring, Jno. Watkins, Sam'll Thompson.
Book 3, p. 16.

REGAN, Francis: Leg.- To son, Francis, 150 acres of Land adjoining the Mill Swamp on the west, now in possession of
my son, Joseph, and also pewter dishes and plates etc. To
son, Joseph a large silver dram cup, and one gun etc. To
son, Richard, five pounds current money. To four daus.
Eliza., Jane, Mary and Faith each one pound, 5 shillings.
To son, John, a pewter dish, pewter plates etc. To wife,
the Plantation I live on, and Land I have rented to Mr.
Thompson and all the rest of my estate, but if she marry
my Plantation and Land to son, John, and part that is
rented to be equally divided. Wife, Jane, Exerx. Made:
19 Mar., 1725/26. Prob.: 16 Aug., 1727. Wit: Wm. Bolden,
Martha Thompson, Elizabeth Regan. Book 7, p. 748.

REIVES, John: Est.- Grace Reives, admr. 15 June, 1720. Giles
Underhill, Samuel Clarke, Henry Meacham. Book 7, p. 27.

REIVES, Timothy: Est.- 19 June, 1717. Estate paid children
of deceased their part. Robert Wynne, Wm. Browne, Jr.
Book 7, p. ___.

REN, Joseph: Est.- 19 Feb., 1750. Thos. Peters, Thos. Peters,
Jr. Book 9, p. 80.

RENOLDS, Grace, widow: Nuncupative will. To daughter, Mary
Reynolds yards of exenburg for her bed. Bequests to kins-
women, Hester Brown, dau., of John Brown, Mary Clark, dau.
of Sampson Clark, Susannah Clark, daughter of Thomas Clark.
Made: 15 Dec., 1711. Prob.: 19 xber, 1711. Wit: Sampson Clark. Book 6, p. 90.

REYNOLDS, Grace: Est.- Amt. due for funeral of herself and
son. 17 Dec., 1712. Samson Clarke. Book 6, p. 130.

REYNOLDS, Robert: Leg.- Age 60 years or thereabouts. To my
wife, my Plantation I live on as long as she is a widdow.

To grandson, Nicholas, the Plantation that my son, Robert,
now lives on when 21 years old. To daughter, Susannah, a
featherbed, 6 pewter dishes, a tankard, 6 spoons, livestock
etc. To daughter, Elizabeth, one cow. To grandson, Robert
Griffin one cow. Wife, Elizabeth, the rest of my estate.
Wit: Jno. Griffin, Agnes Griffin, Henry Baker. Made:
30 Jan., 1702/3. Prob.: 2 Mar., 1702. Book 5, p. 267.

REYNOLDS, Robert: Est.- Signed: Grace Reynolds. 5 July, 1709.
Edward Moreland, John Hancocke. Book 5, p. 414.

RICHARDSON, John: Leg.- To son, Hopkins a round table, 3 cows
etc. To son, Hardy, a bason, 3 cows etc. To son, John,
three cows, pewter bason etc. To wife, Elizabeth, the use
of my Plantation and Land for her life, and at her death
to my son, John. No date. Prob.: 20 Oct., 1747. Wit:
Samuel Maget, Olive Mangum. Book 9, p. 561.

RICHARDSON, William: Leg.- To son, William Richardson, one
negro. Daughter, Mary Wynne, one negro. To son, Joseph
Richardson, one negro, and this Plantation I now live on
after the death of his mother. Mentions, wife, Martha. To
daughter, Mary Wynne a tract of Land..on Nottoway River.
Three youngest daughters, Susannah, Betty and Patty. Wit:
Robert Farrington, Joshua Ellis, Mary Green. Made: 4 Feb.,
1742. Prob.: 18 Feb., 1742. Book 9, p. 548.

RIDDICK, James, Sen.: Est.- By Alice Riddick, admr. 21 Oct.,
1693. Book 4, p. 339.

RIDLEY, Thomas: Est.- By Mary Ridley, admr. 4 March, 1718/19.
Thos. Holt, John Hancocke, Wm. Harris. Book 7, p. 174.

RIDLEY, Thomas: Est.- 20 Nov., 1723. William Seward married
the Exerx. Book 7, p. 485.

RIVERS, William: Leg.- To wife and sweet children all my estate to be equally divided, after my debts are paid. Makes
wife, Elizabeth, Exerx. and Wm. Sandborn, Exer. Children
are all under 18 years old. Wit: John Rickes, George
Rochelle. Made: 9 Aug., 1698. Prob.: 7 March, 1698/9.
(John Rickes, Jr. for above wit.) Book 5, p. 164.

RIVES, George: Leg.- To wife, Frances Rives the use and labor
of two negroes for life, if she marry, to son Geo. Rives
the Land on the north side of Joneshole Swamp, being at the
county line of Thweat's Branch, to south fork of Cherry
Orchard Branch..to Pasmore land, with four negroes, bed,
pewter and 20 pounds. To son, George, the Land and Plantation where I live, 200 acres, with buildings, and 275
acres in Price George County, with four negroes and 20
pounds. To son, Christopher Rives, 400 acres, beginning at
the Old Road on Henry Mitchell's line..down Busby's line
and 235 acres in Brunswick County, on south side of the
Nottoway River, negroes etc. To son, Timothy, 400 acres,
extending to son, John's line at Pasmore's corner, negroes
etc. To daughter, Judith, four negroes, dishes, beds, etc.
Wife have use of plantation for her .widowhood then to be
equally divided among her three sons, Geo., Christopher and
Timothy. To daughter, Frances Rives two negroes and six
plates etc. To brother Timothy 225 acres on Main Fork of
Cherry Orchard Branch, where he now lives. To brother
William Rives, 50 acres where he lives. Makes son, John
Rives, Exer. Made: 14 May, 1746. Prob.: 20 Aug., 1746.

Wit: Thomas Davis, Peter Hawthorne, Chris. Tatum. Book
9, p. 535.

RIVES, John: Est.- By Sarah Rives. 19 June, 1750. Edward
Pettway, Peter Poythress, Henry Mitchell. Book 9, p. 643.

ROBBARDS, John: Leg.- To grandson, John Shands my Plantation
on Otterdam Swamp and four negroes, bed etc. To daughter
Nazarath Shands two negroes. To granddaughter, Mary Shands
one negro. To Susannah Epps two negroes. To Mary Pettway
two negroes. To daughter, Elizabeth Pettway, and her husband and then to her cousin, Elizabeth Pettway, one negro.
To granddaughter, Elizabeth Pettway, one negro. Makes two
sons-in-law, Wm. Shands and Wm. Pettway Exers. Made: 11
Sept., 1740. Prob.: 21 Jan., 1740. Wit: Robert Wynne,
Peter Hawthorne, John Hawthorne. Book 9, p. 263.

ROBERTS, Nathaniel: Leg.- To Thos. Mathews in lieu of deed not
written a small parcell of land between Clay's Branch and
path from Capt. Potter's to Edward Grantham's, and where I
have sold about 80 acres to said Mathews and not confirmed
the title to 80 acres. To Nathaniel Harrison a gray mare
branded T.M. To wife, Elizabeth, all the rest of my land
and all personal estate, and makes her Exer. Made: 19
April, 1693. Prob.: 5 Sept., 1693. Wit: Benj. Harrison,
James Boswell. Book 4, p. 323.

ROBERTS, Nathaniel: Est.- Probate granted to Eliza. Andrews,
and her husband, Bartholomew Andrews on the Will of Nathaniel Roberts, who appointed his Relict, Elizabeth Robberts,
Exer. and she since married to Bartholomew Andrews. 26
Oct., 1694. Book 5, p. 25.

ROBERTSON, Christopher: Est.- Mary Robertson, admr. 21 Feb.,
1727. Signed: Wm. Malone, Edward Farrington, Henry
Gauler. Book 7, p. 784.

ROBERTSON, Christopher: Est.- Thomas Bryan and Mary, his wife,
admr. 20 Aug., 1729. Chris. Tatum, Howell Briggs. Book
7, p. 965.

ROBERTSON, Nathaniel: Est.- Signed: Thos. Freeman, admr. 19
Sept., 1711. Appraisers: James Sammon, Jno. Hawthorne,
Thos. Thrower. Book 6, p. 79.

ROBERTSON, Nathaniel: Leg.- To wife, Elizabeth, the use of
negro until my son, Drury comes of age of 21 years. To son,
Drury Robertson, horse, saddle, bridle, gun and livestock,
sword and Lower Plantation on the south side of south west
Swamp. To child in esse the Upper Plantation and Land. To
wife the remainder of the estate. Made: 2 Jan., 1734.
Prob.: 15 Oct., 1735. Wit: Henry Freeman, Christ. Rob-
bertson, Peter Green. Book 8, p. 527.

ROBINSON, Andrew: Est.- 24 May, 1677. Anne Robinson testified
to the true Inventory of her husband's estate, except what
Mr. Salway carried away for debt and other things sold to
buy corn "For my children to eat". Book 2, p. 113.

ROBINSON, Ann: Est.- 2 April, 1678. Math. Swann, Wm. Newsum.
Book 2, p. 172.

ROBINSON, James: Est.- Thomas Davis, admr. 28 April, 1697.
Wm. Gray, Wm. Foster. Book 5, p. 138.

RODWELL, John: Est.- 18 April, 1703. Wm. Chambers, Robert Crafford, Wm. Jackson. Book 5, p. 277.

ROGERS, Benjamin: Est.- 17 Oct., 1744. Benjamin Ellis, admr. Robt. Judkins, Samuel Maget, Jane Nicholson. Bk. 9, p. 489.

ROGERS, John: Est.- John Rivers, and Mary Rivers, admr. 4 May, 1697. Book 5, p. 138.

ROGERS, Richard: Leg.- To son, John a Neck of Land that runs to ye Crick of one side and the Old Field in ye other, guided with the Mill Path, also a heifer and a gun. To son, Richard, ye Neck of Land yt runs from the Cod of ye Swampe to Barker's path and see to ye ould road, also a heifer and a gun. To son, William, ye Remainder of ye land that passes from ye oulde Rode to Barker's cart path to the head of the Land, also a heifer. To John and Richard beds, rugs etc. To godson, Richard Hide a cow at seventeen years. Sons not to lease or mortgage their land. Daughter, Mary. Bequest to wife, of the Plantation where I live, for her life. Wit: Abraham Heath, Thomas Milton. Made: 27 March, 1678. Prob.: 7 May, 1678. Book 2, p. 174.

ROGERS, William: Leg.- Mentions wife, and makes her Exerx. Mentions sister, Mary Rivers, Nephew Grace Rivers; Nephew Mary Rivers; Nephew, John Rivers. Wit: Robert Nicholson, George Nicholson, Richard Fones. Prob.: 2 Sept., 1701. Book 5, p. 226.

ROGERS, William: Leg.- To my youngest son, William Rogers, my Plantation 400 acres, which I had of my wife, Elizabeth, called his in my life time. To my son, William Rogers, what I had of my former wife to the value of 5 shillings. To my son, Benjamin Rogers to the value of 5 shillings. To my son, Robert Rogers to the value of 5 shillings. To my daughter, Elizabeth Ellis, to the value of 5 shillings. To my daughter, Mary Bennit to the value of 5 shillings. To my daughter, Sarah Bennit, to the value of 5 shillings. To my daughter, Persilla Procktor, to the value of 5 shillings. Son, Joseph Rogers, to the value of 5 shillings. To daughter, Jane Rogers, to the value of 5 shillings. Wife, Elizabeth, all the remainder of worldly goods. Wit: Elizabeth Washington, Priscilla Thomas, Thomas Washington. Made: 8 Jan., 1724/25. Prob.: 17 May, 1727. Bk. 7, p. 706.

ROOKINGS, William: Leg.- Of Flying Point, Surry County. To son, William, my house and land. The rest of the estate to be divided among my three children, viz: Daughter, Elizabeth, son, William, daughter, Jane. If children die before of age, their third of the estate to return to the children of Capt. Nicholas Wyatt, and their heirs. A negro to cousin, Mary Short's children. Son, William to be well educated and daughter a fitting education. Desires that William Badger, of Martin's Brandon, to be admitted to live at my Plantation and look after negroes and Plantation. Desires that Capt. Nicholas Wyatt, or his wife, Francis and William Simmons, and John King be overseers of, and guardian of children. Wit: Edward Greenwood, John Gallow. Prob.: 1 July, 1679. Book 2, p. 213.

ROOKINGS, William: Leg.- To daughter, Elizabeth Rookings, if she marries to her husband, the property that Mr. Bartholomew Clements gave me. To daughter, Susannah and her husband, Charles Hamlin, property known as "Greens", at their death to my son, William Rookings. To daughter Mary Rookings, if she marry to her husband, land at the head of Wm. Knott's Swamp, and at their death to my son, James Rookings. Mentions son James Rookings, daughter, Ann Rookings, daughter Jane Rookings, son, William Rookings. Wife, Ann Rookings. Friends, Coll. Nathaniel Harrison, Capt. Henry Harrison, Mr. William Cocke, Mr. John Simmons, Exers. Wit: John Simmons, George Hagood, Rachell Lewis. Made: 1 Feb., 1715. Prob.: 16 March, 1714. Book 6, p. 224.

ROOKINGS, William: Est.- 19 June, 1750. Charles Lucas, Thos. Shrewsbury, John Collier. Book 9, p. 646.

ROSE, Richard: Leg.- Son, Thomas 28 shillings to his account. To son, Richard, a cow. To Granddaughter, Hannah, bed, cow, etc. To son, Richard all the rest of my estate, if no heirs to granddaughter Hannah, if she die, to daughter, Jane. Mentions wife, Elizabeth. Daughter, Jane Rose, Exerx. Wit: John Nicholson, Jno. Ogburn. Made: 20 Oct., 1736. Prob.: 15 Dec., 1736. Book 8, p. 653.

ROWELL, Edward: Leg.- To son, Edward, 30 shillings. To son, Richard 30 shillings. To daughter, Elizabeth, wife to Matthew Ellis, 30 shillings. To daughter, Mary Rowell, thirty shillings. To daughter, Margaret Rowell, 30 shillings. To daughter, Jemima Rowell, thirty shillings. Son, Samuel Rowell, 40 shillings. Mentions wife, Elizabeth, and makes her Exerx. Wit: Wm. Edwards, Ellen Taylor. Made 20 March, 1727. Prob.: 21 May, 1729. Book 7, p. 927.

ROWELL, Richard: Leg.- To two sons, Robert and Richard a tract of Land in Brunswick County to be equally divided. Land in Surry to be sold, when sons are of age and money divided equally between wife and two sons. Exerx., wife, Mary. Made: 18 Oct., 1743. Prob.: 16 April, 1746. Wit: Jos. John Clinch, Wm. Clinch. Book 9, p. 529.

ROWSUM, James: Est.- 15 Jan., 1727. By Thos. Edmunds, Benjamin Chapman Donaldson, Rich. Norwood, Thos. Allstin. Book 7, p. 778.

RUFFIN, Elizabeth: Leg.- To daughter, Jane Ruffin one negro, new feather bed with curtains, vallance etc. which my son, Robert, promised me to find her by our agreement over the house and other goods to him, also a small table, chest, looking glass, pewter dishes and plates. If no heir to sons, William Ruffin and son, Robert Ruffin. Makes daughter, Jane, Exerx. Wit: William Gray, Jr., Olive Chambers. Made: 29 July, 1711. Prob.: 18 Aug., 1714. Book 6, p. 207.

RUFFIN, Robert: Leg.- To my wife the Plantation I now live on for her life, and at her death to my son, Robert Ruffin, and for want of heirs, to my son, William Ruffin. All the rest of my estate to my two sons, Robert and William, in the land at Pokotink, or Bowling Green Swamp..to Wm. Rowland's path..to Sunken Marsh path, eastward to son, Robert, and the other part to son, William. Gives negro, and silver tumbler to Robert, when he is 21 years old. To son, William, a negro and a silver porringer, when 21 years old. Bequest to daughter, Elizabeth's first born child. Wife to give to daughters as they come of age, or marry. Fra. Mason and Arthur Allen overseers of will. Wife made Exerx. Made: 8 May, 1693. Prob.: 4 July, 1693. Wit: Wm. Chambers, Wm. Newsum, Roger Rawlins. Book 4, p. 310.

RUFFIN, Robert: Leg.- Wife to have the labor of certain slaves for life then to son, John Ruffin. Estate to be equally divided with sons Joseph and Benjamin, and Edmund, daus. Mary, Martha and Elizabeth or survivors of them. To wife, Elizabeth, the remainder of the est, and makes her Exerx. Made: 13 April, 1720. Prob.: 15 Feb., 1720. Wit: John Newsum, James Willson. Book 7, p. 296.

RUGBEE, William: Est.- 12 March, 1687/8. Edward Pettway, Jno. Phillips. Book 4, p. 75.

RYEVES, Timothy: Est.- By Judith Ryeves, admrx. 16 Jan., 1716. George Pasmore, John Hicks, John Harthorne. Bk. 7, p. 43.

SANDS, Samuel: Est.- Leonard Oney, admr. 16 June, 1736. Book 8, p. 617.

SAVAGE, Henry: Est.- Sold by Robert Wynne, sub sheriff. 15 July, 1741. Book 9, p. 355.

SAVIDGE, Charles: Leg.- To Robert Savidge all of my housing and Land. If no issue to return to Loveless Savidge, his brother, also household goods, after my wife's death, and Trooper's Arms, two guns etc. To Samuel Blackgrove a horse and saddle, gun, sword etc. at wife's death and to enjoy his freedom. To wife, household good, and whole estate except bequests to Loveless Savidge. All estate to be divided between Robert and Loveless Savidge at wife's death. Makes wife, Exerx. Friends, Francis Regan and Wm. Davidson overseers of will. Will presented by Elizabeth Savidge, Exerx. Made: 17 March, 1713. Prob.: 17 Sept., 1718. Wit: James Stanton, John Lane, Wm. Ham. Book 7, p. 148.

SAVIDGE, Charles: Est.- Coroner for inquest over the body of said Savidge. Cash due the estate of William Davis, Elizabeth Crips, Exerx. 16 Sept., 1719. Thos. Cocke, Wm. Browne, Jr.

SAVIDGE, Henry: Est.- By Elizabeth Savidge. 18 Nov., 1713. Robert Ruffin, Wm. Rookings. Nich. Smith, admr. Book 6, p. 168.

SAVIDGE, Lovelis: Leg.- To son, Lovelis Savidge all of my land after his mother's death. To daughter, Olive Manggam a pewter dish. To son, Robert Savidge a pewter dish. To grandson, Charles Savidge the same. Lends rest of est. to wife for life, then to son, Lovelis. Wit: John Coker, Anthony Evans, James Bennett. 6 Oct., 1728. Prob.: 21 May, 1729. Book 7, p. 943.

SAVIDGE, Robert: Leg.- To wife, (Mary Savidge) my now dwelling place, 265 acres, and at her death to son, Charles Savidge. Mentions son, Lovelis Savidge. Daughter, Olive Andrews household goods, cattle, etc. Mary Savidge, Exerx. Made: 17 March, 1697/8. Prob.: 3 May, 1698. Book 5, p. 155.

SCARBROO, William: Est.- 15 day of 7br, 1679. Wm. Simmons, Henry Francis. On 6 Jan., 1679, Amy, the wife of Thos. Tias swore that Inventory was correct. Book 2, p. 247.

114

SCARBROW, Edward: Est.- By Daniel Duggard, admr. 20 March, 1716. Nich. Cocke, Richard Lewis, Nich. Davis. Book 7, p. 52.

SCARBROW, Edward: Est.- Paid Mr. Cocke, Mr. John Simmons, Ann Scarbrow. Cash paid Grace Lucas. Dau., Duggard. 18 Mar., 1718/19. Book 7, p. 253.

SCARBROW, Edward: Est.- 17 Aug., 1743. Book 7, p. 450.

SCARBROW, William: Est.- By Ann Scarbrow, admrx. 18 Dec., 1777. John Andrews, John Grantham, Chris. Moring, John Avery. Book 7, p. 86.

SCOGGIN, John: Est.- John Scoggin, admr. 12 Nov., 1725. Will. Tomlinson, John Wilerson, Henry Bedingfield. Book 7, p. 615.

SCOGGIN, John: Est.- By Susannah Scoggin. 19 Apr., 1727. Relict of John Scoggin, admrx. Book 7, p. 698.

SCOGGIN, John: Est.- 21 Feb., 1727. Alex. Chisnall, admr. Henry Bedingfield, John Doby, Daniel Epes. Bk. 7, p. 785.

SCOTT, Adam: Est.- Comfort Scott, admrx. 21 Aug., 1734. Jas. Chappell, Thos. Peters, Wm. Hindes. Book 8, p. 411.

SCOTT, John: Est.- John Bell, aged 37, testified that Mr. John Scott lived at the house of Mr. Robert Crawford, a-bout a month before he went to Maryland - about August 1703 - in conversation with him, Mr. Scott stated that nei-ther his brother, in Glasgow, Scotland, nor anybody else should inherit his estate, but Mr. Robert Crawford, etc. May Court, 1705, Joanna Moore, servant to Mr. Crawford tes-tified that in July, 1703, she heard Mr. Jno. Scott (then a boarder at Mr. Robert Crawford's) say that neither the Queen, his Mother, Brother, or anybody should have his es-tate, except Mr. Robert Crawford, and have all that he had. __ July, 1705.

SEARLE, Richard: Est.- Appraised by Jos. Malden. 12 March, 1684. Wm. Draper. Book 3, p. 18.

SEAT, Joseph: Est.- By Marshall Seat, admr. 15 Apr., 1741. Book 9, p. 305.

SEAT, Robert: Leg.- "My children", wife, Exerx. 11 Oct., 1701. Prob.: 4 May, 1708. Wit: Joseph Seat, Melchisadeck Duche. Book 5, p. 393.

SEAT, Robert: Est.- Ann Seate, Exerx. 6 July, 1708. Book 5, p. 396.

SEATS, Joseph: Leg.- To son, Joseph Seats my now dwelling place, except he die before marriage, then to son, Marchell Seat. To son, Marchell Seat a piece of land formerly land out of Thomas Seat's, called Bair's Neck, if he will live upon it; if he do not live on it, to go to my son, Joseph Seat. To son, Thomas, sheep, and what he has already re-ceived. To son, Billeson Seat one shilling, besides what he has already had. Daughter, Mary Rose, and son, James, one shilling, and what they have already received. Wife, Mable, rem. of est. and to be equally divided, wife and son, Joseph, and Joseph to keep his mother. Friends,

Edward Bayley and son, Joseph Seat, Exers. Made: 27 Nov., 1737. Prob.: 15 Mar., 1737. Wit: Chris. Moring, Wm. Partin, Elizabeth Hux. Book 8, p. 806.

SEBRELL, David: Leg.- To my nephew, Nathaniel Sebrell (not 21) all my Land and Plantation adjoining Samuell Hargrave on Terrapin Swamp on the south side of Blackwater, and negro at twenty one years old, but if he dies to my two sisters, Sussannah Hancock and Sarah Wilson. Mentions brother-in-law, Joseph Hancock. Made: 7 Nov., 1742. Prob.: 17 Nov., 1742. Wit: Wm. Seward, Wm. Drew. Book 9, p. 419.

SEBRELL, Mary: Leg.- To son, Joseph Sebrell, 5 lbs., current money. To son, Benjamin Sebrell five pounds Cur. Money at 21 years old. To daughter, Naomi the remaining part of my ready money; but if she dies to my four sons, Samuel, Moses, Joseph and Benjamin, equally divided. Certified by Jesse Hargrove, who wrote the spoken words. 17 Jan., 1748. Book 9, p. 602.

SELWAY, John: Est.- By wife, Elizabeth. Signed by Coll. Robert Jordan, Maj. Wm. Browne, Justices. 22 June, 1678. Book 2, p. 179.

SELWAY, John: Leg.- To wife, Elizabeth, my estate; but if she have no heir, then to my kinsfolk in England, if any come to Virginia. 10 April, 1678. Prob.: 22 May, 1678. Wit: George Proctor, Eliza. Proctor. Book 2, p. 175.

SERGERTON, William: Est.- Richard Rives, Exer. 16 Apr., 1740. Book 9, p. 152.

SESSOMS, Nicholas: Leg.- To wife, Katherine, for life, the Plantation I live on - 300 acres - at her decease to my daughter, Hannah Black, and for want of issue, to grand-daughter, Mary Black. To granddaughter Hannah Black, doz. spoons, trunk, household goods, an Indian girl, etc.; if she die or marry before of age, to go to my granddaughter, Mary Black. To daughter, Ann Williams, two barrels of pork. To daughter, Mary Black, a negro called "Isle of Wight" etc. To son-in-law, William Williams, after my wife's decease one negro. To grandson, William Williams, my land at, or near, Marshapingo. To grandson, John Black, land on the south side of Bridge Swamp, if no heirs to granddaughter, Mary Black. To granddaughter, Katherine Williams my Plantation on Pegion Swamp, 200 acres, if no issue to my granddaughter, Mary Williams. To son-in-law William Black, all my leather. To two sons-in-law, William Williams and Wm. Black, all my wearing clothes to be equally divided. To friend, Ethelred Taylor, five pounds. To wife, Katherine, and two sons-in-law all the rest of est. to be equally divided. Desires granddaughters to be well educated by Ethelred Taylor, Hannah and Mary Black, and take over the Plantation after my death. He to be overseer of will, with two sons-in-law. Made: 8 Oct., 1715. Prob.: 21 Oct., 1716. Wit: Samuel Cook, John High, Mary Evans. Book 7, p. 33.

SEWARD, Ann: Leg.- To daughter Ann Seward, ten pounds in cash. The rest to five sons and daughter, namely: Christopher Clinch, William, James, Joseph, and Benjamin Seward, and Ann Seward. Made: 20 Aug., 1712. Prob.: 19 Nov., 1714. Book 6, p. 126.

SEWARD, James: Leg.- To son, John Seward one-half of my Tract
of Land I purchased of Thos. Bin's to be laid off next to
Henry Hart's line. To my wife, all the remainder of my
estate for her life, then to son, James. Son, John, not
18 years old. Mentions, "All my children", to child in
esse ten pounds, be it son or daughter. Rest of estate to
wife and makes her Exerx. Will presented by Elizabeth
Seward, Exerx. Made: 25 Aug., 1726. Prob.: 19 Apr.,
1727. Wit: William Gray, Thos. Taylor, Sarah Thorpe.
Book 7, p. 687.

SEWARD, James: Est.- Exers., Thomas Edwards and Elizabeth Edwards. 21 Aug., 1728. Book 7, p. 835.

SEWARD, John: Est.- Mary Seward, admr. 21 Dec., 1699. Book
5, p. 188.

SEWARD, John: Est.- 30 Nov., 1749. John Holt, Chris. Tharpe,
Thos. Davidson. Book 9, p. 632.

SEWARD, William: Leg.- To daughters, Mary Bruton and Eliza.
Holt, each a pewter dish. The Plantation I live on that is
on Banford's Creek..to White Marsh, to Wm. Harrison's to
my grandson, Wm. Seward's line - to my wife, Ann, for her
life, and at her death to my son, William Seward; but for
lack of heirs to my son, Benjamin Seward. To my son,
James, land; if no issue to son, Joseph, - White Marsh
Swamp...to Robert Barham's woods. Rest of estate to my
wife and her five children in law in consideration of her
dowry, children, Wm. Seward, James Seward, Joseph Seward,
Benjamin Seward, and Ann Seward. Makes wife, Exerx. Made:
16 March, 1702/3. Prob.: 4 May, 1703. Wit: Edward
Barrow, Eliza. Barrow, Wm. Gray. Book 5, p. 274.

SEWARD, William: Est.- By Mr. Thomas Holt. 6 July, 1703.
Jno. Lear, Jno. Sugar, Wm. Gray. Book 5, p. 281.

SHARINTON, William: Leg.- To Richard Rives all of my estate,
and make him Exer. Prob.: 19 Mar., 1739. Wit: Chris
Golightly, Wm. Pettway, Wm. Moore. Book 9, p. 119.

SHARP, Francis: Leg.- To son, Francis, 135 acres in Isle of
Wight, and lot and land in the Citty of Williamsburg, that
Mr. Bundel lives on adjoining the Capitall Square (except
35 feet to be laid out of the east end of said lot). House
and Tenement in Williamsburg in occupation of Roadwell,
a shoemaker, and Plantation I now live on called Young
Thomas Smith, I give to son, John Sharp. To sons, Jacob
and William Sharp, lot and land adjoining the market place
in the Citty of Williamsburg, now in the occupancy of John
Rice, Taylor, and 250 acres in Isle of Wight County. Mentions Daughters, Sarah Sharp, Eliza. Garris & Comfort King,
Mr. Charles Binns overseer of Will, and son, Jacob, Exer.
Made: 14 Aug., 1738. Prob.: 20 Feb., 1739. Wit: Thomas
Bell, Wm. Evans. Book 9, p. 115.

SHELLEY, Philip: Est.- 15 Oct., 1712. Paid Phillip Shelley,
John Shelley, Thomas Shelley, Thomas Drew, Richard Taylor,
Joseph Delk, etc. Signed: Nicholas Maget, James Davis.
Book 6, p. 127.

SHELLEY, Phillip, Senior: Leg.- To son, Phillip, 1500 lbs. of
Tobacco, tools, chest, etc. To son, John 1500 lbs. tobacco, tools, chest and half my wearing clothes. To daugh-

ter, Elizabeth Jones bed and furniture. To son, Thomas,
2060 lbs. of tobacco when 21 years old. To daughter, Ann,
at John Sugar's a Bible which was her mother's. Wife,
Leviry and her children to have one-half of my estate, and
makes her Exerx. Son, Thomas. Wit: Thos. Thropp, William
Cockin, Richard Taylor. Made: 7 Mar., 1703/4. Prob.:
4 July, 1704. Book 5, p. 313.

SHELLEY, Phillip: Signed: Sarah Shelley. 25 Nov., 1704. Wm.
Cockin, Charles Jarrett, Rich. Glover. Book 5, p. 323.

SHELLY, Phillips: Leg.- To brothers, John and Thomas Shelley,
200 acres of land, bought from Benjamin Chapman, to be
equally divided; brother, Thomas to have the manner Plantation. Thos. Shelley to have feather bed and furniture.
All wearing clothes, linen and woolens to be equally divided between John and Thomas Shelley, and Thos. Tilton,
and Robert Jones. Wit: Mathew Fones, James Briggs, Wm.
Bennet. Made: 12 July, 1716. Prob.: 15 Aug., 1716.
Book 7, p. 26.

SHEPHERD, William: Est.- William Shepherd, late of the Colony
left an estate. Edward Holloway, Edward Bookey and Fortune,
his wife, made suit to the Court for com. of Administration
on the estate. 21 Dec., 1699. Book 5, p. 188.

SHERLEY, Ralph: Leg.- To wife, Elizabeth, and daughter, Mary,
the produce of 80 hhds. of tob. to be shipped on Captain
Tibbott, and Capt. Morgan's ships and consigned to Mr.
Micajah Perry and Mr. Thos. Lane, merchants etc. To friend,
Henry Tooker and Elizabeth, his wife a bequest. To Henry
Baker and Mary, his wife, a bequest. To Wm. Browne and his
wife, Sarah. To Samuel Stockwell. Friends Henry Baker and
Henry Tooker, Exers. of will. Wit: Samuell Swann, Wm.
Browne. Made: 20 Sept., 1693. Prob.: 28, Sept., 1693.
Book ___, p. ___.

SHERLEY, Ralph: Est.- Probate granted Henry Parker and Capt.
Henry Tooker on the Will of Ralph Sherley. 26 Oct., 1694.
Book 5, p. 24.

SHERRARD, Denis: Est.- 3 March, 1690. Daniel Wade, admr.
Book 4, p. 186.

SHERROD, Arthur: Est.- Charles Mabry, admr. 21 July, 1747.
Chas. Holt, Aug. Hargrave, Wm. Mangum. Book 9, p. 559.

SHOCKEY, Alce: Leg.- To four daughters, Meley Ellis, Eliza.
Bullock, Agnes Barker, and Mary Shockey my wearing clothes.
To grandson, Richard Ellis one cow. To granddaughter, Mary
Ellis, a spinning wheel. To granddaughter, Mary Barker,
an iron pott. To granddaughter, Agnes Barker a sheep. To
granddaughter, Alice Bullock, a bason. To granddaughter,
Mary Bullock, a deep dish and plate. Daughter, Mary Shockey, Exerx. Wit: Benjamin Reekes, Eliza. Saffold. Made:
17 Feb., 1735/6. Prob.: 21 Mar., 1738. Bk. 9, p. 35.

SHOCKYE, Richard: Est.- Alice Shockey, admrx. 20 Oct., 1731.
Thomas Washington, Sampson Lanier, John Justice. Book 8,
p. 138.

SHORT, Susannah: Leg.- Daughter, Mary Harris, to enjoy legacies, and my chest and riding horse. Two grandsons, William and Thomas Harris. To son, Thomas Short, one negro.

Granddaughter, Susannah Short. Rem. of estate to two
grandsons, William and Thomas Short. Grandson, Wm. Harris,
Exer. Wit: Wm. Short, John Woobank, Rich. Bullock. Made:
3 Dec., 1743. Prob.: 21 Mar., 1743. Book 9, p. 462.

SHORT, William: Leg.- To his mother, Mrs. Elizabeth Short,
maintenance for life. Mentions son, William Short, and
gives him Plantation. To daughter, Eliza, Plantation at
Chipeaks Creek, which was had of my wife, Mary Short, when
my daughter is of age, or married. Wife, Mary Short. If
son and daughter die before of age, then the bequest to
sons of my sister, Sarah Midleton, equally divided. Mentions friend, Mr. Thomas Busby, and friend, Mr. Sezar, of
Charles Citty County, and makes them overseers of est.
Wit: Jno. Salway, Thos. Busby, Dan. Roome. Prob.: 28
Mar., 1676. Book 2, p. 106.

SHORT, William: Leg.- To son, William Short, a tract of land
400 acres, where I live and the other parcell at Otterdam -
part in Surry, part in Prince George County, three negroes,
all furniture in the house etc. To son, Thomas Short land
in Prince George County on Monoksnake Creek, 1670 acres.
To first son of son, Thomas, land in Amelia County on
Setler Creek, 400 acres; if he die, to next male heir of
son. If son, Thomas, have no male heir, to heirs of son,
William Short, and five negroes. To first son, of son,
Thomas, three negroes; if no male heir, to his daughters.
To daughter, Mary Harris, the use of room in my dwelling
house for life. To granddaughter, Susannah Short, one negro. To son, Thomas, the west room in my house. To
grandson, William Harris, son of William Harris, tract of
land - 150 acres - where his father now liveth, and one
negro, when he is 18 years old. To grandson, Thomas Harris,
when 18 years old. To grandson, William Short, son of Wm.
Short, four negroes. To granddaughter, Sarah Short, dau.
of Wm. Short, one negro. Granddaughter, Susannah Short,
daughter of Thomas Short. To granddaughter, Martha Short,
daughter of Wm. Short, one negro. Balance of account of
Mr. Bradly & Griffin, in London; and Mr. Richard Hall &
Benj. Hall, in Barbadoes, and Mrs. Elizabeth Willards account to be equally divided between my wife, Susannah, and
sons, William and Thomas. Kinsman, Benjamin Heath. Wit:
Wm. Heath, Richard Jones, Rich. Bullock. Made: 10 April,
1736. Prob.: 16 Sept., 1741. Book 9, p. 365.

SHREWSBURY, Thomas: Leg.- To my wife, Ann, my whole estate and
all Land, houses etc. for life, then to Thomas Shrewsbury,
my brother. Makes boy, William Lurteler, free at 21 years
old. Made 5 Dec., 1694. Prob.: 10 July, 1695. Wit:
John Bentley, Thos. Bentley, Rob. Dowling. Book 5, p. 85.

SHROUSBY, Francis: Leg.- To wife, Katherine Shrousby my Plantation, and all divisions of my land, and when son, Francis, is 21 years old, to each or any of my sons, then the
whole estate divided equally, and wife an equal privilege.
To daughters, Sarah, three cows; to daughter, Elizabeth
two cows, in like manner each son at 21 years. To my
brother, Thomas, a gold ring, or silver spoon, ten shillings cost. To brother, James, a cow, at his death, in-
crease to children. To daughter, Jane, a gold ring. To
daughter, Sarah, a mare. Dau. Jane Rix. Made: 8 Nov.,
1678. Prob.: 4 Mar., 1678. Wit: Samuel Maget, Thomas
Shrousby. Book 2, p. 197.

SHROWSBURY, Francis: Est.- John Vinsent, bound by promise to
Katherine, "My now wife, Relict of Fra. Shrewsbury, late
deceased," provides for Sarah, daughter of said Francis
and her heirs, more than devised to her; and to Thomas,
son of sd. Francis; and Eliza. Daughter of said Francis.
6 May, 1679. Book 2, p. 204.

SIDWAY, Mary: Leg.- To granddaughter, Hannah Harrison, a colt.
To John Kersey, a heifer. Rest of estate to two sons,
Benjamin Harrison, and Thomas Sidway. Makes them Exers.
Made: 1 Mar., 1687/8. Prob.: 29 May, 1688. Wit: Lyddia
Norwood, Samuell Alesbrook. Book 4, p. 41.

SIDWAY, Thomas: Leg.- To wife, Jeane Sidway for her life, and
at her death to William Stringer. Makes
wife, Exerx. Made: 16 Jan., 1694. Prob.: 3 Dec., 1695.
Wit: Benjamin Harrison, Sarah Pedington. Bk. 5, p. 79.

SIDWAY, Thomas: Est.- Thomas Sidway appointed his Relict Jane
Sidway, Exerx. of his Will. She since married to John Griffin. Now, John Griffin and his wife, Jane, ask for admr.
of Thos. Sidway's est. 3 Dec., 1695. Book 5, p. 110.

SIMMONS, Eliza: Leg.- Makes Mr. George Foster, executor of
Will. To daughter, Mary Moring striped gown and petticoat,
side saddle etc. To son, William Simmons, two negroes,
and to keep Mary Haviland, until son, William is 21 years
old. To Eliza. and Sarah Simmons each a Bible. To Eliza.
Evans a couch. To two sons, William and John Simmons the
rest of my estate to be equally divided. To Geo. Foster -
two daughters, Eliza and Sarah. Wit: Maximilian Manfell,
Charles Basse. Made: 16 Sept., 1695. Prob.: 2 Mar.,
1696/7. Book 5, p. 119.

SIMMONS, John: Leg.- To my wife, Rebekah, negroes, household
goods, horses etc. To son, William, all the land where I
now live, and all the Land in Brunswick County, and cattle
and stock on that land, to son, John Simmons, all my Land
in Isle of Wight County, and cattle and livestock on the
Plantation I live on, negroes etc. To Mr. Robert Gray a
colt. All the rest of my estate to be equally divided between my sons, William and John and daughter, Mary Simmons.
Wife Rebekah and son, Wm. Exers. Wit: Benj. Simmons,
John Davis, Jos. Andrews. Made: 18 Oct., 1737. Prob.:
19 April, 1738. Book 8, p. 826.

SIMMONS, John, Jr.: 16 Sept., 1741. Rebecca Simmons, Wm.
Simmons. Book 9, p. 356.

SIMMONS, Mary: Leg.- To grandchild, Mary Simmons, ye daughter
of my son, William Simmons, feather bed, cows, small trunk,
silver bole, half doz. napkins and a fair Bible with her
name upon it, looking glass, gold ring, large chest etc.,
if she die, to return to my father. To John Rutherford a
feather bed. To Frances Gregory a heifer when 17 years old.
Made: 16 Apr., 1677. Prob.: 7 May, 1678. Wit: Maxililian Mansell, Jno. Flood. Book 2, p. 173.

SIMMONS, Thomas: Leg.- To son, Thomas Simmons, the Upper Part
of my Land on Powell's Creek, adjoining Thos. Booth's land.
To son, Joseph, the Lower Part of the Land..to the Creek.
To son, Edward Simmons, bed and furniture. Rest of estate
to Wife and daughter, Elizabeth Simmons. Makes son, Joseph, Exer. Made: 17 Feb., 1725/26. Prob.: 18 Apr., 1733.

Wit: Bernard Sykes, Edward Prince, Edward Prince, Jr.
Book 8, p. 285.

SIMMONS, William: Leg.- To son, William Simmons, all my land
on the North side of Birchen Swamp, and all my land on the
south side of said Swamp..to Myrick's tanyard, also 250
acres on the north side at Bowling Alley, also cows, negro,
fun, etc. To son, John Simmons, all the remainder of my
land I now live on being at Branch at Owen Myrick and 250
acres..at Bowling Alley. To Daughter, Elizabeth, 5000 lbs.
of tobacco when of age, or married. To daughter, Mary
Moring, four ewes. To daughter, Sarah Simmons, 5000 lbs.
of tobacco when of age, or married. I am guardian of Mary
Haviland, and she to be maintained by my son, William and
she to be with my wife; if they die, she is to bound out.
Gives William the water mill, during the life of Mary
Haviland, but at her death to sons, William and John. Hav-
iland, but at her death to sons, William and John. Mr.
Benjamin Harrison and Mr. Chris. Moring, overseers of will.
Wit: Benjamin Harrison, Jr., Maximilian Mansell, Thos.
Sowerby. Made: 15 April, 1693. Prob.: 21 Oct., 1693.
Book 4, p. 340.

SIMSON, John: Est.- Signed: John Brown. 21 Aug., 1717.
Robert Wynne, John Hawthorne, Jno. Hicks. Bk. 7, p. 73.

SISSON, Thomas: Leg.- (First part of this will illegible.) To
daughter, Elizabeth, land in Brunswick County, 134 acres.
To daughters, Ann, Isabel and Mary Sisson, the rest of the
land in Brunswick County. To son, Stephen, what I have before given him and one negro. John Reigns, John Denton and
Peter Simmons to appraise the estate. Appoints sons,
Thomas Sesson, and Wm. Sesson, Exers. Made: 18 Dec.,
1730. Prob.: __ ____, 1731. Wit: John Raines, John Denton, Peter Simmons. Book 8, p. 105.

SISSON, Thomas: Est.- Thos. Sisson, Exer. 14 Aug., 1731.
Book 8, p. 123.

SLATE, Edward: Leg.- To wife, Mary Slate, all my estate for
her life, then to my son, Edward Slate, negroes. Rest and
rem. of est., which wife is to have use of, to be equally
divided with, to grandsons, John, George, Robert Slate and
Robert Kee. Wife, and son Edward, Exers. Made: 9 July,
1747. Prob.: 20 Nov., 1750. Wit: Robert Little, Francis
Little, James Griffin. Book 9, p. 666.

SLEDGE, Charles: Leg.- To son-in-law, John Ellison 75 acres
for his lefe, this land on Pigin Swamp, where he now dwells;
and at his decease, to my granddaughter, Judy Ellison. To
my son, John Sledge, 100 acres of land in Surry, bounded by
Samuel Chappell's land on one side and Coll. Wm. Randolph's
land on the other side. To my daughter, Rebecca Ivy, one
cow. To daughter Mathew Sledge, one cow. To granddaughter
Judy Ellison one cow, rest to wife. Made: 3 Nov., 1725.
Prob.: 16 Feb., 1725. Book 7, p. 623.

SLEDGE, John: Leg.- To my eldest son, Charles Sledge, 150
acres of land where he now lives and negroes. To my son,
Daniel Sledge, part of a tract of 200 acres in Brunswick
County, also pewter dishes, etc. To son, Amos Sledge, 171
acres of land, being a part of the above in Brunswick County. To daughter, Ann Griffin, five pounds. To daughter,
Sarah Sledge, pewter dishes, cows. To daughter, Rebecca,

negroes, and household goods, and 200 acres, where I live,
and at her death, to my son, John Sledge. The rem. of est.
to be divided between, Charles, Daniel, Sarah, John and
Amos. Wife, Exerx. Wit: Hugh Ivey, Thos. Ivey. Made:
27 Dec., 1749. Prob.: 18 Dec., 1750. Book 9, p. 674.

SLEDGE, Mary: Leg.- Makes small bequests to son, John Sledge;
daughter Rebecka Ivie, granddaughter, Judith Ellison, when
the latter is 21 years old. Gives daughter, Martha Hay,
all the rest of the estate; makes son-in-law, Peter Hay,
Exer. Made: 8 Jan., 1726/7. Prob.: 17 July, 1728. Wit:
Edward Prince, Eliza. Prince, Thos. Hay. Bk. 7, p. 826.

SMITH, John: Leg.- To George Williams 200 lbs. of tobacco. To
my son, John Smith, my Plantation, a small gun, etc. If
son die, then to George Williams, and makes latter Exer.
Prob.: 23 July, 1679. Wit: William Thompson, Sion Hill.
Book 2, p. 224.

SMITH, John: Est.- 20 June, 1689. By Mary Smith, Exerx. and
Relict. Book 4, p. 114.

SMITH, John: Est.- By Samuel Thompson. 18 Apr., 1711. James
Jones, Edward Rowell, David Burnett. Margarett Patrick
swore to Inventory of est. she being admr. of the est. John
Smith swore to same. Book 6, p. 50.

SMITH, John: Est.- By Patrick Magarity. 20 Mar., 1716. Mich.
Harris, Wm. Edwards, Jr. Book 7, p. 53.

SMITH, John: (Verbal Will) Sister, Mary, is already taken care
of, therefore give her nothing. Brother, Samuel, is likely
to be a lusty man, and work for his living, therefor gives
him some small memento as David Burnett thinks fit. To
sisters, Elizabeth and Sarah, all the rest of the estate to
be equally divided. Signed by Samuel Thompson. 15 June,
1720. Wit: David Burnett, Mary Magarety, Massy Rowell.
Book 7, p. 273.

SMITH, Nicholas: Leg.- To son, Nicholas Smith, five shillings,
and what he owes me. To son, John Smith 50 acres of land..
upon Cross Swamp, where he first built. To son, Lawrence
Smith, bridle and saddle. To son, William Smith my Plantation and Land where I now live, houses, orchards etc.
and if no heir then to grandson, Arthur Smith, the son of
my son, John Smith. To daughter, Mary, a feather bed etc.
Makes son, William, Exer. Wit: Zacharia Madderra, John
Deberry, Priscilla Madderra. Made: 18 Feb., 1718/19.
Prob.: 18 Nov., 1719. Book 7, p. 227.

SMITH, Richard: Leg.- To wife, Mary Smith, my whole est. and
make her Exerx. To Elizabeth Boun and Richard Sessoms each
a cow. To son, Richard Smith, the Plantation I live on at
my wife's decease. To sons, Thomas Smith and Nicholas
Smith, the land where Thomas Smith now lives. The rest of
est. to wife, Mary. Wit: Will. Davidson, Robert Booth.
Made: 24 Feb., 1712. Prob.: 20 May, 1713. Bk. 6, p. 144.

SMITH, Thomas, Sr.: Leg.- To my sons, Thomas Smith and George
Smith, my estate to be equally divided. Makes son, Thos.
Exer. Made: 29 Sept., 1722. Prob.: 20 Feb., 1722. Wit:
Harmon Horn, Wm. Bynum. Book 7, p. 441.

SNELGROVE, Henry: Est.- Appraised by Chris. Tatum, Peter Tatum,

Francis Maybury. John Doby, admr. 24 Feb., 1720. Book 7, p. 328.

SNIPES, Robert: Est.- By Henry Harrison, Gent., admr. 19 April, 1721. Nich. Maget, Robt. Watkins, John Watkins. Book 7, p. 331, p. 425. Due to the orphans of Melchideck Duche.

SNOW, Josiah: Est.- 5 Nov., 1709. Francis Sowerby, Thos. Collier, Amos Tynes. Book 5, p. 436.

SOLOMON, Lewis: Leg.- To son, William my great coat. To son, Lewis, the rest of my wearing apparel. To daughter, Mary Hill, 20 shillings due from Nathaniel Hawthorne, 100 weight of tob. etc. Daughter, Martha Solomon the rest of my est. Wife, Martha, Exerx. Wit: Thomas Avent, John Avent, Wm. Barlow. Made: 11 Dec., 1742. Prob.: 20 July, 1743.

SOWERBY, Francis: Est.- 11 Aug., 1680. John Vincent, surety for orphans with Jno. Moring, Daniel Room. Wit: Thomas Jordan, Wm. Edwards. Book 2, p. 8.

SOWERBY, Francis: Married Mary, daughter of Thomas Jordan, and with Jane Jordan and himself, petitions the provisions of George Jordan's will, carried out by Thomas Jordan. 5 Nov., 1700. Book 5, p. 213.

SOWERBY, Francis: Leg.- To my son, Francis Sowerby my old Plantation where my father formerly lived, with houses etc. extending from a Red Oak that divides my line and Thomas Collier's land..to Poplar Branch..to Regan's line. To wife, Mary, half the profit of Fruit trees etc. Wife, Mary to have the use of the Plantation, not to sell timber until son, William, is 21 years old, then wife to have one-third for her life. To son, William, the Plantation I live on, except the part to son, Francis, and to heir at 21 years old. Rem. of est. to wife and sons. Wit: Thos. Collier, Richard Rose, Edward Baley, Jr. Made: 12 Sept., 1716. Prob.: 15 May, 1717. Book 7, p. 60.

SOWERBY, Francis: Est.- 19 June, 1723. John Tyus, admr. Thos. Collier, Henry Watkins, Richard Rose. Book 7, p. 453.

SOWERBY, James: Est.- 24 Jan., 1678. Ann Sowerby, admr. Book 2, p. 195.

SOWERBY, James: Est.- By Ann Sowerby. Paid Thos. Sowerby, Jno. Moring, Mr. Thos. Jordan, Nath. Roberts, Wm. Edwards. 1678. Book 2, p. 263.

SOWERBY, John: Leg.- To son, Benjamin, the Land, 120 acres on the south side of Chongsharkin Swamp, called Muddy Branch ad. Wm. Ray, also my gun and sword. To wife, Liddia, the use of my Plantation for her life, at her decease to son, Henry. To daughter, Sarah Owen one cow. To daughter, Jane Deberry, one cow. To daughter, Elizabeth, a cow. To daughter, Mary, trunk, bed and furniture. To granddaughter Anne Sowerby, 20 shillings to teach her to read. Wife to have rem. of estate, and makes her Exerx. Wit: Thos. Sowerby, Nicholas Prockter. Made: 2 Jan., 1726/7. Prob.: 19 July, 1727. Book 7, p. 748.

SOWERBY, Margaret: Married John Battell, the latter has received of John Allen 980 pounds of tobacco 7 caskes, being the whole est. due her, and now John Battell discharges him from all claims. 1 July, 1684. Book 3, p. 2.

SOWERBY, Samuel: Est.- By Jean Sowerby. 18 May, 1743. Book 9, p. 434.

SOWERBY, Thomas: By his will made his Relict, Ann Sowerby Exer. of his estate. Ann Sowerby since married to James Jordan. Now James Jordan and wife, Ann, ask for admr. on Thos. Sowerby's est. 9 July, 1696. Book 5, p. 110.

SOWERBY, Thomas: Est.- 19 Mar., 1719. John Tyus, Mary Tyus. Book 7, p. 264.

SPENSER, Robert: Est.- To daughter, Elizabeth Spenser, land at Blackwater, Surry County (not of age). To daughter, Ann, sheep given daughter, Elizabeth, by Capt. George Watkins, deceased, and spoons, bought of Mr. Place, and chest that came from Accomack..fine thread now aboard Capt. Lavemar's shipp, and be in care of friend, Wm. Edwards, until she is married. Godsons, Henry Browne and James Mason. To Jonas Bennett, his Exers. and administrators. To Martha Whittson, my grandshild, due her from the estate of her deceased father, John Whitson, and cows due from Roger Archer and to remain with the same, he giving bond to Martha Whitson. To William Browne, to Wm. Edwards. To wife, Jane, my land, and makes her Exerx. To wife, Jane, my land, and makes her Exerx. Wit: George Lee, Jno. Phillips (Scotchman), Jane Plow. Made: 5 March, 1678. Prob.: 6 May, 1679. Book 2, p. 207.

SPENSER, Robert (Capt.): Est.- Signed: Jane Jordan, wife to Thomas Jordan, swears it is a true Inventory. 22 7br, 1681. Robt. Ruffin, Wm. Newsum, Jno. Prise, Wm. Gray. Book 2, p. 292.

SPENSOR, Jno.: Est.- 25 Jan., 1675. Thomas Clay, and Elizabeth, his wife, aged 32 years, made deposition on 27 Dec., last that Mr. Jno. Spensor of Lawnes Creek Parish, lay sick at Wm. Hancocke's house and Deponent asked him how he would dispose of his estate, and he said he would leave what he had to his sisters, Mary and Elizabeth. Book 2, p. 104.

SPILTIMBER, ___: Est.- 1 July, 1679. Joseph Rogers, John Phillips. Book 2, p. 19.

SPILTIMBER, Anthony: Leg.- To wife, Mary and daughter, Patte, my cattle, equally divided. Bequest to servant, Richard Tias. Land to be equally divided between my brother, John, and my daughter, Martha, my wife having her third during her life. My daughter, not of age, to be brought up by her brother and wife. Tobacco is owing by Capt. Jennings and by Culbert Flake. Mr. William Thomas to assist my wife and my brother concerning my estate. If my daughter, Martha, dies before coming of age, my brother, John, to have her part. Exers., my wife and my brother, John Spiltimber. Wit: Wm. Hill, George Williams, John Brodie. Made: 30 Mar., 1672. Prob.: 7 May, 1672. Book 2, p. 11.

SPILTIMBER, John: Est.- Eliza. C. Hill made oath of the Inventory of John Spiltimber and signed. 20 July, 1677. Geo. Proctor, Samuel Pla, Geo. Williams, Thos. King. Book 2, p. 139.

SPISPITTLESS, James: Leg.- To Capt. Stith Bolling, my riding
horse to be sold for use of daughter, Jane Bolling. My
three best suits of clothes to be sold by my friend, Henry
Watkins. To goddaughter and cousin, Hannah Pulley. To my
brother, Wm. Pulley the rest of my estate not already given
away, after my debts are paid. Prob.: 21 April, 1725.
Wit: Thos. Collier, Robt. Watkins. Book 7, p. 580.

SPRATLEY, John: Leg.- All my estate in James Citty County to
be equally divided between my three grandchildren, William,
John and Eliza. Spratley & Mary Saunders, daughter of Mr.
Robert Saunders, of Williamsburg, except two cows, I give
to Mary, the wife of Thomas Huse, and a horse to my wife.
To my grandson, John Spratley, all the land I have in Surry
County, after my wife's death. If he live to 18 years, to
have his inheritance; one of my Plantations, my wife is to
let him have, and one negro, and all money made on the
Plantation where Mr. Proctor lives, and be used for schooling of said grandson, John Spratley. To granddaughter,
Eliza., one negro; but wife to have use of the negro for
her life. To my daughter-in-law, Mary Spratley, five
pounds. To Thos. Huse forty shillings. To kinsman, Robert
Saunders, forty shillings. To grandson, John Spratley, a
silver headed cane. To daughter-in-law, Mary Spratley, 14
pounds that her husband, John Spratley owes me on what I
am indebted to Maj. Blair. Wife to sell negroes and divide
the money between my grandsons, John Spratley, and Wm.
Spratley. Wife, Phillis, and Nicholas Maget, Exers. Made:
28 April, 1728. Prob.: 16 Oct., 1728. Wit: John Manggum, Sarah Savidge, Thos. Francis. Book 7, p. 867.

STANTON, James: Leg.- To son, James Stanton, housing and land
and eight pewter plates, chafing dish, large chest, couch
etc. To daughter, Mary Stanton, a feather bed, doz. Pewter plates, one quart tankard, three pewter dishes, porringer etc. To daughter, Ann Stanton, three pewter dishes, one
doz. plates, bed etc. and all the remainder of est. to be
equally divided between my three children, James, Mary and
Ann. Makes son, James, Exer. Wit: Elizabeth Browne, Mary
Stanton, Ann Stanton. Made: 14 July, 1719. Prob.: 16
Sept., 1719. Book 7, p. 215.

STEPHENS, Edward: Est.- 2 May, 1740. Rebecah Stephens, admr.
Christ. Tatum, Wm. Shands, Robert Doby. Book 9, p. 251.

STEPHENS, Edward: Est.- 15 April, 1741. Benjamin Moss and
Rebekah Moss, admrs. Sam. Weldon, James Washington. Book
9, p. 302.

STEWARD, John: Leg.- To son, John the Plantation I live on
after my wife's death, but if no heirs to my son, William
Steward. To son, William, one-half the tract of land where
I dwell, likewise part of same to him. To daughter, Mar-
garet Steward, my Plantation at Otterdam Swamp, where Walter
Cotton liveth, with 135 acres of land, one mare, cows, etc.
To daughter, Mary, the lowermost part of my land at Otter-
dam Swamp, adjoining with Wm. Killingsworth, his line and
135 acres of land. Rem. of estate to wife, Margaret, with
Plantation where I dwell, for her life. Made: 5 Jan.,
1704. Prob.: 8 Nov., 1705. Wit: Rich. Holleman, John
Yorke, John Baker. Book 5, p. 338.

STOKES, Silvanus: Leg.- To eldest son, Jonas Stokes, my Plantation, grist mill, mill stones, and 565 acres of land,

125

houses, orchards, where I lie on the upper part; and at his
death to my grandson, Jones Stokes, with one negro, and
100 acres of land, Jonas Stokes being son of my natural
son, Jones Stokes. To son, Silvanus Stokes, two negroes.
Daughter, Martha Ezell. Grandson, Marcus, son of my son,
Silvanus Stokes, 400 acres of land, the lower part. To
Silvanus Stokes, son of my son, Jones Stokes, one negro.
To Hamlin Stokes, son of my son, Jones Stokes, one negro.
To Jones Stokes, son of my son, Jones, one negro. To
grandson, Silvanus Stokes, son of my son, Silvanus Stokes,
one negro. To my granddaughter, Agnes Freeman, daughter of
my son, Hamlin stokes, one negro. To granddaughter, Agnes
Ezell bed, etc. To sons all the rest of the est. to be
equally divided. Made: 18 May, 1742. Prob.: 21 Mar.,
1748. Wit: Samuel Stokes, John Stokes, David Stokes.
Book 9, p. 604.

STRINGER, William: Est.- 20 Oct., 1714. Book 6, p. 214.

STURDIVANT, Matthew: Est.- Hallum Sturdivant, Admr. John
Hicks, Wm. Moore, Wm. Pettway. 19 May, 1728. Book 7, p.
913.

SUMNER, Francis: Est.- Commission of administration was granted to Coll. Swann, Esq. on the estate of Francis Sumner,
deceased. Signed at Green Spring by Sir Wm. Berkeley, Gov.
16 Mar., 1676. Book 2, p. 119.

SWANN, Matthew: Leg.- To daughter, Elizabeth, wife of John
Drew; and to daughter, Sarah bed vallance, curtains and
negro. To son-in-law, John Drew, six barrels of corn. To
daughter, Mary, wife of William Phillips, and to grandson,
John Phillips, my house and Plantation where I now live;
and to my daughter, Sarah, all the remainder of my land
lying adjoining daughter, Mary, when 18 years old. Made:
14 Dec., 1702. Prob.: 5 Jan., 1702. Wit: Ar. Allen,
Jno. Allen, Robt. Ruffin. Book 5, p. 260.

SWANN, Matthew: Est.- 8 Feb., 1702. Sarah Swann, Exerx. Wm.
Newitt, Robert Crafford, Wm. Chambers. Book 5, p. 264.

SWETT, John: Est.- 6 July, 1697. Signed: Jno. Kicotan and
Mary Kicotan. Book 5, p. 129.

SWETT, Robert: Est.- 15 July, 1696. Signed: By Mary Swett.
James Stanton, Samuel Judkins. Book 5, p. 114.

SWINSOR, Ann: Est.- 5 Sept., 1699. Book 5, p. 181.

TALLETT, George: Est.- 17 May, 1748. William Cornwell, admr.
John Drew, Abraham Mitchell, John Berryman. Book 9, p. 578.

TANNER, Edward: Leg.- To sons, Edward and William, all my Land
and Plantation, and not to be sold. Mentions Wife, mentions son, John, not of age. If children die, then land to
Robert Seate. 1 7br, 1685. Prob.: 15 7br, 1685. Wit:
Thomas Right, Elepabeth Cornwell.

TANNER, Edward: Est.- 21 Dec., 1685. Wife, Jane Tanner, swore
that Inventory was correct. Wm. Hancock, Mathew Swann.
Book 3, p. 35.

TANNER, Edward and William, sons of Edward Tanner, deceased,
acknowledged receipt to Jane Clarke, admr. of the estate

of Jane Tanner, deceased, their late sister, their full
parts in the estate of Jane Tanner. 15 July, 1696. Jane
Clarke, admrx. of the estate of Jane Tanner acknowledges
receipt from Wm. Edwards of Jane Tanner's part of her
deceased father, Edward Tanner's est. Book 5, p. 113.

TARRANT, Nicholas: Est.- 25 Jan., 1718. Elizabeth Mill,
Charles Briggs, Will. Wyche. Book 7, p. 154.

TARVER, Thomas: Leg.- Daughter-in-law, Christian Baly. Mentions Ann Warren. Son, Samuel Tarver and wife, Elizabeth
Tarver. Makes son, Exer. Wit: Robert Bayly, Thos. Waller. Made: 13 Dec., 1711. Prob.: 20 Aug., 1714. Book
6, p. 125.

TATUM, Edward: Leg.- Son, Nathaniel Tatum the Land where he
lives, on Peter Tatum's line to John Young's. To son,
Peter Tatum, the other half, where I live beginning at John
Young's to Joseph's Swamp. Daughter, Elizabeth Tatum, pew-
ter etc. Daughter, Ruth featherbed etc. Wife, Rebekah,
the use of the rest of my est. for life, then to my son,
Peter Tatum. Wit: Chris Tatum, Peter Tatum. Made: 3
Sept., 1736. Prob.: 16 May, 1739. Book 9, p. 62.

TATUM, Peter: Leg.- To son, Edward Tatum, the Plantation
where my mother lived and the other one-half adjoining.
Wife, Sarah, have the use of my Plantation for life.   To
daughters, Sarah, Rebecca, and Wenia, household articles.
To sons, Thomas and Edward, household articles. Mentions
"all my children". Wife, Sarah Tatum, Exerx. Wit: Thos.
Young, Elizabeth Tatum, Mary Heeth. Made: 11 Mar., 1750.
Prob.: 16 April, 1751. Book 9, p. 687.

TAYLER, Walter: Leg.- To wife, Mary, for her life, my Plantation, according to ye first gift of my father-in-law,
Richard Harris, deceased. To son, Richard Tayler, the
rest of the Land. If he die to my daughter, Susan Tayler.
Makes wife, Exerx. Made: 1 Sept., 1680. Prob.:   27 Dec.,
1688. Wit: Ar. Allen, Thos. Drew, Jos. Rogers, John
Phillips. Cocicil: This codicil states that since making
the will, he has another daughter, Elizabeth, and desires
she shall have an equal part in the will. 7 May, 1680.
Prob.: 7 May, 1689. Est. appraised by James Reddick,
Thos. Lawne, Thos. Drew. Book 5, p. 88.

TAYLOR, _____: Est.- 17 Sept., 1746. Nich. Maget and Ann, his
wife, admrs. Peter Warren, Benj. Clark. Book 9, p. 538.

TAYLOR, Edward: Est.- 4 May, 1708. By Margaret Taylor. Wm.
Gray, Timothy Thropp, Wm. Harris. Book 5, p. 392.

TAYLOR, Edward: Est.- Mary Taylor, admr. 19 July, 1727. Thos.
Holt, Christopher Clinch, Thos. Edwards. Bk. 7, p. 740.

TAYLOR, Edward: Est.- John Whitaker, admr. 20 June, 1749.
Wm. Drew, Dolphin Drew, Thos. Brantley. Book 9, p. 608.

TAYLOR, Ethelred: Leg.- To son, Samuel my Plantation on Poha-
tink Swamp by me purchased of the Trustees of the est. of
Joseph John Jackman, deceased, with all land to Coker's
Branch. To son, Henry, all my Land upon the other side of
Coker's Branch ad. James Bruton's and Samuell Cornwell's
land. To son, Ethelred, all my Land upon Lighwood Swamp.
To son, William, the land purchased of Joseph and John

High. To my wife the labor of two negroes for her life, then to be sold and money to be equally divided between my living children. To son, Samuell, two negroes when he is 21 years old, if he give Ethelred fourteen pounds cur. money. Wife, Elizabeth and son, Samuel. To brothers, Samuel and John and my sister, Rebeckah 20 shillings each. To John Clark, Jr. two shillings. Wit: Samuel Thompson, Katherine Sessoms, Ann Edwards, Benjamin Hill. Made: 31 March, 1716. Prob.: 20 June, 1716. Book 7, p. 19.

TAYLOR, John: Leg.- Mentions wife, and makes her Exerx. of est. Brother, William Taylor. Made: 7 Dec., 1680. Prob.: 6 Sept., 1687. Book 4, p. 8.

TAYLOR, John: Est.- John Taylor appointed his wife, Sarah Taylor, Exerx. of his will. Sarah married Thos. Bentley, Jun., who now asks the Court for right of probation in right of his wife. 6 Sept., 1687. Book 4, p. 26.

TAYLOR, John: Est.- Ann Taylor, admr. 16 Feb., 1725. John Chambers, Carter Crafford, John Bamer. Bk. 7, p. 624.

TAYLOR, Richard: Leg.- To wife, Sarah, where she lives with all houses etc. for her life; at her death to my son, Walter Taylor, and all the rest of the land to son, Walter Taylor. To Walter and Richard a weaver's loom and harness. The rest of my est. to my wife and all my children. Sons, John and Thomas to have the benefit of the land until 18 years old. Makes wife, Exerx. Made: 6 May, 1715. 15 Feb., 1715. Wit: Robert Foanes, Thomas Humphrey, Eliza. Taylor. Book 7, p. 46.

TAYLOR, Robert: Est.- LDeloney, Admr. 18 Feb., 1735. Book 8, p. 565.

TAYLOR, Thomas: Leg.- To son, Thomas negroes etc. To son, John, livestock, negroes, furniture etc. To daughter, Elizabeth Chambers, an Indian woman etc. To daughter, Katherine Hobbs, negro, furniture etc. To Mary Tomlinson, wife to John Tomlinson. Est. to be equally divided among my four children, Thomas, John, Elizabeth and Katherine. Makes Thomas and John, Exers. Made: 4 Feb., 1743. Prob.: 16 Jan., 1744. Wit: James Gee, Wyke Hunnicutt, Charles Gee. Book 9, p. 487.

TAYLOR, William: Leg.- To Martha, wife to John Ruffin, My Plantation in Lower Parish, 112 acres to be equally divided among my three brothers, Samuel, Henry and Ethelred. 8 March, 1725. Prob.: 19 May, 1736. Wit: John Ruffin, Peter Robins, Thos. Hall. Book 8, p. 599.

THARPE, Joseph: Leg.- To my wife, Elizabeth, my Plantation and Land where I live, for her life then to my son, Joseph Tharpe. If he die to son, Benjamin Tharpe. To son, William Tharpe, the Plantation where he lives..to Bab's line. If he die without issue, then to my son, Christopher Tharpe. To son, Christopher, all the rest and remainder of land at Pidion Swamp, not already given to son, William. If no issue to my son, Benjamin Tharpe. All the rest of my estate in Virginia and England, to be equally divided between my wife and children, Joseph, Christopher, Banjamin, Dinah Tharpe, Hannah Tharpe, Elizabeth Tharpe. Wife and Jos. Exerx. Made: 17 Aug., 1721. Prob.: 16 Nov., 1726. Wit: Edward Tanner, Robert Inman, Wm. Tanner. Book 7,

p. 662.

THARPE, Robert: Est.- By Sarah Tharpe. 19 Aug., 1719. Thos.
Holt, Wm. Judkins, Jno. Bruce. Book 7, p. 203. (On
21 June, 1721, this estate paid Timothy Tharpe, Joseph
Delk, Sarah Cornwell, Thos. Wright, Joseph Thorp.)

THOMAS, Priscilla: Leg.- To son, William Blunt, one negro.
Sons, Henry, Thomas, and William Blunt, Exers. Wit:
Thomas Edmunds, Evin Thomas. Made: 15 March, 1732. Prob.:
18 Apr., 1733. Book 8, p. 283.

THOMAS, William: Leg.- To son, John Thomas, all my land on
the South side of Meherrin River, featherbed, furniture,
etc. To son, William, my Plantation he now lives on, one
negro my silver-headed cane, watch, books etc. To daughter, Jane Later, 200 acres, joyning Mr. Blunt's land &
Coll. Wm. Harrison's land. To daughter, Rambley Thomas,
one negro, when she is 18 years old, feather bed etc. To
daughter, Ann, a negro. To daughter, Mary, negro. To son,
Henry, the land where Wm. Saunders now lives and land at
Beaverdam, two negroes, one three-pint silver tankard and
six silver spoon etc., all stock at Meherrin to be equally
divided. My desire is that all goods now come in the Bradby, be sold by outcry at Cabbin's Point, to raise money to
pay Mr. Blunt's children. To wife a negro, and rest of
est. for life, be equally divided among my children. Mentions, "three youngest daughters". Makes wife, Priscilla
Thomas, Exerx. Made: 17 Jan., 1719. Prob.: 17 Feb.,
1719. Wit: Thos. Bedingfield, Howell Edmunds, Wm. Blunt.
Book 7, p. 243.

THOMAS, William: Leg.- To son, John Thomas, land in Essex
county on the southwest side of Deep Run that divided said
land from that of Ralph Rouzee, so along the Ferry Road,
also negroes, pistolls, holsters, silver-headed cane, etc.
To son, William, Catlett Thomas, all the residue of Land in
Essex, with land in eastermost side of now ferry, also two
negroes, five silver spoons and my watch. To wife, Elizabeth Thomas, the Plantation I now live on for her life;
at her death, to my son, William. To wife, three negroes,
for her life, at her death to my two sons. To wife, the
residue of the est. To sons, John and William to be of
age at 16 years, and receive their est. They are to be
well educated out of the estate. Wife, Exer. Brother
John Thomas, and uncle Wm. Thompson, trustees. 28 Dec.,
1720. Prob.: 19 Feb., 1723. Wit: Samuel Judkins,
Martha Thompson, Wm. Thompson. Book 7, p. 505.

THOMPSON, John: Leg.- To brother, Samuel Thompson, 50 lbs.
after decease of my wife, 50 lbs. more. To wife the labor
of certain slaves for life. Brother, William Thompson.
Sisters, Catherine and Elizabeth, negroes. (Brother,
Samuel, not living in Surry Co.) Desires that Samuel Al-
sobrooke, son of Samuel Alsobrooke, deceased, be religious-
ly brought up by Exerx. Friends, Maj. Arthur Allen and
Capt. Francis Clements, each a ring. To two brothers-in-
law, Mr. Robert Paine and Mr. Robert Catlett, each a ring.
To wife, certain things given to her by will of Mr. John
Salway, deceased. Wife, Elizabeth Thompson, is made Exerx.
Made: 2 Aug., 1698. Prob.: 7 Nov., 1699. Wit: Geo.
Williams, Jos. Case, Eliza. Prier, Mary Allen, Wm. Fore-
man, Richard Holleman. Book 5, p. 185.

129

THOMPSON, Nicholas: Leg.- To son, Nicholas, 5 shillings. To
daughter, Ann, a half crown. To daughter, Mary, 5 shillings. To son, John, one-third of the remainder of my est.
Wife, Eleanor, all the remainder of estate not disposed of,
and makes her Exer. Made: 4 Aug., 1723. Prob.: 21 July,
1725. Wit: Anne Mathews, Dan. Eelbank. Book 7, p. 591.

THOMPSON, Samuel: Leg.- The land at Cypress Swamp to my brother, Wm. Thompson, not to be sold, but to any shild of his.
To my nephew, Samuel Thompson my entry at Three Creeks, and
land at the head of Crouches' Creek, that I lately escheat-
ed, 200 acres, not to be possessed by him until the death
of my wife, Mary, and the death of his father, Wm. Thompson. To my brother, Wm. Thompson, my land at Meherrin that
I bought of Wm. Braswell, at the death of my wife, Mary.
To cousin, Wm. Mosely, land upon Nottoway River between the
forks of Atamoosack, it being 200 acres, provided he will
come to it and live on it himself; if not, the land to go
to my brother, Wm. Thompson, and cousin, Samuel Thompson,
after his father's death. To brother William Thompson, the
land where Thos. Higgs lives. My wife to enjoy the profits
of all my lands, my brother and cousins to live on them,
then at her death, all the rest of the land not mentioned
in this will to my brother William; where I live to cousin,
Samuel Thompson; if he die, his share to cousins, Katherine Thompson, William Thompson, John Thompson, and Wm.
Mosely and Mary Mosely, equally divided. To my "Necey",
Elizabeth Thompson, a gold ring that was given me by my
father - Posey, being prepared to follow me, W. T. To Wm.
Marriott a seal ring that was my wife's father's ring. To
cousin, Robert Payne, a gold buttons and shirt buckle. To
cousin, Samuel Thompson, all my Doctor's books, Prayer
Books, and Divinity Books, and makes brother, William
Thompson, Exer. Made: 20 Sept., 1720. Prob.: 17 May,
1721. Wit: Wm. Foster, Samuel Alsobrooke. Bk. 7, p. 334.

THOMPSON, William: Leg.- (Will for great part destroyed).
To son, Samuel Thompson...daughter, Katherine...To daughter, Hannah Thompson, 100 acres of land on Deep Branch. To
son, John, 10 acres, after the decease of his mother. To
grandchildren, Samuel and Mary Thompson, the rest of my
estate. To son, John the pistols and gun given him by Wm.
Mosely. Makes wife, Martha, Exer. Made 20 Dec., 1731.
Prob.: 18 Oct., 1732. Wit: Jane Regan, Mary Regan, Mary
Mastin. Book 8, p. 240.

THORNE, Martin: Est.- 15 May, 1685. Appraisement by Robert
Lancaster, Wm. Newsum, Matthew Swann. Book 3, p. 59.

THORNE, Martin: Nuncupative Will, probated by John Findley
and Roger Nichols. Gave all he possessed to Martin Thorne
and to his wife, Margaret. 3 March, 1695. Book 5, p. 89.

THORP, John: Est.- Mary Thorpe, admr. 25 June, 1721. James
Bruton, James Bennett, Joan Gray. Book 7, p. 339.

THORP, William: Est.- Mary Thorp, admr. Zack. Maddera, Wm.
Warren, Thos. King. 20 May, 1724. Book 7, p. 536.

THORP, William: Leg.- My mother, Mary Thorpe. Brother, Joseph
Thorp, not 21 years old. Sisters, Elizabeth Essell, Sarah
Thorp, Olive Thorp, Margaret Thorp, Hannah Thorp. My
father, Timothy Thorp, Exer. Wit: Wm. Seward, James
Hewster, Samson Wilson. 24 Feb., 1726. Prob.: 17 May,

1727. Book 7, p. 708.

THORP, William: Est.- Thomas Thornton and Mary Thornton, admrs.
17 Nov., 1731. Jos. Nicholson, Robt. Jones. Book 8, p.
140.

THREEWETS, John: Est.- Brunswick County. 18 Dec., 1750.
Thomas Jackson, Jr., James Parham, Abraham Peebles. Book
9, p. 677.

THREWETS, John: Leg.- To son, Peter, 325 acres of land on the
south side of Nottoway River, and west side of Cabbib Stick
Swamp. To son-in-law, Robert Newman, 214 acres, where he
now lives on the south side of Nottoway River. To son,
Joel, 450 acres in Brunswick County on the south side of
Three Creeks and one negro. To son, Edward, 175 acres of
land in Surry County on the south side of Nottoway River
and each side of Cabbin Swamp and one negro. To daughter,
Lucy Threwets, one negro and 15 pounds, money. To my son,
John; and my wife Ann, the Plantation I live on and all
the rest of est. Makes them Exers. 14 Nov., 1749. Prob.:
20 Mar., 1749. Wit: Robert Newman, John Threewets, Jr.,
Thos. Oliver. Book 8, p. 623.

THROWER, Edward: Leg.- To my wife, Tabitha, the use of my
Plantation for her life, and my children. Pay my brother's
estate, which William Gilliam is bound for. To my three
sons, Wm. Thrower, John Thrower, and Edward Thrower, after
their mother's death, all land and housing to be equally
divided, when of age. Makes Wm. Thrower, Exer. Wit:
David Sinckler, Fra. Walker. Made: 13 Nov., 1738. Prob.:
21 Feb., 1738. Book 9, p. 6.

THROWER, John: Est.- By Mary Thrower. 13 Aug., 1730. Book
8, p. 20.

THROWER, Tabitha: Est.- William Gilliam, admr. 24 May, 1740.
Book 9, p. 171.

THROWER, Thomas: Leg.- To my son, Thomas Thrower, all my land
that is between Great Neck and Reedy Branch in Prince
George County; if no issue to my daughter, Elizabeth. If
both Thomas and Elizabeth die without heir, to my daughter,
Hester. To son, Thomas, all the land where I live ad.
Stony and Sapponia Creeks, 125 acres. Wife to have her
"Full being on same", for her life; but if she marry, she
is to have only a child's part. To daughter, Elizabeth,
land on the west side of Reedy Creek in Prince George Co.,
if she die, to son, Thomas; if Thomas & Eliza. die to dau.
Hester. Wife, Mary, Exerx. Made: 14 Nov., 1729. Prob.:
15 Apr., 1730. Wit: John Curtis, Wm. Harper, John Freeman. Book 7, p. 1020.

TOMLINSON, Thomas: Leg.- To sons, William Tomlinson, and
Thomas Tomlinson, negroes, furniture etc. To son, Benjamin, the Plantation where I live and one negro. To daughters, Sarah Carter, Elizabeth Moss, and Amy Carter each ten
shillings. To son, Benjamin Tomlinson, my estate not bequeathed, and makes him Exer. Made: 1 Jan., 1750. Prob.:
19 Mar., 1750. Wit: Jos. Carter, Henry Gee. Book 9,
p. 682.

TOMLINSON, William: Leg.- (This will is illegible for the
greater part). To John Tomlinson..to brother, Richard Tom-

131

linson. Wit: Nicholas Partridge, Christ. Tatum, John Mason. Prob.: 20 Dec., 1732. Book 8, p. 249.

TOOKE, John: Leg.- To son, John Tooke, my estate; if he die to my grandson, Joseph Tooke. Daughters, Sarah and Elizabeth Tooke. Granddaughter, Aureola Tooke. John Parsons and Wm. Ezell, Exers. John Parsons and Samuell Sebrell overseers of the will. Made: 17 Nov., 1720. Prob.: 15 Feb., 1720. Wit: James Wilson, John Glover, George Glover. Book 7, p. 308.

TOOKE, William: Est.- 25 Jan., 1675. John Vinson, aged 40 years, or thereabouts, deposed that Wm. Tooke, lately deceased, on his Death bed bequeathed to Jeane Tooke, his wife, his whole estate and made her Exerx. paying unto John and Rebecka Tooke, his son and daughter, one mare and foal. Wit: Joseph Vinsen, Mary Williams. Book 2, p. 104.

TOWERS, John: Leg.- Gives estate to Robert Lacy, and makes him Exer. Five barrels of corn in the house of Roger Delk, and seventy pounds of tobacco. Mr. Bartlett is to pay for Mr. Bland, "being my due for carrying chain in survey of his land etc." 6 Jan., 1675/6. Wit: Robt. Gyles, Rob. Kee. Book 2, p. 103.

TUCKER, Robert: Est.- 15 Aug., 1722. Thos. Collier, sheriff, Thos. Cocke, Arthur Allen. Book 7, p. 415.

TUCKER, William: Est.- 21 Oct., 1719. Mary Tucker, admr. John Hancocke, Thos. Drew, Nich. Thompson. Book 7, p. 230.

TURNER, Daniel: Leg.- To son, John, the Plantation where I live, 200 acres, after my wife's death. To son, Jeames Tucker, 150 acres, the Upper part. To son, David, 200 acres at Poplar Swamp. To John Clark, the lower part at Poplar Swamp. Mentions wife and five children. Wit: Wm. Rose, Wallis Jones, John Clarke. Made: 18 Feb., 1734. Prob.: 15 Oct., 1735. Book 8, p. 530.

TURNER, Daniel: Est.- Thos. Wallace and Sarah Wallace, Exers. 15 Dec., 1742. Robt. Jones, Jno. Newsum. Book 9, p. 421.

TURNER, John: Est.- Thomas Burgess, admr. 17 Mar., 1735. Jas. Chappell, Jane Jones, Rob. Jones. Book 8, p. 577.

TWYFORD, Jno: Est.- Presented by Richard Smith, who married Mary, the Relict of said Twyford, a small neck of land leased by Jno. Byneham for which rent is to be paid etc. Appraised by Anthony Evans, Nicholas Sessoms, Richard Jordan, Jr. 4 Mar., 1678. Signed: Richard Smith, Mary Smith. Book 2, p. 199.

TYUS, John: Leg.- To son, John Tyus, 100 acres of land on the north side of John Shehawken Swamp, beginning at a Creek.. to Bartholomew Andrews' line etc. To my wife, Mary, all the rest of my estate, real or personal, here or in Great Britain or elsewhere for her widdowhood; but if she marry the personal estate to be equally divided between my wife Mary, and my five children: John Tyus, Thomas Tyus, Priscilla Tyus, Joanner Tyus, and Richard Tyus. After his mother's death, I give to my son, Richard Tyus, my land on the north side of Johnshehawken Swamp, 100 acres; to daughter Grace Moss one shilling. To daughter, Elizabeth Tyus, one shilling. Makes wife, Mary, Exerx. Made: 9 June,

1725. Prob.: 16 Mar., 1725. Wit: John Allen, Richard
Lewis, Daniel Duggard. Book 7, p. 631.

TYUS, Mary: Est.- John Tyus, admr. 4 March, 1735/6. John
Nicholson, Charles Lucas, John Collier. Book 8, p. 589.

TYUS, Thomas: Est.- By John Tyus. 20 July, 1726. Jos. Nicholson, Charles Lucas, Richard Lewis. Book 7, p. ___.

TYUS, Thomas: Est.- 18 Feb., 1734/5. John Tyus, admr. Rec.
of the Exers. of John Tyus my portion of my father's estate.
John Chapman, Thos. Edmunds. Book 8, p. 468.

UNDERHILL, Giles: Leg.- Daughter Sary Garritt. To my wife all
my property for her life, then to be divided between John,
Henry, Mary, Elizabeth. Wife, Mary Underhill, Relict,
Exerx., there being no Exer. Wit: Richard Rives, Jonas
Crosland. Made: 27 Jan., 1723. Prob.: 15 April, ___.
Book ___ p. ___.

UPCHURCH, Frances, widdow: By Henry Tooker. 3 Jan., 1691/2.
Torn acct. except clothes and ring given to her daughter,
according to her order at her death. Sworn to by Michael
Upchurch. 1 March, 1691. Charles Jaret, Thos. Lane.
Book 4, p. 258.

UPCHURCH, Michael: Est.- 25 July, 1687. Frances, his Relict,
applies for administration on his est. Book 2, p. 288.

VALENTINE, Nicholas: Est.- 20 July, 1737. John Ruffin, Sheriff. Book 8, p.___.

VASSER, Daniel: Est.- By Robert Wynne, Sheriff. 19 June,
1750. Book 9, p. 644.

VAUGHAN, James: Leg.- To Mrs. Hannah Clinch a gold ring with
letters "I.W.". To daughter-in-law, Lucy Moreland, a gold
ring with letters, "T.V.E.". To James Ransom. To Mrs.
Mary Holt, widow of Capt. Thos. Holt, deceased. To friend
Wm. Seward. (Rem. of will illegible). Book 8, p. 161.
(1731)

VINCENT, Peter: Est.- 3 Aug., 1728. Sarah Vincent, admr. Appraised by John Mayson, Wm. Shands, Wm. Heath, Chris. Tatum. Book 7, p. 851.

VINSON, John: Leg.- Estate to wife, Katherine Vinson, and makes
her Exerx. Fra. Sowerby, Richard Rose, Thos. Sowerby. 20
Oct., 1698. Book 5, p. 173.

VINSON, Katherine: Leg.- To Thomas Rose, son of Richard Rose,
180 acres of land, part of a tract, formerly sold to Richard Rose. To dau., Elizabeth Rose, my wearing clothes,
pewter dishes etc. To my grandchild, Ann Rose, a cow. To
Thomas Sowerby, a cow. To my godson, Charles Reeks one cow.
To Elizabeth Jarrard a looking qlass. To Elias Ogbourne
a bed, blankets etc. To daughter, Jane Reeks, a cow. To
sons, Francis Sowerby and John Sowerby, the remainder of
my estate equally divided, and makes them Exers. Made:
26 March, 1704. Prob.: 6 Nov., 1705. Wit: Mary Oxford,
John Avery, Henry Floyd. Book 5, p. 339.

VIVER, John: Est.- Attached by Jno. Thompson. 3 Oct., 1685.
Book 3, p. 38.

WADE, Daniel: Leg.- To Thomas King my whole estate. Bequest
to friend Nicholas Smith, and makes him Exer. Made: 18
Sept., 1695. Prob.: 3 Mar., 1695. Wit: Thos. Waller,
Geo. Williams. Book 5, p. 88.

WALKER, Humphrey: Est.- 16 May, 1722. Wm. Raines, Jr., Admr.
Richard Pace, Thos. Avent, Richard More. Book 7, p. 396.

WALKER, Timothy: Leg.- To godson, John Phillips, son of William Phillips, my Great Bible, Scimeter and belt and five
shillings. To my friend, Joseph John Jackman, after my
funeral expenses are paid, all the rest of my estate either
here in Virginia or England, or elsewhere. Wit: John
Hatch, Thos. Ridley. Made: 1 Sept., 1706. Prob.: 4
March, 1706. Book 5, p. 362.

WALKER, Timothy: Est.- 30 April, 1707. Henry Sandy, Fra. Regand. Book 5, p. 368.

WALL, Joseph: Leg.- To son, James Wall, 100 acres bought of
Thos. Miller..to the land of James Wall. To son, John Wall,
Bible, Sarment Book, tools etc. To daughter, Elizabeth one
chest, etc. To son, Joseph Wall, 5 shillings. To son,
Richard Wall, 5 shillings. Rest of estate to my wife, and
son, Robert Wall, after my funeral expenses are paid.
Makes son, John Wall, Exer. Prob.: 19 April, 1727. Wit:
Robert Lancaster, Thomas Pittman. Book 7, p. 684.

WALL, Thomas: Nuncupative Will. Made: 9 Nov., 1673. 20 Nov.,
1673 by Richard Hogwood and James Mathews., Put into writing at the request of Francis Hogwood, heir to the estate.
Debts of tobacco due to Lt. Coll. Jordan, Robert Burgess,
Jno. Emerson and Christopher Foster, and they owed him
likewise. Francis Hogwood should take all he had in Virginia, pay his debts, and keep the rest. Wit: Richard
Hogwood, James Mathews. Book 2, p. 37 (a).

WALL, Thomas: Est.- Probate of the will by Francis Hogwood,
given at James City. 7 April, 1674. Book 2, p. 51.

WALLER, Thomas: Leg.- Son, Thomas Waller to pay all debts, and
have pewter bason pewter plates, pewter porringer. To son,
Wm. Waller, 400 lbs. of tobacco. Son, John Waller, one-
half my wearing clothes, 200 lbs. of tobacco and hogs.
To two daughters, Katherine and Sarah Waller, beds and furniture, hogs, cows etc. Daughter, Mary, 10 shillings.
Daughter, Elise, 5 shillings. Daughter, Elizabeth, 5 shillings. All the rest of my estate to my five children: John,
Thomas, William, Katherine and Sarah. Thos. Waller, Exer.
Wit: Wm. Drew, Wm. Allen. Made: 1 Feb., 1720. Prob.:
19 Apr., 1721. Book 7, p. 329.

WALLER, Thomas: Est.- John Ruffin, admr. 29 Dec., 1750. Thos.
Holt, John Newsum, Thos. Binns, Book 9, p. 678.

WALLIS, Thomas, Sr.: Leg.- Son, James, to have the manner
Plantation. The land to be equally divided between my two
sons. If James have no heir, to go to son, John. If John
should die, the land to James. To son, Thomas Wallis, one
shilling. To daughter, Martha iron heaters. To grandson,
Frederick Roberts one cow. To son, William Wallis, one
shilling. Makes wife, Ann, Exerx. Wit: Stephen Hamlin,
James Marsengill. Made: 6 Aug., 1745. Prob.: 16 Jan.,
1749. Book 9, p. 622.

WALLIS, William: Est.- 15 Oct., 1740. Book 9, p. 226.

WAPPLE, John: Est.- By Mary Wapple. 20 June,1716. Wm. Nott, Harry Floyed, George Hagood. Book 7, p. 20.

WARD, Samuel: Leg.- To Daniel Eelbank, my Bible. To Michael Harris, my Psalm Book and my horse. To goddaughter, Mary Gilbert, daughter of Roger Gilbert, one cow. Friend, Nicholas Magget, the remainder of my estate, and makes him Exer. Made: 13 April, 1720. Prob.: 15 June, 1720. Wit: Michael Harris, John Dance, Dorothy Gilbert. Book 7, p. 268.

WARD, Thomas: Leg.- To wife, Elizabeth the benefit of my Plantation until my son, Thomas Ward, comes of age, and afterward she is to have one-third of the land. To son, Thomas, one-half of my land I live upon with housing, long gun, household goods, etc. To son, John Ward, the other one-half after his mother's death. Rest of estate to be equally divided between my wife and children. As for my land, the survivors to have all. Friends, James Reddick and Joseph Richeson, overseers of my will. Made: 20 Feb., 1675. Prob.: 4 July, 1676. Wit: John Person, James Stringfield. Book 2, p. 118.

WARD, Thomas: Est.- Probate granted Mrs. Elizabeth Ward on the estate of her husband, deceased, Thos. Ward's Will. Signed: at Green Spring by Sir. Wm. Berkeley. 16 Mar., 1676. Book 2, p. 119.

WARREN, Allen: Leg.- To my wife, bed & furniture, my riding horse, saddle and bridle, etc. To son, Allen Warren, all the land I hold in this county, bed & Furniture, where I now lie, one negro, my Trooper's Arms, and enjoy his inheritance at once. To my son Allen Warren, 3 bbls. of corn. To son, Robert, all the Land I hold in Prince George County, sell the negro girl and money to Robert, 808 lbs. of tobacco in the hands of Mr. Bridger, Sherrif in Isle of Wight, and to remain with mother until 21 years old. If she marry to have estate at 18 years of age. Wife and four daughters, Sarah, Elizabeth, Lucy and Mary, to have the rest of my estate. Wife Exerx. Wit: Sam. Sands, Chas. Binns, Thom. Foster. Made: 16 Dec., 1732. Prob.: 15 Aug., 1733. Book 8, p. 325.

WARREN, Allen, Jr.: Est.- By Anne Warren. 16 Jan., 1733. Sam. Taylor, Nich. Thompson, Wm. Batten. Book 8, p. 345.

WARREN, Allin: Est.- 21 Mar., 1738. John Little, Anne Little, Alias Warren, Exers. Book 9, p. 47.

WARREN, Edward: Leg.- To be buried by wife, Grace Creed. Appoints loving friend, Nicholas Meriweather, Exer. To four daughters-in-law my wearing apparel. Jolindy to have her first choice in my whole est. after my debts are paid. To son-in-law, William Creed the rem. of my estate. Orders the executor to do the best way for sd. son, if he die in minority, then it shall fall to his sister, Mary Creede. If she die, to her three sisters. Have some entertainment for guest at the funeral. Memorandum. Edward Warren, his debts paid, gives to Martin Johnson his wearing apparel. Geo. Jordan, Robt. Spensor. Made: 15 April, 1676. Prob.: 18 Apr., 1676. Book 2, p. 114.

WARREN, Edward: Est.- Probated granted to Ni. Meriweather on
the Will of Edward Warren, deceased, signed at James City
by the Gov. 14 June, 1676.

WARREN, Elizabeth: Leg.- To son, John Warren, 30 acres of land
that runs up to Hall Cabbin..To son, Robert Warren, all the
remaining part of my land. To son, William Warren, two
sheep. To granddaughter, Mary Warren, a trunk. To grandson, Thomas Warren a featherbed etc. To son, Joseph Warren
an iron pot. To grandson, James Davis, a cow. To son,
Robert, all the remainder of the estate, and makes him Exer.
Made: 21 Aug., 1724. Prob.: 21 Oct., 1730. Wit:
Michale Harris, Allen Warren, Catherine Harris. Book 8, p.
60.

WARREN, Jno.: Est.- By Mary Warren. Relict and Administratrix.
Appraisement by James Reddick, Richard Briggs, Richard Harris. John Price sworn before Capt. Law. Baker. Presented
3 9br, 1674. By Jno. Denfield, who married sd. Relict.
Book 2, p. 64.

WARREN, John: Est.- Com. of administration granted Mary Warren
on the estate of her deceased husband, Jno. Warren. Signed
at James Citty by the Gov. 18 June, 1675. Book 2, p. 82.

WARREN, John: Est.- Sarah Warren, admrx. 9 Mar., 1731. Mich.
Harris, Wm. Smith, Robt. Gray. Book 8, p. 168.

WARREN, John: Est.- By Stevenson Buxton. 21 May, 1735. John
Simmons, Jr., Thos. Eldridge, Jr. Book 8, p. 498.

WARREN, Robert: Est.- Robert Warren, admr. 15 May, 1728.
Nich. Maget, Gil. Gray, W. Gray, Jr. Book 7, p. 810.

WARREN, Thomas: Leg.- To son, William Warren, where I live
and the land between the two Swamps, 80 acres, after the
death of my wife. To son, John Warren, the land called
Rich Neck, where he now lives. To son, Joseph Warren my
land lying upon Peterfells, and buck point, between Hog
Pen Swamp and Wild Swamp, 90 acres. To son, Robert Warren,
land between Hull Cabbin and shee cabbins, 40 acres. To
wife, Elizabeth Warren, all the rest of my estate. Makes
her Exerx., with son, William. Wit: Nich. Smith, John
Deberry, Nich. Maget. Prob.: 16 Aug., 1721. Book 7, p.
362.

WARREN, William: Est.- 2 June, 1702. Prob. by James Warren,
admr. Rich. Smith, Geo. Williams. Book 5, p. 260.

WARRIN, Allen: Leg.- To son, Benjamin the Plantation I live on
and all land, 100 acres; makes him Exer. Made: 15 Mar.,
1737/8. Prob.: 16 Jan., 1744. Wit: Thos. Warren, John
Warren, Thos. Barham. Book 9, p. 488.

WARWELL, Thomas: Est.- Wife, Elizabeth, admr. 1C 7br, 1675.
Fra. Mason, Jno. Hunnicutt, Jno. Phillips, John Pulitson.
Book 2, p. 87.

WASHINGTON, Eliza: Est.- Bv Thomas Washington. 15 Oct., 1735.
Pd. to Geo. Washington, John Washington, Thomas Washington,
William Washington, Arthur Washington, Dau. Eliza. Lanier,
Priscilla Lanier, Faith Baldwin, Mary Heart, Ann Steavens,
bed to Thomas Steavens, son of Thomas Steavens, to Thomas
Lanier, son of Robert Lanier. Book 8, p. 529.

WASHINGTON, Elizabeth: Leg.- Son, George, pewter dishes and a silk handkerchief. To son, Richard, 3 ells of holland. To son, John, chest, jugs, etc. To son, Thomas, featherbed & furniture, chest of drawers, seal skin trunk etc. To son William Warren, 3 pewter dishes and 2 plaits. To son, James 3 cows, pot racks etc. To son, Arthur, one large Bible and Common Prayer Book etc. To daughter, Elizabeth Lanier, gold ring, cold still etc. To daughter, Priscilla Lanier, 40 shillings worth. To daughter, Faith Barker, large bason. To daughter, Ann, a book called "Christ's Famous Title", and a golden chain. Daughter, Mary Hart. Dau. Ann Washington. Son, Thos. Washington Exer. Wit: Benj. Reeks, Thos. Drinkard, Robt. Clary. Prob.: 21 May, 1735. Book 8, p. 496.

WASHINGTON, Richard: Leg.- To son, George Washington, 300 acres of land on the west side of Nottoway Swamp..below John Barnes land, one negro, and livestock, for his life, then to son, Richard Washington, all land he hath in his possession, his full share of est. To son, John Washington, 150 acres of land at Pokefield Branch, and stock in possession, and two negroes. To son, Thomas Washington, the Land and Plantation where I now live, being at Blackwater Swamp, at foot bridge to widdow Evans..to Pocoson..to Mill Branch, not to sell or lease for seven years, and two negroes, and he to buy a negro for Ann Washington, also six leather chairs Horse Arms etc. To son, James Washington, 165 acres at Seacock Swamp, not to mortgage or sell for seven years. To son, Arthur Washington, all the remaining part of land below Thomas Washington, on Blackwater, 300 acres, not to sell or lease for seven years; also 200 acres between Geo. Washington and Flaggy Run, 6 leather chairs, and tables, chest, etc. also three negroes. Daughter Elizabeth Lanier, 200 acres of land on the west side of Mill Branch, where she now lives. To son-in-law, Sampson Lanier, 200 acres in Isle of Wight County on the east side of Flaggy Run..to Robt. Rix's line. To daughter, Priscilla Washington, negroes, horses, goods etc. To daughter, Ann Washington household goods etc. To daughter, Faith Barker, sheep etc. To daughter, Mary Hart, one negro; grandson, Thomas Lanier one negro; gr. sons, Arthur Sampson, Richard and Samuel each a cow. To grandson, John Washington 250 acres of land in Isle of Wight County at the mouth of Nottoway River. To Richard and Joseph Barker, each a cow. Wife, negroes, goods etc. Ch. - Geo., John, Thomas, William, James, Arthur, Priscilla, and Ann. John Simmons and Howell Edmunds overseers of will. Made: 9 Nov., 1724. Prob.: 19 May, 1725. Wit: Howell Edmunds, Dan. Eelbank, Richard Shaky. Book 7, p. 583.

WASHINGTON, Richard: Est.- 18 Aug., 1723. Elizabeth Washington choice for legacy. J. Simmons, Nich. Cocke, Jos. Nickolson. Book 7, p. 593.

WASHINGTON, Richard: Est.- Geo. Washington and Thomas Washington, Exers. 20 Mar., 1733. Benjamin Edwards, John Ruffin. Book 8, p. 361.

WASHINGTON, Thomas: Est.- This est. lying in Brunswick County. Agnes Washington, admr. 20 June, 1749. Wm. Mosely, Benj. Mosely, Thos. Clanton. Book 9, p. 609.

WASHINGTON, Thomas: Est.- 27 Jan., 1748. Edward Baily, Benj. Reeks. Book 9, p. 613.

WATHEN, James: Leg.- To daughter, Anne Wathen, 20 pounds,
    current money to buy a negro; if she die to seven years, to
    return and be in the hands of Mr. Nicholas Cocke. Wife to
    have the remainder of est. Makes wife, Mary, Exerx. Wit:
    Nicholas Cocke, Elizabeth Lanier, Mary Rawlings. Made:
    18 Feb., 1723. Prob.: 18 Mar., 1723. Book 7, p. 519.

WATKINS, ___: Leg.- Desires to be buried in the Chancel of
    the church at Lawnes Creek Parish, as predecessors have
    been, in the Chancel of the Parish Church where they dwelt.
    Bequest to wife, Elizabeth and to goddaughter, Elizabeth
    Spensor, daughter of Robert Spensor. To cousin Charles
    Barham, son of my Uncle, Capt. Charles Barham. Residue of
    estate to be divided equally between my wife, Elizabeth,
    and cousin, Christopher Watkins, of White Hart Co't in
    Long Lane, London; but if wife is with child, the cousin's
    part to such child. My land to my wife for her life, and
    then to my child, if any; in default, to be sold and pro-
    ceeds sent to cousin, Watkins, or his heirs. Gift of 1000
    lbs. of tobacco to Lawnes Creek Church, to be laid out in
    Plate, also 1000 lbs. of tobacco to Capt. Charles Barham.
    To John Price, 300 acres of land surveyed for Peter Greene,
    to lie next to Sunken Marsh Mill 7 Clothes. To Wm. New-
    sum a coat. To friends Wm. Sherwood 20 shillings for a
    ring. Exers., wife, Elizabeth and Uncle, Capt. Charles
    Barham. Made: __ Sept., 1673. Prob.: 20 Nov., 1673.
    Wit: Wm. Sherwood, Jennette Davis. Book 2, p. 36.

WATKINS, George (Capt.): Est.- Inventory presented by Mrs.
    Eliza. Watkins, late wife and Exerx. Appsm. by Wm. Thomson,
    Randall Holt, and Fra. Mason. 7 Jan., 1673. In 7 7br,
    1675, admr. of est. was presented by Mr. Robert Ruffin,
    "who married ye Relict". Book 2, p. 46.

WATKINS, Henry: Est.- John Watkins, admr. 20 Mar., 1678.
    Book 2, p. 198.

WATKINS, Henry: Est.- Presented by John Watkins, Inventory. 6
    May, 1679. Jno. Moring, Nicholas Witherington, Thos.
    Sowerby. Book 2, p. 205.

WATKINS, Henry: Est.- 18 April, 1744. Book 9, p. 465.

WATKINS, James: Leg.- To Eliza. Webb, two cows, if she stay
    out her time. To goddaughter, Susannah Greene, Richard
    Greene's daughter, one cow. To wife, Judith Watkins, all
    the rest of my estate, and makes her Exerx. Sworn to by
    Maximilian Mansell, Adam Heath.

WATKINS, James: Est.- 15 April, 1724. Book 7, p. 526.

WATKINS, John: Leg.- To my son, Robert, my Plantation where
    I now live and ye Plantation at Indian Field that he hath
    now in possession, reserving ye wife, Elizabeth, use of
    Plantation where I live for her life, adjoins Ja. Chestetts
    to the Swamp, where Mr. Thos. Collier's mill stands, to the
    Deep Bottom Branch..to Jas. Davis, where he did lately live
    ..to Mr. Will. Edwards, to Indian Field Swamp..also my
    place where Jno. Parr now lives and land on the east side
    of Colt's Branch, a negro, household goods, silver tankard,
    gold ring, twelve pewter plates and dishes, wall table,
    six leather chairs, and larg looking glass. To son, John,
    the Plantation where John Cooke live and my Plantation
    where James Davis did lately live, when son John is 21

years old, and 1060 lbs. of tobacco. To my son, Henry,
my Plantation at Blackwater Swamp, bought of Robert Warren,
when 21 years old, and negro. If son, Henry, die, the negro to son, William. To son, William, my Land on the south
side of Cypress Swamp and Tyus' Branch, when 21 years old,
and one negro. To daughter, Mary, one negro when 21 years
old, or married. To daughter, Elizabeth, one negro, one
cow and 500 lbs. of tobacco. To wife, Elizabeth, household goods and two negroes. To my wife, goods coming from
England for tobacco I sent home to be equally divided between wife and children. Made: 5 Nov., 1703. Prob.:
5 Mar., 1708. Wit: Nich. Maget, John Watkins, Jr., Eliza.
Skelton. Book 5, p. 407.

WATKINS, John: Leg.- To brother, Henry Watkins, all the Land
I have on the south side of that Swamp where I now live.
To brother, Robert Watkins, an amount out of the estate to
40 shillings. The use of the Plantation where I now live
to my wife Ann, for her life, then to my brother, Henry
Watkins and my gun. Wife to have all the rem. of est.
Wit: Nicholas Maget, Francis Sowerby, Mary Judkins.
Made: 12 May, 1722. Prob.: 20 June, 1722. Bk. 7, p.401.

WATKINS, John: Leg.- To son, John Watkins, all the land that
my mother-in-law holds as her dower. Bequest to child in
esse. Wife, Mary, Exerx. Wit: Robert Wager, Thos. Bage,
Benj. Nicholson. Made: 18 June, 1748. Prob.: 16 Jan.,
1749. Book 9, p. 619.

WATSON, Thos.: Est.- Presented by Thos. Avent, Richard Moore,
James Odyan. 18 Feb., 1718. Book 7, p. 178.

WEATHERS, Thomas: Leg.- To son, William, the Plantation where
I live, land purchased of John Jones. To son, Benjamin,
the Plantation purchased of Jeremiah Ellis. To son,
Thomas, the Plantation and Land on Spring Swamp, purchased
of Thos. Atkinson. To son, William the feather bed where
I lie and a horse. To son, Michael, a young colt, and cow
and calf. To daughter, Susannah, one cow. To sons, Benjamin, John, Isaac, and Reuben, to each a cow. All the
rest and remainder of estate to wife for her life, or
marriage, then to be equally divided between wife, Lidia,
and the children. Made Wife, and son, Wm. Exers. Made:
26 Oct., 1744. Prob.: 17 Oct., 1744. Wit: Wm. Pettway,
Edward Pettway, Rich. Rives. Book 9, p. 481.

WEAVER, Henry: Est.- By John Weaver. 20 May, 1719. John
Mason, Giles Underhill, Nicholas Partridge. Bk. 7, p. 186.

WEAVER, John: Leg.- To son, John Weaver, 20 shillings. To
son, William Weaver, 20 shillings. To daughter, Joyce
Callihan, 20 shillings. To dau., Elizabeth Weaver - Grandson, John Weaver, one-half the land I bought of Thos. Tomlinson, which land his father was possessed with, before
his death etc. To son, Edward Weaver the other one-half
of the land. To son, Stephen Weaver, the estate if John
die. If grandson, John Weaver, die without heirs, his
portion to go to my youngest son, Stephen Weaver. Wife,
Elizabeth Weaver, Exerx. Prob.: 17 Feb., 1719. Wit:
John Mason, Gilbert Hay, William Weaver. Bk. 7, p. 244.

WEBB, Nicholas: Est.- By LDeloney, admr. 15 Jan., 1734. W.
Rookings, Thomas Allstin, Jos. Washington. Bk. 8, p. 443.

WEBSTER, Thomas: Est.- By Thos. Sidway, admr. 23 Aug., 1677.
Hes. Bunnell, Jno. Tayler. Book 2, p. 193.

WEEKS, Stephen: Leg.- To Timothy Isold, son of Timothy Isold,
one hog. To his brother, Michael Isold, one hog. To
Mary Braderton, daughter of Henry Braderton, one hog. Makes
Timothy Isold, and Edward Tanner, appraisers of the estate.
To wife, Mary Weeks, the rem. of my est. after my debts are
paid. Made: 20 May, 1676. Prob.: 4 September, 1677.
Wit: John Oasse, Judith Oase. Book 2, p. 141.

WEEKS, Thomas: Leg.- Bequests to loving friends, Thos. Foseraft, and Thomas Gray, and makes them Exers. To Joan Gray,
daughter of Francis Gray. Wit: Wm. Thompson, Jno. Thomson. Made: 1 March, 1675/6. Prob.: 2 May, 1676. Book
2, p. 114.

WEST, Sarah: Leg.- To son, Nicholas Lanier my glazing tools,
barber's bason etc. To daughter, Mary Hill, one cow, and
planks. To daughter, Sarah West, the remainder of my estate; if no heir to son, Nicholas and dau., Mary. Daughter, Sarah, Exerx. Made: 20 Aug., 1744. Prob.: 19 June,
1750. Wit: Thos. Allstin, Wm. Rookings. Book 9, p. 642.

WESTON, William: Est.- By Eliza. Weston. 3 Jan., 1727/8.
Sam. Thompson, Mich. Harris, Wm. Marriott. Book 7, p. 784.

WHITE, Charles: Leg.- To my eldest son, John White, all my
Land and Plantation where I live; if no issue then to next
oldest and then to the youngest. My desire is that my wife
have the use of my Plantation, and the north part of my
land for her life. To son, Charles, livestock and horse
sold to Christopher Rowling. To daughter, Elizabeth bed &
bedding etc. when 18 years old, or married. If she die to
my wife and four youngest children. To daughter, Ann Raw-
ling, a steer. Rest of estate to my wife and four youngest
children: Walter, Mary, William and Thomas White. Wife,
Exerx. Wit: Roger Williams, John Case. Made: 26 Jan.,
1709/10. Prob.: 2 May, 1710. Book 6, p. 8.

WHITE, Charles: Est.- Appraisement presented by Naomy White.
2 May, 1710. Signed: Naomy Case, on 4 July, 1710. Book
6, p. 25.

WHITE, Charles: Leg.- To my grandson, Charles Holsworth, one
negro and ten pounds in money. To my granddaughter, Mary
Holsworth, one negro in possession of her father, Charles
Holsworth and ten pounds, money. To my son, Robert White,
my Plantation and Land where I live, also land on Seacock
Swamp, and eight negroes. To my daughter, Jane Clinch, the
use of three negroes for her life, then to be equally divided among her children, also a riding horse etc. To my
grandson, Wm. Clinch, one negro. To son, Robert, two of
my best beds, 67 pounds money, a horse and all debts due
me, also a desk, table and dishes. Bequests to gr. children, Charles and Mary Holdsworth. Son-in-law, James Clinch
and son, Robert, Exers. Wit: Richard Cocke, Hartwell
Cocke, Katherine Piland. Made: 28 March, 1747. Prob.:
15 April, 1747. Book 9, p. 552.

WHITE, John: Leg.- Bequest to Francis Mason. To John, the
son of John Price, a mare formerly my sister Mary White's.
To John Price, Son., one-half of what is due from him to
me. To Robert Caufield fifty shillings. To my sisters,

140

Lucy Corker and Mary White, my whole estate to be equally
divided. Makes them Exerxs. Made: 1 April, 1679. Prob.:
6 May, 1679. Wit: Fra. Tayler, Phillip Shelby. Book 2,
p. 203.

WHITE, John: Leg.- To my brother, William White, my wearing
apparel and a chest. To my cozen John Humphrey, son of my
sister, Mary Humphrey, 30 shillings for learning, to the
two eldest of my sister, Mary's children 20 shillings to
be for learning. To my sister, Elizabeth White, five
pounds money. To my brother, Walter White, a bridle and
saddle, and my great coat. To my cozen Chris. Moring The
Whole Duty of Man. To Jane Moring a Prayer Book. To my
brother, Charles White's three children each 20 shillings
to put them to school. To Thomas and Mary Wrenn, each a
Bible. To brother Walter White's three children, to each
20 shillings. Brother, Charles White, Exer. Made: 14
March, 1727/8. Prob.: 17 April, 1728. Wit: Nich. Maget,
Matthew Metcalf, Fran. Regan. Book 7, p. 800.

WHITE, John: Leg.- To my son-in-law, Thomas Lawrence, bed,
15 cattle, 2 horses, hoggs, etc. To cozen, Sarah Hays, one
heifer. To grandson, Wm. Morris, one heifer. To grandson,
John Lawrence, pewter plates, bed, etc. To granddaughter,
Elizabeth Lawrence pewter dishes, etc. at Hubard Farrall's.
Rest of my estate to Thomas Lawrence. Made: 8 Dec., 1729.
Prob.: 18 Feb., 1729. Wit: Lawrence House, William Renn,
E. Wingfield. Book 7, p. 1005.

WHITE, Mary: Leg.- To Eliza., wife of Mr. Nicholas Cocke,
chest, gold ring, silver shoe buckles etc. To Mary Holt,
daughter of Thos. Holt, pewter dishes, gold ring, large
fire dogs, and money due me from said Thomas Holt, after the
death of her father, and she to discharge a debt to Mr.
Wm. Dawkins of London, also my great chest. To Katherine
Holt, daughter of Thos. Holt, one black horse, three pewter dishes, small chest etc. To Martha Holt, daughter of
Thomas Holt, pewter dishes etc. To Lucy Holt, daughter of
Thomas Holt, leather chairs and pewter dishes. To Francis
and Thomas Holt, sons of Thomas Holt, bed I lie on, and
pewter dishes. To Thomas Holt one-half the money due me,
and make him Exer. Wit: Francis Price, Elizabeth Holt, Jr.
Made: 5 March, 1720/21. Prob.: 21 June, 1721. Book 7,
p. 343.

WHITE, Thomas: Leg.- His estate to be divided between his wife,
Phillis and children: Thomas, Mary, Rebecca, and Elizabeth.
Sister-in-law, Elizabeth Ruffin, have the land, and manage-
ment of daughter, Rebecca, and her estate, and place daugh-
ter Elizabeth, and her estate with whom she please. Mr.
Robert Lancaster to have the care of son, Thomas, and daugh-
ter Mary, and their estates. Makes wife, Phillis, Exerx.
Elizabeth Ruffin and Robert Lancaster, overseers of the
will. Made: 7 May, 1694. Prob.: 4 Sept., 1694. Wit:
Thos. Bage, W. Edwards, John Thompson. Book 5, p. 20.

WHITE, Walter: Leg.- To wife, Hannah, two negroes for her life,
then equally divided among all my children: Benjamin,
Henry, Lucy, Joe and Nanny. Wit: Rich. Cocke, James
Clinch. Made: 23 Sept., 1743. Prob.: 18 Sept., 1745.
Book 9, p. 511.

WHITE, William: Leg.- To Thomas Smith, the son of Will. Smith,
a cow. To Willi. Smith, my wearing apparel etc. To my

wife the rest of the est. Wit: Robert Parke. 16 9br, 1677. Book 2, p. 153.

 WHITEHEAD, Robert: Est.- By Elizabeth Whitehead, admrx. John Threeweet, Solomon Wynne, Jollum Sturdivant. 21 April, 1731. Book 8, p. 93.

WIGGINS, Sarah: Makes Gifts as follows: to eldest son, John Bayley, to dau., Eliza. Cooper, to Daughter, Mary Wiggin, to son, William Wiggin. 16 May, 1711. Wit: Richard Hide, Jno. Phillips. Book 6, p. 56.

WIGGINS, Thomas: Leg.- To son, Richard Wiggin, a piece of Land at Johnchehocan Swamp where he dwelleth, 140 acres, part of Land I bought of Mr. John Simmons. To son, John Wiggin, a Plantation at Johnchehocan, which I lately made there and all the remaining part I hold there, and part bought of Mr. John Simmons. To son, Thomas Wiggin, 100 acres of land at Johnchehocan..to a road that comes from Jno. Parsons, also Plantation bought from John Simmons. To my son, William, after my wife's death, Sarah Wiggins, three-fourths of the Plantation where I dwell; the other one-fourth to my son, John Wiggins. To daughter, Eliza. Cooper, two ewes. Daughter, Mary Wiggins, one cow, when sixteen years old. To daughter, Sarah, a cow when sixteen or married. Sons, William and John each a mare at 18 years old. Made: 31 Jan., 1710/11. Prob.: 25 Feb., 1710. Wit: Will. Cocke, Thos. Cocke. Book 6, p. 41.

WILKASON, John: Verbal Will. All of his estate to his wife, Elizabeth for her life, then to his son, Mathew Wilkason. 7 May, 1700. Hump. Folpe, Richard Green, Thos. Adkins. Book 5, p. 203.

WILKINSON, John: Est.- By Eliza. Wilkinson, admrx. 2 July, 1700. Richard Bullock, Adam Heath. Book 5, p. 210.

WILLIAMS, Charles: Leg.- Daughter, Elizabeth Champion 5 lbs. Daughter, Mary Seward, one horse. Grandson, Charles Champion, bed, gun etc. Son-in-law, Benjamin Champion, wearing clothes. Child in esse, whether boy or girl, 100 acres in Lawnes Creek Parish, if it dies to granddaughter, Elizabeth Champion. All estate here or in England, to be equally divided between my wife, Elizabeth and child in esse. Wife made Exerx. Made: 14 Dec., 1720. Prob.: 16 Aug., 1721. Wit: Wm. Gray, James Vaughan, Bartlett Moreland. Book 7, p. 357.

WILLIAMS, David: Leg.- Bequest to Wm. Harris, orphan of one gun and two pewter dishes. To wife, Martha Williams, my whole estate to be divided between her and her children. Child in esse to have equal portion with my wife and daughter. 28 Dec., 1675. Prob.: 28 March, 1676. Wit: James Murray, Jno. Twyford. Book 2, p. 106.

WILLIAMS, George: Est.- 25 May, 1703. Nath. Harrison, Samuel Thompson. Book 5, p. 282.

WILLIAMS, Jones: Leg.- To brother, Edmund Hubbard, one negro. To my kinsman, John Tyler, one negro. To my brother, Edmund Hubbard my Plantation at Meherrin and an account due me from Abraham Saul. A horse had of John Stevens to my kinswoman, Ann Hunt, and all jewels, gold, silver, goods and chattels. Makes "My kinsman, George Hunt" Exer. Wit:

Edward Harper, Mathew Edloe, John Macon. Made: 8 Nov., 1717. Prob.: 21 May, 1718. Book 7, p. 121.

WILLIAMS, Lewis: Est.- Mrs. Elizabeth Merriweather has made suit to the Court that Commissioners be appointed in right of the orphans of the deceased. Mr. Robert Caufield and Mr. Arthur Allen appointed. Mrs. Eliza. Meriweather to qualify. 16 June, 1679. Book 2, p. 216.

WILLIAMS, Roger: Leg.- To son, Roger, all my Land he now lives on, and he pay his brother, George Williams, 500 lbs. of tobacco. If no issue to surviving brothers. Wife, Mary Williams, to have the use of my Plantation, housing and land where I live, for her life, then to my son Samuell, if no heirs, to my son, George. After my debts are paid the remainder of my estate to be divided between my wife and children. Wife and son, Roger, Exers. Wit: Nich. Smith, Benj. Foreman, Rand. Revell. Made: 24 Oct., 1706. Prob.: 5 March, 1708. Book 5, p. 411.

WILLIAMS, Roger: Leg.- Gives wife use of all Lands and Plantation for her life; at her death to my son, Thomas and one negro. If no heir, negro to my three daughters, Eliza. Bage, Mary Lancaster, wife of Law. Lancaster and Jane Williams. To daughter, Elizabeth Bage one negro for her life, then to granddaughter, Eliza. Lucy Bage. To daughter, Mary Lancaster, wife of Lawrence Lancaster, one negro; if no heirs to three children, Thomas Williams, Eliza. Bage, and Jane Williams. Daughter, Jane Williams one cow. Son, Thomas, a negro. Wife, Exerx. Made: 7 Aug., 1744. Prob.: 20 March, 1744. Wit: Wm. Jordan, John Sharpe, Robt. Gray. Will presented by Katherine Williams. Book 9, p. 497.

WILLIAMS, William: Leg.- To son, Lewis Williams, 40 acres adjoining his own land up Wet Slash to Green Swamp. To daughter, Hester, my Plantation where I live with one-half the remaining part of land and one negro. Son, William, to have the use of the other part of the land for seven years then to my daughter, Lidia. Gives daughter, Lidia, into the care of Wm. Newsum's wife until of age, or married and teach her to read the Catechism. To daughters, Anne, Katherine, Mary, Hannah, Unity, and Faith, each five shillings. Sons John and William five shillings each. Mentions five children, Lewis, Wm., Eliza, Lidia, and Hester. Friend, Wm. Edwards and son, Lewis Williams, Exers. Made: 17 Nov., 1740. Prob.: 16 April, 1741. Wit: Wm. Edwards, John Johnson. Book 9, p. 294.

WILLIAMSON, Guthbert: Est.- Hallum Sturdivant, Elizabeth Sturdivant. 16 June, 1736. John Rottenbury, Susannah Rottenbury. Book 8, p. 636.

WILLIAMSON, John: Leg.- To Elizabeth Sturdivant, wife of Hollum Sturdivant, some ells of ozenburg. To daughter, Susannah Rottenbury, wife of John Rottenbury, 241 acres of land on the south side of Nottoway River where they now live and 100 ells of brown ozenburg. To daughter, Edith Williamson, one negro, bed, horse and 15 pounds. Daughter, Hannah Fox, wife of Richard Fox an account at the store of Thos. Eldridge, four negroes, and my Troopers Arms. To my son, Cuthbert Williamson (a large stain makes this bequest illegible). Brother Cuthbert Williamson, and friend Robert Green supervisors of my will until son, Cuthbert is of age

21 years. Wit: Judith Harper, Edward Farrington. Made:
30 Jan., 1731. Prob.: 17 May, 1732. Book 8, p. 196.

WILLS, George: Est.- Joshua Nicholson, admr. 18 March, 1746.
John Collier, Henry Collier, Thos. Sowerby. Book 9, p. 550.

WILSON, Anne: Leg.- To Robt. Bootman & Anne Bootman, son and
daughter of Jno. and Sarah Bootman, all my possessions in
Carolina except cows and sheep. They go to Robert Willson
and Ann Wilson, son and daughter of Isaac Willson and his
first wife, Ann. Jno. Tooke and Sam. Cornell, Exers. Wit:
Richard Smith, John Phillips. 21st day of 5th mo. 1702.
Book 5, p. 248.

WILSON, Sampson: Est.- By Sarah Wilson. 18 Sept., 1750. Wm.
Drew, Dolphin Drew, John Newsum. Book 9, p. 663.

WINDOM, Griffin: Est.- By Mary Windom, admrx. 19 April, 1721.
Thos. Binns, John Bamer. Book 7, p. 230.

WINKELLS, William: Leg.- To son, Isack Winkels the land where
I live, and saddle etc. To son, James Winkels, five pounds,
horse, pig, sow etc. To son, John Winkels the Plantation I
live on after my wife's death. To daughter Frances Winkel
a cow and ewe. To daughter, Elizabeth Winkel, cows, etc.
To dau. Amy, Mary, cows. To wife, Easter, the rest of my
estate. Made: 30 Apr., 1733. Prob. (not legible). Wit:
James Chappell, Will. Burgis, James Turner. Bk. 8, p. 323.

WITHERINGTON, Nicholas: Leg.- To my grandson, William Foster,
a gun and heifer. Wife Catherine, Exerx. Made: 15 Feb.,
1711/14. Prob.: 20 Aug., 1714. Wit: Samuel Thompson,
William Foster. Book 6, p. 107.

X WOARD, John: Leg.- To daughter, Jane Ellis. To Mary Jackson.
Wife, Exerx. Wit: Robert Wynne, Wm. Jones. Made: 30
Aug., 1715. Prob.: 15 Feb., 1715. Book 5, p. 264.

X WOARD, John: Leg.- To daughter, Jane Ellis, one shilling. To
Mary Jackson, wife of John Jackson all of my estate, makes
her Exerx. Made: 30 Aug., 1715. Prob.: 15 Feb., 1715.
Wit: Robert Wynne, William Jones. Book 6, p. 264.

WOMBWELL, John: Leg.- Of Isle of Wight Co. To sons, Benjamin,
Joseph, Joshua, John each one shilling. Daughters, Martha
and Mary Wombwell. Wife, Mary, Exerx. 21 Jan., 1746. Wit:
Wm. Brady, Edward Pittman, Wm. Flake, John Giles, Matthew
Jordan. Book 9, p. 543.

WOMBWELL, John: Est.- 16 June, 1747. Benj. Bell, Wm. Little,
John Gwaltney. Book 9, p. 558.

WOOBANK, Robert Smith: Est.- 17 July, 1750. Charles Lucas,
Thos. Sowerby, Joshua Nicholson. Book 9, p. 660.

WOOD, Josiah: Est.- Charges of Wood and his wife to Jno. Dunfields's estate. 1 July, 1690. His daughter, Mary Wood,
Wm. Browne, administered on est. in right of Mary Browne,
next of kin. Book 4, p. 147.

WOODARD, William: Est.- John Woodard, admr. 19 July, 1727.
Wm. Parham, Isaac Hall, John Threewet. Book 7, p. 745.

WORD, John: Est.- By Mary Jackson. 19 Sept., 1716. Book 7,

p. 27.

WORDEN, Amy: Est.- 26 Oct., 1741. Book 9, p. 418.

WOULVES, Thomas: Nuncupative Will. Mentions wife, Barbary.
Desires debts to be paid. 7 July, 1691. Signed: Ann
Cockerham, Mary Brulon. Book 4, p. 213.

WRAY, William: Est.- 21 Apr., 1742. Martha Ray, Exerx. Book
9, p. 403.

WREN, Joseph, Sr.: Leg.- To son, Thomas Wren, 50 acres on
Robin's Branch. To sons, Joseph, William, George, John,
Francis each one shilling. Dau., Susannah Heath, one shill-
ing. To daughter, Elizabeth Rawser, bed & furniture. To
Susannah Rawser, daughter of Elizabeth Rawser. Daughter,
Mary Daniel. Son, James Wren, Exer. Made: 23 Dec., 1749.
No date of probate. Wit: Samuel Peete, Lazarus Drake,
John Hinds. Book 9, p. 636.

WRENN, John: Est.-Signed: Eliza. Wrenn, 'admrx. 15 July,
1713. David Andrews, William Howell. Book 6, p. 158.

WRENN, John: Est.- 17 Dec., 1729. Charles White, Elizabeth
White, Howell Briggs, W. Johnson. Book 7, p. 995.

WRENN, Richard: Leg.- To wife a horse on Hog Island, bridle,
saddle. To daughter, Mary, five shillings. Wife and five
children to have the rest of the est. Wife and brother
John Ogburne, Exers. Made: 16 April, 1717. Prob.: 19
Mar., 1717. (Will presented by Mary Wrenn, Exerx.) Wit:
Robert Inman, Ed. & Wm. Tanner. Book 7, p. 111.

WRIGHT, Thomas: Leg.- Wife, Mary, to have one negro for her
life, then to set free. Eldest son, Timothy Wright a
horse and hogs. To son, Thomas Wright, one shilling. To
son, Joseph Wight one shilling. Wife, Mary, Exerx. Wit:
Robert Snipes, Joseph Seat, Thomas Seat. Made: 5 Aug.,
1714. Prob.: 18 Mar., 1714. Book 6, p. 135.

WRIGHT, Timothy: Est.- Thomas Wight, admr. 18 Dec., 1717.
Wm. Harris, John Bruce, John Hancocke. Book 7, p. 83.

WYCHE, Henry: Leg.- To daughter, Hellinor, livestock, bed &
furniture, and the Land and Plantation I live on with Pewter dishes etc. To son, William, all my books, Trooper's
Arms, etc. To daughter, Sarah, one cow. To son, George
two steers, and to his son, Peter, a cow. To my daughter,
Sarah, a cow; and to her son, Henry, a cow. To my son,
Henry, a horse, old bed, pewter, etc. to my son, James,
the rest of the horses and livestock, and all the rest of
my estate after paying debts and legacies. Makes James
Exer. Wit: Jane Green, Henry Bedingfield. Made: 1 Aug.,
1712. Prob.: 18 Mar., 1714. Book __, p. ___.

WYCHE, James: Leg.- To daughter, Amy Jackson, her husband
Ambrose, one negro for life, then to her heirs. To my
daughter, Tabitha Lucas, one lamb. To my eldest son,
James, the lower part of my land at Flagg Gutt..below Great
Island to John Tharp's path. To daughter, Martha Bridges
one ewe lamb. To daughter, Elizabeth Johnson, one negro.
To my youngest son, Nathaniel Wyche, the remainder of the
land and two negroes. To daughter, Sarah, one ewe. To
daughter, Ann, a negro. To daughter, Frances, one ewe,

negro etc. To daughter, Rebecca, one negro. To wife, Elizabeth, the remainder of the estate. Son, James and Nathaniel Wyche. Made: 24 Feb., 1748. Prob.: 20 June, 1749. Wit: James Terrell, William Pettway. Book 9, p. 611.

WYCHE, James: Est.- 15 May, 1750. Jos. Thorpe, Mary Tiller, Sam. Alsobrooke. Book 9, p. 644.

WYCHE, William: Leg.- To son, Cyrill, all my Land and three slaves. Wife, Judith, to have the labor of the three negroes until Cyrill is 21 years old. Rest of estate to wife, Judith, and "all my children", after debts and funeral expenses are paid. Made: 21 Feb., 1719-20. 15 Feb., 1720. Wit: Richard Parker, Henry Bedingfield, Richard Parker, Jr. Book 7, p. 299.

WYCHE, William: Est.- Richard Parker, Jr., surviving husband of Judith Parker, Exer. 16 Feb., 1731. Wit: Jos. Witherington, Jos. Gee. Book 8, p. 164.

WYNN, Thomas: Leg.- To my son, Thomas Wynn, land on the north side of Surry County, 200 acres, and horse and gun. To my wife a gold ring, one negro for her life, horse, etc. To granddaughter, Leweresy Wynn, one cow. To granddaughter, Martha Wynn, one cow. Wife, Agnes. Son, Robert Wynn. The rest of my estate to be equally divided amongst "my children". Makes son, Robert, Exer. Presented by Richard Bland, admr. Wit: John Roberts, John Hicks, Wm. Moor. 18 Feb., 1716. Prob.: __ ____, 1718. Book 7, p. 117.

WYNNE, Robert: Est.- By John Brown. Sworn to by Robert Wynne. 21 June, 1727. Wm. Smith, Thos. Willson, Charles Kimbell. Book 7, p. ___.

WYTHERINGTON, Katherine: Leg.- To my grandson, William Foster; but if he die, or not return from sea, then to Joseph Witherington, my kinsman. To William Gray, a debt. To Mary, wife of William Gray. Friend, Samuel Thompson, Exer. Made: 5 Jan., 1713/14. Prob.: 17 ____, 1713. Wit: Samuel Cooke, Robert Payne. Book 6, p. 179.

YOUNG, John: Leg.- Estate to his wife, Tabitha Young. 4 Sept., 1714. Agnis Farmer, Mary Ellis, Clement Lanier. Book 6, p. 238.

INDEX

(?), Abraham 29
(?), Beck 29
(?), Dina 29
(?), Frank 29, 46
(?), Isaac 29
(?), Jack 29, 93, 94
(?), Jacob 29
(?), Jamey 29
(?), Jane 20
(?), Joe 29
(?), John 60
(?), Judy 29
(?), Nanny 29
(?), Robbin 94
(?), Tom 5, 20, 29
(?), Will 29
Adams, Ann 1
  Eliza 1
  Mary 1, 32
  Patrick 5, 24, 25
  Peter 32
  Sarah 1
  Susannah 1
  Thomas 1
  Thos. 1
  William 1
  Wm. 1
Addams, Peter 82
Adkins, Eliza 2
  Jane 2
  Joan 2, 65
  Joane 1
  Mary 2
  Rachel 2
  Richard 2
  Thos. 65, 142
  William 2
Adrews, John 18
Alderson, Elizabeth 2
  Jillian 2
  Wm. 82
Alesbrook, Samuell 120
Alexander, Samuel 38
Allen, (?) 5
  Ann 3, 4
  Ar. 10, 93, 126, 127
  Arthur 3, 4, 10, 12, 15,

Allen (cont.)
  Arthur 28, 29, 35, 37, 41,
    93, 97, 99, 114, 132, 143
  Arthur (Maj.) 129
  Eliza 28
  Elizabeth 3, 5, 27
  James 2, 3, 29, 35
  Jno. 86, 126
  John 2, 3, 4, 27, 35, 92,
    93, 123, 133
  John (Capt.) 100
  John (Col.) 52
  John (Coll.) 5
  Joseph 2, 3, 4, 97
  Katherine 2, 3, 28
  Mary 3, 4, 129
  Sarah 4
  Wm. 4, 5, 96, 134
Allistin, Thos. 87
Allstin, John 58
  Mary 52, 98
  Thomas 58, 98, 101, 102,
    139
  Thos. 113, 140
Allston, Thomas 56
Allvirs, Thomas 30
Alsbrook, Samuell 14
Alsobrook, John 43
  Sam. 55
  Thos. 85
Alsobrooke, Joan 75
  Sam. 146
  Samuel 75, 129, 130
  Thomas 14
Alstin, Thomas 3
  Thos. 3
Amos, Mary 5
Amry, Charles 58
  Edward 99
  Jno. 82
  Ruth 5
  Thos. 99
Anderson, Eliza. 5
  Ingumbred 5
  James 21, 22, 37, 82, 91
  Mary 5, 83
  Thomas 26

Anderson (cont.)
  Thos. 10
Andrews, (?) 39
  Amie 6
  Ann 6
  Barth. 7
  Barthol. 48
  Bartholomew 6, 111, 132
  Benj. 9
  Benjamin 6
  David 14, 39, 52, 59, 80,
    145
  David, Jr. 14, 52
  Dorothy 7, 83
  Eliza. 111
  Elizabeth 5, 10, 11
  James 10
  Jean 6
  John 6, 23, 28, 50, 62, 115
  Jos. 54, 120
  Joseph 6
  Martha 6, 90
  Mary 52
  Olive 114
  Ollaf 6
  Priscilla 90
  Rebecca 90
  Rich. 51
  Richard 8
  Robert 5, 6, 7, 59
  Thomas 6, 59, 83
  Thos. 55
  William 6, 60
  Wm. 6
Andros, David 59
Andross, Mary 11
Andrus, Wm. 105
Archer, Roger 124
Argebrook, Samuell 77
Arnall, Wm. 82
Arnoll, George 19
Ashe, Mary 23
Atkins, Thos. 58
Atkinson, Aaron 7
  Absalom 72
  Absolom 7
  Amos 7
  Benjamin 7
  Christopher 7
  Daniel 7, 63
  Elizabeth 7
  Jacob 7, 63
  John 7, 49, 89
  Reuben 7
  Thomas 7, 35, 36
  Thos. 139
  William 7
  Wm. 26, 92
Atkison, Anges 7
  Elizabeth 7
  Lucy 7
  Mary 7
  William 7
  Wm. 7

Atkisson, Elizabeth 7
Attkins, Elizabeth 7
Avent, John 123
  Thomas 12, 20, 31, 42, 123
  Thos. 12, 49, 85, 94, 134,
    139
Averis, John 10
  Richard 10
Averiss, John 65
Avery, Ann 27
  Elizabeth 59
  George 8
  Hannah 90
  Jane 8
  Jean 74
  John 7, 8, 25, 74, 115, 133
  Richard 8, 28
  Thomas 7
  Thos. 7
  William 8
Bacon, Nathaniel 16
Badcock, James 50
Badger, William 112
Bage, Eliza 8
  Eliza. 24, 143
  Eliza. Lucy 143
  Sarah 14
  Thomas 59
  Thos. 139, 141
Bagley, Edward 25, 55
  Edward, Jr. 6
  Elizabeth 8
  George 8
  Hue 8
  Hugh 8
  Peter 2, 7, 8
  Sarah 8
  Thomas 8
Bagly, Joan 1
Bailes, Henry 105
Bailey, Anselm 9
  Anselm, Jr. 40, 65
  Benjamin 7, 9, 40, 44
  Ed. 41, 72
  Edward 101
  Elizabeth 9
  Hannah 9
  Jane 9
  John 15
  Mary 9
  Sarah 9
  Thomas 9
  Walter 9
Baily, Edward 137
  John 87
Bain, William 13
Baker, (?) (Captain) 44
  (?) (Mrs.) 54
  Alice 9
  Anne 9
  Catherine 10
  Edward 9
  Elizabeth 9, 10
  Hen. 54, 79

Baker (cont.)
  Henry 9, 10, 38, 74, 82,
    101, 110, 118
  James 4, 5, 25, 65, 68,
    107
  Jas. 4
  John 9, 125
  Law. (Capt.) 79, 136
  Lawrence (Capt.) 2, 42,
    60, 71
  Mary 9, 37, 54, 118
  Sarah 9, 54
  Susannah 9
  William 9
Baldwin, Faith 136
  Wm. 86
Baley, Anselm 2
  Edward, Jr. 123
  Elizabeth 83
  Jno. 3
  John 2
  Thos. 86
Balfour, James 24
Ball, (?) 97
Baly, Christian 127
  Edward 48
Bamer, Anne 10
  Hannah 10, 30
  John 50, 92, 128, 144
  Mary 10, 30
  William 10
Bard, Sarah 82
Barefoot, Noah 39
Barham, Charles 12, 30, 35,
    73, 138
  Charles (Capt.) 5, 138
  Eliza. 30
  Elizabeth 30
  John 30
  Mary 30
  Robert 12, 30, 117
  Thos. 136
Barker, Agnes 10, 11, 118
  Catherine 6
  Elizabeth 11
  Faith 11, 137
  George 11
  Grace 10, 11, 39, 84
  Henry 11
  Jehu 11
  Jethro 65
  Jethro, Sr. 39
  Joel 11, 17, 20
  Joell 50, 67
  John 10, 37, 55, 65, 66
  Joseph 137
  Joshua 11
  Joshuay 11
  Josiah 10, 11, 82
  Josiah C. 11
  Josie 10
  Mary 11, 118
  Prisselah 21
  Richard 10, 11, 137

Barker (cont.)
  Sarah 6, 11
  William 11
  Wm. 88
Barkers, John 11
Barler, John 40
Barlow, Elizabeth 19
  John 12
  Nathaniel 11
  Sarah 12
  William 11, 12
  Wm. 11, 12, 108, 123
Barmer, John 19
Barnes, Henry 36
  Jane 12
  John 20, 38, 81, 137
  Sarah 12
  Susannah 12, 19
Barrick, Geo. 109
Barrow, Edward 117
  Eliz. 117
  Elizabeth 73
  Sarah 30
Bartlett, (?) 132
  Alice 12
  Walter 79
Barton, Ann 21
  Wm. 36
Baser, Samuel 35
Bass, Charles 64
Basse, Charles 120
  John 85
Battell, John 123, 124
  Mathew 12
Batten, Wm. 135
Battle, Elizabeth 6
  Faith 12
  Mary 93
Battles, Charles 93
Batts, Elizabeth 13
  John 12
  Martha 12, 13
  Mary 13
  William 13, 15, 56
Battwell, John 98
Bayley, Ed. 6, 74
  Edward 51, 59, 116
  Jno. 90
  John 142
  Mary 87
  Robt. 73
  Thos. 6
Bayly, Edward 83
  Robert 127
Beaumont, Bluitt 39
Beberry, John 76
Beckett, Charles 89
Beddingfield, Thos. 10
Bedingfield, Grace 10
  Henry 21, 56, 76, 94, 115,
    145, 146
  Isabel 13
  Mary 21
  Nathaniel 13

149

Bedingfield (cont.)
  Thomas 13, 82
  Thos. 28, 80, 129
Bee, John 12
Beech, Wm. 81
Belbank, Daniel 91
Belinsbe, Mary 105
Bell, Amy 13
  Ann 13
  Balaam 13
  Benj. 144
  Benjamin 13, 25, 44
  Burrel 13
  Burrell 13
  Eliza. 13
  Hannah 13
  James 13
  John 14, 23, 90
  Mary 13
  Richard 13
  Sarah 13
  Thomas 14, 23, 24, 40, 117
  Thos. 29
  Wm. 13
Benitt, Mary 96
Bennet, Richard 101
  Wm. 118
Bennett, Ann 14
  Benjamin 14
  James 35, 114, 130
  John 41
  Jonas 124
  Richard, Sr. 23
Bennit, Mary 112
  Sarah 112
Benson, Samuel 35
  William 88
Bentley, John 27, 35, 119
  Thomas 80
  Thos. 18, 89, 91, 119
  Thos., Jr. 128
Berkeley, William 56
  William (Sir) 19
  Wm. 30
  Wm. (Sir) 126, 135
Berrick, Geo. 64
Berriman, Augustine 75
  John 75
Berry, Eleanor 14
  Henry 34
Berryman, Ann 14
  Augustin 76
  Elizabeth 15
  John 14, 44, 126
  Joseph 14
  Katherine 15
  Lucy 14
  Margaret 14
  Robert 15, 76
  William 14
Betts, William 82
Bin, Thos. 117
Binam, Eliza. 94
Bineham, John 75

Binford, Thomas 42
Binham, James 98
Binne, Chas. 29
Binns, Charles 13, 20, 25,
  44, 51, 63, 68, 69, 73,
  76, 106, 107, 117
  Chas. 49, 50, 63, 135
  Elizabeth 15
  Jane 15
  Martha 15
  Sally 15
  Sarah 15
  Thomas 12, 28, 44
  Thos. 15, 20, 75, 76, 93,
    97, 106, 134, 144
Binum, Agnes 74
  James 74
Bird, Mary 16
  Thos. 16
  William 16
  Wm. 41
Bishop, (?) 12
  Mary 11
Black, Hannah 116
  John 116
  Mary 116
  William 116
  Wm. 116
Blackburn, Benjamin 16
  Faith 16, 22
  John 16
  Joseph 9, 16
  Mary 22
  Wm. 22
Blackburne, William 14
Blackgrove, Samuel 114
Blair, (?) (Maj.) 125
  Arch. 45
  Archibald 47
  Arthur 3
Blake, Honor 103
Bland, (?) 132
  Robert 76
  Sarah (Madam) 2
Blandford, John 100
Blewer, John 71
Blow, Eliza. 16
  Geo. 108
  George 74
Blunt, (?) 44
  Ann 17, 18
  Anne 18
  Benjamin 17
  Elizabeth 17, 18
  Henry 17, 129
  John 17
  Lucy 17
  Priscilla 18
  Rich. 22, 45, 57
  Richard 18, 47, 74
  Thomas 25, 129
  Thos. 12, 20, 21, 51
  William 17, 25, 129
  Wm. 17, 40, 129

150

Bobbitt, Thomas 61
Bock, Launselett 26
Bockey, Edward 30
Bolden, Elizabeth 6
  Wm. 6, 109
Boldin, Wm. 5
Bolling, (?) 22
  Alexander 18, 23
  Ann 23
  Drury 18
  Eliza. 19
  Elizabeth 69
  J., Jr. 19
  Jane 23, 125
  John 18, 23
  Robert 18, 19
  Robert (Col.) 47
  Stith 22, 69
  Stith (Capt.) 125
  Stith, Jr. 51
Bookey, Ed. 8
  Edward 62, 77, 118
  Fortune 19, 118
Booky, Edward 91
Booth, Robert 122
  Thos. 120
Bootman, Anne 144
  Jno. 144
  Robt. 144
  Sarah 144
Borreman, Sarah 65
Boston, Mary 32
Boswell, James 111
Boun, Elizabeth 122
Bowman, James 87
  Jane 19
Boyce, Jno. 53
  Mary 53
  Sarah 9
Boyd, James 5
Boykin, Edward 63
  Elizabeth 40
Boyseau, Holmes 82
Bozeman, James 87
Bradby, Joseph 5
  Sarah 67
Braddy, Katherine 51
  Patrick 35
  William 51
Braderton, Henry 140
  Mary 140
Bradly, (?) 119
  Benj. 18
Brady, Eleanor 19
  Eleanor (Mrs.) 19
  Patrick 78
  Wm. 144
Branch, Elizabeth 99
  Geo. 89
  George 38
  John 41
Brandon, Martin 66, 112
Brantley, Elizabeth 19
  Priscilla 19

Brantley (cont.)
  Thos. 127
Brashare, John 34
Braswell, Wm. 130
Braxup, Nathaniel 43
Bray, David 5
  Elizabeth 4
  Frances 4
  James 3, 4
  Thos. 4
Brebray, Charles 57
Brewer, Wm. 37
Brewton, Anne 20
  Elizabeth 20
  Geo. 20
  Martha 20
  Mary 20
  Sarah 20
Bridger, (?) 135
  Arthur 3
  Elizabeth 3
  James 3
  Jos. 20
  Joseph 3, 4
  Martha 3
  Samuell 3
  William 3
  Wm. 3, 56
Bridges, James 77
  Martha 145
  Susannah 64
  Timothy 64
  Wm. 81, 105
Briggs, Amy 22
  Ann 21
  Benjamin 21
  Charles 1, 16, 100, 127
  Geo. 21
  George 21, 82
  Hannah 21
  Henry 17, 22, 74, 86, 90
  Howel 23
  Howell 20, 34, 45, 60, 85,
    90, 108, 111, 145
  James 30, 97, 104, 118
  John 21
  Lucy 21, 22, 60
  Margery 21
  Marie 21
  Mary 21, 22
  Nath. 62
  Nathaniel 21
  Richard 79, 136
  Robert 21
  Sam. 86
  Sam'll. 51
  Samuel 18, 20, 21, 74
  Samuell 9, 88
  Thomas 21, 22
  William 21
  Wm. 37, 57
Brittle, John 64
  Joyce 103
  Wm. 103

Brodie, John 124
Brooks, Abigail 86
  John 22
Brotherton, Mary 1
Brown, (?) (Col.) 39
  Ann 22
  Ed. 63
  Edward 31, 51
  Henry 25, 95
  Hester 109
  Jno. 63
  John 39, 71, 95, 105, 109,
    121, 146
  Mary 16, 22, 24
  Rebecca 22
  Wm. 8, 106
  Wm., Jr. 19
Browne, (?) (Capt.) 96
  (?) (Major) 48, 52, 83
  Ann 23, 24
  Anne 23, 32
  Berkeley 87
  Eliza 23
  Elizabeth 22, 23, 24, 32,
    125
  Henry 22, 23, 24, 25, 124
  Jane 22, 23, 25
  John 10
  Martha 24
  Mary 23, 24, 32, 82, 86,
    144
  Rebecca 24
  Thos. 67
  Will. 83, 91
  William 23, 25, 51, 84, 124
  William (Capt.) 96
  William, Jr. 23, 54, 62
  Wm. 17, 23, 24, 25, 48, 53,
    71, 72, 75, 76, 84, 105,
    108, 118, 144
  Wm. (Capt.) 32, 54, 75
  Wm. (Coll.) 84, 105
  Wm., Jr. 32, 72, 84, 91,
    109, 114
  Wm. (Lt. Col.) 41
  Wm. (Maj.) 48, 87, 116
Browns, Wm. (Coll.) 99
Bruce, Jacob 64
  Jno. 129
  John 38, 85, 92, 94, 99,
    145
Brulon, Mary 145
Bruson, Wm. 25
Bruton, Ann 25
  Elizabeth 25
  Ja. 28
  James 13, 28, 127, 130
  Martha 25
  Mary 25, 28, 117
  William 12
  Wm. 25
Bryan, Mary 111
  Thomas 111
Bullifant, Thos. 51

Bullivant, Sarah 85
Bullock, Alice 118
  Eliza. 118
  Mary 25, 118
  Rich. 119
  Richard 8, 142
Bundel, (?) 117
Bunnel, Hezekiah 28
Bunnell, Hes. 140
  Hezekiah 103
  Jane 28
Bunnill, Jean 26
Burd, Ann 74
Burgess, Ann 26
  Robert 134
  Thomas 26, 132
Burgis, Will. 144
Burk, Thos. 78
Burnell, Hezekiah 28
Burnett, David 90, 122
Buryber, Thos. 70
Busby, Thomas 119
  Thos. 94, 119
Bush, Nich. 105
Bushup, John 93
Butler, Joyce 26
  Robert 10
  Robt. 19
  Wm. 79
Butterell, William 23
Butts, Thomas 45
Buxton, Stevenson 136
Bynam, Eliza. 54
  John 23
Byneham, Jno. 132
Bynton, Lucy 26
Bynum, Agnes 50
  James 50
  John 54, 61
  William 55
  Wm. 122
Byrd, (?) 26
Byrum, James 76
  Mary 76
  Wm. 61
Byton, Richard 29
Callaham, Frances 26
  Nich. 26
Callahan, Francis 26
Callihan, Joyce 139
  Nicholas 26
Camer, Francis 77
Cannon, (?) 27
  Joanna 26
Cargill, David 27
  Eliza. 27
  Elizabeth 67
  John 23, 36, 46, 47, 52,
    101, 102
Carlile, Elizabeth 27
Carpenter, Wm. 31
Carpinder, Wm. 28
Carpinter, Mary 27
  Wm. 99, 101

Carr, Jno. 88
Carrell, Benjamin 85
  James 107
  Jno. 27
  John 85
  Joice 27
  Joseph 27
  Katherine 27
  Mary 27
  Samuel 27
Carroll, Phillis 77
  Wm. 64
Carter, Amy 131
  Eliza. 28
  Geo. 28
  George 75
  Jos. 131
  Sarah 131
Carteright, Eliza. 28
  Elizabeth 28
  Hezekiah 28
  Mary 28
  Rich. 28
  Richard 28
Cartwright, Elizabeth 28
  Mary 28
Cary, (?) 82
  Ann 45
  Henry 45
Case, John 20, 101, 140
  Jos. 129
  Naomy 140
Casely, Elizabeth 28
  Mary 28
  Mickel 28
  Sarah 28
Cash, Rueben 21
Catlett, Robert 129
Caufield, Eliza. (Mrs.) 93
  Elizabeth 29
  Rob. 75
  Robert 5, 20, 32, 35, 58,
    85, 140, 143
  Robt. 43, 44, 79
Caulfield, Robert 10
Chambers, Elizabeth 29, 128
  John 59, 79, 128
  Margery 29
  Martha 29
  Mary 29, 74
  Olive 113
  William 1, 15
  Wm. 19, 29, 86, 87, 98, 112,
    114, 126
Champion, Anne 84
  Benj. 44, 65
  Benjamin 142
  Charles 29, 142
  Elizabeth 142
  John 15
  Lucy 84
Champton, Anne 29
  Charles 29
  Elizabeth 29

Champton (cont.)
  John 29
  Mary 29
Chapman, Benj. 16, 52
  Benjamin 14, 38, 118
  Jno. 54
  John 9, 10, 19, 30, 40, 86,
    133
  John (Capt.) 14
  Mary 29
Chappel, Elizabeth 22
Chappell, Benjamin 30
  Drury 30
  Eliza. 30
  Elizabeth 30
  Emelie 30
  James 1, 21, 30, 79, 82,
    144
  James, Jr. 21, 82
  Jas. 115, 132
  John 30
  Mary 22, 30
  Rebecca 21
  Robert 30
  Sam. 91
  Samuel 79, 121
  Sarah 30
  Thomas 30
  Thos. 21
Charles, Jno. 89
Cheetam, Marmaduke 36
Chessutt, Annie 30
  Elizabeth 30
  John 30
  Phebe 30
  Sarah 30
Chestetts, Ja. 138
Chestnutt, Alex. 31
Child, John 25
Chisnall, Alex. 115
Chissett, James 30
Christ, Tobias 86
Churchill, Hannah 67
Claiborne, Auf. 5
Clanton, Agnes 30
  Edward 30, 57, 104
  Joanah 30
  Mary 30
  Nathaniel 30, 93, 104
  Richard 30
  Sarey 104
  Thos. 137
Clare, Thomas 98
Clark, Benj. 127
  Benjamin 80
  Elizabeth 80
  Hanah 106
  Hannah 31
  Henry 59
  Jno. 103
  John 13, 97, 132
  John, Jr. 128
  Jos. 105
  Jos. Sampson 63

Clark (cont.)
  Mary 31, 109
  Sampson 109
  Samuel 31
  Susannah 109
  Thomas 109
  Thos. 31
Clarke, Ann 70
  Banjamin 31
  Edward 47
  Elizabeth 31
  Henry 58
  Jane 31, 126, 127
  Jno. 46
  John 65, 66, 72, 75, 132
  Joseph 40
  Robert 91
  Samson 109
  Samuel 109
  Thomas 64
  Thos. 72, 87
  Wm. 31, 71, 82
Clary, Benjamin 32
  Charles 32
  Elizabeth 32
  Joseph 32
  Martha 32
  Robt. 137
  Thos. 64
  Wm. 31, 108
Clay, Elizabeth 124
  Judith 38
  Thomas 124
Claye, Elizabeth 32
Clements, (?) (Capt.) 11
  Ales 32, 33
  Ann 32
  Bartholomew 112, 113
  Benj. 57
  Benjamin 32, 45, 101
  Elizabeth 33, 94
  Fra. 8
  Francis (Capt.) 78, 94,
    129
  Henry 33
  Jno. 96
  John 96
  Judith 101
  Lucy 33
  Lydia 32
  Mary 32
  Samuel 1
  Samuell 32, 33
  Thos. 32, 56
  William 40
  Wm. 32, 33
Clemmons, Samuell 40
Clemons, John 91, 103
Clerk, Benjamin 40
Clinch, Ann 33
  Chris. 23
  Christ 73
  Christopher 66, 105, 116,
    127

Clinch (cont.)
  Eliza. 33
  Elizabeth 66
  Hannah 66
  Hannah (Mrs.) 133
  James 140, 141
  Jane 33, 140
  John 33
  Jos. 33, 86
  Jos. John 113
  Margaret 33
  Mary 33
  William 6, 33, 64
  Wm. 33, 80, 113, 140
Cling, Elizabeth 14
Coates, Joseph 33
  Mary 33
Cobbs, Eliza. 24
Coche, Nich. 115
Cock, Thos. 49
Cocke, (?) 115
  (?) (Capt.) 24
  Ann 34, 53
  Benj. 27
  Benjamin 13, 42
  Catherine 34
  Eliza. 141
  Elizabeth 33, 34, 73
  Frances 34
  Hannah 34
  Hartwell 23, 140
  Henry 24
  Isabella 34
  Jane 22
  John 34, 35
  Jonathan 94
  Katherine 73
  Lemuel 22, 24, 34
  Martha 34
  Mary 34
  Nich. 36, 52, 91, 137
  Nicholas 31, 34, 73, 98,
    138, 141
  Rich. 141
  Richard 23, 24, 33, 34, 140
  Richard (Capt.) 24
  Samuel 84
  Susannah 34
  Thomas 91
  Thos. 26, 27, 28, 67, 73,
    78, 96, 106, 114, 132,
    142
  Thos. (Capt.) 52
  Thos. (Col.) 34
  Walter 34
  Will. 142
  William 22, 33, 42, 53,
    113
  William Walter 52
  Wm. 26
Cocker, Frances 34
  Wm. 34
Cockerham, Ann 35, 145
  Elizabeth 35

Cockerham (cont.)
  Mary 35
  Priscilla 35
  Thomas 59
  Timothy 35
  Wm. 28
Cockes, Will 63
Cockin, William 43, 118
  Wm. 118
Cocks, John 59
Coggin, Elizabeth 27, 35
Coging, Will 96
  Wm. 96
Coker, John 3, 29, 37, 114
  John, Jr. 35
  Margaret 3
  Margarette 35
  Priscilla 36
  Thomas 35
  William 35
  Wm. 35
Colleck, John 58
Collier, Ann 3
  Charles 36
  Elizabeth 36, 52, 108, 109
  Grace 36
  Henry 36, 144
  Jane 36
  Jeane 36
  John 27, 88, 90, 113, 133,
    144
Collier, Mary 36
  Sarah 21, 36
  Thomas 52, 88, 90, 98, 123
  Thos. 24, 47, 63, 64, 77,
    80, 123, 125, 132, 138
  William 36, 109
  Wm. 109
Collins, John 5, 29, 98
Coockins, William 35
Cook, Amy 37
  Elizabeth 37
  Hannah 37
  Henry 37
  James 37
  Joanna 37
  Mary 37
  Rebeccah 37
  Rubin 37
  Samuel 116
  Sarah 37
  Susannah 37
  Wm. 41
Cooke, Benjamin 4
  Catherine 4
  Elizabeth 37
  Jno. 85
  John 6, 56, 65, 138
  Samuel 146
  Thos. 96
  William 56
Cooper, Eliza 22
  Eliza. 142
  Elizabeth 22, 37, 71

Cooper (cont.)
  James 30
  Jas. 87
  John 37
  Martha 37
  Thomas 37
  William 37
  Wm. 108
Corker, Jno. 89
  Judith 38
  Lucy 38, 141
  Susannah 38
Cornell, Catherine 38
  Elizabeth 38
  Isaac 19
  Katherine 38
  Mary 38
  Sam. 144
  Samuel 20, 77
  Samuell 19
  Susanna 38
Cornhill, Samuel 98
  Samuell 98
Cornwell, Aaron 38
  Elepabeth 126
  Eliza. 38
  Jacob 4, 38
  John 4, 38
  Mary 4
  Moses 38
  Mourning 4
  Sam. 62, 87
  Samuel 14, 38, 78
  Samuell 50, 75, 87, 127
  Sarah 58, 129
  William 126
Coron, Joseph 93
Cortrock, Robert 82
Cotten, Elizabeth 39
  Jane 38
  Mary 71
  Thomas 11, 38, 39
  Walter 39
  William 39
Cotton, Mary 39
  Thos. 2, 65
  Walter 125
Coullop, Thos. 70
Craffoed, Carter 74
Crafford, Carter 15, 29, 86,
    97, 104, 128
  Carter, Jr. 39
  Constance 39
  John 39, 44, 74
  Margaret 39
  Mary 39, 104
  Robert 65, 86, 95, 112, 126
Crawford, Ludwick 38
  Robert 115
Crawley, David 68, 75
Crede, Mary 72
Creed, Grace 135
  Mary 5
  William 135

155

Creed (cont.)
  Wm. 39
Creede, Mary 135
Crewes, Catherine 39
  Elizabeth 39
  Feeby 39
  Phoeby 39
Crews, Elizabeth 39
  John 39
  Mary 40
  Thos. 42
  William 39, 40
Cripps, Elizabeth 40
  John 40
  Mary 40
  Wm. 49, 102
Crips, Elizabeth 16, 114
  Elizabeth, Jr. 16
  Marriott 92
  William 16
  Wm. 16
Croifford, Carter 41
Crosland, Jonas 133
Crudge, Wm. 60
Crus, Thos. 55
Cruse, Thos. 55
Cryer, Geo. 104
Curtis, John 131
Curby, Richard 40, 41
Current, Matthew 27
Daingerfield, (?) (Mrs.) 4
Dance, John 135
Daniel, Mary 145
Davee, Thomas 35
Davidson, John 40
  Thomas 40, 64
  Thos. 77, 100, 117
  Will. 122
  Wm. 16, 114, 141
Davis, Arthur 40, 43
  Dolphin 64
  Edward 85
  Elizabeth 40, 41
  Frances 40
  Henry 41
  James 6, 33, 41, 51, 117,
    136, 138
  Jane 41
  Jas. 138
  Jennette 138
  Jno. 103
  John 20, 40, 41, 53, 66,
    70, 95, 105, 120
  Margaret 40
  Margery 74
  Mary 33, 40, 41
  Nath. 72
  Nathaniel 41
  Nich. 74, 115
  Peter 40
  Rebecca 41
  Rich. 53
  Robert 40, 41
  Roland 61

Davis (cont.)
  Rowland 61
  Solomon 88
  Thomas 70, 81, 95, 111
  Thos. 42, 85
  William 41, 114
Dawkins, Wm. 141
Dawson, John 32, 34
  Mary 34, 52, 109
Deans, James 69
Deberry, Jane 123
  John 122, 136
Delk, John 42
  Joseph 15, 42, 92, 99, 105,
    117, 129
  Rebecca 42
  Roger 35, 60, 79, 96, 99,
    132
Delke, Roger 87
Deloney, Lewis 31
Denfield, Jno. 136
Dennis, Nathaniel 42
  Wm. 39
Denton, Edmond 107
  Elizabeth 42
  Jno. 107
  John 121
Dering, James 25
  Nicholas 40
DeWell, Thomas 42
Dewell, Wm. 68
Dickens, Bindlord 47
  Binford 42
  Elizabeth 42
  Hildy 42
  James 42, 47
  Jarns 42
  Sary 42
Dickeson, Edward 42
Dickins, Israel 29
Dickson, Mary 54
  William 53
Dinkins, Charles 42
  James 42
  Margaret 43
  Sanders 43
  Thomas, Jr. 43
  William 43
Dobe, John 43
  John, Jr. 43
  Robert 43
Doby, John 115, 123
  Peter 43
  Robert 43, 125
  Robt. 48
Doelong, Wm. Briggs 45
Dole, Mary 43
Doles, Peter 43
  Rachel 43
Dolling, John 94
Don, Thomas 104
Donaldson, Benjamin Chapman
    34, 113
  Mary 30

Doois, Jno. 51
Dovell, Thomas 35
Dowling, Rob. 119
Drake, Lazarus 145
Draper, Wm. 115
Dredge, Wm. 16
Drew, David 13, 44
  Dolphin 127, 144
  Dolphine 27
  Edward 44, 46, 97
  Elizabeth 43, 44
  Faith 44
  James 2
  John 27, 39, 44, 75, 105,
    106, 126
  Judith 44
  Mabell 43, 44
  Martha 44
  Mary 43, 44
  Newitt 97
  Sarah 43
  Richard 35, 79
  Thomas 2, 4, 43, 54, 97,
    117, 127
  Thos. 45, 71, 127, 132
  Will. 43, 96
  William 14, 44, 96
  Wm. 3, 15, 27, 29, 44, 45,
    64, 79, 104, 106, 116,
    127, 134, 144
Drinkard, Thos. 137
Drummond, Wm. 106
Drumond, John 69
Duce, Phyllis 44
Duche, Melchideck 123
  Melchisadeck 115
  Melchisideck 87
Duchee, Ann 44
Dudley, Faith 109
Duell, Wm. 40
Dues, Phyllis 44
Dugall, Eliza. 13
Dugan, Sarah 22
Duggard, (?) 115
  Daniel 115, 133
Dun, (?) 26
Duncan, Daniel 44
  Elizabeth 44
  Jennett 44
  John 44
  Nathaniel 44
  Peter 44
Dunfields, Jno. 144
Dunford, John 34, 43
  Mary 44
Dunn, (?) 26
  Jno. 26
  John 57
  John, Sr. 26
  Thomas 26, 57, 98
  Thos. 2, 26
Dunston, (?) 2
E-(?), E. 48
Eacolls, Robert 93

Ealy, James 44
Eaton, Mary 24
  William 24
  Wm. 24
Eaves, Elinor 56
Edloe, Henry 23
  Jane 24
  John 24
  Mathew 143
  Philip 24
  Rebecca 23, 24
  William 24
Edmonds, Ni. 17
  Nicholas 17
Edmund, David 45
Edmunds, Ann 45
  Anne 18, 51
  Christian 45
  Elizabeth 17, 45
  Faith 45
  Howell 17, 18, 20, 83,
    88, 129, 137
  John Edmondgrey 45
  John Edmundgrey 45
  Mary 21, 45
  Nicholas 45, 53
  Phyllis 45
  Sarah 45
  Susannah 45
  Thomas 13, 73, 95, 97,
    117, 129
  Thomas (Capt.) 89
  Thos. 22, 33, 51, 113,
    133
  Wm. 45, 76
Edwards, (?) 42, 71
  Ann 46, 87, 94, 104, 128
  Banjamin 46
  Benj. 46
  Benjamin 15, 137
  Eliza. 46
  Elizabeth 46, 47, 60, 96,
    117
  Hannah 47
  Jno. 46
  John 14, 45, 46, 47, 86,
    93, 94, 97, 102, 104
  Joseph 14
  Mary 46, 47, 68, 104
  Micajah 46
  Nath. 45, 53, 68
  Nathaniel 46, 47
  Newitt 35, 96, 97, 100,
    106
  Rebecca 47
  Sarah 45, 46, 47, 50
  Tho. 1
  Thomas 50
  Thos. 31, 46, 59, 66, 85,
    92, 99, 105, 106, 127
  W. 141
  Will 105, 138
  Will. 138

Edwards (cont.)
  William 1, 45, 56, 66, 97
  William, Jr. 23, 47
  Wm. 2, 10, 20, 28, 29, 40,
    45, 46, 50, 53, 59, 71,
    73, 84, 93, 94, 96, 97,
    101, 103, 105, 106, 108,
    113, 123, 124, 127, 143
  Wm. Jr. 31, 103, 122
  Wm. Newitt 96
Eelbank, Dan. 130, 137
  Daniel 91, 135
Eelbeck, (?) (Rev. Mr.) 23
  Henry 23
Eggleston, Benj. 69
  Elizabeth 69
Eldridge, Anne 47
  Elizabeth 47
  Jane 47
  Judith 47
  Martha 47
  Mary 47
  Richard 47
  Tho. 62
  Thomas, Jr. 43
  Thomas, Sr. 43
  Thos. 15, 68, 143
  Thos., Jr. 136
  William 47
  Wm. 47
Elis, James 104
Elles, Elizabeth 47
Elley, James 79
Ellico, James 76
Ellis, Ben. 89
  Benj. 17, 62
  Benjamin 112
  Caleb 36
  Ed. 91
  Elizabeth 41, 112
  Hart. 95
  Isabella 41
  James 41, 49, 84, 96, 108
  Jane 144
  Jere. 50
  Jeremiah 26, 48, 61, 82,
    139
  Jeremiah, Jr. 49
  Joshua 110
  Mary 47, 68, 146
  Mathew 41
  Matthew 113
  Meley 118
  Mildred 47
  Richard 118
  Sara 65
  Thomas 41
Ellison, John 121
  Judith 122
  Judy 121
Elmes, Judah 47
Emerson, Faith 48
  Jno. 134
  John 48

Emerson (cont.)
  John 48
Emery, Benj. 48
  Green 48
  Susannah 48
Emmerson, John 48
Emry, Thomas 12
Epes, Daniel 70, 115
  Mary 60
Eppes, Daniel 69, 95
  Richard 95
  Sarah 95
  Susannah 95
  Thos. 48
  William 95
  Wm. 101
Epps, Daniel 5, 26
  Mary 48
  Rebecca 61
  Susannah 111
  Wm. 41
Essell, Elizabeth 31, 130
Eustace, James 105
Evans, (?) (Widdow) 137
  Abraham 11, 55
  Ann 48
  Anthony 35, 76, 83, 114,
    132
  Benjamin 48, 50, 51
  Edward 82
  Elinor 70
  Elizabeth 3, 48
  John 48, 51, 69, 74
  Mary 49, 116
  William 14, 48, 51
  Wm. 117
Evens, Mary 49
Evins, Anthony 50
  John 50
  Mary 49
  William 50
Ezel, Elizabeth 49
  John 49
  Lucy 49
  Mary 49
  Sarah 49
  Timothy 49
  William 49
Ezell, Agnes 126
  Edward 49
  Elizabeth 19, 49
  Geo. 61
  George 42
  Martha 126
  Mary 49, 50
  Michael 19, 98
  Rebeckah 49
  Timothy 7
  William 19, 49
  Wm. 49, 79, 132
Ezelle, Rebecker 48
Farloe, Joseph 27
Farlow, Joseph 35
Farmer, Agnes 50, 98

Farmer (cont.)
  Agnis 146
  Isaac 98
  Thomas 108
  Thos. 50
Farrall, Hubard 141
Farrell, Charles 35
Farrington, Edward 107, 111,
    144
  Robert 107, 110
  Robt. 61
Fatherbe, Anne 50
  Elizabeth 50
  Martha 50
  Mary 50
  William 50
Faulcon, Jane 50
  Nich. 50
  Nicholas 50
Fawcett, Jno. 19
Fealds, Ann 40
  Richard 40
Featherstone, Susan 94
Fellows, Robt. 75
Felps, Callepe 50
  Eleanor 50
  Francis 50
  John 50
  Mary 50
  Nathaiel 50
  Richard 50
  Thomas 50
  William 50
Ferraby, Ann 51
Ferribee, Ben. 54
Fichett, Haner 59
Field, Jane 11
Fields, Green 40
  Jean 51
  Richard 40
Figgers, Thoas. 17
Figures, Barth. 88, 92
  Bartho. 62
  Bartholomew 13, 28
  Elizabeth 11
  Hannah 51
Fillips, Nath. 57
Findley, John 130
Finnie, Alex. 87
Fitchett, Elizabeth 75
  John 55
  William 54
Fitchit, Mary 51
Fiveash, Francis 51
  Mary 51
  Peter 51
Flacke, Robert 26
Flake, Culbert 124
  Elizabeth 51
  Margaret 92
  Robert 92
  Thomas 92
  Wm. 144
Fleacher, James 70

Flefelce, John 70
Flood, Ann 25, 53
  Eliza 53
  Elizabeth 52, 53
  Fortune 25, 53
  Jane 18, 52, 53
  Jno. 120
  Joanna Joyce 99
  John 17, 25, 51
  Joice 52
  Mary 52, 74
  Robert 52
  Tho. 82
  Thomas 7, 36, 83, 85
  Thos. 7, 53, 72, 99
  Walter 25, 48, 78, 83
  Water 28, 82, 83
Floyd, Harry 40, 76, 108
  Henry 18, 64, 133
Floyed, Harry 135
Foanes, Robert 128
Folpe, Hump. 142
Fones, Mathew 118
  Richard 112
Foons, Robert 97
Foorman, Will. 89
Forbush, Eliza. 53
  Elizabeth 53
  James 108
  Jas. 5
  John 53
  Theoph. 103
  Theophilus 53
Ford, Edward 54
  Jos. 45
  Joseph 44, 54
  Mary 53, 54
  William 54
Fordman, Wm. 99
Foreman, Benj. 143
  Benjamin 54
  Will. 84
  William 14, 62, 63
  Wm. 129
Forman, Hester 54
  Will. 5
  William 77
Forrington, Robt. 61
Fort, Elias 50, 51
  Elizabeth 83
  George 54, 55
  Holiday 54
  John 83
  Mary 54
  Phillis 51
  Richard 54, 55
  Sarah 30, 54
  Thomas 54, 55
  William 54
Fortt, Elizabeth 54
Foscroft, Thos. 42
Foseraft, Thos. 140
Foster, Alice 54
  Ann 30, 55, 97

159

Foster (cont.)
  Chris. 83, 92
  Christopher 11, 48, 134
  Eliza. 55
  Elizabeth 55
  Faith 55
  Fortune 55
  Geo. 5, 6, 8, 26, 40, 43,
    120
  George 14, 32, 39, 59, 71,
    74, 97, 120
  Grace 11, 55
  Henry 55
  Jno. 55
  John 55
  Mary 54, 55
  Robert 11, 55
  Thom. 135
  Thomas 55
  Thos. 32
  William 8, 39, 55, 84, 85,
    144, 146
  Wm. 14, 15, 26, 59, 111,
    130
Fowler, Jos. 43
Fox, Hannah 143
  Mary 94
  Richard 143
Francis, Hen. 30
  Henry 114
  Jane 10
  Thos. 125
Freele, John 58
Freeman, Agnes 126
  Henry 29, 81, 111
  John 58, 81, 94, 131
  Thos. 111
  William 56
Friday, John 50, 73
Frowman, Will. 108
Furbross, Theophilus 53
Furbush, George 53
Further, Geo. 6
  Margaret 6
Futerell, Gilian 56
Gale, Simon 60
Gallow, John 112
Garrett, George 10
  Martha 10
Garroll, Thomas 46
Garris, Eliza. 117
Garritt, Sary 133
Gary, Richard 37
Gaul, Henry 63
Gauler, Henry 7, 60, 111
Gee, Charles 58, 128
  Hanah 56
  Henry 131
  James 128
  Jos. 146
George, Sarah 56
Gibbs, Ann 74
  Nath. 60
Gibson, Thos. 74

Gilbert, Anne 57
  Dorothy 135
  Elizabeth 57
  Hannah 57
  James 57
  Joanah 56
  Johanna 37
  John 56
  Martha 57
  Mary 57, 135
  Roger 96, 98, 135
  Thomas 56
  William 57
  Wm. 102
Gilbird, Dorothea 102
Giles, John 144
Gilliam, Amy 57
  Ann 57
  Burrell 57
  Charles 57
  Elizabeth 57
  Fortain 57
  Hansille 57
  Hincha 22
  Hinche 57
  Hinsha 18
  Hinshaw 93
  Isom 57
  John 18, 30, 93
  John, Jr. 92
  Ledea 57
  Levy 57
  Lydia 57
  Mary 57
  Millie 57
  Priscilla 57
  Samuell 57
  Sarah 21, 57
  Thomas 57
  Tibatha 57
  Walter 57
  William 131
Gillom, Hincha 18
Girly, Robert 66
Glover, George 78, 132
  John 35, 78, 102, 106, 132
  Rich. 118
  Sarah 20, 57
Goldne, Thomas 22
Golightly, Chris 117
Good, John 27
Goodman, Elizabeth 58
  Rebecca 37
  William 36, 37
Goodrich, E. 14
Goodwin, John 77
  Sarah 77
Goodwyn, Francis 58
  John 58, 82
  Mary 58
  William 58
Gord, Harry 58
  Nathaniel 58
  William 58

Gordon, Mary 58
Goring, Charles 58
  Jno. 5, 73
Gourd, Mary 58
Grantham, Edward 111
  Elizabeth 58
  Eloner 58
  Joanne 58
  John 58, 115
  Sarah 59
  Steven 59
  Thomas 58, 59
Graves, Adam 5
Gray, Benjamin 7
  Charles 60
  Edmund 60
  Eliza. 20
  Elizabeth 19, 59
  Gra. 59
  Francis 59, 140
  Gil. 136
  Gilbert 59, 60
  Henry 65
  James 60
  Joan 130, 140
  Jos. 60
  Joseph 60
  Lidie 59
  Lucy 24
  Mary 59, 60, 146
  Priscilla 60
  Robert 1, 27, 60, 90, 120
  Robt. 60, 136, 143
  Thomas 60, 140
  Thos. 60
  W., Jr. 136
  Will. 59
  William 15, 24, 55, 56,
    117, 146
  William, Jr. 95, 96, 113
  Wm. 28, 29, 38, 59, 60, 66,
    71, 79, 92, 95, 97, 111,
    117, 124, 127, 142
  Wm., Jr. 44, 66
Green, Abraham 93
  Ann 60
  Benj. 61
  Benjamin 61
  Burrell 61
  Elizabeth 61
  Faith 60
  Frederick 61
  James 61
  Jane 61, 145
  John 87
  Lewis 63, 100
  Lewis, Jr. 100
  Lewis, Sr. 100
  Mary 61, 110
  Mildend 61
  Nathaniel 61
  Olive 61
  Peter 60, 63, 100, 111
  Richard 48, 142

Green (cont.)
  Robert 143
  Susannah 48
  William 60
  Wm. 61
Greene, Edward 8, 16, 36
  John 12, 32, 42, 94, 98
  Peter 138
  Richard 138
  Robt. 10
  Susannah 138
  Wm. 29
Greenwood, Edward 112
Gregory, Barbara 61
  Frances 120
Grice, Ann 61
  Faithy 61
  Francis 61
  John 61
  Robt. 25
Griffin, (?) 119
  Agnes 110
  Ann 121
  Elizabeth 62, 87
  James 87, 89, 121
  Jane 120
  Jno. 110
  John 35, 59, 87, 104, 120
  Mary 61
  Rob. 87
  Robert 105, 110
  Sarah 87
Griffis, Edward 62
  Jane 62
  John 62
  Mary 62
  Travis 62
Griffith, John 23
Grimes, Robert 22
Grimmer, Robert 23
Griswitt, Ann 62
  George 62
  Thomas 62
  Walter 62
Grizzard, John 40
Gronswolt, Gerardt 84
Groves, Mary 38
  Phoebe 62
Guillidge, Lucy 37
Guillum, John, Jr. 100
Gulledge, John 84
  Lucy 85
Gulley, Lucey 62
  Robert 62
Gully, Elizabeth 62
  Robert 6, 62
Gutheridge, John 41
Guttre, Daniel 62
Gwaltney, Benj. 63
  James 63
  Jean 15
  John 144
  Mary 49, 63
  Ruth 63

Gwaltney (cont.)
Thomas 22
Thos. 49
William 51
Wm. 63
Gyles, Robt. 132
Hadly, John 102
Hagood, Francis 34
George 113, 135
Hagwood, Fra. 48
Hall, Benj. 119
George 63
Isaac 144
Judith 63
Lewis 63
R. 98
Richard 119
Thos. 128
William 63
Halleman, John 65
Halloman, Ann 64
Margarett 64
Samuell 64
Thomas 64
Thos. 64
William 64
Halso, William 34
Ham, Richard 83
Wm. 114
Hamilton, Geo. 101
Hamlin, Ann 34, 53
Ann (Mrs.) 104
Charles 113
Stephen 62, 134
Thomas 22, 23, 52
William 64
Wm. 28
Hancell, John 103
Hancock, Duegates 64
Duejates 64
Eliza. 64
Fanny 64
Henry 64
James 64
John 100
Joseph 116
Martha 64
Mary 64
Sussannah 116
William 55, 64
Wm. 64, 126
Hancocke, Eliza. 104
Elizabeth 64
Jane 73
John 7, 12, 38, 64, 73,
   87, 94, 110, 132, 145
Mary 104
Will. 48
William 20, 33
Wm. 29, 38, 42, 124
Handcocke, Jos. 65
Hanersly, John 70
Hanniford, Elizabeth 76
Hansford, Martha 73

Hansford (cont.)
Wm. 73
Hardin, Benjamin 65
Martha 64
Sarah 64
Harding, Richard 108
Hardy, Wm. 5
Hare, Wm. 28
Harebottle, Thos. 51
Haregrave, Margaret 76
Hargrave, Aug. 118
Benj. 65
Bray 32, 75, 97
Jesse 65
John 93
Joseph 65, 72
Lemeull 65
Mary 65
Rich. 71
Richard 80, 93
Samuel 65
Samuell 116
Hargrewe, Samuell 87
Hargrove, Augustine 7
Jesse 116
Samuell 15, 38
Harny, Sara 65
Harper, Edward 143
John 13
Jos. 92
Judith 144
Wm. 131
Harris, (?) 97
Catherine 136
Edward 23, 30, 32
Eliza 2
Henry 65
Jane 65, 66
Jno. 15
John 66, 80
Joseph 2, 37, 65
Joshua 37
Margarette 66
Mary 65, 66, 118, 119
Mich. 30, 52, 78, 88, 96,
   122, 136, 140
Michael 32, 35, 36, 40, 59,
   80, 91, 135
Michale 136
Richard 44, 127, 136
Sarah 65
Thomas 118, 119
Thos. 89, 100
Unity 65
Will. 99
William 71, 118, 119
Wm. 8, 31, 102, 110, 119,
   127, 142, 145
Harrison, (?) (Coll.) 53, 78
Ann 67
Banj. 67
Banjamin 46
Ben. 48

Harrison (cont.)
  Benj. 17, 28, 57, 72, 87,
    100, 111
  Benja. 56
  Benjamin 12, 63, 67, 68,
    86, 120
  Benjamin, Jr. 121
  Eliz. 98
  Elizabeth (Mrs.) 14
  Hannah 67, 86, 120
  Henry 14, 18, 25, 56, 66,
    67, 68, 91, 94, 98, 123
  Henry (Capt.) 14, 52, 77,
    113
  James 4, 5
  John 68
  Martha 68
  Mary 68
  N. 50
  Nath. 23, 28, 53, 56, 67,
    68, 82, 87, 98, 142
  Nathan. 35
  Nathaniel 4, 16, 46, 52, 66,
    86, 87, 111
  Nathaniel (Coll.) 113
  Nathaniel (Maj.) 77
  Priscilla 96
  Sarah 67
  Solomon 101
  William 68
  Wm. 60, 104, 107
  Wm. (Coll.) 129
Hart, Ann 68
  Elizabeth 68
  Faith 39
  Henry 13, 69, 97, 103, 117
  John 68, 69
  Joseph 68
  Lucy 68, 69
  Lydia 68
  Mary 68, 69, 88, 98, 137
  Moses 69
  Priscilla 68, 69
  Rebekah 88
  Robert 23, 63, 69
  Sarah 68, 69
  Thomas 2, 27, 68, 69
  William 68
  Wm. 44, 49, 63, 68
Harton, Eliz. 71
Hartwell, Elizabeth 69
Harvey, Will. 8
  William 36
  Wm. 48
Hassell, John 90
Hatch, John 54, 134
Hathorn, John 107
Hatly, John 69, 105
Hatty, John 19
Haviland, Mary 69, 120, 121
Hawkes, Thomas 3
Hawkins, Solomon 36
Hawthorne, Elizabeth 70
  Jno. 111

Hawthorne (cont.)
  John 111, 114, 121
  Joshua 69
  Nathaniel 69, 123
  Peter 13, 69, 111
  Pether 41
  Rebecca 41, 70
  Robt. 10
Hay, Alex. 38, 105
  Gilbert 139
  John 22
  Mary 62
  Martha 122
  Peter 122
  Thos. 122
Hays, John 44
  Sarah 141
Haywood, George 32
Heart, Mary 136
Heath, Abraham 70, 112
  Adam 8, 25, 36, 48, 49,
    65, 138, 142
  Benjamin 119
  Elizabeth 70
  John 70
  Margery 56, 70
  Sarah 70
  Susannah 145
  William 37, 56
  Wm. 70, 133
Heeth, Mary 127
Heiden, Mary 70
  Heigh, Mary 75
Hewster, James 130
Heydon, Mary 70
Hickman, Mary 108
Hicks, Christiana 70
  Daniel 11
  Daniell 70
  Denias Christiana 70
  Isodenias Christiana 70
  Jno. 121
  John 59, 69, 71, 107, 114,
    126, 146
  Joseph 70
  Joshua 71
  Rebeckah 71
  Robert 70
  Robt. 94
  Thomas 70
  William 70
Hide, Banj. 71
  David 33, 38, 71
  Jean 71
  Mary 71
  Richard 34, 39, 112, 142
  Richard, Sr. 34
Higgs, Thos. 130
High, Hannah 71
  John 71, 116, 127, 128
  Joseph 71, 127, 128
Hill, Benjamin 128
  Eliza. 94
  Eliza. C. 124

Hill (cont.)
  Elizabeth 92, 94
  Hannah 21, 71
  John 47
  Mary 123, 140
  Miel 37
  Priscilla 71
  Robert 72, 94
  Sarah 47
  Sion 40, 54, 86, 122
  Wm. 124
Hindes, Wm. 115
Hinds, John 145
Hinman, Robert 37
Hix, Elizabeth 71
  Robert 75
Hobbs, Katherine 128
Hodg, James 71
  Margott 71
  Mary 71
Hodge, James 72
  John 37
  Margaret 37
Hodges, Jno. 82
Hodgood, Frances 72
  George 72
  Richard 72
  William 72
Hogood, Ann 72
  Francis 72
  John 72
  Richard 72
Hogwood, Elizabeth 40
  Fra. 5
  Francis 134
  George 40
  Joan 40
  Richard 134
  William 40
Holder, Richard 38
Holdsworth, Charles 140
  Mary 140
Holesworth, Charles 8
Holleman, Henry 72
  Josias John 72
  Martha 72
  Mathew 72
  Rich. 74, 125
  Richard 72, 108, 129
  Robert 72
  Samuell 72
  Thomas 72
  Thos. 63, 72
Holliman, Marie 72
  Unity 72
Hollingsworth, Henry 25
Holloway, Edward 62, 118
Holmes, Robert 35
Holsworth, Charles 140
  Mary 140
Holt, (?) (Capt.) 9
  Ann 73
  Benjamin 73, 80
  Charles 64, 72, 73

Holt (cont.)
  Chas. 84, 118
  Eliza 28, 93, 117
  Eliza. (Mrs.) 29
  Elizabeth 33, 58, 80
  Elizabeth Ann 73
  Elizabeth, Jr. 141
  Frances 73, 93
  Francis 141
  Henry 13, 73
  James 73
  John 33, 71, 72, 102, 117
  Joseph 72, 73
  Katherine 93, 141
  Lucy 73, 84, 93, 141
  Martha 9, 141
  Mary 73, 93, 141
  Mary (Mrs.) 133
  Rand. 31
  Randall 5, 58, 138
  Sarah 73, 84
  Susannah 102
  Thomas 3, 9, 31, 33, 58,
    141
  Thomas, Jr. 93
  Thos. 1, 15, 44, 71, 73,
    93, 95, 105, 110, 127,
    129, 134, 141
  Thos. (Capt.) 32, 66, 133
  William 58, 88
  Wm. 28, 31, 46, 47, 50, 73,
    80, 88, 97, 103
Honeycutt, John 84
Hood, Mary 74
  Thos. 48
Hook, Mary 81
Horn, Harmon 61, 122
  Mary 61, 76
Horne, Mary 65
Horton, Daniel 27
  Martha 73
  Thomas 75
Hosier, Edman 98
Hoskins, Ann 86
  Elizabeth 74
Houlsworth, Mary 74
  Walter 74
House, Isaac 20
  Laurence 105
  Lawrence 141
  Samuel 80
  Thos. 105
Houseman, Stephen 77
Howard, Benj. 69
Howell, Ann 74
  Edmond 70, 75
  Elizabeth 75
  Joannah 75
  John 18
  Joseph 75
  Olive 74
  Susannah 74
  Thomas 75
  Thos. 1, 56

Howell (cont.)
  William 14, 80, 145
Howes, Margarett 75
Howse, Margaret 83
Howser, Sarah 109
Howlon, Sam 12
Hubard, Mathew 106
Hubbard, Edmund 142
Hudson, Daniel 39
Hugato, James 1
Huggins, Will. 103
Hulme, Wm. 42
Humphrey, Elizabeth 79
  John 141
  Mary 75, 141
  Thomas 128
Huniford, Elizabeth 76
  Philip 58
Hunnicutt, Ann 15, 75, 76
  Aug. 29
  Augustin 76
  Augustine 29, 86
  Augustine, Jr. 72
  Augustus 86
  Elizabeth 75, 76
  Jno. 136
  John 5, 40, 80
  Katherine 75, 76
  Margaret 72
  Martha 75, 76
  Mary 75
  Oysteen 95
  Robert 75, 95
  Wyke 128
Hunniford, Elizabeth 76
  Hugh 49, 51, 95, 102
  Jane 76, 95
  Katherine 76
  Wm. 92
Hunt, Ann 142
  Benj. 61
  Benjamin 61
  Elizabeth 61, 76
  Faith 101
  Fortune 82
  George 76, 142
  John 45, 76
  John, Jr. 61
  Mary 76
  Sarah 76, 77
  Thomas 11
  Thos. 76
  William 61, 100
  Wm. 27, 51
Hurdell, Wm. 50
Hurdle, Benjamin 77
  Christian 77
  Martin 77
  Wm. 77, 95
Huse, Mary 125
  Thomas 125
  Thos. 125
Hutchings, Sarah 77
Hutchins, Francis 90

Hutchins (cont.)
  Jane 90
Hux, Elizabeth 116
  Ironmonger 77
  Thos. 28
  Thos., Sr. 60
  Wm. 36
Iles, Wm. 103
Ingles, James 73
Ingram, John 40
Inman, John 9, 77
  Mary 77
  Robert 88, 128, 145
  Sarah 77
Irby, John 17, 22
  Mary 17
Ironmonger, John 59
  Mary 77
  Susannah 77
  Thos. 42, 74
Isell, Mich. 90
Isold, Michael 140
  Timothy 140
Isriell, Timothy 1
  Timothy, Sr. 1
Issiell, Timo. 99
Ivey, Hugh 44, 122
  Thos. 122
Ivie, Hugh 11
  Rebecka 122
Ivy, Rebecca 121
Izzard, Elizabeth 37
  Michael 37
Jackman, Elizabeth 3
  Joseph John 27, 31, 87, 134
  John 127
Jackson, Ambrose 145
  Amy 145
  George 77
  John 77, 88, 93, 100, 144
  Mary 144
  Robert 93
  Samuel 77
  Thomas, Jr. 131
  Wm. 94, 112
Jacquelin, (?) (Mrs.) 52
James, John 49
Jaret, Charles 133
Jarrard, Elizabeth 78, 133
  John 78
  Sarah 78
  Thomas 78
Jarratt, (?) 81
Jarrell, Catherine 78
  Jean 78
  Julian 78
  Thomas 46
  Thos. 46
Jarrett, Anne 109
  Charles 29, 79, 87, 118
  Elizabeth 79
  Faith 78
  Ferdinando 79
  Geo. 79

165

Jarrett (cont.)
George 78
Hannah 78
Henry 78
Jane 78
Jno. 78
John 25, 27, 64, 78, 109
Margery 79
Martha 78, 79
Mary 78
Micaell 1
Richard 78
Sarah 79
Thomas 43
Jarrod, (?) 53
John 21
Jeffres, Joseph 79
Lucy 79
Rebecca 79
Richard 79
Jeffry, Robt. 69
Jelks, Richard 93
William 80
Jenkins, Samuel 39
Jennings, (?) (Capt.) 124
Johnson, Aaron 80
Ann 32
Elizabeth 80, 145
Grace 80
Isaac 78
John 10, 11, 39, 143
Leveton 80
Martha 80
Martin 29, 86, 96, 97, 104, 135
Mary 80
Moses 36, 57, 80
Peter 80
Phillis 85
Richard 80
Samuell 85
Thomas 10, 32, 80
W. 145
William 59
Wm. 59
Joles, Sylvester 21
Jones, Betty 81
Catern 81
Catherine 39
Charles 60
Charles Henry 5
David 41, 81, 82
Elizabeth 76, 82, 101, 118
Elizabeth, Jr. 101
Henry 39, 81, 82
Howell 81, 93
James 31, 62, 84, 88, 89, 96, 122
Jane 81, 132
John 8, 70, 76, 91, 139
Judah 8
Mary 81, 88
Philip 89
Prudence 81

Jones (cont.)
Rebecca 81
Rich. 70
Richard 8, 34, 70, 81, 82, 119
Richard, Jr. 98
Robert 1, 30, 81, 82, 91, 93, 96, 101, 118
Robert, Jr. 81
Robt. 79, 131, 132
Sarah 45, 81, 82, 83, 89
Thomas 70, 81
Thos. 22
Wallis 132
William 58, 144
Wm. 26, 47, 144
Jordan, (?) (Lt. Coll.) 134
Ann 124
Ar. 86
Arthur 48, 83, 85, 99
Charles 83
Eliza. 83
Elizabeth 82, 83, 84, 100, 118
Geo. 28, 135
Geo. (Lt. Coll.) 48
George 72, 84
Hannah 83
Ja. 84
James 48, 122, 124
Jane 24, 124
Martha 84
Mary 25, 83, 84
Matthew 144
Priscilla 83, 84
Rachel 83
Richard 9, 28, 44, 119
Richard, Jr. 132
Richard, Sr. 76
River 82
Robert 6, 83, 118
Robert (Coll.) 116
Sarah 83
Thomas 83, 123, 124
Thos. 48, 59, 123, 124
Wm. 68, 82, 143, 144
Jorden, (?) (Lt. Coll.) 72
Joyner, Elizabeth 19
Judgson, Elizabeth 76
Mary 76
Judkin, Charles 51
Robert 51
Judkins, Ann 84
Anne 84
Charles 13, 85, 92
Elizabeth 66, 84
James 84
Jane 84
Jean 84
Jno. 89
John 50, 85, 92
Lidia 84
Mary 139
Nich. 84

166

Judkins (cont.)
Rob. 88
Robert 14, 28, 39, 91, 92, 96, 103
Robt. 56, 60, 62, 112
Sam 89
Sam'll. 91
Samuel 1, 92, 103, 105, 126, 129
Sarah 76, 84
William 84
Wm. 42, 71, 105, 129
Jurden, Ann 25
Justice, Eliza. 27
Elizabeth 26, 27
Jean 26
Joanna 26
John 27, 118
John, Jr. 27
Lydia 26
Mary 26, 27
Sarah 27
Kae, Bruton 25
John 25
Mary 25
Robert 26
Kate, Ann 85
Kavenaugh, Arthur 31, 85, 94
Kee, Rob. 132
Robert 121
Kelly, Wm. 81
Kerney, Elizabeth 85
Joannah 85
Micajah 85
Phillis 85
Kersey, John 120
Kicotan, Jno. 126
Mary 126
Kiggin, Phebe 39, 85
Killingsworth, (?) 65
Avis 85
John 37, 85
Will. 20
William 37
Wm. 18, 125
Killinsworth, Wm. 60
Kilpatrick, Lydia 85
Kimball, Alice 95
Charles 95
Joseph 1
Sarah 1
Kimbell, Charles 146
Kinchen, Wm. 108
Kindred, Katherine 86
Mary 85
Sam. 85
Samuel 46, 86
King, (?) (Dr.) 92
Benj. 90, 91
Benjamin 86, 91
Comfort, 117
Deborah 6, 30, 86
Deborak 91
Elizabeth 86

King (cont.)
Faith 54, 86
Henry 13
James 86
Jane 86
John 5, 16, 31, 36, 62, 109, 112
John, Jr. 5
Joseph 86
Mary 86
Richard 5
Sarah 86
Thomas 41, 134
Thos. 86, 124, 130
William 86
Kirby, Richard 40
Kitchen, Benjamin 86
John 66
Sarah 86
Kitching, John 32
Knight, Daniel 61, 87
Densie 61
Nate. 59
Nath. 28, 48
Samuel 86
Knot, Mary 3
Knott, Christian 87
William 30, 32
Wm. 27, 31, 56, 69, 79, 87, 113, 135
Wm., Jr. 86
Wm., Sr. 86
Lacaster, William 87
Lacey, Robert 38
Lacie, George 87
Mary 87
Lacy, Robert 132
Lainer, Sampson 107
Lancaster, Ann 88
Elizabeth 87, 88
Joseph 87
Judith 31
Laurence 43
Law. 143
Lawrence 143
Mary 87, 88, 143
Robert 22, 29, 65, 130, 134, 141
Robert, Jr. 3, 31
Robt. 9
Samuel 29, 87, 88
Samuell 3
Land, Curtis 19, 77
Custis 69
John 88
Mary 88
Rebeckah 88
Thomas 88
William 88
Lande, Sarah 15
Lane, Jean 55
John 88, 114
Joseph 46, 72, 88
Mary 88

Lane (cont.)
  Tho. 46
  Thomas 97, 103
  Thos. 31, 39, 118, 133
  Thos., Jr. 55
Lanier, Clement 146
  Eliza. 136
  Elizabeth 137, 138
  John 50
  Nicholas 140
  Priscilla 136, 137
  Robert 11, 37, 98, 136
  Sampson 99, 118, 137
  Sarah 10, 11
  Thomas 37, 136, 137
  Thos. 88
Lanser, Sampson 102
Lashley, Hannah 10, 11
  Patrick 65, 84
  Walter 88, 90
  Wm. 106
Later, Jane 129
Lather, Jane 36, 88
  John 28, 36, 65
Laughter, Jane 9
Lavemar, (?) (Capt.) 124
Lawne, Thos. 127
Lawrence, Elizabeth 141
  John 141
  Thomas 141
Ldeloney, (?) 102, 128, 139
Ldelong, (?) 52
Ldelony, (?) 67
Leath, Elizabeth 88
  John 88
  Sarah 88
Ledderdale, (?) 24
Lee, George 98, 107, 124
  Godfrey 78
  Robert 48
Legrand, John 56, 107
Lester, Andrew 21, 45, 47
Lewis, Mary 87
  Rachell 113
  Richard 32, 56, 87, 94,
    115, 133
Liles, Wm. 71
Litel, Frances 44
Littel, Francis 77
Little, Ann 95
  Anne 135
  Beaz 89
  Benj. 89
  Benjamin 89
  Boaz 95
  Elizabeth 89
  Francis 121
  John 23, 34, 63, 88, 135
  Katherine 89
  Patience 89
  Robert 44, 89, 121
  William 7, 23
  Wm. 63, 89, 144
Littleboy, Robert 37

Loftin, Clee 90
  Cornelius 74, 90
  Elizabeth 90
  Mary 90
  Rebekah 90
  Sarah 90
  Wm. 89
Long, Arthur 2
  Edward 90
  Eliza 90
  Geo. 96
  George 6, 90
  Mary 6
  Mary Ann 90
  Mercy 90
  Thomas 90
  William 90
Longbottom, John 90
  Jones 90
  Samuel 90
  Samuell 90
  Thomas 90
Longwell, Lu. 21
Looshas, Wm. 22
Lother, Henry 90
  Jane 90
Louis, Miles 1
Lowery, James 64
  Judeth 65
Lucas, Ann 90, 91
  Charles 28, 36, 37, 71, 89,
    90, 91, 94, 113, 133, 144
  Eliza 13
  Elizabeth 90, 91
  Grace 91, 115
  Hannah 90, 91
  Martha 90
  Mary 91
  Tabitha 145
  William 13, 90
  Wm. 22, 90
Ludwell, (?) (Coll.) 45
  Phillip 46
Lukelasco, Martha 91
Luper, Phillyp 81
Lurteler, William 119
Lyle, George 91
  Judith 91
  Judy 62
  Thomas 91
  Wm. 30, 62
Lynsey, Richard 38
Mabry, Charles 118
Macdaniell, Daniell 51
  John 51
Macham, Elizabeth 91
Mackdaniell, Daniel 38
Mackenny, Morgan 18
Macklemore, Abraham 48
Macklin, Wm. 105
Maclin, James 107
  John 37, 107
Macon, John 143
Macheden, Anne 22

Maddera, Zachariah 41
  Zacharias 15, 98
  Zack. 130
Madderra, Priscilla 122
  Zacharia 122
Madders, Zach 33
Maddery, Joanna 77
Maderna, Zacharias 86
Madra, Joanna 77
  John 77
Magarety, Mary 92, 122
Magarity, Patrick 122
Maget, Ann 91, 127
  Fortune 91
  Nich. 19, 25, 32, 34, 51,
    53, 55, 56, 60, 71, 72,
    75, 76, 88, 96, 98, 106,
    108, 123, 127, 136, 139,
    141
  Nicholas 9, 62, 90, 94,
    104, 117, 125, 139
  Sam. 76, 88
  Saml. 62
  Samuel 10, 17, 28, 79, 92,
    110, 112, 119
  Samuell 45, 60
Magett, Nich. 78
Magget, Faith 19
  Nicholas 135
  Samuel 89
  Samuel, Sr. 86
Maggett, Nicholas 19, 36
  Sam. 18
Magot, Samuell 50
Malden, John 108
  Jos. 12, 70, 115
Mallone, Daniel 92
  Drury 92
  Nathaniel 92
  Thomas 92
  William 92
Mallory, Frances 85
Malone, Agnes 92
  Amey 92
  Anne 92
  Elizabeth 92
  Hannah 92
  John 92
  Milly 92
  Sarah 92
  Wm. 26, 111
Malsen, Jos. 91
Manfell, Maximilian 120
Manggam, Olive 114
Manggum, John 125
Mangum, Olive 92, 110
  Wm. 118
Mansell, Maxililian 120, 121
  Maximilian 138
Marable, Elizabeth 69
  Geo. 69
  Geo., Jr. 69
  Henry Hartwell 69
  Mary 69

Marler, Robert 62
Marlow, Nathan 38
  Robert 100   .
Marriett, William 1
Marriott, (?) (Maj.) 106
  (?) (Major) 32
  Alice 92
  Allice 92
  Mary 36
  Mathias 56
  Sarah 36
  Thomas 36
  William 36
  Wm. 10, 66, 130, 140
Marsengill, James 134
Martiall, Rob. 73
Martin, Sarah 92
Mason, (?) (Capt.) 81
  Elizabeth 93
  Fra. 20, 29, 40, 71, 80,
    84, 97, 99, 113, 136, 138
  Francis 16, 28, 37, 80, 140
  James 15, 97, 124
  John 41, 66, 96, 132, 139
  Joseph 58
  Phebe 93
  Sam. 85
Masongall, James 83
Mastin, Mary 130
Mathews, (?) 111
  Anne 130
  James 134
  Thomas 44
  Thos. 59, 111
Mathias, Edward 89
Mathis, Thos. 107
Matthews, Edward 89
May, John 58
Maybry, Cornelius 93
  Ebrill 93
  Elizabeth 93
  Emidia 93
  Rebecca 93
  Rebeccak 93
  William 93
Maybury, Ann 93
  Charles 93, 94
  Eleanor 94
  Elizabeth 94, 100
  Frances 100
  Francis 55, 69, 70, 93, 107,
    123
  George 93, 94
  Hancha 94
  Hanchey 94
  Hinchey 100
  Hinshaw 93
  Judith 93, 94
  Mary 93
  William 94
Maygaratery, Patrick 89
Maynard, John 92
Mayson, John 133
McDonnae, Henry 14, 39

169

Mcexodon, Ann 23
Meacham, Henry 109
Meade, Honour 94
Measell, Luke 88
Meazle, Elizabeth 94
  Luke 54
  Sarah 94
Megarety, Mary 94
Mercer, John 61
  Stephen 27
Mercey, John 61
Meriweather, David 32
  Eliza 32
  Eliza. (Mrs.) 143
  Fra. 94
  Jane 32
  Mary 32
  Ni. 19, 38, 48, 136
  Nich. 109
  Nich. (Maj.) 32
  Nicholas 94, 135
  Sarah 32
  Wm. 32
Merrill, Thos. 91
Merriweather, Elizabeth
  (Mrs.) 143
Mersingale, James 70
Messer, Robt. 72
  Unity 72
Metcalf, Matthew 56, 141
Meyrich, Owen 8
Middleton, George 28
  John 69
  Katherine 94
  Thos. 69, 104
Midleton, Sarah 119
Miles, Alice 95
Mill, Elizabeth 127
Miller, Rich. 103
Mills, John 19
Milton, Thomas 112
Minard, John 70
Minton, Wm. 80
Mitchell, Abraham 126
  Henry 26, 33, 37, 60, 74,
    110, 111
  Henry, Jr. 33
  James 22
  Mary 95
  Robert 22
  Robt. 18
  William 18
Mithcell, Henry 70
Mizel, Richard 68
Mizell, Deborah 95
Moody, Blanks 86, 91
  Charity Pemlum 91
  Joseph 24
Moonk, Rich. 39
Moor, Wm. 146
Moore, Alice 95
  Elizabeth 95
  Francis 90
  Joanna 115

Moore (cont.)
  Rich. 60
  Richard 139
  Thos. 13
  Wm. 117, 126
Mooring, John 39
More, Richard 12, 134
  William 28
Moreland, Ann 12, 95
  Bartlett 12, 66, 85, 142
  Edward 14, 31, 44, 60, 62,
    110
  Elizabeth 95
  John 12
  Katherine 95
  Lucy 95, 133
  Margaret 85
  Margarett 66
  Martha 95
  Thomas 12, 95
  Thos. 15
Morgan, (?) (Capt.) 118
  Richard 96
Moring, Chris. 80, 115, 116,
    121, 141
  Christopher 88
  Christopher, Jr. 59
  Jane 141
  Jno. 48, 55, 99, 101, 106,
    109, 123, 138
  John 8, 14, 20, 23, 41, 48,
    51, 53, 74, 84, 86, 91,
    108
  Mary 120, 121
Morland, Edward 48
Morley, Catherine 32
  Elizabeth 32
Morning, Chris. 74
Morrell, Elizabeth 96
  George 96
  John 96
  Mary 96
  William 96
Morris, Rich. 29
  Richard 12
  Travis 62
  Wm. 141
Morrison, Charles (Coll.) 58
Morroll, Mary 6
Mosely, Benj. 137
  George 103
  Mary 130
  Wm. 130, 137
Moss, Benjamin 125
  Eliza 16
  Elizabeth 131
  Grace 132
  Henry 96
  Martha 96, 106
  Nath. 45
  Rebekah 125
  Thomas 96
  Wm. 28, 91, 96
Mountfortt, Joseph 73

Mountfortt (cont.)
Lucy 73
Moyee, John 58
Moyel, John 58
Moyer, John 73
Mumford, James 109
Joseph 34
Munger, Spenser 96
Murfrey, Lemon 34
Murphy, Simon 104
Murray, James 142
Muzelwhite, Elizabeth 31
Mylone, Ann 39
Myrick, Owen 121
Nelson, James 30
John 30
New, John 102
Tabitha 102
Newburn, Jos. 15
Newby, Jeane 19
Sarah 19
Newett, Wm. 66, 71
Newit, Wm. 65
Newitt, Eliza. 97
Elizabeth 97
Frances 97
William 103
Wm. 65, 97, 126
Newman, Robert 131
Newsom, Tapphenas 73
Newsum, Ann 97
Anne 97
Jno. 132
Joel 97
John 1, 15, 29, 59, 70, 71,
73, 74, 88, 94, 106, 114,
134, 144
Martha 73
Philip 86
Robert 97
Sarah 97
Tapphanas 73
Thomas 97
William 2, 9, 15, 69
Wm. 26, 29, 43, 85, 86, 97,
104, 111, 114, 124, 130,
138, 143
Newsume, Robert 55
Thomas 55
Newsums, Wm. 65, 82
Newton, Mary Lucie 97
Robert 78
Samuel 29, 37
Niblet, Tabitha 3
Nicholas, Roger 99
Nicholls, John 27
Sarah 98
Nichollson, Elinor 49
Nichols, Benjamin 51
Robert 77
Roger 130
Wm. 77
Nicholson, Ann 41, 52
Benj. 139

Nicholson (cont.)
Benjamin 98
Eliza. 20
Elizabeth 52, 98
George 2, 16, 52, 112
Hannah 98, 107
Henry 52
James 6, 52, 76
Jane 98, 112
John 27, 65, 98, 99, 113,
133
Joice 52
Jos. 28, 94, 131
Joseph 36
Joshua 20, 28, 98, 99, 144
Joyce 98
Mary 52, 59, 98
Parks 98
Robert 27, 41, 52, 59, 102,
112
Robt. 17
Sarah 20
Nichoss, John 60
Nickolson, Jos. 137
North, Katherine 99
Norton, Henry 76, 83
Norwood, Edward 99
Eliza. 16
George 82, 99
Lyddia 120
Lydia 99
Mary 99
Rich. 113
Richard 99
Sarah 99
Wm. 28
Norwoods, George 53
Nuby, Jean 37
Oase, Judith 140
Oasse, John 140
Odyan, James 139
Ogbourne, Elias 133
Elizabeth 99
Ogburn, Elizabeth 64
Jno. 113
Ogburne, John 145
Oliss, Elizabeth 99
Oliver, Mandlin 99
Mary 99
Onails, Elizabeth 78
Oney, Leonard 114
Orchard, Jno. 28
John 28
Ostin, Francis 56
Robert 56
Owen, Catherine 100
Elizabeth 100
Hannah 51
Jane 99
John 19, 85, 100
Katherine 88
Robert 51
Sarah 123
William 100

Owen (cont.)
  Wm. 79
Owens, (?) 83
Owing, Rob. 83
Oxford, Mary 133
Oysten, Francis 98
Pace, Richard 11, 12, 20,
  134
Pack, Christopher 100
  Graves 100
Page, John 29, 48
Paine, Eliza 93
  Robert 129
Panhup, Gregory 13
Pardon, Elizabeth 98
Parham, Ann 13, 100
  Ephraim 13
  Frances 100
  Gower 100
  James 100, 131
  John 88
  Lewis 61, 100
  Lina 100
  Matthew 100
  Phebe 100
  Wm. 42, 70, 144
Parke, Elizabeth 100
  Mary 43
  Robert 35, 142
  Robt. 43
Parker, Ann 101
  Daniel 25
  Drury 101
  Frederick 101
  Henry 118
  Judah 101
  Judith 87, 100, 146
  Martha 101
  Mary 101
  Peter 101
  Rich. 45, 108
  Rich., Jr. 69
  Richard 91, 146
  Richard, Jr. 146
  Sarah 101
  Thomas 101
  Thos. 54
  William 101
  Wm. 101
Parks, Samuel 79
Parr, Jno. 138
  John 30
Parsons, Francis 87
  Jno. 142
  John 132
Partin, Eliza. 107, 108
  Wm. 116
Partridge, Nich. 73, 93
  Nicholas 11, 102, 132, 139
  Nicholas, Jr. 11
  Thos. 96
Pasfield, Jeane 101
  Mary 101
  Nicholas 10, 32

Pasmore, George 114
  John 9, 10
Patrick, Margarett 122
Payne, Robert 130, 146
Paynter, John 38
Paynton, John 105
Peacock, Katherine 86
Peacocke, Catherine 39
Peck, Elizabeth 92
Pedington, Sarah 120
Peebles, Abraham 131
  Sarah 102
Peete, Samuel 30, 101, 106,
  145
Pelling, Wm. 47
Penenton, Edward 102
  George 102
  John 102
  Mary 102
  William 102
Penington, Mary 3
  Thos. 78
Pennenton, Thos. 79
Penneton, Thos. 69
Pennington, Phillis 54
Peoples, Ann 94
  Wm. 60
Pepper, Elizabeth 102
  Jane 102
  Jussy 102
  Rebeccah 102
  Sarah 102
Perry, Margaret 43
  Micajah 46, 118
Person, Benjamin 102
  Elizabeth 102
  Francis 102
  Jacob 102
  John 135
  Joseph 102
  Mary 102
  Samueal 102
  Samuel 100
  Sarah 102
  Thomas 102
  Thos. 102
  William 102
Pestel, Ann 102
  John 102
Pestell, John 49
  Sussannah 102
Peters, Thomas 45
  Thos. 91, 109, 115
  Thos., Jr. 109
Pettaway, Ann 95
  Edward 61, 103
  Edwards 103
  Elizabeth 95
  John 95
  Mary 95
  Phebe 95
  Robert 95, 103
  Selah 95
  Wm. 95

Petteway, Wm. 42
Pettway, Edward 50, 85, 88,
  111, 114, 139
Eliza. 103
Elizabeth 103, 111
Fortune 103
Jane 103
John 103
Joyce 103
Mary 103, 111
Micajah 103
Robt. 85
Ruth 103
Sarah 103
William 103, 146
Wm. 103, 111, 117, 126,
  139
Petway, Elizabeth 107
Robert 63
Wm. 108
Pharlow, Eliza 103
Phelps, Richard 25
Phillips, (?) 87
Alias 104
Alice 40
Ann 101, 104
Anne 104
Eliza. 103
Elizabeth 104
Faith 52
Hannah 54
Jno. 40, 114, 124, 136,
  142
John 5, 12, 16, 35, 36, 37,
  42, 49, 54, 66, 71, 74,
  109, 124, 126, 127, 134,
  144
Joseph 54
Mary 52, 108
Mathew 104
Nath. 65
Nathaniel 86
Ruth 103
Sarah 104
Swann 104
Thomas 103
Thos. 54
William 126, 134
Wm. 27, 86, 104
Pickerill, Hanah 104
Piddington, Thos. 87
Pidington, Abigail 105
Pierce, Mary 30
Piland, Geo. 32, 50
James 10, 58
Katherine 140
Martha 105
Mary 73, 105
Priscilla 105
Richard 105
Pinginton, Edmond 105
Edwards 105
John 105
Pingington, Tabitha 105

Pitt, Ann 31
Charles 31, 38, 75, 76
Joseph 105
Lucy 105
Milea 105
Pittman, Benj. 72
Edward 144
Thomas 37, 134
Thos. 3, 64, 101
Thos., Jr. 96
Thos., Sr. 70, 74
Wm. 64, 72, 108
Pkttaway, Elizabeth 103
Pla, Samuel 124
Place, (?) 124
Plow, (?) (Mrs.) 56
Jane 124
Jane (Mrs.) 63
Samuel 56, 86
Pollard, Arthur 65
Poole, Richard 19
Porch, Henry 105
James 105
Margery 105
Porche, Henry 105
Portch, James 5
Portis, Elizabeth 105
Potter, (?) (Capt.) 111
(?) (Mrs.) 52
Ann 105
Roger 36, 59
Roger (Capt.) 55
Potway, Wm. 84
Poythras, David 42, 43
Poythress, Peter 111
Prentice, (?) 24
Prescott, Ann 106
Rachel 106
Pretlow, Thos., Jr. 89
Price, David 86
Elizabeth 96
Francis 76, 93, 141
John 29, 64, 104, 138, 140
Martha 89
Mary 15
Susannah 19
Wm. 19, 97
Prier, Eliza. 129
Prince, Edward 121, 122
Edward, Jr. 121
Eliza. 122
Prise, Jno. 124
Pritchard, Casey 106
Elizabeth 106
John 106
Richard 106
Pritchett, Morris 47
Prockter, Nicholas 54, 123
Procktor, Joshua 83
Persilla 112
Proctor, (?) 56, 92, 125
Eliza. 116
Geo. 56, 86, 124
George 5, 92, 116

Proctor (cont.)
  Hannah 106
  Joan 3
  Joseph 54
  Joshua 53, 84
  Josiah 83
  Katherine 106
  Mary 73, 86, 106
  Nicholas 5, 6, 106
  Richard 53, 106
  Robert 106
  Sarah 106
  Wm. 5
Prosser, Wm. 61
Pulister, John 94
Pulistone, Ann 106
Pulitson, John 75, 136
Pulley, Hannah 125
  William, Jr. 42
  Wm. 30, 78, 104, 125
Pully, Mary 106
Pyland, Eliza. 20
  James 19
Rainer, John 105
Raines, John 107, 121
  Richard 100
  Wm. 64
  Wm., Jr. 134
Ramey, William 107
Randal, Eliza 107
Randall, Mary 61, 107
  Peter 107
  Robert 74
  Robt. 10
Randol, Mary 107
Randolph, (?) (Capt.) 50
  Wm. (Coll.) 121
Ransom, Catherine 107
  Elizabeth 107
  Gwathmey 107
  James 44, 133
  Mary 107
  Richard 27
Rawlin, Mary 36
Rawlings, Ann 140
  Elinor 107
  Eliza. 82, 108
  Gregory 87, 90, 99, 107
  Jno. 107
  John 26, 36, 56, 82
  Mary 82, 87, 99, 107, 108,
    138
  Wm. 87
Rawlins, Roger 114
Rawser, Elizabeth 145
  Susannah 145
Ray, Affiah 108
  Fra. 108
  James 81
  Lenard 108
  Martha 145
  Marthy 108
  Susannah 6
  Wm. 50, 123

Rea, Francis (Maj.) 98
Read, Samuell 47
Reade, Mary 47
  William 47, 101
  Wm. 47, 108
Reddick, Alice 108
  Geo. 96
  James 43, 127, 135, 136
  James R. 79
  Mary 96
Reding, Mary 108
Reekes, Benjamin 118
Reeks, Benj. 108, 137
  Charles 133
  Elizabeth 108
  Faith 108
  Jane 108, 133
  Jean 52
  Thos. 52
Regan, Daniel 109
  Eliza. 109
  Elizabeth 109
  Faith 109
  Fran. 141
  Francis 46, 114
  Jane 109, 130
  Jeremiah 109
  John 109
  Joseph 109
  Mary 109, 130
  Richard 109
Regand, Fra. 134
Reigns, John 121
Reives, Eliz. 71
  Geo. 69
  Grace 109
Renn, William 141
  Wm. 80
Resbe, Richard 108
Revell, John 51
  Rand. 143
Revelle, John 51
Reynolds, Elizabeth 110
  Grace 110
  Mary 109
  Nicholas 110
  Susannah 110
Rice, David 15
  John 117
Richardson, Alex. 1, 99
  Arthur 79, 102
  Betty 110
  Elizabeth 110
  Hardy 110
  Hopkins 110
  Joseph 110
  Joseph, Jr. 54
  Martha 110
  Patty 110
  Susannah 110
  Wm. 60
Richeson, Joseph 135
Rickes, John 110
  John, Jr. 110

Ricks, Richard 88
Riddick, Alice 110
　James 35, 71
Ridley, Mary 110
　Thos. 134
Rieves, Arsilla 71
Riggon, Joseph 101
Right, Thomas 126
River, John 60
Rivers, Elizabeth 110
　Grace 112
　John 112
　Mary 112
　Robert 98
　Wm. 84
Rives, Christopher 110
　Frances 110
　Geo. 69, 95, 110
　John 110
　Judith 110
　Rich. 139
　Richard 95, 116, 117, 133
　Sarah 111
　Timothy 110
　William 110
Rix, Jane 119
　Robt. 137
Robberts, Elizabeth 111
Roberts, Elizabeth 111
　Frederick 134
　John 146
　Mary 96
　Nath 123
　Nathaniel 6
　Willet 22
Robertson, Christ. 111
　Drury 111
　Elizabeth 111
　Nath. 92
Robins, Peter 128
Robinson, Anne 111
Rochell, Geo. 37, 61, 67
　George 2, 86
Rochelle, George 110
Rodwell, J. I. 35
Roe, James 34
Rogers, Benjamin 85
　Elizabeth 28, 112
　Jane 112
　John 16
　Jos. 127
　Joseph 28, 44, 112, 124
　Mary 112
　Robert 112
　Sarah 28
　Thomas 69
　William, Sr. 23
　Wm. 28
Rome, Mary 72
Rooking, Wm. 114, 140
Rookings, (?) 87
　Ann 98, 113
　Elizabeth 52, 112
　Ellen 27, 42

Rookings (cont.)
　James 3, 37, 42, 113
　Jane 112, 113
　Jas. 87
　Mary 113
　Susannah 113
　W. 139
　William 13, 14, 32, 42, 98
　Wm. 5, 27, 68, 72, 87, 101,
　　105, 106, 140
Rooks, Jane 104
　Thos. 104
Room, Daniel 123
Roome, Dan. 119
　Daniel 83
Roscow, (?) (Mrs.) 4
　Mary 4
　Wm. (Coll.) 4
Rose, Ann 73, 133
　Elizabeth 8, 113, 133
　Francis 20
　Hannah 113
　Henry 50
　Jane 113
　John 71
　Mary 50, 115
　Rch. 52
　Richard 7, 8, 14, 46, 82,
　　123, 133
　Thomas 7, 113, 133
　Thos. 60
　William 8, 20, 84
　Wm. 8, 54, 70, 78, 88, 102,
　　132
Rosser, John 21
Rottenbury, (?) 143
　John 143
Rowell, Edward 27, 38, 75, 81,
　　101, 122
　Elizabeth 113
　Jemima 113
　Katherine 38
　Margaret 113
　Mary 113
　Massy 122
　Richard 33, 75
　Robert 113
　Samuel 113
Rowland, Elizabeth 106
　Mary 47
　Simon 8
　William 14, 47
　Wm. 113
Rowling, Christopher 140
Rouzee, Ralph 129
Ruffin, Ann 45
　Benjamin 114
　Edmund 22, 45, 114
　Elizabeth 114, 141
　Faith 60
　Jane 113
　John 25, 39, 50, 73, 89,
　　104, 106, 107, 114, 128,
　　133, 134, 137

175

Ruffin (cont.)
  John (Capt.) 5
  Joseph 114
  Martha 114, 128
  Mary 114
  Robert 2, 15, 29, 66, 71, 82,
    86, 94, 95, 97, 106, 138
  Robt. 28, 40, 66, 124, 126
  Sarah 97
  William 113
  Wm. 60, 88, 101
Rutherford, Jno. 30
  John 74, 120
Ryeves, Judith 114
Saffold, Eliza. 118
Salway, (?) 92, 111
  Jno. 119
  John 129
Sammon, James 5, 81, 107,
  111
Samon, James 58
  Mary 107
Sampson, Arthur 137
Sanburne, Samuel 36
  Sarah 36
Sandborn, Wm. 110
Sands, Sam. 135
Sandy, Henry 134
Saul, Abraham 45, 142
Saunders, Mary 125
  Robert 125
  Wm. 16, 37, 87, 102, 129
Savage, Wm. 98
Savidge, Charles 9, 16
  Elizabeth 114
  Henry 90
  Loveless 114
  Mary 114
  Sarah 125
Scarbo, William 74
Scarbro, Edward 10, 71
Scarbroo, Edward 82
Scarbrough, Joanna 26
  Joannah 27
  Wm. 27
Scarbrow, Ann 115
Scoggin, Susannah 115
Scogging, Frances 65
  John 65
  Richard 65
  William 65
Scott, Bethyer 43
  Comfort 115
  Jno. 115
  John 43
  John, Sr. 43
  Robt. 60
Seale, Jos. 64
  Joseph 42, 48
Seat, Jos. 60
  Joseph 12, 116, 145
  Marshall 115
  Thomas 115, 145
Seate, Ann 115

Seate (cont.)
  Robert 126
Seats, Billeson 115
  James 115
  Mable 115
  Marchell 115
Sebrell, Benjamin 116
  Daniell 106
  Joseph 116
  Moses 116
  Naomi 116
  Nathaniel 116
  Samuel 38, 116
  Samuell 132
Sebriel, Mary 64
  Nath. 64
  Nathaniel 64
Seldon, Joan 48
Selway, Elizabeth 116
Sesome, Nicholas 9
Sesshings, Ann 42
Sessom, Thomas 95
Sessoms, Katherine 116, 128
  Nicholas 83, 132
  Richard 122
  Thos. 100
Sesson, Thomas 121
  Wm. 121
Sessums, Nich. 76
Seward, Ann 117
  Benjamin 116
  Elizabeth 117
  Hannah 3
  James 116
  Jas. 105
  John 25, 28
  Joseph 116
  Mary 73, 117, 142
  William 27, 33, 102, 110,
    116
  Wm. 26, 43, 44, 45, 66, 71,
    75, 85, 116, 117, 130, 133
  Wm., Jr. 45, 89
Sezar, (?) 119
Shahankon, John 6
Shaky, Richard 137
Shands, John 111
  Mary 111
  Nazarath 111
  Nazareth 58
  William 58
  Wm. 41, 48, 111, 125, 133
Sharp, Jacob 117
  John 16, 26, 103, 117
  Sarah 117
  William 117
  Wm. 78
Sharpe, John 143
Shaw, Rebecca 58
  Robert 58
Shehawcon, John 33
Shehawken, John 132
Shehawkin, John 54
Shelby, Phillip 141

Shelley, Ann 96, 118
  John 96, 100, 117, 118
  Phillip 10, 29, 89
  Phillip, Jr. 96
  Phillip, Sr. 96
  Sarah 118
  Thomas 100, 117, 118
  Thos. 118
Shelly, Mary 79
  Phillip 27
  Thomas 79
  Wm. 4
Shelton, Edward 13
  John 99
Sherley, Elizabeth 118
  Mary 118
Sherwood, (?) 5
  Wm. 138
Shockey, Alice 118
  Mary 118
Shoker, Richard 26
Shorsby, John 82
  Thomas 82
  Thos. 82
Short, Eliza 119
  Elizabeth 119
  Martha 119
  Mary 112, 119
  Sarah 119
  Susannah 119
  Thomas 118, 119
  William 7
  Wm. 8, 25, 34, 65, 67, 70, 119
  Wm., Jr. 8
Shrewsbury, Ann 119
  Fra. 120
  Francis 120
  Katherine 120
  Thos. 113
Shrousby, Elizabeth 119
  James 119
  Jane 119
  Katherine 119
  Thomas 119
Shrowsbury, Eliza. 120
  Thomas 120
Shugars, Elizabeth 43
  John 43
Sidway, Jane 120
  Jeane 120
  Thos. 120, 140
Sikes, Henry 40
Simmons, Benj. 120
  Edward 120
  Elizabeth 14, 39, 120, 121
  Frances 33
  J. 137
  James 69
  Jno. 73
  John 6, 14, 18, 19, 23, 41, 68, 77, 85, 94, 108, 113, 115, 121, 137, 142
  John, Jr. 6, 136

Simmons (cont.)
  Joseph 120
  Lucy 34
  Peter 121
  Rebecca 120
  Rebekah 120
  Sarah 34, 120, 121
  Stephen 106
  William 18, 23, 69, 89, 112, 120, 121
  Wm. 53, 69, 89, 101, 114, 120
Simons, William 74
Sims, Amos 91
Sinckler, David 131
Sisson, Ann 121
  Elizabeth 121
  Hannah 101
  Isabel 121
  Mary 121
  Stephen 121
  Thos. 121
Skelton, Eliza. 139
Skilltimber, (?) 95
Skinner, Mary 49, 71
  Wm. 5
Slate, George 121
  John 41, 121
  Mary 121
  Robert 121
Sledge, Amos 121, 122
  Charles 91, 122
  Daniel 121, 122
  John 122
  Mary 31
  Mathew 121
  Sarah 121, 122
  Rebecca 121
Smalley, Michael 64
Smith, Ann 71
  Arthur 4, 107, 122
  Arthur, Jr. 3
  Eliza. 53
  Elizabeth 3, 39, 71, 86, 107, 122
  Francis 16
  George 122
  Henry 87
  Jno. 20
  John 16, 39, 49, 71, 92, 95
  John (Maj.) 56
  Lawrence 16, 122
  Mary 39, 122, 132
  Nich. 106, 114, 136, 143
  Nicholas 86, 90, 95, 134
  Rich. 136
  Richard 4, 132, 144
  Samuel 122
  Sarah 122
  Tho. 48, 53
  Thomas 117, 122, 141
  Thos. 53, 94, 106, 122
  Thos., Jr. 48
  Will. 141

Smith (cont.)
  Willi. 141
  William 122
  Wm. 33, 101, 136, 146
Snipes, Lucy 6
  Jos. John 75
  Robert 6, 59, 145
  Robt. 59
Sollowman, Betty 80
Solomon, Martha 123
Sorrows, Henry 62
Sowerby, Ann 48, 123, 124
  Anne 123
  Benjamin 108, 123
  Elizabeth 123
  Fra. 80, 133
  Francis 24, 108, 133, 139
  Henry 6, 108
  James 82
  Jane 91
  Jean 124
  Jeremiah 109
  John 8, 50, 54, 133
  Liddia 123
  Lydia 99
  Mary 24, 123
  Sam. 89
  Sarah 82
  Thomas 26, 37, 82, 133
  Thos. 86, 121, 123, 133,
    144
  William 123
Spain, John 63
Spane, Mary 62
Speed, Wm. 106
Spencer, Robert 38
Spenser, Ann 124
  Elizabeth 124
  Jane 124
Spensor, Elizabeth 124, 138
  Mary 124
  Robert 138
  Rogt. 135
Spiltimber, Martha 124
  Mary 124
  Patte 124
Spittles, James 19
Spratley, Eliza. 34, 125
  John 91
  Mary 34, 125
  Phillis 125
  William 125
  Wm. 125
Squire, Roger 9
Stanley, Ethill 96
Stanly, Wm. 65
Stanton, Ann 125
  J∩. 77
  James 71, 103, 114, 126
  Mary 125
Steavens, Ann 136
  Thomas 136
Stegall, John 81
Stephens, Rebecah 125

Stephenson, Ann 43
  Benjamin 43
  John 43
  Martha 43
  Peter 43
Stevens, John 142
Steward, Margaret 125
  Mary 125
  Richard 27
  William 125
Stewart, Chales 20
  Richard 37, 42
Stoke, Silvanus 126
Stokes, David 126
  Hamlin 126
  John 126
  Jonas 90, 125, 126
  Jones 126
  Marcus 126
  Samuel 126
  Silvanus 13, 74, 90, 126
Stokey, Richard 26
Stranford, Anthony 106
Stransford, Alice (Mrs.) 106
Stringer, William 67, 120
Stringfellow, Jane 66
Stringfield, James 135
Strinkfeler, Sara 16
Sturdevant, Matthew 10
Sturdivant, Daniell 21
  Elizabeth 143
  Hallum 126, 143
  Hollum 92
  Jollum 142
  Mary 61
Sturdyvaut, Holan 97
Sugar, Elizabeth 96
  John 44, 64, 118
Sugars, John 29, 60
Summons, Charles 53
Surcutt, Katherine 42
Sutpork, Robert 54
Swann, (?) (Coll.) 83, 126
  Elizabeth 126
  Fra. 56
  Madan Mary 99
  Mary 126
  Math. 111
  Mathew 1, 19, 85, 104
  Matthew 97, 130
  Sam. 106
  Sampson 10
  Samuel (Maj.) 10
  Samuell 10, 30
  Samuell (Capt.) 35
  Sarah 104, 126
  Thomas (Coll.) 59
  Thos. 10
  Thos. (Capt.) 84
Swanns, (?) (Col.) 82
Sweet, Wm. 82
Swett, Mary 126
Sykes, Bernard 121

178

Taberer, Thos. 96
Taner, Edward 20, 127, 128
Tanner, Ed. 145
  Edward 127, 128, 140
  Jane 126, 127
  John 30, 126
  William 126
  Wm. 96, 128, 145
Tapley, Adam 105
Tarver, Elizabeth 9, 127
  Mary 9
  Samuall 9
  Samuel 127
  Thos. 90
Tate, Barbaby 23
Tatum, (?) 74
  Chris. 42, 85, 94, 95, 111,
    122, 127, 132, 133
  Christ. 74, 125
  Christopher 60, 70, 71, 74
  Elizabeth 127
  Henry 42
  Nathaniel 127
  Peter 122
  Rebekah 127
  Robert 70
  Ruth 127
  Sarah 127
  Thomas 127
  Wenia 127
Tavor, Thos. 77
Tayler, Elizabeth 127
  Fra 141
  Jno. 140
  John 31
  Mary 127
  Richard 127
  Samuel 104
  Susan 127
Taylor, Ann 66, 128
  Edward 66
  Edwards 73
  Eliza. 15, 128
  Elizabeth 128
  Ellen 113
  Elli 46
  Eth. 46
  Ethelred 15, 116, 128
  Fra 10, 29, 42
  Francis 60, 103
  Harris 66
  Henry 13, 127, 128
  John 66, 102
  Katherine 128
  Margaret 127
  Margarett 66
  Margret 73
  Mary 66, 127
  Pennellope 58
  Rebeckah 128
  Rich. 43
  Richard 4, 117, 118
  Sam. 63, 135
  Samuel 127, 128

Taylor (cont.)
  Samuell 128
  Sarah 128
  Thomas 66
  Thos. 117
  Thso. 105
  Walter 45, 66, 71, 128
  William 30, 127
Terrell, James 146
Tharp, John 145
  Timothy 73
Tharpe, Benjamin 128
  Chris. 117
  Christopher 128
  Dinah 128
  Elizabeth 128
  Hannah 128
  Jos. 128
  Sarah 129
  Timothy 71, 129
  William 128
Thoma, William Catlett 129
Thomas, (?) 51
  Ann 129
  Benjamin 51
  Elizabeth 129
  Evin 129
  Henry 51, 129
  John 129
  Jordan 27
  Mary 129
  Mourning (Mrs.) 4
  Priscilla 18, 112
  Rambley 129
  William 18, 51, 124
  Wm. 5, 10, 18, 20, 73
Thompson, (?) 46, 109
  Ann 130
  Catherine 129
  Eleanor 130
  Eliza. 91
  Elizabeth 129, 130
  Hannah 13, 130
  James 92
  Jno. 96, 97, 133, 140
  John 5, 12, 14, 41, 44, 84,
    103, 130, 141
  Katherine 89, 130
  Martha 109, 129, 130
  Mary 130
  Nich. 132, 135
  Nicholas 106
  Posey 130
  Sam 77
  Sam. 66, 92, 106, 140
  Saml. 47
  Sam'll 109
  Samuel 28, 33, 41, 84, 122,
    128, 129, 142, 144, 146
  Samuell 10, 32, 33, 34, 40,
    41, 47, 59, 65, 77, 84
  William 63, 88, 122, 129
  Wm. 28, 65, 76, 83, 86, 89,
    129, 130, 140

179

Thompson (cont.)
  Wm., Sr. 77
Thomson, Elener 58
  Nicholas 58
  Wm. 99, 138
Thorne, Margaret 130
  Martin 58
  Thomas 37
Thornton, Mary 6, 131
  Thomas 131
Thorp, Hannah 130
  Joseph 37, 129, 130
  Margaret 130
  Mary 130
  Olive 130
  Sarah 130
  Timothy 37, 130
  Wm. 49
Thorpe, Jos. 146
  Joseph 37
  Mary 130
  Sarah 117
  Timothy 60
Threeweet, John 142
Threewet, John 144
Threewitt, John 70
  Thos. 77
Threewitts, Ann 61
Threwets, Ann 131
  Edward 131
  Joel 131
  Lucy 131
  Peter 131
Throop, Timothy 127
Thropp, John 26
  Thos. 118
Throuston, (?) 32
Thrower, Eliza. 131
  Elizabeth 131
  Hester 131
  Mary 131
  Thos. 111
  Wm. 131
Tias, Amy 114
  Richard 124
  Thos. 114
Tibbott, (?) (Captain) 118
Tiller, Mary 146
Tilton, Thos. 118
Tomlinson, Benjamin 131
  Jno. 102
  John 128, 131
  Mary 128
  Richard 131
  Thomas 37
  Thos. 139
  Will. 115
  William 5
  Wm. 85
Tooke, Aureola 132
  Elizabeth 132
  Jeane 132
  Jno. 144
  John 9, 12, 19

Tooke (cont.)
  Joseph 37, 132
  Rebecka 132
  Sarah 132
  Wm. 19, 132
Tooker, (?) (Maj.) 37
  Elizabeth 118
  Henry 12, 45, 118, 133
  Henry (Capt.) 118
Tortt, George 48
Treewets, John, Jr. 131
Tucker, Charles 59
  Mary 132
  Robert 87
  Sarah 8
Tuke, Averelah 102
  Joseph 102
Turner, David 132
  James 144
  Jeames 132
Twet, Wm. 46
Twy, John 32
Twyford, Jno. 142
  Mary 132
Tyas, Ann 89
  John 10, 89
  Sarah 89
  Thomas 40
Tyler, John 142
Tynes, Amos 123
  John 51
  Thos. 95
Tyus, Elizabeth 132
  Joanner 132
  John 22, 23, 55, 67, 71,
    123, 124, 133
  Mary 124, 132
  Priscilla 132
  Richard 132
  Thomas 132
Underbill, Giles 58
Underhill, Elizabeth 133
  Giles 66, 73, 81, 109, 139
  Henry 133
  John 133
  Mary 133
Underwood, Mary 37, 85
  Rosemond 80
Vahan, Stephen 49
Vahn, Elinor 49
Vandinan, Mary 42
Vaser, Samuel 35
Vaughan, Elizabeth 20
  James 66, 95, 142
  Mary 66
Vaughn, (?) 20
  Eliza. 20
  Henry 20
  James 85
Vaughnn, Henry 20
Vick, Geo. 102
Vincent, John 38, 123
  Sarah 133
Vines, Thos. 107

180

Vinsen, Mary 43
  Thomas 43
Vinsent, John 120
Vinson, John 92, 132
Wade, Daniel 118
Wage, John 34
Wager, (?) 91
  Robert 27, 91, 139
  Robt. 104
Walker, Fra 131
  Geo. 78
  George 83
  Jane 32
  Thos. 19
Wall, (?) (Coll.) 45
  Elizabeth 134
  James 134
  John 29, 134
  Jos. 96
  Joseph 3, 72, 83
  Richard 134
  Robert 134
Wallace, Sarah 132
  Thos. 132
Waller, (?) 99
  Alice 48, 106
  Elise 134
  Elizabeth 134
  John 7, 134
  Katherine 134
  Mary 48, 106, 134
  Sarah 134
  Thomas 9, 76
  Thos. 3, 9, 48, 66, 101,
    106, 127, 134
  William 134
  Wm. 134
Wallis, Ann 134
  James 134
  John 134
  Martha 134
  William 134
Walters, William (Col.) 32
Walthall, Henry 93
Wapool, John 56
Wapoole, John 4
Wapple, John 31, 32, 76
  Mary 135
  John 27, 31, 32, 76
Ward, Benj. 40
  Elizabeth 135
  Elizabeth (Mrs.) 135
  John 135
  Thos. 135
  William 40
Warde, Thos. 26
Warren, Allen 15, 28, 32, 41,
    106, 136
  Ann 26, 39, 127
  Anne 135
  Edward 5
  Elizabeth 32, 135
  Grace 19
  James 136

Warren (cont.)
  Jane 32, 41
  Jno. 1, 99
  John 1, 2, 41
  Jolindy 135
  Joseph 136
  Lucy 135
  Mary 135, 136
  Ogburn 32
  Peter 24, 58, 90, 127
  Robert 6, 8, 15, 26, 32,
    33, 54, 135, 139
  Samuel 50
  Sarah 135, 136
  Thomas 6, 41, 46
  Thos. 47, 91, 136
  William 9, 137
  Wm. 1, 90, 106, 130
Warrin, Benjamin 136
Warwell, Elizabeth 136
Washington, (?) 82
  Agnes 137
  Ann 137
  Arthur 82, 136, 137
  Elizabeth 112
  Geo. 136, 137
  George 84, 137
  James 7, 14, 125, 137
  Jas. 72
  John 136, 137
  Jos. 139
  Priscilla 137
  Richard 9, 83, 106
  Samuel 137
  Thomas 112, 116, 118, 136
  Thos. 137
  William 136
Washyer, Jos. 49
Water, (?) (Col.) 32
Wathen, Anne 138
  Mary 138
Watkins, (?) (Capt.) 5
  Ann 139
  Christopher 138
  Eliza. 52
  Eliza. (Mrs.) 138
  Elizabeth 138, 139
  Fortune 91
  George (Capt.) 124
  Henry 8, 14, 106, 123, 125,
    139
  James 70
  Jno. 8, 43, 52, 109
  John 20, 51, 58, 123
  John, Jr. 139
  Judith 138
  Mary 139
  Robert 9, 14, 36, 51, 96
  Robt. 123, 125, 138, 139
  William 139
Wattel, Joseph 104
Watts, James 27
  John 106
Weathers, Benjamin 139

181

Weathers (cont.)
  Isaac 139
  John 139
  Lidia 139
  Michael 139
  Reuben 139
  Susannah 139
  William 139
  Wm. 139
Weaver, Edward 102, 139
  Elizabeth 139
  John 7, 26, 27, 58, 60,
    69, 73
  Stephen 139
  William 139
Web, Robert 90
Webb, Eliza. 138
  Robert, Jr. 90
Weeks, Mary 140
  Robert, Sr. 90
Welche, Siril 57
Weldon, Sam. 125
Welling, Wm. 27
Wells, Robert 13
Were, Joseph 54
Wesson, Edward 40
West, Francis 93
  John 93
Weston, Eliza. 140
Wharton, Thomas 5
Wheler, Benj. 69
Whitaker, Elizabeth 5
  John 127
White, Benjamin 141
  Charles 14, 23, 25, 141,
    145
  Elizabeth 38, 140, 141,
    145
  Hannah 141
  Henry 141
  Joe 141
  Jno. 26
  John 11
  Lucy 141
  Mary 38, 140, 141
  Mary (Mrs.) 28, 93
  Nanny 141
  Naomy 140
  Phillis 141
  Rebecca 141
  Rebeckah 54, 141
  Rebekah 88
  Robert 140
  Thomas 140
  Walter 40, 140
  William 140
Whitehead, Elizabeth 142
Whittington, John 100
Whitson, Jno. 20
  John 82, 124
Whittson, Martha 124
Wiggin, (?) 33
  John 142
  Mary 142

Wiggin (cont.)
  Richard 142
  Thomas 142
  William 142
Wiggins, John 34, 142
  Mary 142
  Richard 34
  Sarah 8
  Thomas 8
  Thomas (Admr.) 8
  William 142
Wiggs, Henry 37
Wight, Joseph 145
  Thomas 145
Wigins, Richard 36
Wilbourne, John 29
Wilerson, John 115
Wilkason, Elizabeth 142
  John 66
  Mathew 142
Wilkinson, Eliza. 142
Willards, Elizabeth (Mrs.) 119
Williams, Ann 13, 116
  Anne 143
  Charles 31, 70
  Chas. 29
  Christopher 88
  David 89
  Eliza 143
  Elizabeth 142
  Faith 143
  Geo. 16, 19, 40, 129, 134,
    136
  George 12, 19, 26, 75, 122,
    124, 143
  Hannah 143
  Hester 143
  Jane 143
  Joanna 26
  John 143
  Jones 81
  Katherine 116, 143
  Lewis 5, 82
  Lidia 143
  Martha 142
  Mary 29, 32, 116, 132, 143
  Mary, Jr. 86
  Nicho. 56
  Richard 26
  Robt. 18
  Roger 88, 92, 140
  Sam'l. 51
  Samuell 143
  Thomas 40, 143
  Thos. 65
  Unity 143
  William 40, 84, 116
  Wm. 5, 9, 40, 143
Williamson, Cuthbert 143
  Edith 143
  Vallentine 90
Willie, Wm. 33
Willis, William 13
Willison, Jestes 50

182

Wills, John 44
Willson, Ann 144
  Isaac 144
  James 19, 20, 78, 79, 114
  Jone 48
  Nicholas 44, 103
  Robert 144
  Sampson 60, 71
  Thos. 146
Wilson, Ann 144
  Elizabeth 35
  James 132
  James, Jr. 89
  Jannett 103
  Jno. 3, 100
  Nicholas 34
  Nicholas (Col.) 34
  Samson 73, 130
  Sarah 116, 144
Windom, Mary 144
Windum, Griffin 97
Wingfield, E. 141
Winkel, Elizabeth 144
  Frances 144
Winkells, Amy 144
  Easter 144
  Mary 144
Winkels, Isack 144
  James 144
  John 144
Witherington, Catherine 144
  Elizabeth 78
  Jane 78
  Jos. 51, 146
  Joseph 52, 78, 146
  Katherine 53
  Ni. 42
  Nich. 52, 53
  Nicholas 5, 8, 20, 30, 85,
    138
Witherinnton, Nicho. 104
Woddrop, Ann 33
  Elizabeth 34
Wombwell, Benjamin 144
  Joseph 144
  Joshua 144
  Martha 144
  Mary 144
Woobank, John 119
  Robert 34
  Robert Smith 52
Wood, George 45
  Mary 144
Woodbank, R. Smith 53
Woodward, Hannah 80
  John 144
  Richard 102
Worden, James 39
  John 51
  Rebecca 26
Woulves, Barbary 145
Wray, George 5
Wren, Francis 145
  George 145

Wren (cont.)
  James 145
  John 145
  Joseph 145
  Thomas 145
Wrenn, Eliza. 145
  Elizabeth 6
  Mary 141, 145
  Thomas 141
  Thos. 103
Wright, Mary 145
  Thos. 129
Wyat, Richard 79
Wyatt, Francis 112
  Nicholas (Capt.) 112
Wyche, Ann 145
  Charles 24
  Cyrill 146
  Elizabeth 146
  Frances 145
  Geo. 69
  George 31, 145
  Hellinor 145
  Judith 19, 146
  Nathaniel 145, 146
  Peter 145
  Rebecca 146
  Sarah 145
  Will. 127
  William 145
Wynn, Agnes 146
  Martha 146
  Leweresy 146
  Robert 43, 146
Wynne, John 92
  Mary 110
  Robert 33, 82, 92, 94, 107,
    109, 111, 114, 121, 133,
    144
  Solomon 70, 92, 142
  Thomas 82, 100
  Thos. 77, 94
  Thos. (Capt.) 95
  William 14
  Wm. 61
Yorke, John 125
Young, John 127
  Tabitha 146
  Thos. 127
Youron, Elizabeth 74

ADDITIONS

Lile, Hannah 89
Lisbon, Thomas 81
Mabry, Francis 48, 93
Mabry, Mary 48

Nance, Wm. 2, 101
Napkin, Edward 70, 76, 96
Simmons, John (Maj.) 56
Stockes, (?) 102